GROUP LITIGATION IN EUROPEAN COMPETITION LAW

GROUP LITIGATION IN EUROPEAN COMPETITION LAW

A Law and Economics Perspective

Sonja E. Keske

intersentia

Antwerp – Oxford – Portland

Distribution for the UK:
Hart Publishing Ltd.
16C Worcester Place
Oxford OX1 2JW
UK
Tel.: +44 1865 51 75 30
Email: mail@hartpub.co.uk

Distribution for the USA and Canada:
International Specialized Book Services
920 NE 58th Ave. Suite 300
Portland, OR 97213
USA
Tel.: +1 800 944 6190 (toll free)
Tel.: +1 503 287 3093
Email: info@isbs.com

Distribution for Austria:
Neuer Wissenschaftlicher Verlag
Argentinierstraße 42/6
1040 Wien
Austria
Tel.: +43 1 535 61 03 24
Email: office@nwv.at

Distribution for other countries:
Intersentia Publishers
Groenstraat 31
2640 Mortsel
Belgium
Tel.: +32 3 680 15 50
Email: mail@intersentia.be

Group Litigation in European Competition Law. A Law and Economics Perspective
Sonja E. Keske

ISBN 978-94-000-0084-1
D/2010/7849/75
NUR 827

ACKNOWLEDGMENTS

This book was written as PhD thesis at the Erasmus University Rotterdam and successfully defended on 15 December 2009. Heartfelt thanks to my supervisor Prof. Roger Van den Bergh for his support and guidance throughout the major part of my PhD career and Prof. Michael Faure for stepping in and helping me to bring this project to a successful end. General thanks to all members of the Rotterdam Institute of Law and Economics as highly appreciated colleagues and friends. Particularly Louis Visscher often had to endure my company and I am very grateful for his patience and advice on numerous occasions. Alessio Pacces made me laugh even on rainy days. Wicher Schreuders and Marianne Breijer always had my back in administrative issues and their work was indispensable. General thanks also to the EDLE group, especially the first year comrades for making the test run a great experience. To my friends Hanneke Luth, Sharon Oded and Franziska Weber for helping me out in matters large and tiny. Last but not least, I am indebted to my family and friends, especially Andreas Strub, for always encouraging me and also for being prepared to forgive one or the other social lapse on my part. I fear that thanking each and every person which has done me great service throughout the last years might require a second book to be written. If one or the other does feel short-changed here, please accept my apology and provide me the opportunity to express my gratitude to you in person.

FOREWORD

Prof. Roberto Pardolesi[*]

There are two basic approaches to deterring socially harmful behaviour: enforcement by public agencies and litigation by private parties. Most countries use both approaches, though to varying degrees. The United States of America characteristically relies on private enforcement across the board: these litigation options are less relied upon in the European Union (EU), where public enforcement tends to be the favoured lever.

Common sense suggests, by and large, that private enforcement, if effectively designed, will lead to an increased probability of detecting illegal conduct and accuracy of fact-finding. This, in turn, would increase the workload of the courts and trial costs for private parties.

However, in the antitrust field there may be more arguments for public enforcement than in other areas. On the one hand, public enforcement is commonly deemed superior in pursuing the objectives of deterrence (more investigative powers, more effective sanctions, better control of their measure, more reliable commitment), and in clarifying the content of the antitrust prohibitions. On the other hand, even if better suited to pursue corrective justice, private enforcement might work poorly. Reasons for this include: if victims of antitrust law infringements are private consumers, harm and causation are typically not obvious to the victims; the detection of infringements requires investigation by experts, and public authorities are often better prepared (and informed: but this is a contentious issue) than the victims; and, since the total harm caused by infringements of competition law is often spread across many victims, even well-informed victims have little incentive to bring damages claims.

The final stroke against private enforcement is even more devastating: facilitating access to civil courts in antitrust cases increases the risk that private damage actions will be abused by competitors. In fact, plaintiffs are often competitors or takeover targets of defendants. They may have an incentive to employ private enforcement strategically, in order to: 1) prevent large potential competitors from

[*] Professor at the LUISS Guido Carli University – Italy.

entering their market or competing vigorously; 2) extort funds from successful rivals; 3) improve contractual conditions; 4) enforce tacit collusive agreements; and, 5) respond to existing suits, or hostile takeovers. The extent to which firms strategically abuse the antitrust laws under private enforcement depends crucially on the structure of damage awards in private antitrust cases. Where available, punitive damages (and the variation on the same theme, represented by disgorgement of profits) reduce firms' incentives to violate antitrust laws, but also increase their incentives to use antitrust laws strategically against their rivals. The actions that are taken to extort money are often resolved through the payment of a "tax on success" for the firms whose positions are sought after by competitors. However, taxes on success discourage investment and innovation, which harms consumers.

Moreover, it has been recently claimed that in the EU the accumulation of sanctions (which over time have been consistently aggravated) and damages might have an over-deterrent effect. Suppose, for the sake of clarifying this non-obvious argument, that a firm with an annual turnover of € 100 million joins a cartel (which is expected to last 7 years) and imposes an overcharge of, say, 15%. Apply a reasonable discount rate of 8%. The total expected profit from the participation to the cartel will be ca. € 84 million. Taking note that, in Europe, the average fine for a cartel member climbed in 2007 to € 75 million, one should consider that the firm risks paying a € 10 million fine (10% of the yearly total turnover, which might be referred to a host of products, beside the cartelized one), plus damages for € 84 million, plus legal costs of 10 to 20% of the awarded damages, plus reputational loss, plus wasted managerial resources in handling litigation: a total bill of over € 120 million. Carrying out such a computation forces the conclusion that too much is simply too much.

To further darken the picture, critics have pointed out that, where private enforcement is widespread, private actions too often result in remedies that provide lucrative attorney's fees but secure no real benefits for overcharged purchasers, are parasitic and "dramatically overreaching" (Kovacic).

Yet, as remarked by other commentators, administrative fines will often be insufficient to achieve the optimal level of deterrence. Diffuse recidivism strongly supports the idea that cartelizing is a promising activity. Looking at the 18 cartels which were the subject of decisions during the years 2005 to 2007, and assuming an overcharge of between 5% to 15%, the European Commission (2009) has estimated a total harm ranging from around € 4 billion to € 11 billion. Taking the middle point of this overcharge range – 10% – provides a conservative estimate of consumer harm of € 7.6 billion due to these cartels. This harm should be compared to the total amount of fines, which is € 5.9 billion. This comparison hints at the conclusion that cartelizing is still convenient, especially if one considers cartels which are not discovered.

Accordingly, there seem to be considerable advantages to having a system in place for private actions. First, private enforcement of competition laws can be a formidable deterrent to such conduct. Second, they help to ensure that the victims of unlawful conduct are compensated. Third, allowing private actions relieves some of the enforcement burden from public competition agencies, which do not always have sufficient funding to pursue every matter that is worth pursuing.

This being the case, private claims for damages caused by antitrust violations should provide, to say the least, a complement to public enforcement. Actually, this is the view recently adopted by the European Commission. In its view, compensation of antitrust damages is to be regarded as fundamental. Victims (all victims of all breaches of Article 101 and 102 TFEU in all sectors of the economy) should get full restoration of the prejudice suffered; and law-abiding businesses should not suffer from a competitive disadvantage. An increased level of actions for damages will also have the effect of increasing deterrence for potential infringers. Purporting to implement a "genuinely European system", the Commission emphasizes its commitment to preserve an effective public enforcement. The crucial role of the public authorities remains the main pillar; however, it should be complemented by a second pillar, private damages actions, never mind whether relying, or not, on a prior finding of an infringement by a competition authority (and thus both follow-on and stand-alone suits).

In this work, Sonja Keske explores the 'philosophic' foundations of this approach. The scenario is extremely complicated. Some issues – such as fault requirement, fee shifting and, to a lesser degree, the standing of indirect purchasers (but cf. the German experience) appear relatively undisputed. Other issues still raise bitter discussions.

Among them, a pivotal role is to be ascribed to collective redress. Whereas the necessity to provide for means of collective redress amenable to all categories of victims of competition law infringements goes without saying, the means to achieve this goal are hotly debated, not only in the antitrust framework, above all because of concerns about misuse of the system.

Keske's work focuses precisely on the uneasy fate of group litigation in the antitrust field. The problem is multi-faceted, and exposed to the risk of unmanageability. Abiding by the scientific imperative of reducing complexity, and deploying the armoury of law and economics, she privileges the perspective of deterrence. As the author candidly recognizes, such one-dimensional analysis largely neglects other relevant aspects. But the insights it provides are significant, and extremely challenging. A telling example: the shyness of the Commission in preferring an opt-in system, because of the avowed evils of the American class-action style, is to be scrutinized through the paradigm of mandatory procedures, where all the members of the concerned group are automatically represented in the collective suit. No surprise, then, that the analysis evolves toward unexplored frontiers, like auction mechanisms in determining the agent responsible for the final relief.

Harsh as it may appear in its uncompromising trajectory, Keske's work is a precious start of a still long journey.

CONTENTS

LIST OF ABBREVIATIONS

Art.	Article
ATE (insurance)	After-the-event (insurance)
BB	Betriebs-Berater
BGB	Bürgerliches Gesetzbuch (Civil Law Code)
BGH	Bundesgerichtshof (Federal Court of Justice)
BGHZ	Collection of decisions by the BGH
BörsG	Börsengesetz (Stock Exchange Act)
BRAO	Bundesrechtsanwaltsordnung (Federal Lawyer's Act)
BVerfG	Bundesverfassungsgericht (Federal Constitutional Court)
CA	Competition Act
CAFA	Class Action Fairness Act
CAT	Competition Appeal Tribunal
CAT R	Competition Appeal Tribunal Rules
CDC	Cartel Damage Claims company
CFI	European Court of First Instance (now: General Court)
CFAO	Conditional Fee Arrangements Orders
CFAR	Conditional Fee Arrangements Regulations
Commission	European Commission (Commission of the European Communities)
Community	Community of the European Union
CPR	Rules on Civil Procedure
e.g.	exempli gratiā (for example)
EC	European Community
ECJ	European Court of Justice (now: Court of Justice of the European Union)
EC Treaty	Consolidated version of The Treaty Establishing the European Community
Ed.	Editor
et al.	et alii / et aliae (and others)
EU	European Union
European Commission	Commission of the European Communities
FCA	Federal Competition Authority (Bundeskartellamt)
FRCP	Federal Rules of Civil Procedure (US)

GLO	Group Litigation Order
GWB	Gesetz gegen Wettbewerbsbeschränkungen (Competition Law)
GRUR	Gewerblicher Rechtsschutz und Urheberrecht
i.e.	id est (that is)
KapMuG	Gesetz über Musterverfahren in kapitalmarktrechtlichen Streitigkeiten (Capital Market Test Case Act)
LEC	Ley de Enjuiciamiento Civil
LEI	Legal Expense Insurance
LG	Landgericht (Regional Court)
LSC	Legal Services Commission
Member States	Member States of the European Union
NJW	Neue Juristische Wochenzeitschrift
OECD	Organisation for Economic Co-operation and Development
OJ	Official Journal of the European Union
P.E.	Private Enforcer
PD	Practice Direction
OLG	Oberlandesgericht (Higher Regional Court)
R&D	Research and Development
RVG	Rechtsanwaltsvergütungsgesetzes (Law on remuneration of lawyers)
TEU	Consolidated Version of the Treaty on the European Union
TFEU	Consolidated Version of The Treaty on the Functioning of the European Union
Treaty of Lisbon	Treaty of Lisbon amending the Treaty on European Union and the Treaty establishing the European Community
UK	United Kingdom
UrhG	Gesetz über Urheberrecht und verwandte Schutzrechte (Law on Copy Rights and Related Rights)
US	United States of America
USA	United States of America
U.S.C.	United States Code
UWG	Gesetz gegen den unlauteren Wettbewerb (Law Against Unfair Competition)
VBER	Vertical Block Exemption Regulation
ZPO	Zivilprozessordnung (Rules on Civil Procedure)

PREFACE

The economic losses caused to society by competition law infringements are significant. A few exemplary estimates may assist in clarifying the amounts at stake. For example, in the United Kindom (UK), annual losses due to monopolistic behaviour are estimated to be between £ 4.5 billion and £ 9 billion.[1] Enforcement of competition law is perceived as being able to reduce these losses. In the United States of America (USA), the yearly benefit, or avoided losses, achieved by the albeit not perfect enforcement system is estimated at US$ 50 to US$ 100 billion per year.[2] For Australia, the OECD estimates the yearly benefit of their effective competition policy at 2.5 percent of gross domestic product (GDP).[3] In Europe, 2.5 percent of GPD would amount to around € 396 billion per year. Whatever the exact figures may be, it is safe to say that such figures are anything but "peanuts." Therefore it is crucial that efficient enforcement systems are developed that sufficiently deter harmful anticompetitive practices and minimise the corresponding social welfare losses.

Due to the potential for such enormous losses, several avenues by which to achieve efficient enforcement of competition rules are currently being pursued by European legislators. First, there has been a tendency towards strengthening the investigative powers of competition authorities.[4] Second, like the UK and Ireland, other Member States are discussing the possibility of using criminalisation of competition law infringements as a tool to achieve more efficient and effective deterrence against anticompetitive behaviour.[5] A third avenue, which is being strongly pursued not only by the European Commission,

---

1. Organization for Economic Co-operation and Development, "Report on the Nature and Impact of Hard Core Cartels and Sanctions against Cartels under National Competition Laws," (2002) 7, 2.Organization for Economic Co-operation and Development, "The Role of Competition Policy in Regulatory Reform, OECD Reviews of Regulatory Reform, Reform of the United Kingdom " (2002) 55. Available at: www.oecd.org/dataoecd/2/61/27068497.pdf.
2. See Baker, "The case for antitrust enforcement," *Journal of Economic Perspectives* 17 (2003): 27.
3. Renda, et al, "Making antitrust damages actions in the EU more effective. Study in support of the impact assessment of the EC White Paper on antitrust damages actions," (2007) 92.
4. Wils, "Is criminalization of EU competition law the answer?" *World Competition: Law and Economics Review* 28 (2005): 117, 136.
5. See for example the contributions by Luna and DeLong, discussing the risks and costs connected to an overextension of criminal law. Luna, *Overextending the Criminal Law. Go Directly to Jail: The Criminalization of Almost Everything.* ed. Healy. Washington DC: Cato Institute (2004), 1; DeLong, *The New 'Criminal' Classes: Legal Sanctions and Business*

is to increase competition law enforcement and its deterrence effect by strengthening private enforcement. It is in pursuing this last avenue where the introduction of a group litigation mechanism plays a vital role. As a consequence, increased information regarding the most efficient way to design a group litigation mechanism, the benefits and costs incurred by choosing one specific variation over other alternatives, and what other legal rules and principles will affect the overall performance, are paramount. Some answers to these questions are presented in this book.

The goal of group litigation, as it is discussed in Europe, is to utilise the long grown and well-established basics of tort regulation as they exist in the various Member States to foster private enforcement. Other avenues may also be taken to enforce competition law. For example, Competition Authorities could be endowed with more resources and power. Alternatively, public enforcement could be improved by instigating solutions to perceived inefficiencies of public enforcement. Criminal law could be made applicable. Also, additional public bodies could be created and charged with the task of investigating markets and firms to detect competition law infringements. However all these avenues are beyond the realm of this book. The concern here is with the question of, if and how private actions for damages may assist to protect competition and thereby ultimately benefit the consumer. To be more precise, the focus is on the potential role group litigation mechanisms in actions for damages could play. In order to concentrate on this question, it is of course necessary to omit detailed investigations of other important and currently discussed issues, such as the still ongoing debate of private versus public enforcement. Moreover, other debated features of private actions for damages, inter alia: the correct way to calculate damages, whether or not to allow for a passing-on defence, or all the different possibilities to finance such litigations, are not dealt with in depth in this analysis. There are many other excellent pieces of work, which I refer to when applicable, which do deal with these matters.

Current developments on the European level, as well as in individual Member States suggest that soon there will be some form of private enforcement with group litigation in actions for damages due to competition law infringements in most if not all Member States. This is the starting point of this analysis. The use of class actions in antitrust law is a well known and established concept in the USA and other common law countries, such as Canada or Australia. However, group litigation in general and especially in competition law cases has not been widely used in the European Union Member Staes. Therefore, empirical research into the (in-)effectiveness of group litigation in the case of infringement of

---

Managers. Go Directly to Jail: The Criminalization of Almost Everything. ed. Healy. Washington DC: Cato Institute (2004), 9.

European competition law remains a point of research for the future, once different systems are introduced and allowed to operate sufficiently long in the various Member States.

The analytical approach used in conducting the theoretical analysis throughout this book involves a Law and Economics approach. This approach is founded on various streams of legal and economic literature concerned with, not only competition policy, but also the theory of crime and punishment, as well as litigation theory. These streams are then combinined to develop an integrated and consistent framework. As a consequence, the analysis in this book focuses on the goal of deterrence, rather than that of compensation, and also on stand-alone actions rather than follow-on actions.[6] The efficiency of substantive rules of competition law or their public enforcement is not evaluated. Rather, the analysis rests on the assumption that the imposition of the optimal fine, as developed in deterrence theory, will lead to total welfare increase by increasing compliance with competition laws and only allowing total welfare enhancing breaches. Another assumption made is that public enforcement as it exists is not perfect and does not detect and/or deter all infringements, so that private enforcement may increase deterrence as a second enforcement pillar. Further research may provide more detailed insights into the costs and benefits of such enforcement of competition law activities and allow a more accurate evaluation of the effects on total welfare. It may also allow a cost-benefit comparison of private versus public enforcement. Moreover, just as in the case of competition law, the firm will be treated as one entity, not taking in account considerations that are dealt with in the stream of corporate governance literature and others. The harmonisation costs or costs of legal change are also not taken into account. These can differ greatly from one legal system to another and would have to be weighed against any increase in total welfare the specific group litigation systems may bring about.

Despite these limitations of the analysis conducted here, many of the obstacles to efficient group litigations discussed under the chosen approach are also relevant for follow-on actions as well as for other areas of law than competition law. Moreover, the insights developed here within the context of pursuing the goal of deterrence will also be highly relevant to any analysis or evaluation where compensatory justice is set as the overriding goal. In that case, the trade-offs between the features that make a particular litigation mechanism efficient or effective and compensatory justice are most relevant. While not the focus of this analysis, at least the former, but sometimes also the latter side of these trade-offs are identified in this work. Moreover, these issues are also discussed in the

6 A focus on stand-alone actions is a consequence of focusing on the goal of deterrence, as will be shown in Chapter 3.

analysis of the legal changes proposed by the European Commission and in the legal comparison of the regimes implemented in the USA, UK and Germany. The analysis therefore is also able to provide insights for other approaches.

The book is structured as follows. Chapter 1 provides an overview of the placement of the topic in the context of the general debate about enforcement of competition law and the recent developments concerning private enforcement of competition law in the European Union. In chapter 2, the general framework used throughout this book is established. Relevant terms and concepts are defined and the general legal and economic framework established. Chapter 3 applies the framework established in the previous chapter to analyse generalised forms of existing forms of group litigation mechanisms, i.e. collective actions and representative actions. The insights gained in this analysis are then used to develop a form of group litigation, which is designed to be more efficient than previous forms, i.e. a market based mechanism combined with auctions. In chapter 4, the proposals made by the European Commission in the Green Paper and the ensuing White Paper are measured against this benchmark as developed in chapter 3, to provide an analysis as to whether they will generate efficient deterrence. As deterrence is not the primary goal for the Commission's position, also other goals as defined by the European Commission and potential legal obstacles are described and discussed with regard to the results developed in chapter 3. Chapter 5 provides a legal comparison of group litigation mechansims found in three selected legal systems: the USA, UK and Germany. The book concludes in chapter 6 by reaching some overall conclusions and policy implications of the results.[7]

[7] Legislative and policy developments as well as case law could only be taken into account until August 2009. Advances after that have not been incorporated, except for the notation changes brought about by the Lisbon Treaty coming into effect December 2009.

CHAPTER 1

ENFORCEMENT OF EUROPEAN COMPETITION LAW

A. THE RATIONALE OF EUROPEAN COMPETITION LAW

1. PROTECTION OF COMPETITION

The Organisation for Economic Co-operation and Development (OECD) states that "there is general consensus that the basic objective of competition policy is to protect and preserve competition as the most appropriate means of ensuring the efficient allocation of resources - and thus efficient market outcomes - in free market economies. While countries differ somewhat in defining efficient market outcomes, there is general agreement that the concept is manifested by lower consumer prices, higher quality products and better product choice."[8]

In the European Union, Article 3(1)(g) of the *Treaty Establishing the European Community* provided that one of the activities of the Community, in order to achieve the objectives set out in Article 2 of that Treaty was the implementation of "a system ensuring that competition in the internal market is not distorted". In consequence, the main aim of not only European competition law was generally regarded to lie in the protection of competition in markets from restrictions.[9] With the Treaty of Lisbon,[10] which came into force December 2009, the *Treaty on European Union* (TEU)[11] and the *Treaty establishing the European Community,* (EC Treaty) were amended and the EC Treaty was

8 Organization for Economic Co-operation and Development, "Competition Policy and Efficiency Claims in Horizontal Agreements" Paris, 1996), 5. Available at: www.oecd.org/dataoecd/1/4/2379526.pdf.

9 Budzinski, "Monoculture versus diversity in competition economics," *Cambridge Journal of Economics* 32 (2007): 295, 295; Langen and Bunte, *Kommentar zum deutschen und europäischen Kartellrecht.* Luchterhand (2001), no. 53; Emmerich, *Kartellrecht,* München: Beck (2001), 1; Van Den Bergh and Camesasca, *European competition law and economics: a comparative perspective,* London: Sweet & Maxwell (2006), 5 f, 16 ff.

10 OJ 2007/C 306/1. The treaty was signed in 2007 and came into effect 01.12.2009.

11 Consolidated Version of the Treaty on the European Union OJ 2008 C115/13.

renamed as *Treaty on the Functioning of the European Union* (TFEU).[12] Article 3 EC Treaty was abolished in the process. This prompted critical voices fearing that the reform would compromise the system of undistorted competition and European competition law. Even though a protocol was annexed to the TFEU, the *Protocol on the Internal Market and Competition*[13], in which it is explicitly stated that "the internal market as set out in Article 3 of the Treaty on European Union includes a system ensuring that competition is not distorted", critics argue that courts may not place the same value on a mere protocol in the interpretation of the treaty and its objects as they have done in the past with Article 3(g) EC Treaty, as part of the first Articles referring to the principles of the treaty.[14] Others, especially the official side, argue that the whole Article 3 EC Treaty essentially was replaced by Article 7 TFEU, Article 13(1) and Article 21(3) TEU, and with regard to competition policy, by the legally binding protocol on competition, so that competition policy remains just as important as it was.[15] With regard to the actual competition rules, mainly a renaming of the unchanged Articles of the EC Treaty took place, the old Article 81 and Article 82 EC Treaty now being Article 101 and Article 102 TFEU, respectively. Overall, it seems that "the principle of an open market economy with free competition" (as stated several times in the consolidated versions of TEU, TFEU and annexes, e.g. Article 119 TFEU) may be regarded as generally still being applicable, and competition law remaining uncompromised, at least in the short run.[16] In the end it remains to be seen, how the courts will react to the excision of Article 3(g) EC Treaty and the new *Protocol on the Internal Market and Competition.*

That competition in the market will lead to an efficient allocation of resources is an economic concept. Competition law restricting anti-competitive behaviour of market participants is undoubtedly heavily based on economic theory. The notions that cartels or monopoly power may be undesirable from a societal point of view are rooted in the realisation that these deviations from competition in the market lead to welfare losses and inefficiencies. The idea that competitive markets generate benefits for society by increasing welfare and economic growth,

---

12 Consolidated Version of the Treaty on the Functioning of the European Union, OJ 2008, C 115/47.

13 Protocols OJ 115/203.

14 Riley, A. The EU Reform Treaty and the Competition Protocol: Undermining EC Competition Law CEPS Policy Briefs, Politics and Institutions, *CEPS Policy Brief* No. 142, September 2007.

15 Statement by European Commissioner for Competition Neelie Kroes on results of June 21–22 European Council – Protocol on Internal Market and Competition, MEMO/07/250.

16 Kurpas, Sebastian, The Treaty of Lisbon – How Much 'Constitution' is Left? An Overview of the Main Changes (December 11, 2007). *CEPS Policy Brief*, No. 147, December 2007. Amtenbrink, Fabian and Van de Gronden, Johan. Economic Law and the Treaty of Lisbon I: Competition and Internal Market. Tijdschrift voor Europees en Economisch Recht, Vol. 56, pp. 323–329, 2008–9.

can be traced back (at least) to the seminal work of Adam Smith.[17] Since then, economic theory has been developed further and has grown into a large set of specialised parts of economic theory. In the 1950s, traditional industrial economics developed the so called 'structure-conduct-performance paradigm', which heavily influenced competition laws for a substantial time.[18] The basic idea was that there was a structural relationship between market structure, behaviour of firms in the market and market outcome. The lessons drawn from that theory were that the most important thing for competition law to achieve and protect is the appropriate market structure, which, if maintained, would eventually lead to the desired market outcomes. However, it was soon realised that the theory was insufficient to describe actual developments.

In response, new theoretical foundations were researched and new industrial economics was developed. Within this paradigm, the behaviour of firms in the market is analysed. However, there is a lack of consensus, even in economic theory, as to what form of efficiency should be the ultimate subject of protection. A number of different types of efficiencies have been posited: static efficiency, which includes the classical theories on monopoly power and the resulting allocative inefficiency;[19] productive efficiency, relating to efficiency in the production process;[20] and, dynamic efficiency,[21] which relates to innovations and developments which may have even larger impacts on an economy than static efficiency.[22] Between these goals, the lines are blurred and conflicts can arise. Productive efficiency, where the costs of production are reduced per unit because large amounts are produced (so called *economies of scale)* can lead to allocative inefficiency, when this advantage of size leads to a natural monopoly with monopoly prices and lower quantities produced than in a competitive

17 Möschel, *Recht der Wettbewerbsbeschränkungen,* Köln: Heymann (1983), 42.

18 At least until recently, also the EU competition law was protecting certain market structures, if it does not still do so. See Behrens, *Theoretische und Praktische Probleme einer Ökonomisierung der Kartellrechtsanwendung. Internationalisierung des Rechts und seine ökonomische Analyse.* eds. Eger, et al. (2008), 457, 462. See also Court of First Instance of the European Communities, *Case T-201/04 Microsoft Corp. v Commission of the European Communities* (2007) no. 664, referring to the protection of certain market structures.

19 Allocative efficiency requires that manufacturers produce and sell products that society wants in the amount and at the price that society wants, which means that productions is aligned with consumer preferences.Hubbard and O'Brien, *Microeconomics,* London: Prentice Hall (2008), 10.

20 Productive efficiency refers to a situation in which a good or service is produced at the lowest costs possible. *Ibidem*, 10.

21 Dynamic efficiency refers to an adequate balance between short run concerns (static efficiency) with concerns in the long run (focusing on encouraging research and development). Stiglitz and Walsh, *Economics,* New York: W. W. Norton (2006), 457 f. For a discussion on dynamic efficiency see also Audretsch, et al, "Competition policy in dynamic markets," *International Journal of Industrial Organization* 19 (2001): 613.

22 Foer, "The Goals of Antitrust: Thoughts on Consumer Welfare in the US," *American Antitrust Institute Working Paper No. 05-09* (2005).

market.[23] Another example is the conflict between static efficiency and dynamic efficiency in the area of research and development (innovation). In this case firms conducting costly and risky research projects, for example in the pharmaceutical industry, need to be granted a temporary monopoly on their products (usually through patent rights) and allowed to earn supra-competitive profits for a certain time period, in order to give sufficient incentives for firms to develop desired products.[24]

Since its inception, the development and application of competition law, however, has not been limited to one particular branch of economic theory. The beginnings of European competition law were heavily influenced by the ordo-liberal view on competition, which focused on the market structures necessary to generate rivalry in the markets and the necessity to regulate and control these market structures.[25] Since then, the basic concepts underlining European competition law have undergone changes and developments. The two most recent of these, are the hotly debated so called '*more economic approach*', and the shift towards placing more emphasis on the protection of consumers. The latter will be discussed in greater detail in the next section.

The '*more economic approach*' relates to the idea that firms' behaviour itself should be evaluated and the effects of certain behaviour on the market should be assessed. This approach opened the way for efficiency arguments to be included in the assessment of firms' conduct.[26]

Despite the seemingly multiple different economic theories, certain aspects of economic theory are met by wide consensus in the world of economics and may be called standard economic theory,[27] which will be applied here.[28]

---

23 Behrens, *Theoretische und Praktische Probleme einer Ökonomisierung der Kartellrechtsanwendung* 457, 464.

24 On the potential conflicts of the different efficiency concepts see alsoVan Den Bergh, *European competition law and economics: a comparative perspective*, 29 f.

25 See Pera, "Changing Views of Competition, Economic Analysis and EC Antitrust Law," *European Competition Journal* 4 (2008): 127.

26 European Commission, "Communication from the Commission, Notice, Guidelines on the application of Article 81(3) of the Treaty (2004/C 101/08)," *OJ* 47 (2004): 97, no. 24 und 33. For Article 82 see: European Commission, "Discussion Paper on the Application of Article 82 of the Treaty to Exclusionary Abuses." Brussels, (Online Publication) (2005), no. 84.

27 It seems most of new industrial economic theory, game-theory and microeconomic insights fit that description, which can be found in any textbook on microeconomics and new industrial organisation. See for example Tirole, *The theory of industrial organization.* Lipczynski, *Industrial organization: competition, strategy, policy.* Pindyck, *Microeconomics.* Rubinstein, *Theory of Games and Economic Behavior.*

28 See Chapter 2 section C on the economic framework used in this analysis for details.

2. TOTAL VERSUS CONSUMER WELFARE

Another important discussion currently taking place in Europe, and a matter of dispute in the USA,[29] is whether the welfare approach taken in competition law should be that of consumer welfare or total welfare. This dialogue is also connected to the discussion described above concerning the 'more economic approach.'[30]

The use of total welfare or an efficiency standard is aimed at maximising total welfare to society in a Kaldor-Hicks[31] sense. Kaldor-Hicks improvements refer to changes that result in some members of society winning and some members of society losing, but where the welfare gains outweigh the losses. Therefore, when there is a Kaldor-Hicks improvement, the winners could compensate the losers and still be better off than before the event. For that reason, this is also called potential Pareto improvement.[32] Focusing on the total welfare of society implies that a wealth transfer from one part of society to another has no impact, as it does not influence the welfare of all members of society as a sum. In the area of competition law the use of the Kaldor-Hicks approach to efficiency allows firms to engage in conduct that does result in dynamic efficiency, for example by providing increased incentives for innovation, but which leads to higher prices for consumers, at least in the short run. The aim according to this standard is to increase the sum of the consumer and producer surplus and therefore total welfare.

On the other hand, a pure and narrow consumer welfare approach could prohibit any conduct by firms that would lead to a transfer of wealth from consumers to producers. There are a couple of different ways in which a narrow consumer welfare approach can be implemented. When the consumer welfare standard is defined as allowing only Pareto improvements then the above-mentioned behaviour by firms will not be allowed. Under this approach, the gain of one part of society (producers) will only be allowed when the other part of society (consumers) is not made worse off. Apart from practical problems of such an

---

29 See Farrell and Katz, "The economics of welfare standards in antitrust," *Competition Policy International* 2 (2006): 3. Heyer, "Welfare standards and merger analysis: Why not the best?" *U.S. Department of Justice Working Paper* (2006). Available at SSRN: http://ssrn.com/abstract=959454.

30 For an overview see Vanberg, "Consumer Welfare, Total Welfare and Economic Freedom–On the Normative Foundations of Competition Policy," *Freiburg Discussion Papers on Constitutional Economics* (2009). Available at: www.eucken.de/publikationen/09_03bw.pdf.

31 Named after the economists Nicholas Kaldor (1908–1986) and John Hicks (1904–1989). A Kaldor-Hicks improvement is achieved, when – *theoretically* – those made off better through the change could fully compensate those made off worse and still be better off.

32 Pure Pareto-improvement will be described below. See footnote 37 and acc. text.

approach, the so-called Pareto improvement[33] requirement would put an enormous limitation on any changes of the *status quo*.[34]

A second interpretation of the consumer welfare approach could be that it aims at maximising consumer surplus. This would be along the line of prohibitions of excessive prices, for example. In such a setting, consumers would always have to win and losses of producers would not be taken into account.[35] Again, such an approach could lead to unwanted outcomes when dynamic efficiency is taken into consideration, unless the future benefits of consumers that result from temporary producer surpluses are adequately taken into account. For example, consumers can be made worse off when they have to endure higher prices due to a patent protected monopoly for a certain period of time, but at the same time consumers would still be made worse off if patents were abandoned and innovative activity plummeted as a consequence.

Like the literature, the approach in reality seems not to be clear-cut. In the USA, total welfare is sometimes interpreted as consumer welfare.[36] There also are voices that argue that in fact consumer welfare usually does correlate with total social welfare, so that enhancing the latter would automatically also increase the former.[37] In addition, the normative foundations of European competition law are criticised as not being well developed.[38] In a number of statements, the European Commission seems to follow the line of thought, that efficient allocation of resources and consumer welfare will be correlated.[39] However, other Commission statements could lead to different conclusions, especially

---

33 Named after the Italian economist Vilfredo Pareto (1848–1923). A pareto improvement is said to be achieved when at least the situation of one person can be improved, without making any other individual worse off. Pareto-efficiency is achieved when no further pareto improvements are possible.

34 Van Den Bergh, *European competition law and economics: a comparative perspective* 40 f.

35 In that respect, the voiced argument might be included that individual members of society not only act as consumers, but can also be shareholders and employees of firms, in turn benefiting from producer surplus. As such, the focus on consumer welfare might be slightly less favourable also for members of society intuitively assumed to be only consumers.

36 See Behrens, *Theoretische und Praktische Probleme einer Ökonomisierung der Kartellrechtsanwendung* 457, 468; as an example see Bork, *The antitrust paradox: A policy at war with itself*, Basic Books New York (1978).

37 Foer, *The Goals of Antitrust: Thoughts on Consumer Welfare in the US* 19 f. Available at SSRN: http://ssrn.com/abstract=1103510.

38 For a discussion, see Kerber, *Should Competition Law Promote Efficiency? Some Reflections of an Economist on the Normative Foundations of Competition Law. Economic Theory and Competition Law.* ed. Drexl. Cheltenham: Edward Elgar (2009), 93.

39 Neelie Kroes, "Damages Actions for Breaches of EU Competition Rules: Realities and Potentials Opening speech at the conference 'La reparation du prejudice cause par une pratique anti-concurentielle en France et à l'étranger: bilan et perspectives ', Cour de Cassation" 17 Oct 2005), Neelie Kroes, "Enhancing Actions for Damages for Breach of Competition Rules in Europe, SPEECH/05/533" Available at: http://europa.eu/rapid/

those stating that consumer welfare should be given priority.[40] Additionally, the current case law does not seem to clarify the predominance consumer welfare should have in the application of competition law. In *British Airways*, the European Court of Justice (ECJ) considered that "Article 82 EC [EC Treaty] is aimed not only at practices which may cause prejudice to consumers directly, but also at those which are detrimental to them through their impact on an effective competition structure, such as is mentioned in Article 3(1)(g) EC [EC Treaty]."[41] Later the court of first instance clarified that "it must be borne in mind that it is settled case-law that Article 82 EC [EC Treaty] covers not only practices which may prejudice consumers directly but also those which indirectly prejudice them by impairing an effective competitive structure."[42]

The major problem in the discussion of which consumer welfare standard should be applied is that there is an absence of a clear-cut definition of 'consumer welfare'. What exactly counts as hindering or fostering consumer welfare, and what concept should be given priority when conflicts arise between a form of efficiency and consumer welfare, as defined, should be decided upon and made explicit. Consumer welfare that includes long-run gains, for example from dynamic competition, will come much closer to the total welfare standard since it also has to take into account the producer surplus. This is in contrast to a limited definition that includes just the short-run consumer surplus.[43] If the Commission really wants to pursue that goal as a priority, such a definition would be vital, however, to allow sensible decision-making and to increase legal certainty.

The substantive rules of competition law may be focusing on various different criteria and definitions of consumer welfare, at various times. The approach chosen for the analysis in this thesis is that of total welfare, i.e., the sum of consumer and producer surplus. This approach will allow for so called 'efficient breaches' of competition law, where the profit for the infringing firm outweighs

pressReleasesAction.do?reference=SPEECH/05/512&format=HTML&aged=1&language=EN &guiLanguage=en.

40 Mario Monti, "European Commissioner for Competition Policy, A reformed competition policy: achievements and challenges for the future" Brussels, 28 October 2004), Available at: http://europa.eu/rapid/pressReleasesAction.do?reference=SPEECH/04/477&format=HTML &aged=1&language=EN&guiLanguage=en. Neelie Kroes, "Consumers at the heart of EU Competition Policy SPEECH/08/212" 22 April 2008), Available at: http://europa.eu/rapid/ pressReleasesAction.do?reference=SPEECH/08/212&format=HTML&aged=0&language=EN &guiLanguage=en.

41 ECJ 15.03.2007, C-95/04,(British Airways/Commission), no. 106.

42 Court of First Instance of the European Communities, *Case T-201/04 Microsoft Corp. v Commission of the European Communities*, no. 664.

43 Canoy, et al, "Dominance and Monopolization," *Tilec Discussion Paper DP 2004–022* (2004), 7. Available at www.tilburguniversity.nl/tilec/publications/discussionpapers/2004–022.pdf.

the losses caused to society at large. Moreover, enforcement activities that would lead to more costs than they could create benefits in terms of deterrence are considered inefficient and therefore undesirable from a social point of view. The choice for a total welfare approach is motivated by several reasons.

First, standard economic theory applies total welfare concepts when analysing the effects of certain firm's behaviour in the market. It is the standard approach adopted in the Law and Economics literature when analysing legal rules.[44] Redistribution mechanisms, which should "take from the rich and give to the poor", are usually advocated to be outside the realm of competition and even private law.[45] This is because otherwise the incentives structures of market players and the functioning of markets would be distorted.[46]

Second, as can be seen from the description above, the consumer welfare approach, even if it were to be strictly applied in European competition law, is not yet clearly defined. Whether consumer welfare is harmed by the short-run monopoly prices allowed by a patent, or increased by the incentives provided for innovation, are amongst the many aspects that would have to be decided upon in the definition. Depending on the definition, it is possible that the consumer welfare approach closely mirrors the total welfare approach, so that the choice between these two approaches may be of less importance.

Third, whether the substantive criterion is harm to consumers or restriction of effective competition in the markets, the total welfare criteria may still be applied when the issue of enforcement is discussed. Arguably, allowing for efficient breaches would then entail that the law protecting consumers would be infringed and the gain for the infringer would outweigh the losses caused to consumers. This may be seen as being in conflict with the law focusing on consumer welfare in the short-run. However, the difference between substantive law and its enforcement should also be taken into account. Enforcement of a law that prohibits some certain unwanted behaviour can also be designed to pursue different objectives than the underlying substantive law. Amongst these objectives may be the punishment of offenders for their wrongdoing, deterrence of other potential infringers or infringements, and also some form of justice goal. This may imply the extortion of illegal profits gained by the offender through the

44 Kerber, *Should Competition Law Promote Efficiency? Some Reflections of an Economist on the Normative Foundations of Competition Law* 93, 104 f.
45 Cooter and Ulen, *Law and Economics*, Pearson (2003), 7 f.
46 See Kaplow and Shavell, "Fairness versus welfare," *Harvard Law Review* 114 (2000): 961.

infringement. These are the classical arguments, not only for sanctions imposed in public proceedings, but also for proclaimed goals of tort law.[47]

Fourth, although inefficient markets cause costs to be borne by a number of different members of society enforcement mechanisms are also costly. Enforcement costs may be borne by society at large. In particular, public enforcement as a state activity typically is financed through general tax revenues. If calculating costs are those incurred by the whole of society, including: competitors, small and medium enterprises that have business relations with the infringer, and end consumers, then it seems reasonable to contrast these with the total welfare of society, and not just a part of society. Under this approach, enforcement mechanisms that will increase total welfare should be given preference. That again implies a total welfare approach.

Lastly, the choice of which member of society in which function should be given more rights compared to other members in other functions seems to be a political one, and is not to be answered here. The total welfare approach remains relevant, and will still reveal important information about the costs and benefits of certain choices compared to other choices, even if a political choice were to be made that would favour a different welfare approach.

B. ENFORCEMENT OF COMPETITION LAW IN THE EUROPEAN UNION

In the last years, European competition law has been reformed and made more sophisticated. Spurred by developments concerning the substantive law, the importance of evaluating and subsequently reforming the enforcement instruments has been increasingly recognised throughout the decade. It is uncontroversial that the debate about the 'best' competition law rules remains meaningless, apart from it being a nice theoretical exercise, if enforcement is lacking or inefficient. One of the most important reform steps taken in this regard was EC Regulation 1/2003, which came into force 1 May 2004 and modernised the European enforcement system.[48] With this regulation, the Member States abolished the notification system under Article 101 TFEU (ex

47 See Polinsky and Shavell, *Punitive Damages. Tort Law and Ecomomics, Encyclopedia of Law and Economics*. ed. Faure. Cheltenham: Edward Elgar Publishing Limited (2009), 228, 228 f. Kionka, *Torts in a Nutshell*, St. Paul: Thomson West (1999), 5 ff. Kötz, *Ziele des Haftungsrechts*. in *Festschrift für Ernst Steindorff*. ed. Baur. Berlin: Walter de Gruyter & Co. (1990), 643, 643 f.

48 Council of the European Union, *Council Regulation (EC) No. 1/2003 of 16 December 2002 on the implementation of the rules on competition laid down in Articles 81 and 82 of the Treaty* (2003).

Article 81 EC Treaty), decentralised enforcement giving more responsibility to the national competition authorities and courts, and made Article 101 TFEU (ex Article 81 EC Treaty) and Article 102 TFEU (ex Article 82 EC Treaty) directly applicable.

Public enforcement still predominates the enforcement of competition law in the European Union. However, the decentralisation of enforcement mechanisms, and the consequential decisions of the ECJ, has meant that private enforcement mechanisms have become more important. This form of enforcement has to take place before the national courts of the Member States, following national procedure. This spurred the interest in the prospects and obstacles of private enforcement in the Member States, however with a focus on actions for damages and less so on other possible legal remedies. In 2004, a study (*Ashurst Study*)[49] was undertaken to identify obstacles to private enforcement in the Member States. The findings led to the result of "astonishing diversity and total underdevelopment"[50] of effective systems for private damage claims in the Member States. In the wake of the Ashurst Study there have only been some limited developments designed to increase private enforcement in the Member States.

The principle of private enforcement of Community law rights in addition to their enforcement by the public authorities reaches back to the 1963 *Van Gend & Loos* judgment,[51] in which the ECJ held that the EC Treaty not only established the rights and duties of Member States, but also directly for individuals. The landmark 2002 *Courage* decision,[52] examined the right for damages due to competition law infringements. In this judgement, the EJC clarified the existence of a right to sue for damages due to European competition law infringements. In its decision, the ECJ also considered that private enforcement can "make a significant contribution to the maintenance of effective competition in the Community".[53] Furthermore, that "the full effectiveness of Article 85 of the Treaty [now Article 101 TFEU] and, in particular, the practical effect of the

49 The study is frequently referred to as the "Ashurst Study", as it was the law firm Ashurst conducting the study. Waelbroeck et al, "Study on the Conditions for Claims for Damages in Case of Infringement of EC Competition Rules: Comparative Report, Open Procedure COMP/2003/A1/22, Ashurst Study for Directorate General Competition of the EU Commission, London, England," (2004) Available at: www.europa.eu.int/comm/competition/antitrust/others/private_enforcement/comparative_report_clean_en.pdf.

50 "Ashurst Study"*Ibidem*, 4. Available at http://ec.europa.eu/comm/competition/antitrust/others/actions_for_damages/national_reports/spain_en.pdf.

51 European Court of Justice, *Case 26/62 Algemene Transport- en Expeditie Onderneming van Gend & Loos v Nederlandse administratie der belastingen* (1963).

52 European Court of Justice, *Case C-453/99 Courage Ltd v Bernard Crehan [2001] ECR I-6297* (2001).

53 *Ibidem* no. 34.

prohibition laid down in Article 85(1) would be put at risk if it were not open to any individual to claim damages for loss caused to him by a contract or by conduct liable to restrict or distort competition." In a later judgement, the so-called *Manfredi* judgement,[54] the ECJ reconfirmed the importance of actions for damages. However, the question of how private enforcement could or should play a role in enforcement of competition law in Europe remained open.

In December 2005, the European Commission issued a Green Paper "Damages actions for breach of the EC antitrust rules".[55] The release of the Green Paper initiated a discussion as to obstacles and possible changes to enhance private actions for damages. Following the Green Paper and the resulting debate, a White Paper was prepared and published in 2008.[56] In it, the Commission presented its vision as to what legal changes are necessary and desirable.[57] If the Commission decides to take a next step going beyond a mere suggestion, these proposals have the potential to have a profound impact on the national legal systems of Member States. In 2009, after receiving support by the European Parliament,[58] the Commission was expected to present legislative measures in the near future.[59]

In light of these developments in Europe, old discussions have resurfaced, with new features and questions attached. The questions raised include: Why should private enforcement be enhanced in the first place? Should it be designed so as to replace public enforcement, or does it pursue completely different goals and act as a mere and completely independent complement? Or is its function something in between? These questions have already been addressed in the classic debate about public versus private enforcement.[60] In the following section, an overview is given of the classic public versus private enforcement dispute and its specific features in the area of private enforcement of competition law.

---

54 European Court of Justice, *Cases C-295/04 to C-298/04 Vincenzo Manfredi and Others v. Lloyd Adriatico Assicurazioni SpA and Others ECR I-6619* (2006).

55 European Commission, "Green Paper: Damages actions for breach of the EC antitrust rules," (2005), COM(2005) 672 final.

56 European Commission, *White Paper on Damages actions for breach of the EC antitrust Rules COM(2008) 165 final, SEC(2008) 404.*

57 See Chapter 4 for a detailed discussion of the propositions laid out in the White Paper.

58 See Press-Release: Antitrust: Commissioner Kroes welcomes the European Parliament's cross-party support for damages for consumer and business victims of competition breaches, MEMO/09/135, 26/03/2009.

59 See e.g. www.martindale.com/antitrust-trade-regulation-law/article_Jones-Day_692038.htm.

60 Public enforcement refers to the detection and sanctioning of illegal conduct by public enforcement agencies, such as the police or competition authorities. Private enforcement refers to such enforcement activities outside the public law realm, such as legal actions by private individuals or by consumer associations.

1. THE CLASSIC DEBATE: PRIVATE VERSUS PUBLIC ENFORCEMENT

Taking a step back from the current discussion about the most appropriate tools with which private enforcement should be enhanced, the underlying issue of the potential of private enforcement *vis-à-vis* public enforcement comes once again to the fore. The question to be answered first is whether private enforcement may be able to substitute for public enforcement of European competition law. Currently this may be said to be the case in antitrust enforcement in the USA, where 90 percent of all antitrust cases are of a private nature.[61] If not, the next question would be whether private enforcement may act as a suitable complement to the public enforcement, which currently clearly predominates in the EU.[62]

The debate about private versus public enforcement of competition law also hinges on the question which goal is to be achieved by which mechanism. Broadly speaking, often commentators argue that while public enforcement is concerned primarily with deterrence and punishment, private enforcement is concerned with compensation and justice for victims. However, legal theory also sometimes includes deterrence as one of the functions of tort law, as well as the function to at least deprive the offender of its illegal gain.[63]

From an economic point of view, which is the approach taken in this thesis, the goal of any enforcement activity is mainly that of deterrence. When offenders are efficiently deterred from committing the undesirable offence, the losses incurred by members of the society are minimised and therefore total welfare to society is maximised. Compensation, in the form of the compensatory damages awarded to a plaintiff for harm caused by the defendant, for example, then is only a matter of distribution between members of the society, but not in itself relevant for the total welfare of a society as a whole. Such a (re-)distribution, from an economic point of view, is not completely irrelevant, however. It plays an important role where it influences the incentives for certain behaviour by the members of

---

61 Van Den Bergh, *European competition law and economics: a comparative perspective*, 325.

62 Segal and Whinston, "Public vs. private enforcement of antitrust law: A survey," *Stanford Law and Economics Olin Working Paper No. 335* (2006), 1. Available at http://ssrn.com/abstract=9520671. Van Den Bergh, *European competition law and economics: a comparative perspective*, 325.

63 For example skimming-off procedures in Germany are brought by associations under civil law, even though their predominantly preventive function is acknowledged. See Stadler, "Grenzüberschreitender kollektiver Rechtsschutz in Europa," *JuristenZeitung* 64 (February 2009): 121. For an economic analysis of skimming-off procedures, mainly focusing on criminal procedures, see Bowles, et al, "Forfeiture of Illegal Gain: An Economic Perspective," *Oxford Journal of Legal Studies* 25 (2005): 275.

society, or leads to an efficient risk distribution, for example. Distribution issues therefore form a tool with which to reach the primary goal of efficient deterrence, rather than it being a goal in itself. Consequently, most of the economic and Law and Economics literature concerning public versus private enforcement focuses on the potential for private enforcement to achieve deterrence as a goal.

1.1. Advantages of public enforcement

Private enforcement as a substitute, or a complement, to public enforcement has been a point of deliberations in the Law and Economics literature since the seminal work of Gary Becker and George Stigler in 1974.[64] In their work, the authors focused on the deterrence effect of private enforcement, and argued that it could be just as, or even more, efficient than public enforcement when correctly designed. According to the authors, the prerequisites for such effective private enforcement entail setting the damages awarded in court so as to exceed the actual harm caused in order to account for the low probability of detection, and granting the damages awarded to those private parties who play an active role in detection and conviction.[65] This positive view of private enforcement as potential substitute to public enforcement, however, has been frequently challenged in the ensuing debate during the past four decades.

In response, Landes and Posner[66] argued that the general efficiency of private enforcement will be more restricted than Becker and Stigler proposed, especially where large investments are necessary to increase the probability of detection. They further hinted towards possible problems concerning duplications of efforts, a race to the courts, waste of resources and over-enforcement.[67]

Much later, Posner[68] also pointed to other problems of private enforcement, such as the trade-off or conflict between providing the right incentives for private enforcement (which are directly influenced by the amount of damages awarded) and setting the penalty faced by the infringer (which equals the amount of damages awarded) at an optimal level.

---

64 Becker and Stigler, "Law enforcement, malfeasance, and compensation of Enforces," *The Journal of Legal Studies* 3 (1974): 1.

65 See *Ibidem*, 14.

66 Landes and Posner, "The Private Enforcement of Law," *The Journal of Legal Studies* 4 (1975): 1.

67 See *Ibidem*.

68 Posner, *Economic analysis of law*, Boston: Little, Brown and Company (2003), 632.See also Shavell, "Social versus the Private Incentive to Bring Suit in a Costly Legal System, The," *The Journal of Legal Studies* 11 (1982): 333.

Following these initial assessments of private versus public enforcement, a number of arguments supporting the supremacy of public over private enforcement were developed. These shall be presented here.

1.1.1. Private incentives to sue are lacking

The classic argument why public enforcement activities may be more efficient than private enforcement concerns the different incentives to detect and sanction offences. Public enforcement is thought to dominate private enforcement because the individual plaintiff does not have the social welfare in mind when suing for damages.[69] The individual harmed by certain conduct will generally only decide to file suit against the offender when such an action will provide more benefits to themselves as the injured party than it entails in costs. A simple example may be that a victim having incurred a loss of € 5 is not expected to incur litigation costs of €100 in order to sue for damages.[70] This leads to a subset of problems. There will be inadequate investment in litigation because the private plaintiff does not consider the total costs and benefits to society, but merely his own expected costs and expected gain from litigating. This can lead to under-investment in enforcement activities, because the deterrence effects of such suits on other potential offenders, enhancing legal certainty and similarly beneficial aspects of successfully challenging a certain illegal conduct in court, are not taken into account by the private party. When these effects are taken into account, the total benefit to society may well exceed the costs of litigation the potential plaintiff faces, so that litigation would be desirable from a total social point of view. Furthermore, there may be additional costs the individual faces on top of the enforcement costs. For example, firms harmed by a competition law infringement by an important business partner may fear retaliation and therefore be reluctant to commence action even if the harm would justify the costs and they possess sufficient relevant information and evidence. This may especially be the case when economic dependencies exist.[71]

On the other hand, the deviation of incentives to engage in enforcement activities by private parties may also lead to over-investment in litigation in some cases. An example of this would be when competition law is used as a shield to protect the plaintiff from a strong competitor rather than to protect competition itself.[72]

---

69 Wils, "Should private antitrust enforcement be encouraged in Europe?" *World Competition* 26 (2003): 473, 482; Segal, *Public vs. private enforcement of antitrust law: A survey* 1, 7. Available at http://ssrn.com/abstract=952067; see also Shavell, *Social versus the Private Incentive to Bring Suit in a Costly Legal System, The* 333.

70 In these cases the rational plaintiff will remain *rationally apathic*, see section 3.2 in chapter 2.

71 Van Den Bergh, *European competition law and economics: a comparative perspective*, 331.

72 Möschel, "Law and Market Organization: The Historical Experience in Germany From 1900 to the Law Against Restraints of Competition (1957)-Comment," *Journal of Institutional and*

While direct competitors and close business partners are likely to have sufficient knowledge to detect an infringement and the necessary resources and motivations to sue, these private enforcers are also the ones which may benefit the most from using competition law strategically. Due to the prospective gains, private parties may have increased incentives to use competition law rather as a shield than as a sword, i.e. to abuse competition law to prevent strong competition.[73] The risk of unmeritous suits will have to be incorporated in the creation of the optimal group litigation mechanism. Another example would be a case where the aim of the plaintiff is merely to extract a settlement from the defendant by threatening costly litigation although the case has little or no merits.[74] Here, the individual plaintiff does not incorporate into his reckoning the total costs to society that his behaviour triggers. This includes unnecessary costs invested in this rent-seeking behaviour (for example the lawyers costs) and the costs of deterring legal behaviour that would be beneficial to society.

Since the individual plaintiff is generally considered not to incorporate the total costs and benefits to society into his decision, it follows that private enforcement activities will deviate from the optimal level. This deviation of the private incentive to sue from that of society is a pitfall that public enforcement may cure, as public enforcement agents could consider total costs and benefits to society.

1.1.2. Lack of information on the victims side

Another argument for public enforcement concerns problems of information. In tort law, the victim of an offence is usually assumed to be aware of the harming act and the responsible offender. A classic example would be a traffic accident. However, while these arguments are valid in some instances they can be much less true for other victims and offences. Examples where this is not the case include damages caused by violations against environmental protection regulations or end-consumers harmed by a price-cartel at the manufacturer level. In such cases, specialised enforcement agents such as public enforcement agents may be in a much better position to detect and prosecute violations against the law. They often possess greater knowledge, experience, resources and powers to do so, than individual parties. This is especially the case for competition law infringements that are not obvious and subject to a *per se* prohibition. In such cases a more profound analysis and subsequent balancing of positive and negative effects of a certain conduct to society is demanded, and

---

Theoretical Economics 151 (1995): 21, 23; Ginsburg, "Comparing antitrust enforcement in the United States and Europe," *Journal of Competition Law & Economics* 1 (2005): 427, 435.

73 This argument has frequently been made, seeSnyder and Kauper, "Misuse of the Antitrust Laws: The Competitor Plaintiff," *Michigan Law Review* 90 (1991): 551;Ginsburg, *Comparing antitrust enforcement in the United States and Europe* 427, 435 f.

74 For a more detail analysis of such nuisance suits, see section 2.2.2 in chapter 3.

much more extensive information and knowledge required. Where such information is not directly available but has to be acquired, public authorities are often assumed to have an advantage over private parties.[75] They regularly have greater investigative power than individuals and are specialised in performing an analysis of potentially anti-competitive behaviour.

Public enforcement also offers additional tools to enhance revelation of information. Where information advantages on the side of private parties exist, they can and already often are taken advantage of, also in public enforcement activities. For example, any natural or legal person can file a complaint for breach of European competition law to the European Commission, which invokes a duty for the European Commission to react to that complaint.[76] Another important tool can be found in the leniency programs offered by public enforcers, which incentivise the most informed parties, the offenders themselves, to disclose the information. Leniency programs have frequently been reported as successful mechanisms to increase detection,[77] in both the EU and the USA. Thus far, they exhibit great potential to further destabilise already unstable cartel agreements, enhancing the general deterrence effect.

1.1.3. Limited sanctions in private enforcement

A third important argument favouring public over private enforcement relates to the necessity to set the sanction to be imposed on the infringer at the optimal level in order not to under-deter illegal behaviour and not to over-deter beneficial conduct. The principle idea for deterrence of unwanted behaviour is that the sanction imposed on the potential infringer has to be large enough to outweigh the potential gains from the law infringement. So that after weighing the expected benefits and costs the potential offender will decide to refrain from breaking the law.[78] The optimal level of sanction, ensuring that only breaches of law that are beneficial to society as a whole from a total welfare perspective will take place, is the level of sanction that forces the potential infringer to internalise the total harm done to society. That in turn requires that the optimal sanction be

---

75 Prichard, *Private Enforcement and Class Actions.* in *Canadian Competition Policy: Essays in Law and Economics.* eds. Prichard, et al. Butterworths (1979), 217, 237.

76 Wils, *Should private antitrust enforcement be encouraged in Europe?* 473, 486. Segal, *Public vs. private enforcement of antitrust law: A survey* 1, 5. Available at http://ssrn.com/abstract=952067.

77 Spagnolo, "Leniency and whistleblowers in antitrust," *Centre for Economic Policy Research (CEPR) Discussion Paper No. 5794*(2006), 2. See Kroes, "Enforcement of Prohibition of Cartels in Europe," *Proceedings of 2006 EU* (2006). Available at www.iue.it/RSCAS/research/Competition/ 2006(pdf)/200610-COMPed-Kroes.pdf.

78 The economics of deterrence will be presented in greater detail in section C of chapter 2. Here, only the general and basic arguments for public enforcement shall be presented.

at least as large as the total harm done to society in monetary terms.[79] Unfortunately, the sanction imposed in private enforcement, for example through individual actions for damages, generally captures only those harms borne by those individuals that can and do file suit. Other damages caused to society, for example the so called *dead weight loss* incurred due to monopoly prices,[80] are not incorporated in the private sanction. Even if multipliers are used, as for example treble damages in the USA,[81] public enforcement still may allow for a better fine tuning of the imposed sanction than would be feasible in private damages actions with a fixed multiplier.[82]

Additionally, settlements agreed upon between plaintiff and defendant may be far from optimal from a social welfare perspective, irrespective of the merits of the case. A settlement agreement between the parties that satisfies the plaintiff and the defendant alike may not have the same deterrence effects that the outcome of the trial would have had. Individuals may prefer to settle even though society would have preferred the case being tried.[83] Therefore, even if offenders are certain they will have to compensate all victims that step forward, some illegal conduct causing damages to society can still be beneficial to potential offenders. Since they are still not forced to incorporate the total harm caused to society into their cost-benefit calculation.

Public fines, on the other hand, have the potential to be set at adequate levels in order to deter efficiently. If the public fine is set at the optimal level, the optimal sanction will be imposed on the offender in just one costly proceeding, rather than in numerous individual and costly trials before the courts. This adds to the efficiency of the overall enforcement activities, by reducing the costs of doubled efforts that would arise in several proceedings.

1.1.4. Specific public sanctions needed

Fines or sanctions in form of financial payments to be made by the convicted also face the risk that the wrongdoer may escape part or all of his liability because

---

79 The optimal sanction would also have to take into account the probability of detection, which is often less than one. For the full economics of the optimal sanction, see section C of chaper 2 below.

80 The dead weight loss refers to the loss in total social welfare when a market is not in the competitive equilibrium. For a discussion see Leslie, "Antitrust Damages and Deadweight Loss," *Antitrust Bulletin* 51 (2006), 521.

81 As done in the US. For a discussion of treble damages see Polinsky, "Detrebling Versus Decoupling Antitrust Damages: Lessons from the Theory of Enforcement," *Georgetown Law Journal* 74 (1986): 1231.

82 Wils, *Should private antitrust enforcement be encouraged in Europe?* 473, 481.

83 In addition to potentially too low settlement amounts, deterrence effect of settlements may also be inhibited when settlements are not made public or because settlements may not set a precedence.

he[84] is unable to pay the total amount. The optimal monetary sanction, equal to the total harm done to society, can in some cases surmount the wealth of the offender. The actual expected fine a potential offender takes into account when contemplating whether or not to break the law is limited to his own wealth. If that is less than the expected benefit, the illegal conduct will likely seem beneficial to the potential infringer, despite the fact that total harm caused to society would be much larger. Private enforcement has little alternatives to offer in such cases, but public enforcement may resort to other mechanisms. One of these is the use of criminal sanctions.[85] The threat of imprisonment on top of monetary sanctions could cure this obstacle to efficient deterrence. The imposition of criminal fines, however, is traditionally restricted to public enforcement activities. Therefore, in this regard public enforcement also has an advantage over private enforcement.

Finally yet importantly, enforcement through specialised public authorities is considered to add more to the development and clarification of the law than private suits. This is for reasons connected to the different incentives to sue or to enforce. The general interests of society are less likely to be an issue in private actions before the courts, where the interest of the individual plaintiff will be dominant. These interests may strongly deviate from those of society, as discussed above. This may be a problem especially in the case of competition law enforcement.[86]

Summing up, it may be argued that public enforcement is absolutely necessary to achieve efficient deterrence, as it can help to close some gaps that may persist if enforcement were only to take place through private actions. Therefore, private enforcement, as it generally is constructed, is unsuitable to act as perfect substitute for public enforcement. However, as it is currently designed, public enforcement may also be insufficient on its own. Therefore, there is likely to be a growing role for private enforcement. This may all the more be the case, when private enforcement is changed and designed in a way to be more efficient, or when other goals than that of deterrence are pursued through law enforcement.

84 The terms he or she are used throughout the text to refer to both female and male persons.

85 For example Shavell, "Criminal law and the optimal use of nonmonetary sanctions as a deterrent," *Columbia Law Review* (1985): 1232; Wils, *Is criminalization of EU competition law the answer?* 117,145.

86 For a general assessment, see Wils, "The Relationship between Public Antitrust Enforcement and Private Actions for Damages," *World Competition* 32 (2009): 3.

1.2. *Advantages of private enforcement*

In many cases, the injured party will have a large information advantage over a public authority with regard to the detection of a law infringement.[87] A clear example could be a competition law infringement concerning refusal to deal.[88] In such a case, the retailer is instantly aware of the conduct of his opponent, while a competition authority would have to invest considerable resources to detect that infringement. As already mentioned, such private information may be voluntarily supplied to the public authorities. In addition to the option to file complaints with the authorities, positive experiences are claimed with private claims for injunction as well.[89] Private claims for damages, which are the focus in the current discussion and this thesis, may be an additional and possibly overall more efficient avenue to utilise private information advantages where they exist, thus increasing the number of prosecuted cases and consequently increasing deterrence.

As explained above, from an economic perspective, compensation of victims is only important to the extent that fear of its payment engenders deterrence. Nevertheless, sound arguments also exist for private enforcement when taking deterrence as a major objective. More particularly, private enforcement may be a beneficial complement to public enforcement. If public enforcement were perfect, the optimal number of cases would be prosecuted and optimal sanctions would be imposed, leading to optimal deterrence. However, when public enforcement is not efficient or even effective enough, enhancing private enforcement may remedy pitfalls of public enforcement in Europe.

The level of sanction imposed on offenders can also be positively influenced by using private enforcement as complement to public enforcement. Commentators have repeatedly raised concerns that the current fines imposed by competition authorities are not high enough to efficiently deter firms from engaging in anti-competitive behaviour.[90] Apart from further increasing fines or even introducing

---

87 McAfee, et al, "Private v. public antitrust enforcement: A strategic analysis," *Journal of Public Economics* 92 (2008): 1863, 1864 f; Brodley, "Antitrust Standing in Private Merger Cases: Reconciling Private Incentives and Public Enforcement," *Michigan Law Review* 94 (1995): 1, 35.

88 Refusal to deal refers to the practice of refusing or denying supply of a product to a purchaser, usually a retailer or wholesaler, often used in order to enforce other restrictions, such as retail price maintenance.

89 Reporting positive experiences in Austria and Germany:Eilmansberger, "The Green Paper on Damages Actions for Breach of the Ec Antitrust Rules and Beyond: Reflections on the Utility and Feasibility of Stimulating Private Enforcement through Legislative Action," *Common Market Law Review* 44 (2007): 431, 437.

90 A frequent argument of proponents of criminal sanctions, see Wils, *Is criminalization of EU competition law the answer?* 117, 145. Möschel, "Kommentar: Erweiterter Privatrechtsschutz im Kartellrecht," *Wirtschaft und Wettbewerb* (2006): 115, 115.

prison sanctions, follow-on private claims for damages in the wake of decisions taken by competition authorities may also form a partial remedy to address this. Thereby the deterrence effect could be enhanced through the use of such complementary sanctions.

Stand-alone private claims on the other hand may at least lead to some punishment when no prosecution through competition authorities takes place. There are a number of reasons why a specific case, even it is brought to the attention of the competition authorities, may not be pursued. Limited resources can be a source for such an omission. Public authorities working under budget constraints may not be able to deal with all cases brought to their attention.[91] The case selection and invested efforts may also be biased.[92] The selection of cases to be investigated may be biased towards more prestigious cases in light of the self-interest of the agencies.[93] Moreover, it may be path-dependant. It has been noted that a large number of competition law infringement are detected by the competition authorities when investigating a previously discovered and related violation.[94] Once investigations are started, there may also be a tendency to find an infringement, due to the confirmation bias,[95] or a desire to justify invested resources. Private enforcement may capture some of those cases that otherwise may escape the enforcement system. Complementary private enforcement permits more cases to be investigated and more infringements to be punished by drawing more resources to enforcement compared to public enforcement alone and thereby leads to a closing of the enforcement gap.[96]

---

91 Traditional argument, see Coffee Jr, "Rescuing the Private Attorney General: Why the Model of the Lawyer as Bounty Hunter Is Not Working," *Maryland Law Review* 42 (1983): 215, 217 f; Böge and Ost, "Up and Running, or is it? Private enforcement-the Situation in Germany and Policy Perspectives," *European Competition Law Review* 27 (2006): 197, 197.

92 Wils, "The combination of the investigative and prosecutorial function and the adjudicative function in EC antitrust enforcement: A legal and economic analysis," *World Competition* 27 (2003): 201, 212 f.

93 See Lande and Davis, "An Evaluation of Private Antitrust Enforcement: 29 Case Studies," *Interim Report Submitted to the Antitrust Modernization Commission* (2006), 4. Available online at www.antitrustinstitute.org/recent2/550b.pdf; Eger and Weise, "Limits to the private enforcement of antitrust law," *German Working Papers in Law and Economics* (2007), 4. Available at: www.bepress.com/gwp/default/vol2007/iss2/art3.

94 See Schinkel, "Effective Cartel Enforcement in Europe," *World Competition* 30 (2007): 539, 565 f.

95 The confirmation bias is described in the psychological and cognitive sciences as tendency to select and interpret new information in a way as to confirm prior beliefs. See for example Camerer, "Behavioral economics: Reunifying psychology and economics," *Proceedings of the National Academy of Sciences of the United States of America* 96 (1999): 10575.

96 See Schinkel, *Effective Cartel Enforcement in Europe* 539, 548, stating "Civil servants in the agencies have to set priorities on the basis of limited information, budgets and time". See also Jones, "Private Antitrust Enforcement in Europe: A Policy Analysis and Reality Check," *World Competition* 27 (2004): 13, 21.

Lastly, another major advantage of private enforcement through actions for damages, compared to public enforcement through fines or possibly also criminal sanctions, is that the former can also lead to compensation of the victims and therefore to corrective justice.[97] The major objective of corrective justice is to compensate parties that suffered harm due to the unlawful conduct of another. Depending on the value society attaches to that goal, private damages suits may be preferred to an indirect compensation of victims, for example through the redistribution of collected public fines. The latter could lead to a compensation relatively unrelated to the actual amount of individual damage sustained. In such cases, private enforcement has large advantages over public enforcement. However, as will become clear in the analysis of the optimal group litigation below, the goals of compensating individual victims and at the same time providing adequate incentives for private enforcement may not be reconcilable. In such cases, society will have to make a choice about which goal should be given precedence.

2. THE RIGHT PRIVATE ENFORCEMENT AS COMPLEMENT TO PUBLIC ENFORCEMENT

The classic debate over private versus public enforcement was heavily based on the existing mechanisms of private and public enforcement alike. At least in theory, both systems could be improved. For example, public enforcement agents could be endowed with more resources, so that the enforcement gap could be reduced. On the other hand, maybe private enforcement could be designed as to give incentives to private actors that are better aligned with those of society in order to pursue more beneficial private claims. It is this second possibility, i.e. ways to enhance private enforcement that is the topic of this thesis. The focus being placed here is on the optimal design of a group litigation mechanism.

Leaving public enforcement to the realm of *ceteris paribus*, the question answered is how group litigation mechanisms should be designed in order to reach optimal deterrence. Again, while this goal may not be the foremost goal for current legislators, it is the choice paradigm in which to conduct an economic analysis. Compensation as a goal will be discussed as far as relevant and the analysis conducted with regard to the goal of deterrence. Additionally many valuable insights for the efficiency of group litigation mechanisms when the goal is that of corrective justice will be highlighted. For example, the same obstacles to detection and litigation of damages due to competition law infringements limit

97 As envisioned by the European Commission, seeEuropean Commission, *White Paper on Damages actions for breach of the EC antitrust Rules COM(2008) 165 final, SEC(2008) 404*, COM(2008) 165 final, SEC(2008) 404, 3. Critical:Wils, *Should private antitrust enforcement be encouraged in Europe?* 473, 486 ff.

the degree to which either goal, compensation or corrective justice, can be achieved. Moreover, necessary trade-offs between effectiveness or efficiency of private enforcement and the goal of corrective justice for individuals will be demonstrated.

When designing such a group litigation mechanism, some deviations from the traditional private two-party dispute may be required, even if only theoretically possible. For example, the way in which the amount of damages to be awarded to private plaintiffs is established will have a great effect on the efficiency of such a system. Some commentators fear that when the damages awarded exceed the actual harm imposed on the plaintiff, private parties may have inefficiently high incentives to sue.[98] However, when damages awarded will only be based on the individual harm suffered and not connected to the optimal sanction, exclusive private enforcement will lead to under-deterrence.[99] As the analysis shows, the critical point in all these exercises is that in order to reach sufficient, or even efficient, deterrence effects through the means of claims for damages, a departure form the idea of damages as just compensation for inflicted harm will be necessary. However, the general principle of *restitutio ad integrum* still dominates in most European countries. Although the deterrence function of tort law is recognised, it remains thus far subsidiary to the goal of compensation.[100]

The optimally designed group litigation as a tool of private enforcement is discussed in great detail in the following chapters. It is shown how private enforcement may then act as complement, or even a substitute, to public enforcement.

3. THE DEVELOPMENT IN THE EUROPEAN UNION

In the previous part, the old debate that resurfaces now, although possibly with new or different clothes in some places, was revisited. We now turn to an overview of the recent developments in the discussion of private enforcement of competition law in the European Union.

Currently, in regard to the utilisation of private enforcement, the European Commission places a greater value on the goal of compensatory justice than on

---

98 Kalven Jr and Rosenfield, " The Contemporary Function of the Class Suit," *The University of Chicago Law Review* 8 (1941): 684, 684 f. Micklitz and Stadler, "The Development of Collective Legal Actions in Europe, Especially in German Civil Procedure," *European Business Law Review* 17 (2006): 1473, 1476, 1482.

99 Wils, *Should private antitrust enforcement be encouraged in Europe?* 473, 483.Van Den Bergh, *European competition law and economics: a comparative perspective*, 330.

100 Magnus, *Unification of tort law: Damages, Principles of European Tort Law*, The Hague, London, Boston: Kluwer Law International (2001), 185 ff.

the goal of deterrence. In light of current European developments and the connected discourses being held on the national as well as the supra-national level, the value attached to the goal of corrective justice seems to justify at least some costs connected to changes concerning actions for damages due to competition law infringements. However, how legal changes may be incorporated into the existing cultural and legal framework or, when not, whether the peculiarities of damages due to competition law infringements are large enough to justify special legal provisions outside traditional tort law, is still debated.[101] Moreover, the Member States are likely to be given some leeway to be able to incorporate the proposed measures into their legal systems, so that slight variations may persist from Member State to Member State. For all these upcoming changes, the debate about the most relevant features of private enforcement will be paramount in providing sufficient information for informed decision making.

Traditional means to pursue corrective justice, i.e. the general provisions of tort law, are often regarded as inadequate to effectively deal with the complex, risky and consequently costly undertaking to establish a competition law infringement and to proof the resulting harm.[102] Indeed, in the 2004 Ashurst Study, the obstacles to private enforcement of competition law in the Member States were identified and private enforcement of competition law was found to be in a state of "total underdevelopment".[103] Subsequently, several avenues to enable and encourage private parties to seek compensation in front of courts have been explored and debated in the EU. These include changes to substantive or procedural law, for example concerning standing or time limitations, as well as non-legal, such as the establishment of legal aid funds for specific purposes or private insurance for legal costs. In its Green Paper, the Commission sketched the perceived obstacles to private actions for damages and invited a discussion

101 Eilmansberger, *The Green Paper on Damages Actions for Breach of the Ec Antitrust Rules and Beyond: Reflections on the Utility and Feasibility of Stimulating Private Enforcement through Legislative Action* 431, 442; Micklitz, *The Development of Collective Legal Actions in Europe, Especially in German Civil Procedure* 1473, 1473; Joint Working Party of the Bars and Law Societies of the United Kingdom ("JWP"), "Response to the Commission White Paper on Damages Actions for Breach of the EC Competition Rules," (2008), 3. Available at: http://ec.europa.eu/comm/competition/antitrust/actionsdamages/white_paper_comments.html.

102 Focusing on the problems of financing such lawsuits: Riley and Peysner, "Damages in EC antitrust actions: who pays the piper?" *European Law Review* 31 (2006): 748. See also:Eilmansberger, *The Green Paper on Damages Actions for Breach of the Ec Antitrust Rules and Beyond: Reflections on the Utility and Feasibility of Stimulating Private Enforcement through Legislative Action* 431, 446 ff.

103 "Ashurst Study" Waelbroeck, *Study on the Conditions for Claims for Damages in Case of Infringement of EC Competition Rules: Comparative Report, Open Procedure COMP/2003/A1/22, Ashurst Study for Directorate General Competition of the EU Commission, London, England*, 1, 84. Available at http://ec.europa.eu/comm/competition/antitrust/others/actions_for_damages/national_reports/spain_en.pdf.

on possible solutions, which were elaborated in the annexed Staff Working Document.[104] The Green Paper was followed by a White Paper, in which the Commission after deliberation of the comments on the Green Paper and an extensive impact assessment focused the proposals on specific measures.[105] The White Paper will be discussed in greater detail in chapter 4. In this section, an introduction into the debate that took place on the European as well as national levels shall be provided, focusing on the main issues that are or were to be solved.

Some of the proposals focused on ways to reduce the costs of litigation faced by potential plaintiffs (contingency fees and other financing mechanisms; one-way fee-shifting). Others were meant to increase the incentives to sue in general (types of damages awarded) or for specific types of plaintiffs (passing-on defence and standing of indirect consumers). Methods to ease the complexity of establishing a competition law infringement (disclosure rules; access to evidence) were also discussed. Most importantly for our purposes was that also the introduction of some form of group litigation was mooted. The effects of each option individually not only depends on its specific design but also on its combination with others. A rough summary of some major points in the discussion shall therefore suffice here.

3.1. *One way fee-shifting*

In the Green Paper, the Commission opened the discussion about an adequate cost and fee-shifting rule in cases of claims for damages due to competition law infringements. The most common fee-shifting rule in the Member States is the so-called English rule, whereby the succumbing party in a trial has to bear all or part of costs of the prevailing party.[106] In combination with high risks and large costs connected to a trial concerning an alleged competition law infringement, such a rule can have a great discouraging effect on potential plaintiffs. Therefore,

---

104 European Commission, *Green Paper: Damages actions for breach of the EC antitrust rules*, COM(2005) 672 final; European Commission, "Commission Staff Working Paper, Annex to the GREEN PAPER Damages actions for breach of the EC antitrust rules, (COM(2005) 672 final)," (2005).

105 European Commission, *White Paper on Damages actions for breach of the EC antitrust Rules COM(2008) 165 final, SEC(2008) 404*, COM(2008) 165 final, SEC(2008) 404; European Commission, "Commission Staff Working Paper accompanying the White Paper on Damages actions for breach of the EC antitrust rules," (2008), COM(2008) 165 final, SEC (2008) 405.

106 "Ashurst Study"Waelbroeck, *Study on the Conditions for Claims for Damages in Case of Infringement of EC Competition Rules: Comparative Report, Open Procedure COMP/2003/A1/22, Ashurst Study for Directorate General Competition of the EU Commission, London, England*, 1. Available at http://ec.europa.eu/comm/competition/antitrust/others/actions_for_damages/national_reports/spain_en.pdf.

one way fee-shifting, in which that rule is only applied to a losing defendant is debated.

This idea is not entirely new and has been widely discussed in the Law and Economics literature, with regard to its merits concerning encouragement of lawsuits, as well as its potential to increase unmeritous suits.[107] The basic arguments are the following. One-way fee-shifting reduces the expected costs of the plaintiff concerning the bringing of a claim and thereby encourages litigation. However, not all plaintiffs may need such encouragement. Competitor plaintiffs using competition law strategically would also benefit from such a rule. Moreover, apart from well-founded suits, unmeritous suits would also be encouraged precisely because they reduce the expected costs of filing suit for the potential plaintiff. This is because he is protected from having to bear the opponents costs, unless some safeguards against abuse (such as limiting the application of the fee-shifting rule to plaintiffs that did not act unreasonable) are in place.

3.2. *Financing mechanisms*

The magnitude of expenses connected to the establishment of a breach of competition law, which typically requires the deployment of not only legal but also economical experts, can act as a deterrent for potential plaintiffs. Private individuals may not be able to pre-finance such expenditures. The issue of financing mechanisms was not directly addressed in the Green Paper, but opened up for consideration and debate in the following White Paper.[108] Amongst options to be considered by the Member States were contingency fees, legal aid mechanisms or insurance systems. All of these issues have been addressed in the legal and economic literature, while the majority of Law and Economics literature focused on contingency fee arrangements and their effects.

Contingency fee arrangements, whereby the lawyer bears the burden of financing the lawsuit in exchange for a percentage of the awards granted in the damage claim, relieve the plaintiff of pre-financing obligations and the risk connected to

---

107 Snyder and Huges, "The English rule for allocating legal costs: evidence confronts theory," *Journal of Law, Economics, & Organization* 6 (1990): 345. Wagener, "Modelling the effect of one-way fee shifting on discovery abuse for private antitrust litigation," *New York University Law Review* 78 (2003): 1887. Feuerstein, "Two-Way Fee Shifting on Summary Judgment or Dismissal: An Equitable Deterrent to Unmeritorious Lawsuits," *Pepperdine Law Review* 23 (1995): 125.

108 European Commission, *Commission Staff Working Paper accompanying the White Paper on Damages actions for breach of the EC antitrust rules*, COM(2008) 165 final, SEC (2008) 405, 17.

loosing the case at trial.[109] The effects of such a fee arrangement are heavily debated in the Law and Economics literature. Such fee systems obviously are less feasible for individual claims with very low values, unless they can be bundled. A common criticism against contingency fees is their potentially negative impact on the principal-agent problems between client and lawyer.[110] However, other commentators see the contingency fee arrangement as a partial solution to the principal-agent problem.[111] Opinions also differ with regard to the effect of contingency fee arrangement on the incentives to file unmeritous suits. Obviously, when the plaintiff is secured against any costs of the litigation, he may be more willing to pursue suits that have little or no merits.[112] However, other authors claim that contingency fees may reduce or at least not exacerbate the incentives to file unmeritous suits, when the lawyer acts as a kind of gatekeeper.[113]

Legal aid or insurance systems are similarly problematic and debated. While reducing disincentives for plaintiffs to file suit, they also may encourage unmeritous suits, as the plaintiff does not have to take the costs of the litigation into account. Total welfare can only be increased when the costs incurred by society due to more litigation activities are outweighed by the deterrence effects created by that litigation activity.[114] Before-the-event legal expense insurance can influence the bargaining position between opposing parties, by making the threat to sue credible even in those cases, where the claim itself would otherwise have a negative expected value, because the plaintiff will not have to bear the

---

109 Discussing risk-shifting properties: Danzon, "Contingent Fees for Personal Injury Litigation," *The Bell Journal of Economics* 14 (1983): 213. Halpern and Turnbull, "Legal fees contracts and alternative cost rules: An economic analysis," *International Review of Law and Economics* 3 (1983): 3. Generally:Rubinfeld and Scotchmer, *Contingent fees. The New Palgrave Dictionary of Economics and the Law.* ed. Newman. London: Macmillan (1998), 415.

110 Schäfer, "The Bundling of Similar Interests in Litigation. The Incentives for Class Action and Legal Actions taken by Associations," *European Journal of Law and Economics* 9 (2000): 183, 194 f. See also Miller, "Some agency problems in settlement," *The Journal of Legal Studies* 16 (1987): 189. Contrary: Polinsky and Rubenfield, "A note on settlements under the contingent fee method of compensating lawyers," *International Review of Law and Economics* 22 (2002): 217.

111 See for example Rubinfeld, *Contingent fees* 415. Gravelle and Waterson, "No Win, No Fee: Some Economics of Contingent Legal Fees," *The Economic Journal* 103 (1993): 1205. Schwartz and Mitchell, "Economic Analysis of the Contingent Fee in Personal-Injury Litigation, An," *Stan.L.Rev.* 22 (1969): 1125.

112 Legal Expense Insurance or Legal Aid might have similar effects.

113 Miceli, "Do contingent fees promote excessive litigation," *The Journal of Legal Studies* 23 (1994): 211, who found no support for excessive litigation; Kritzer, "Contingency fee lawyers as gatekeepers in the civil justice system," *Judicature* 81 (1997): 22, stating that 50% of the cases were turned down by lawyers working on contingency basis, due to lack of merits.

114 For an analysis seeVan Velthoven, "Legal cost insurance and social welfare," *Economics Letters* 72 (2001): 387.

litigation costs.[115] This effect would work in cases that have little merits and are started in order to extract a settlement offer from the defendant, as well as in meritous cases.[116] After-the-event legal expenditure insurance is not likely to have the same effect, as the insurance companies can be expected to only offer insurance in cases where they consider the probability of winning to be large. It should be noted, however, that many legal expense insurance policies (at least before-the-event insurances) do not provide coverage for competition law cases. This may be due to the complexity of cases and the difficulties in assessing the expected value of such cases. Moreover, they also often require a minimum value of the case, which may not be met in case where small and widely scattered damages occurred to end consumers due to a competition law infringement.

Another possible alternative are professional litigation funders, who have become increasingly important in the recent years. Their "*modus operandi*" can be regarded as an investment in a risky endeavour, typically rewarded by a contingency payment. These forms of financing also lead to a shift of risk and costs away from the plaintiff while at the same time the professional litigation funders will also thoroughly investigate the risks and chances connected to an investment into a specific case. Therefore, they are also likely to prefer financing the litigation of cases with a larger probability of winning, and at the same time also cases with a larger total value.

3.3. *Types of damages awarded*

A first issue with regard to damages awarded would be which types of harms can be compensated, i.e. whether only harm caused to direct purchasers can be compensated or whether also indirect purchasers may be compensated.[117] As this question is strongly connected to the issue of the passing-on defence, it will be discussed in detail in that section.[118] Other types of harm that would have to

115 Negative Expected Value cases refer to cases where the costs of litigation are expected to outweigh the prospective benefits, either because the probability of winning the case at trial is low (the case has little merits) or because the litigation costs are simply too large compared to the expected outcome. For an overview see Bebchuk, "Negative Expected Value Suits," *NBER Working Paper Series Paper No. W6474*(1998). Available at SSRN: http://ssrn.com/abstract=226219.

116 In Germany, where Legal Expense Insurance plays a very important role for financing litigation, the experience seems to have been exactly that LEI stimulates litigation.Kilian, "Alternatives to Public Provision: The Role of Legal Expenses Insurance in Broadening Access to Justice: The German Experience," *Journal of Law and Society* (2003): 31, 45 f.

117 Indirect purchasers of the good in question are consumers, that did not buy directly from the manufacturer (or competition law infringing firm), but from intermediaries, for example in the downstream market such as retailers. Just as the product in question might go trough a whole distribution chain from producer to end-consumer, so may the increased prices due to a restriction of competition in the upstream markets be passed on.

118 See section 3.4 below.

be included in order to reach the optimal sanction to efficiently deter anti-competitive conduct would also include the harm caused to competitors or the deadweight loss.[119]

Other issues that need to be decided upon relating to the damages awarded are connected to the way damages will be quantified, for example whether damages can be aggregated, and the amount of damages that can be awarded, for example whether interest is granted or multipliers are used. In July 2008, the European Commission issued a tender invitation to investigate methods to quantify damages due to competition law infringements, which is expected to provide much needed insights and recommendations.[120]

Just like the general debate on private enforcement of competition law, also the discussion about adequate damages due to competition law or antitrust infringements divided commentators into two slightly different approaches: those who analyse damages with the goal of deterrence in mind,[121] and few who focus on the goal of corrective justice.[122] While the former view necessitates that, in order to efficiently deter, the damages awarded should be based on total costs imposed on society due to the infringement,[123] the latter view focuses on the more traditional individual harm based methods and the idea of *restitutio ad integrum* to establish the amount of damages. Harm-based or gain-based methods to determine damages, as they were introduced as point of deliberation in the Green Paper, reach the compensation and deterrence goal to differing degrees.[124] When the illegal gains to the infringer exceed the costs imposed on private parties as victims of the infringement, a gains based estimation of damages, such as disgorgement of profits, would be preferable from a strict deterrence point of view.[125] Moreover, individual harm may be more difficult to quantify and prove than the illegal gain, so that a gains based estimation could

119 See Renda, *Making antitrust damages actions in the EU more effective. Study in support of the impact assessment of the EC White Paper on antitrust damages actions*, 415.

120 See http://ec.europa.eu/competition/antitrust/actionsdamages/index.html.

121 The classic Law and Economics approach. See e.g. Landes, "Optimal sanctions for antitrust violations," *The University of Chicago Law Review* 50 (1983): 652; Baker, "Private information and the deterrent effect of antitrust damage remedies," *Journal of Law, Economics, & Organization* 4 (1988): 385.

122 European Commission, *White Paper on Damages actions for breach of the EC antitrust Rules COM(2008) 165 final, SEC(2008) 404*, COM(2008) 165 final, SEC(2008) 404, 3.

123 See chapter 2, section C and also Polinsky and Shavell, "Should Liability Be Based on the Harm to the Victim or the Gain to the Injurer?" *Journal of Law, Economics, & Organization* 10 (1994): 427.

124 Again, the economics relating to optimal deterrence and the optimal sanction will be discussed in section C of chapter 3 in greater detail, while in this section only crude and general ideas will be presented.

125 Assuming the goal is absolute deterrence, which excludes efficient breaches of competition law. See Camilli, "Optimal Fines in Cartel Cases and the Actual EC Fining Policy," *World Competition* 29 (2006): 575.

lead to a higher probability of conviction. However, the lack of a direct link between harm and illegal gain leads to inaccurate compensation of plaintiffs. In addition, gains based methods for quantifying damages also bear no systematic relationship to the total harm caused to society, so that in cases where the gain is smaller than the harm, under-deterrence could result.

Other deliberations include the possibility to award multiple (double or treble) damages, in order to incorporate the low probability of detection, to increase the level of deterrence and to further motivate victims to undertake the complex and risky task of litigation.[126] However, mandatory doubling of damages constitutes only an extremely crude method to account for the low probability of detection, which differs greatly depending on the anti-competitive conduct in question[127] and on whether private litigation takes place as stand-alone or follow-on suits.[128] Moreover, the risk of unmeritous suits also increases with the amount of expected gain from litigation, as it makes any litigation more profitable and the threat of litigation more credible.

Less disputed in the European Union are questions relating to pre-judgment interest. Pre-judgement interest is, contrary to the USA, normally granted in the Member States of the European Union, in accordance with the goal of fully compensating the victim, although the dates from which pre-judgement interest is granted differ.[129]

3.4. *Passing-on defence and standing of indirect buyers*

Possibly influenced by the famous US cases *Illinois Brick v. Illinois* and *Hannover Shoe*,[130] where standing to sue was denied to indirect purchasers, the Green Paper and the annexed Working Paper discussed the passing-on defence and indirect purchaser standing as possible obstacles to private damage claims due to competition law infringements. In the White Paper, the Commission opted for

126 German Monopolies Commission, "Das allgemeine Wettbewerbsrecht in der Siebten GWB-Novelle, Sondergutachten der Monopolkommission gemäß, §44 Abs. 1 Satz 4 GWB," (2004) 40 ff; Paulis, *Policy Issues in the Private Enforcement of EC Competition Law. Private Enforcement of EC Competition Law.* ed. Basedow. Alphen aan den Rijn: Kluwer Law International (2007), 7, 13.

127 See Renda, *Making antitrust damages actions in the EU more effective. Study in support of the impact assessment of the EC White Paper on antitrust damages actions*, 177 ff; Easterbrook, "Detrebling antitrust damages," *Journal of Law & Economics* 28 (1985): 445.

128 As in follow-on suits the infringement has already been detected by public authorities, the detection rate has to be equal to one in the follow-on proceeding.

129 For an overview and anlaysis of pre-jdugment interest see Renda, *Making antitrust damages actions in the EU more effective. Study in support of the impact assessment of the EC White Paper on antitrust damages actions*, 436 ff.

130 U.S. Supreme Court, *Illinois Brick Co. v. Illinois, 431 U.S. 720* (1977); U.S. Supreme Court, *Hanover Shoe, Inc. v. United Shoe Machinery Corp., 392 U.S. 481* (1968).

allowing the passing-on defence in cases of direct purchasers as plaintiffs and a general but rebuttable assumption of full passing-on in cases of indirect purchaser claims, shifting the burden of proof in both cases on the defendant.[131] The likely effects of this decision will be discussed in greater detail in chapter 4, while in this section a general overview shall be given over the issues discussed.

Businesses harmed by a competition law infringement, for example distributors as direct buyers paying supra-competitive prices due to a price cartel on the manufacturer level, may be able to pass all or part of their additional costs on to indirect buyers, such as the end consumer. Being sued for damages by direct buyers, the defendant may invoke this fact as the so called passing-on defence and thereby reduce the damages to be paid to the plaintiff by the amount of costs passed on to direct consumers.

The passing-on defence insures that the direct buyer does receive compensation only for the actual harm caused to him and therefore would mirror the legal landscape of damages in torts as existent in the Member States. It also would follow the reasoning that the same harm should not be compensated twice, in case the indirect purchasers harmed by the same infringements would also sue for damages. For such reasons, some commentators support the passing-on defence.

At the same time, it has been frequently argued that allowing a passing-on defence entails the risk that the party closest to the infringement and therefore the best informed party with lower costs to sue may have too little incentives to file suit.[132] Direct buyers may already be hesitant to file damages claims, either because of fear of retaliation,[133] or because they benefit from the restriction of competition in the upstream markets themselves.[134] At the same time, the more distant indirect buyers, for example end consumers, may never file suit for their damages.[135] Overall, calculating and proving accurate damages along a

131 European Commission, *White Paper on Damages actions for breach of the EC antitrust Rules COM(2008) 165 final, SEC(2008) 404*COM(2008) 165 final, SEC(2008) 404.

132 Such arguments are made by Landes and Posner, "Should Indirect Purchasers Have Standing to Sue under the Antitrust Laws - An Economic Analysis of the Rule of Illinois Brick," *The University of Chicago Law Review* 46 (1978): 602;Werden and Schwartz, "Illinois Brick and the Deterrence of Antitrust Violations - An Economic Analysis," *The Hastings Law Journal* 35 (1983): 629; Lopatka and Page, "Indirect Purchaser Suits and the Consumer Interest," *Antitrust Bulletin* 48 (2003): 531.

133 Renda, *Making antitrust damages actions in the EU more effective. Study in support of the impact assessment of the EC White Paper on antitrust damages actions*, 471.

134 As, for example, competitors outside a price cartel might also be able to profitably increase their price (umbrella effect).

135 Schinkel and Rüggeberg, "Consolidating Antitrust Damages in Europe: A Proposal for Standing in Line With Efficient Private Enforcement, Amsterdam Center for Law & Economics Working Paper No. 2006–04," *World Competition: Law and Economics Review* 29

distribution chain may become a very complex task.[136] In consequence, potential competition law infringers would face a low probability of ever being held liable and under-deterrence would result. Therefore, it has been suggested to prohibit the passing-on defence, often connected to a restriction of standing to direct purchasers.[137]

3.5. *Access to evidence*

Competition law infringements are likely to pose larger obstacles as regard to establishment of cause and resulting harm than other torts, especially in stand-alone suits. Legal provision concerning access to evidence in competition cases therefore may be a crucial tool to enhance or hinder private claims for damages. Civil law tradition, as opposed to the common law tradition, relies on information gathered during the process and often severely restricts the possibilities for plaintiffs to extract evidence from the defendant.[138] Very broad and general pre-trial disclosure regimes, as they are available in the USA, are fairly alien to many Member States. Broadening discovery rules could help to overcome initial information asymmetries between plaintiffs and defendants and allow fact-findings that are more accurate. Moreover, as the economic literature states, the incentives to settle increase when parties' estimations of the likely outcome of the trial converge,[139] thereby reducing overall costs of litigation. The reason lies in the effect that settlement is more likely when the opposing parties have similar assessment of the likely outcome of the case when it proceeds to trial and broad discovery rules can reduce information asymmetry between the parties, leading to more assessments that are similar.

However, broad discovery rules also may enable plaintiffs to pressure defendants, for whom the discovery procedure can entail considerable costs, into settlements

---

(2006): 395, 402. Findings by Lande and Davis, that recoveries of direct purchasers greatly outweigh recoveries by indirect purchasers seem to support that idea. SeeLande, *An Evaluation of Private Antitrust Enforcement: 29 Case Studies* 1.

136 Fisher, "Economic Analysis and Antitrust Damages," *World Competition* 29 (2006): 383, 388. See also Hellwig, *Private Damage Claims and the Passing On Defense in Horizontal Price Fixing Cases: An Economists Perspective. Private Enforcement of EC Competition Law.* ed. Basedow. Alphen aan den Rijn: Kluver Law International (2007), 121.

137 See for example the discussion in Germany, Chapter 5, Sectoin C.

138 For example Germany leaves collection of evidence to parties. Court orders the parties may achieve to compel the other party to provide documents are restricted to extremely narrowly defined and precisely described documents. See: "Ashurst Study" Waelbroeck, *Study on the Conditions for Claims for Damages in Case of Infringement of EC Competition Rules: Comparative Report, Open Procedure COMP/2003/A1/22, Ashurst Study for Directorate General Competition of the EU Commission, London, England,* 1. Available at http://ec.europa.eu/comm/competition/antitrust/others/actions_for_damages/national_reports/spain_en.pdf.

139 Priest and Klein, "The Selection of Disputes for Litigation," *The Journal of Legal Studies* 13 (1984): 1, 1 ff.

even if the merits of the case are uncertain.[140] Consequently, the risk of abuse increases.[141] Other issues debated in the Green Paper concerning that context include the availability of information gathered by the European Commission or national competition authorities and possibilities to reduce the burden of proof on the claimant's side.[142] In the White Paper, the Commission opted for several options to ease the burden on plaintiffs with regard to the access to evidence.[143] A minimum disclosure *inter partes* should be ensured, in line with general rules on legal procedures in many Member States. Moreover, final decisions taken by public bodies, such as the European Commission or national competition authorities should be made binding for national courts in cases of follow-on actions for damages. The necessity for plaintiffs to proof fault of the defendant should be reduced, so that only an *excusable error* could eliminate liability of the defendant.

3.6. *Group litigation mechanisms*

The last feature that the Commission generally opened for discussion in the Green Paper and narrowed down to specific proposals in the White Paper are group litigation mechanisms. These are the main subject of this thesis and are described and analysed in depth throughout the following chapters. Therefore, it may suffice here to say that the proposals of the European Commission in the White Paper include: representative actions brought by qualified entities, for example consumer associations, on behalf of the victims; and opt-in collective actions brought by one or more victims on their own behalf and on behalf of other victims.

C. SUMMARY

This chapter provides a brief overview of the placement of the thesis topic in the current discussion about private enforcement of competition law. As the enforcement of competition law may not absolutely be looked at separately from the actual goals of competition law, a quick overview has been given of relevant matters of discussion, i.e., what is the actual subject of protection in European competition law and what weights are given to consumer versus producer welfare. Next, private enforcement of competition law was described as part of

---

140 Wagener, *Modelling the effect of one-way fee shifting on discovery abuse for private antitrust litigation* 1887, 1887.

141 Ginsburg, *Comparing antitrust enforcement in the United States and Europe* 427,437.

142 European Commission, *Commission Staff Working Paper accompanying the White Paper on Damages actions for breach of the EC antitrust rules*, 23 ff.

143 European Commission, *White Paper on Damages actions for breach of the EC antitrust Rules COM(2008) 165 final, SEC(2008) 404*, 4f.

the classic debate about private versus public enforcement. Advantages of private and public enforcement *vis-à-vis* each other were described and related to the specific issue of competition law infringement. As was noted, the strength of the arguments depends very much on the specific design of both private and public enforcement mechanisms. Last, the current developments and issues of debate and reform concerning private enforcement of competition law on the European level were briefly described.

After this overview of placement of the topic of group litigation in the broader context of enforcement of European competition law, the next chapter will introduce the framework used for the analysis of group litigation as conducted in chapter 3 and applied in the following chapters, including definitions of relevant concepts and terms.

CHAPTER 2

GROUP LITIGATION: A GENERAL LEGAL AND ECONOMIC FRAMEWORK

In this section, the general framework of the analysis is presented and the most important concepts are defined. This framework is required in order to identify the specific features a group litigation mechanism would need to entail in order to achieve efficient deterrence effects. Therefore, in the first section the general definitions of terms connected to group litigation mechanisms as they are used here are given. In the second section, a broad overview of the legal framework used for the analysis as a starting point is described. In the last section, the economic framework is presented in detail.

A. DEFINITION OF GENERAL CONCEPTS

> "For he went in many guises, and won renown under many names"
> J.R.R. Tolkien, *Lord of the Rings*

Recently, countries both within the EU and beyond have been faced with relatively new problems that have challenged the sometimes long grown legal traditions of civil procedure. In the age of globalisation, technological developments have lead to an opening of tight knit and small communities to the world. Mass production and exchange on the world market take place with modern technologies and amongst anonymous parties. Consequently, it has become possible for very large numbers of people to become victims of just one particular incidence. Courts faced legal claims that exceeded the possibilities of traditional means to bundle similar interest into one procedure. In the light of the special needs that emerged and the general underlying legal system, different group litigation mechanisms have been developed and incorporated. A large diversity exists in reality, and even more forms are theoretically possible, as a multitude of features can be regulated individually and only in combination shape a particular system. To clarify the concepts used, some basic principles and definitions are introduced here.

1. THE TYPES OF GROUP LITIGATION

The first criterion that will be used to distinguish different forms of group litigation is the nature of the representative. Joinder procedures occur when several victims file individual suits, but their suits are bundled into one procedure (either voluntarily or by order of the court). If the group of harmed individuals (group members) is represented by only one (or relatively very few) of the group members, so that this so called lead plaintiff and/or the lawyer are the main driving forces behind the action, the form will be considered to be that of a collective action. If an association, organisation or public body is the main actor and files suit on behalf of the group members then it is a representative action.

1.1. Joinder procedures

Joinder procedures are already commonly conducted in many Member States. Litigants can decide to bring a suit together in one trial against the same defendant, when legal or factual questions of the case are common. Typically, such procedures are only allowed where basic questions of facts to be determined are common to all individual claims, such as the question of liability for instance. Each plaintiff may each have their own lawyer representing them, or they can decide to be represented by the same lawyer or association. The critical fact is that the individual claims remain fully intact over the proceeding to the same extent as they are in traditional civil litigation. Consequently, claims are filed and tried on an individual basis. The individual plaintiffs remain the opponent of the defendant, can change their legal representative, settle with the defendant or withdraw their claim as though it was an individual procedure. However, it is possible for the group to coordinate their efforts through contractual agreements. Victims and their lawyers do not become anonymous, as they may in other forms of group litigation, and the different claims are not merged into one.

Joinder procedures have long been included amongst the mechanisms of civil procedure in many Member States. The obstacles to private damage claims identified in the Ashurst-Study[144] apparently have not been overcome by allowing joinder procedures. This may be why the Commission in its White Paper[145]

144 See Waelbroeck, *Study on the Conditions for Claims for Damages in Case of Infringement of EC Competition Rules: Comparative Report, Open Procedure COMP/2003/A1/22, Ashurst Study for Directorate General Competition of the EU Commission, London, England.* Available at: www.europa.eu.int/comm/competition/antitrust/others/private_enforcement/comparative_report_clean_en.pdf.

145 European Commission, *White Paper on Damages actions for breach of the EC antitrust Rules COM(2008) 165 final, SEC(2008) 404.*

focused on the development of representative actions and collective actions. These systems are described below.

Some other forms of existing group litigation mechanisms are very close to the principles of joinder as well. Test case procedures, for example, lead to the selection of one of the many individually filed suits, in which some issues common to all the individual claims are decided upon. Plaintiffs, made aware of each other through an association, can also decide to bring a lawsuit jointly, or it may be possible for them to assign their claims to the association for enforcement. Examples include so-called *Sammelklagen*, as they exist in Germany[146] and Austria.[147] Depending on the specific design, such mechanisms are either closer to joinder procedures or closer to representative actions with a requirement for victims to explicitly express their wish to be represented by the association and possibly to provide proof and evidence with regard to their claims.

This form of bundling similar claims into one proceeding is not analysed explicitly here for several reasons. First, many of the obstacles to the more traditional individual actions for damages also inhibit the efficiency of joinder procedures. Second, experience has shown that these mechanisms have not been significantly effective in those countries, where actions for damages due to competition law infringements have been available for a long time.[148] Moreover, these experiences are akin with those using these procedures in other areas of law.[149] Third, the whole discussion about enhancing private enforcement of European competition law rests on the findings that these existing mechanisms are not completely sufficient.

1.2. Representative actions

In many Member States certified bodies, such as consumer associations, are already endowed with selected rights to act on behalf of victims of illegal behaviour. Very often, these rights are limited to cease and desist orders and to

---

146 Koch, "Non-Class Group Litigation Under EU and German Law," *Duke Journal of Comparative and International Law* 11 (2001): 355, 360. See also Günter Hörmann, "Sammelklagen im Energie- und Versicherungsrecht" in: Kollektive Rechtsdurchsetzung – Chancen und Risiken, Bamberg, 79–88.

147 See B. Pirker-Hörmann and P. Kolba, "Österreich: Von der Verbandsklage zur Sammelklage" in: Kollektive Rechtsdurchsetzung – Chancen und Risiken, Bamberg, 199–211.

148 Ashurst Study Waelbroeck, *Study on the Conditions for Claims for Damages in Case of Infringement of EC Competition Rules: Comparative Report, Open Procedure COMP/2003/A1/22, Ashurst Study for Directorate General Competition of the EU Commission, London, England*, speaking of a "total underdevelopment", 1.

149 See for example the Test-case procedure in Germany and the Group Litigation Order in the UK, discussed in Chapter 5.

specific areas of law. For example, in France, associations are granted standing to bring claims in the general interest of consumers (*intérêt collectif des consommateurs*).[150] However, although damages to the collective could be claimed, courts typically granted only reimbursement for expenses.[151] Therefore, the experiences with such claims remained limited. In Spain, since the reform of the law on civil procedure (LEC 2001), representative actions for damages have been introduced in the area of consumer protection.[152] Represented parties in both cases, however, will have to enforce their title for damages against the defendant individually.

As the Commission discussed and proposed in its White Paper, one option is that certified associations could be granted standing to represent their members or even larger groups.[153] The Commissions preferred option for establishing the group of those represented is through opt-in procedures, while in special cases also unidentified victims may be represented.[154] The alternative of representation of unidentified victims would make opt-in solutions unfeasible. The certified body envisioned by the Commission is an association, such as a trade or a consumer association. In that definition, it acts according to and in adherence to its written statutes, which could form the basis of certification. The financing of activities of such associations often is done through membership fees, and frequently supplemented by public subsidies. To attract members, associations typically offer services, such as information through publications, consultancy services, and representation in representative actions.

In this analysis, the definition adopted will be as followed. A representative action is an action brought by an association or specified body on behalf of a group of victims. The important distinction to joinder procedures is that the association is the main actor and initiator. In representative actions as defined here, the incentives for the association that are inherent in the system become very important and greatly influence the effectiveness and efficiency of any representative action. *Ad hoc* associations, as defined by the European

---

150 See Cafaggi and Micklitz, "Administrative and Judicial Collective Enforcement of Consumer Law in the US and the European Community," *EUI Law Working Paper No. 2007/22*(2007), p 24. Available at SSRN: http://ssrn.com/abstract=1024103; Wagner, *Kollektiver Rechtsschutz – Regelungsbedarf bei Massen- und Streuschäden. Auf dem Weg zu einer europäischen Sammelklage?* eds. Casper, et al. Munchen: European law publishers GmBH (2009), 41, 73 ff.

151 Beuchler, *Länderbericht Frankreich.* in *Das Verbandsklagerecht in der Informations- und Dienstleistungsgesellschaft.* eds. Micklitz andStadler. Münster: Landwirtschaftsverlag (2005), 57, 57.

152 See Mom, *Länderbericht Spanien.* in *Das Verbandsklagerecht in der Informations- und Dienstleistungsgesellschaft.* eds. Micklitz andStadler. Münster: Landwirtschaftsverlag (2005), 655.

153 See European Commission, *Commission Staff Working Paper accompanying the White Paper on Damages actions for breach of the EC antitrust rules*, 18 ff.

154 *Ibidem*, 18 ff.

Commission,[155] will not be considered as a separate option in this analysis. This is because *ad hoc* associations may resemble, depending on their specific design, various other forms of group litigation. They may approximate joinder procedures (for example when victims themselves form the association *ad hoc* for administrative purposes in joinder procedures), or collective actions (for example when lawyers form the association and ask a premium in the form of a percentage of the aggregate value of the damages achieved by the represented victims).

1.3. Collective actions

Collective actions (or class actions) are actions brought by one member of the group that is to be represented in the action. The so-called *lead plaintiff* belongs to the group and represents the interest of himself as well as that of all group members. A classic example would be the class action system, as it exists in the USA. This scenario allows lawyers to take a very dominant role, to the extent that the lawyer may even be able to choose the lead plaintiff for the group litigation that they themselves initiate. This is especially the case when victims are less informed and knowledgeable. Then there may be a large possibility that the active party motivating the litigation is the lawyer, rather than the victims. Therefore, in collective actions, the main actors will be the lead plaintiff and/or the lawyer. In such cases, the incentive structures guiding the decisions taken by the lawyer and the lead plaintiff play an important role.

While the US class action system is typically characterised by opt-out systems, the Commission's proposal includes an opt-in collective action. In this case, other victims have to be notified of the proceeding and decide to opt-in, in order to become a represented member of the group. Experiences with collective actions in the Member States are generally limited and recent.[156]

2. ESTABLISHING GROUP MEMBERSHIP

Another important criterion, which is relevant whenever plaintiffs are not bringing their claims themselves, is under what conditions they will be eligible to be part of the represented group. Again, these systems can be constructed in many different ways, so that although technically taking one particular form,

---

155 European Commission, *White Paper on Damages actions for breach of the EC antitrust Rules COM(2008) 165 final, SEC(2008) 404*, 4.

156 For example Sweden introduced allegedly as first Member State an opt-in class action in 2003 (Lag (2002:599) Om Grupprättegång). Denmark introduced a similar class action with generally opt-in, and an opt-out solution in special circumstances in 2008.

they may resemble other forms in their effect. Here a general distinction will be made between opt-in, opt-out and mandatory regimes.

2.1. Opt-in systems

Opt-in systems require the victims, upon notification, to express their wishes to take part in a group litigation procedure. In the internet age, this may be as simple as filling in a legal form that states a wish to be represented in a group litigation. However, it may also require victims do much more, for example provide the specifics and evidence concerning their claim, or fill out extensive legal forms. Another option is one, where victims assign their rights to litigate their claim to some other party acting on their behalf. However, the latter system resembles much more the course of a joinder procedure.

In general, opt-in procedures require a minimum of activity on the side of the victims, who have to inform themselves about the consequences of opting-in, spend at least some time in filling out forms and in some cases possibly accept liability for financial participation. This will be the major difference in the definition used in this analysis compared to opt-out procedures.

Given the fact that individual damages can in some cases be widespread and very small in amount, a large risk of using an opt-in procedure in the case of small claims is that victims will remain passive and the group finally represented will be relatively small.

2.2. Opt-out systems

Contrary to opt-in procedures, opt-out procedures require the represented members of the group only to become active, if they do not wish to be part of the group.

Opt-out procedures can be designed in a way that would make them similar to opt-in or even joinder procedures. For example, if individuals are required to file individual claims against the defendant after liability (or potentially also the damage amount per represented party) has been established in a group proceeding, the opt-out system will have a similar effect to test case procedures. If victims need to become active, by filling out forms, providing proof for their claim and eligibility to participate in the group in order to receive their damage awards, then the system will have similar effects as an opt-in system, even though the "opt-in" would take place in a latter stage. If opt-in and opt-out procedures are designed to take place at the same period in the proceeding and individuals need to be sent individual letters inquiring whether they want to opt-out (or opt-in), the difference between these two mechanisms becomes smaller.

Therefore, in this analysis, opt-out procedures are generally assumed to not require victims to become active, unless they do not wish to be represented in the group proceeding.

Depending on the way notification and certification are regulated, the members of the group may become anonymous and detached from the trial. Again, victims ideally should inform themselves about the possible consequences of their choice. Splitting the costs ex ante over all those represented, as under opt-in, becomes much more difficult in the context of an opt-out procedure, since all parties may not yet be identified. Therefore, this can only be done ex post. The major risk with opt-out systems is that created by inadequate notification systems. Notification can take place through direct contacts with each potential group member (when the relevant data is available to the initiator of the action), or be attempted indirectly through mechanisms such as advertisements in newspapers. Notification therefore can be more or less exact and might become very costly, depending on the case at hand and possible number of victims. If the notification system is insufficient, there is a risk that members of the group represented in the proceeding and bound by the subsequent legal decision may not even have been aware of the proceeding.

2.3. Mandatory systems

Mandatory procedures do not allow victims to exempt themselves from representation. All those described as members of the group are automatically represented and they cannot opt-out of the proceedings.

Such a mandatory representation is not very common in traditional civil law tort actions for damages. However, other litigation mechanisms do exist that have legal effects on victims without their prior consent, such actions on behalf of the public interest or affected groups, however this usually restricted to injunctive relief. An example would be the German *Verbandsklage*, where §33 Abs. 2 GWB grants standing to associations to bring claims for injunction on behalf of a group of competitors. Similarly, in cases of infringements of the law against unfair competition and competition law (§§10 UWG, 34a GWB), associations have standing to bring skimming off procedures before the court.[157] In these cases, the association earns a fee to compensate for their expenses, but any other award must be passed on to the state.[158] Here, the association might also be interpreted as enforcing rights that actually would have originated elsewhere,

157 Skimming-off procedures refer to claims to retrieve the illegal gain by the law infringing party.

158 Van Boom and Loos, *Effective Enforcement of consumer law in Europe.* in *Collective Enforcement of Consumer Law.* eds. Van Boom andLoos. Europa Law Publishing (2007), 231, 250. See Eichholtz, *Die US-amerikanische Class Action und ihre deutschen Funktions-*

without the expressed consent of the original right holder. Although participation in these cases may be considered to be mandatory, none of the existing systems described here seem to preclude the individual enforcement of the rights as well.

A mandatory group litigation system is not envisioned by the Commission and due to the important legal questions it raises, would almost certainly meet strong opposition amongst the Community. However, there may be benefits to such a system compared to opt-in and opt-out systems, as discussed in chapter 3.

3. REMUNERATION OF LAWYERS

In this thesis, three general ways to remunerate lawyers for their efforts are discussed, hourly fee arrangements, conditional fee arrangements and contingency fee arrangements. The latter two concepts are sometimes mixed up, so that a definition of how these concepts are used is in order. The line between the different systems of conditional and contingency fees can often be blurred and they may be used to form mixed variations. Additionally, often due to established principles of freedom of contract, parties often may contract for different kind of payment methods. However, not all of these may be considered to be recoverable by the winning opponent under the British cost shifting rule (loser pays) in all countries.

3.1. Hourly fee arrangements

In most Member States of the European Union, lawyers are generally paid through an hourly fee arrangement, granting them a certain amount of payment for each hour worked.[159] In some countries, like in Germany, there are also general regulations on the quantum of these fees. There, these rules also form the basis of the amount of fees that can be recovered by the winning opponent under the British cost-shifting rule.

3.2. Conditional fee arrangements

Contingent or conditional fee arrangements in this analysis are understood to refer to rather to "no win, less fee" arrangements, as opposed to contingency fee

äquivalente, Tübingen: Mohr Siebeck (2002), 274. Wagner, *Kollektiver Rechtsschutz – Regelungsbedarf bei Massen- und Streuschäden* 41, 80.

159 The code of the European Association of Lawyers prohibited *pactum quota litis*, and many Member States only recently began to soften their strict ban, for example by introducing forms of conditional fee arrangements. Emons and Garoupa, "The economics of US-style contingent fees and UK-style conditional fees," *Centre for Economic Policy Research (CEPR) Discussion Paper No. 4473* (2004), 327.

arrangements which are more clearly "no win, no fee", although the line between these two may be thin. Contingent fee agreements grant the lawyer some kind of success bonus and are otherwise based on the hourly fee system. Such systems exist in the UK and also have been recently introduced in Germany.[160]

3.3. *Contingency fee arrangements*

Contingency fee arrangements are understood to refer to agreements that provide the lawyer with no fee, in case his client looses, and a (typically) larger fee[161] in case the client wins. This system is known from the USA, where the lawyer's payment is usually determined as a percentage of the amount in dispute, rather than being based on hourly fees. As is the case in other contingent or contingency fee systems, the larger fee in case of success has to be interpreted at least partially, as compensation for the risk taken by the lawyer.

4. THE TYPES OF VICTIMS

Different types of competition law infringements can harm different sets of victims. As the nature of these can play an important role in the effectiveness or efficiency of a specific group litigation mechanism, the victims also need to be incorporated in the analysis. Broadly speaking, six types of victims harmed can be distinguished.[162] First, direct purchasers (generally other businesses) can incur losses when they sell less of their products at higher prices due to an increased price for their input factor. Second, customers that refrain from buying the product in question or switched to less favourable substitutes are harmed. Third, customers of firms outside a cartel, that have also raised their prices under the price umbrella, are harmed as they also have to pay supra competitive prices. Fourth, indirect purchasers of the infringing firm(s) products may have to pay part of the overcharging that have been passed on by the direct purchasers. Fifth, suppliers to the infringing parties sell less of their products when output is reduced by the offending party. Last, competitors can be harmed by anti-competitive conduct when certain illegal behaviour is aimed at reducing their ability to enter or compete on the market, or simply has that effect.[163] Depending

160 See Chapter 5 on the regulations in these countries.

161 Research has shown that such contingency fee arrangements in the US can lead to effective hourly rates up to thousands of dollars. See Brickman, "Effective Hourly Rates of Contingency Fee Lawyers: Competing Data and Non-Competitive Fees," *Washington University Law Quarterly* 81 (2003): 653.

162 There can, however, be many more, for examples shareholders that are negatively affected, or employees.

163 For types of victims of an infringement of Article 82 ECT see, Mackenrodt, *Private Incentive, Optimal Deterrence and Damage Claims for Abuses of Dominant Positions– The Interaction between the Economic Review of the Prohibition of Abuses of Dominant Positions and Private*

on the specific case in question, such as how much of the larger costs can be passed on from direct to indirect purchasers, only few or all of these types of victims may be harmed by a certain type of conduct.

The nature of the types of victims can also change. A direct purchaser will very often be another firm, such as a retailer, but in some cases direct purchasers may also be private persons, such as end consumers. Customers refraining from buying the product in question because of the non-competitive prices being charged can be both companies as well as private individuals.

The distinction between the victims is relevant to the analysis wherever the nature of the victims influences the extent to which certain advantages or disadvantages of group litigation can arise. A company in business relationship with the infringer will often consume larger amounts of the product affected by the competition law infringement, have a more direct relationship with the offender, possess better knowledge about the market and competition law, and have larger resources available for litigation than a private end consumer has. For these reason, the abilities and incentives of victims to detect infringements and to act upon the detection differ largely.

B. THE LEGAL FRAMEWORK

1. THE TYPES OF INFRINGEMENTS

Naturally, the first legal basis taken into account in this analysis are the regulations governing European Competition Law, namely Article 101 TFEU (ex 81 EC Treaty) and Article Article 102 TFEU (ex 82 EC Treaty).[164] These regulations form the basis on which illegal conduct has to be deterred and which violations of law form the legal basis of actions for damages.

However, a simple distinction between these two rules often will not suffice. There is a variation in the range of possible infringements under European competition law. This variation will have a different effect in regard to the possibilities available for private enforcement. Throughout the analysis, trade-

---

Enforcement. in *Abuse of Dominant Position: New Interpretation, New Enforcement Mechanisms?, Series: MPI Studies on Intellectual Property, Competition and Tax Law.* eds. Mackenrodt, et al. Berlin: Springer (2008), 165 f. For a classification of victims in cartel cases, see Connor, *Global price fixing,* Berlin: Springer (2008), 80 ff.

164 This section shall only provide a quick and basic introduction. For more detailed information, please see Van Den Bergh, *European competition law and economics: a comparative perspective*; Motta, *Competition policy: theory and practice,* Cambridge: Cambridge University Press (2004); Jones and Sufrin, *EC Competition Law: text, cases and materials,* Oxford: Oxford University Press, USA (2007).

offs are necessary between generalisation and a case-by-case analysis. Therefore, in the analysis, reference will be made to which forms of group litigation will be better suited to deal with, or what problems are connected to, specific types of infringements of Article 101 TFEU (ex 81 EC Treaty) and Article Article 102 TFEU (ex 82 EC Treaty). In the end, it may depend on real life experience as to which type of cases may be grouped together and treated in a similar fashion with regard to private enforcement and which cases may need an altered approach.

Breaches of Article 101 TFEU (ex 81 EC Treaty) and Article Article 102 TFEU (ex 82 EC Treaty) can be broadly categorised into three categories. Those involving horizontal agreements, vertical agreements, and abuses of a dominant position.

1.1. Horizontal agreements

Cartel agreements are one form of horizontal agreement or collusive behaviour that is typically prohibited by competition regulation. Such cooperative anti-competitive behaviour includes price fixing, output restriction, the freezing of existing market shares, market division, targeted actions against rivals, and non-price competition restrictions, such as agreements concerning advertising. The effects of all these forms of horizontal agreements can be described as allowing firms to jointly enjoy a market power they would not have otherwise, leading to larger prices and reduced output, and consequently welfare losses.[165] These agreements can harm all types of potential victims, as described above, depending on the type of infringement and specifics of the case in question.

Article 101(1) TFEU prohibits agreements between undertakings, decisions by associations of undertakings, and concerted practices that have the restriction of competition either as their objective, or as their effect. The guidelines clarify that agreements having the restriction of competition as their object, either through price fixing, output restriction or market or costumer sharing, will fall under Article 101(1) TFEU without the necessity to analyse their specific effects.[166] Therefore, especially hard-core cartel agreements fall under almost a *per se* prohibition of Article 101(1) TFEU. An exemption is made for those agreements fulfilling the requirements of Article Article 101(3) TFEU. Article 101(3) TFEU applies to agreements that contribute to the improvement of production or distribution of products, or to the promotion of technical or economic progress, as well as granting consumers a fair share of the benefits.[167] However, the

---

165 Van Den Bergh, *European competition law and economics: a comparative perspective*, 155 ff; Motta, *Competition policy: theory and practice*, 137.

166 European Commission, "Commission Notice – Guidelines on the applicability of Article 81 of the EC Treaty to horizontal cooperation agreements (2001/C 3/02)," *OJ* (2001) no. 18.

167 *Ibidem* no. 31 ff.

restrictions on competition must be indispensable to each of these benefits and may not make the elimination of competition for that product possible. With regard to certain types of agreements in specific industries, the fulfilment of these requirements is legally presumed and they therefore fall under so called *block exemptions*.[168] Courts are bound by these block exemptions, while national competition authorities may withdraw the exemption under certain circumstances.[169]

Horizontal cooperation agreements can be either explicit in nature (a direct agreement between the cartelists, which is seldom), or implicit (which is more common, where cartelists do not directly communicate with each other). The former may be easier to establish in court, as in such cases the effect of the agreement does not have to be proven, proving the purpose of the agreement suffices.[170] An explicit agreement may be proven by providing documents that establish or relate to the agreement. Such documents may be recovered either in a prior public proceeding or potentially in a trial through discovery procedures, when the existence of such documents is reasonably certain. For the establishment of a tacit agreement, some form of invitation to achieve a common goal of one party to the agreement to the other must be established.[171] An explicit agreement therefore may be easier to prove than an implicit agreement, provided that the evidence for the former is accessible.

For the potential plaintiff, however, it would also be necessary to have an idea of whether the alleged infringement falling under Article 101(1) TFEU may potentially be exempted as fulfilling the conditions of Article 101(3) TFEU, or as falling under one of the block exemptions. This could make the assessment more complex and consequently more costly. On the other hand, as all conditions of Article 101(3) TFEU have to be fulfilled cumulatively, it would be sufficient to establish to a reasonable degree that one of the conditions will not be met.

1.2. Vertical agreements

Vertical restraints typically take the form of an agreement between firms on different levels of the supply chain. These may be contracts between producers

---

168 European Commission, "Block Exemptions for Horizontal Agreements: Commission regulation No 2658/2000 of 29 November 2000 on the application of Article 81 (3) of the Treaty to categories of specialisation agreements," (2000); European Commission, "Commission regulation No 2659/2000 of 29 November 2000 on the application of Article 81 (3) of the Treaty to categories of research and development agreements," (2000).

169 European Commission, *Communication from the Commission, Notice, Guidelines on the application of Article 81(3) of the Treaty (2004/C 101/08)* 97, no. 36 f.

170 *Ibidem*, no. 2 and 20 ff.

171 *Ibidem*, no. 15.

and their wholesalers and or retailers. Vertical restraints will in most cases be beneficial to both parties to the contract, and only harm third parties, if at all.[172] However, vertical restraints can also be overall beneficial in many cases, or at least also exhibit efficiency gains that would have to be weighed against the potential anti-competitive effects. In fact, empirical evidence suggests that the majority of vertical agreements enhance welfare.[173] Vertical restraints can raise concerns with regard to reduction of competition as they may be used to protect a position of market power in one market, or to extend it into other markets, thereby reducing total welfare. For example, exclusive dealing contracts may create barriers to entry in the market.

Article 101(1) TFEU also applies to vertical agreements that may affect trade between Member States and that prevent, restrict or distort competition. In light of the ambiguity that vertical restraints can exhibit and the fact that many vertical restraints can be total welfare enhancing, the Commission adopted an economic approach to vertical restraints in its 2000 "Guidelines on Vertical Restraints", recognising their potential pro-competitive effects.[174] A number of vertical agreements are presumed to be beneficial overall and are exempted from the application of Article 101(1) TFEU under the Vertical Block Exemption Regulation (VBER).[175] These block exemptions provide a safe harbour for suppliers (or buyers in certain cases) with a market share of less than 30 percent (Article 3 VBER), where the agreement does not contain hard core restrictions as defined in Article 4 or certain non compete regulations laid down in Article 5. In a public procedure, the Commission may withdraw the block exemption in special cases, where the agreement falls under Article Article 101(1) TFEU and does not fulfil the requirements of Article 101(3) TFEU however. Following the general guidelines on the application of Article 101(1) EC Treaty, courts do not

172 For example all agreements avoiding vertical externalities such as the problem of double-marginalisation, when both producer and retailer have some market power, leading to larger prices and less products sold, in turn leading to less profit for both parties, than had they jointly agreed upon a price/quantity. See, e.g. Motta, *Competition policy: theory and practice*, 307 ff.

173 Cooper, et al, "Vertical Restrictions and Antitrust Policy: What About the Evidence?, Vanderbilt Public Law Research Paper No. 05–32," *Competition Policy International* 1 (2005): 45; Lafontaine and Slade, "Exclusive contracts and vertical restraints: Empirical evidence and public policy," *Handbook of Antitrust Economics*, P. Buccirossi (Ed.) Cambridge: MIT Press (2008).

174 See European Commission, "Guidelines on the application of vertical restraints, Official Journal of the European Communities (2000/C 291/01)," *OJ* (2000). Although the Guidelines will not be binding for courts, it can be assumed that courts are likely to take the Commission's approach with regard to the assessment of certain types of infringements into consideration, especially when private enforcement is just developing.

175 European Commission, "Commission Regulation (EC) No 2790/1999 of 22 December 1999 on the application of Article 81(3) of the Treaty to categories of vertical agreements and concerted practices," *OJ* (1999). In addition, specific Block Exemptions regulations have been enacted for certain industries, which will not be considered here.

have the same ability; therefore block exemptions are binding on courts, also in the case of vertical agreements.[176] For all cases not falling under the Block Exemptions Regulations, the Commission adopts an economic approach for establishing the overall effect of a specific agreement, considering negative and positive effects. The Commission acknowledges the following possible negative effects: market foreclosure or barriers to entry; reduction of inter-brand or intra-brand competition; and inhibiting market integration.[177]

On the other hand, the Commission mentions non-price competition and improved service quality as positive effects. The Commission also cites that this may provide the solution to different forms of free riding behaviour and furthermore it could provide economies of scale in distribution, curb capital market imperfections and ensure uniformity and quality standardisation.[178]

Vertical restraints are less likely than horizontal agreements to be covert,[179] so the probability of detection can be assumed to be considerably larger. Other market participants are likely to notice such conduct that may affect them negatively. However, as these kinds of infringements follow more a rule of reason approach, establishing the illegality of a certain observed conduct may be more complex, and consequently costly.[180]

1.3. Abuse of a dominant position

Article 102 TFEU prohibits the abuse of a dominant position by one or more undertakings. Article 102 TFEU mentions the following particular examples of abusive behaviour: imposing unfair prices or trading conditions; limiting production or markets or innovation; special trade conditions for specific customers; and imposing supplementary obligations on the contracting party that have no connection with the subject of the contracts (tying).

---

176 European Commission, *Communication from the Commission, Notice, Guidelines on the application of Article 81(3) of the Treaty (2004/C 101/08)* 97, no. 2 and 36;European Commission, *Guidelines on the application of vertical restraints, Official Journal of the European Communities (2000/C 291/01)*, no. 71 ff.

177 *Ibidem* no. 103 ff.

178 *Ibidem* no. 115 ff.

179 As already stated by Kauper and Snyder, " An Inquiry into the Efficiency of Private Antitrust Enforcement: Follow-on and Independently Initiated Cases Compared," *Georgetown Law Journal* 74 (1985): 1163, 1164.

180 Ginsburg (2005) observes that "experience shows that when plaintiffs had to prove the challenged practices harmed competition, they were very rarely able to do so", Ginsburg, *Comparing antitrust enforcement in the United States and Europe* 427, 438.

The Commission's guidelines in relation to the application of Article 82 EC Treaty (now Article 102 TFEU) to exclusionary conduct[181] identify the following as specific forms of abuse of a dominant position: types of exclusive dealing, tying and bundling, predation practices, refusal to supply and margins squeezes. In the application of Article 102 TFEU, the Commission incorporates the efficiency claims brought by the undertaking in question into its assessment.[182]

Infringements of Article 102 TFEU, as opposed to Article 101 TFEU, commonly impose direct harm on competitors. This is especially the case for all types of behaviour that can be subsumed under exclusionary abuses. Therefore, in many cases of abuse of dominance, the probability of detection is likely to be very high, as the conduct is easily observable, including the resulting harm. Often, evidence supporting the assessment of the conduct will be in the hands of the primary victims of the infringements. Also, the market power of the company in question is probably known to other actors in the market – if not insofar as its legal definition, then possibly at least in regard to its economic consequences. On the other hand, the competitor plaintiff may also have to be regarded with greater caution, as they may have larger incentives to abuse competition law, for example using it to impose costs on a particular competitor, or lessening the competitive pressure exerted by a strong competitor.

There are also other cases in which plaintiffs would have a very hard time detecting an infringement and the resulting harm, for example in cases of abuse of a dominant position that leads to the inhibition of innovation and consequently to losses caused by dynamic inefficiency. Forms of exploitative abuses can cause harm directly to consumers.[183] These are likely to be less detectable and generally more difficult to assess.

2. OTHER RELEVANT REGULATIONS

Other regulations relevant to group litigation mechanisms include, amongst others, general rules on civil procedure, general rules on tort law and regulations concerning the conduct and reimbursement of lawyers or associations.

When using theory to design the optimal group litigation for a certain type of competition law infringement, a choice has to be made upfront about which boundaries of a legal system are to be treated as given. That choice obviously

181 European Commission, "Communication from the Commission, Guidance on the Commission's enforcement priorities in applying Article 82 of the EC Treaty to abusive exclusionary conduct by dominant undertakings 2009".

182 *Ibidem*, no. 28 ff.

183 Jones, *EC Competition Law: text, cases and materials*, 316 ff.

greatly influences the outcome of the subsequent analysis, but is unavoidable if a minimum relevance to the current discussion within Europe is to be maintained.

As mentioned above, the effects, both positive and negative, of the proposed changes to enhance private enforcement of competition law through the avenue of private claims for damages, depend on their specific design, and on their combination. It should be clear at this point that making reasonable statements about the effects of one specific tool to enhance private enforcement, especially concerning the introduction of a group litigation mechanism, will often necessitate the incorporation of changes or limitations in other features of the private enforcement design as well. Moreover, when studying the effectiveness of a particular group litigation mechanism, other features of the private enforcement system have to be taken into account. Therefore, it will sometimes be unavoidable during the course of analysis to incorporate effects not primarily caused by the group litigation mechanism itself.

The basic starting point to this analysis will be that of traditional actions for damages, as they have been developed. The very basic and common concept behind these regulations is that a victim of a harm caused by an illegal act of another has the right to be compensated.[184] Compensation should be given for the full harm caused (unless the victim is partially responsible as well). However, the victim should not be able to gain from the fact that harm was caused, and therefore should not receive more than actual damages. Such so-called unjust enrichment is also explicitly made impossible by Community Law.[185] Following the concept of *restitutio ad integrum*,[186] the goal is to put the victim in a position he/she would have been in had the damage-causing incident never occurred.

However, sometimes such compensation may not be possible or feasible. If, for example, the damages to the individual victim are so low that the costs of litigating, awarding or transferring the individual amounts would exceed

---

184 See for example the general provision of the German BGB, §823, stating that who unnlawfully and intentionally or negligently violates someone else's right has to compensate the victim for the resulting harm (Wer vorsätzlich oder fahrlässig das Leben, den Körper, die Gesundheit, die Freiheit, das Eigentum oder ein sonstiges Recht eines anderen widerrechtlich verletzt, ist dem anderen zum Ersatz des daraus entstehenden Schadens verpflichtet).

185 *Courage* Judgement, European Court of Justice, *Case C-453/99 Courage Ltd v Bernard Crehan [2001] ECR I-6297*, no. 30: "In that regard, the Court has held that Community law does not prevent national courts from taking steps to ensure that the protection of the rights guaranteed by Community law does not entail the unjust enrichment of those who enjoy them". See also discussion in European Commission, *Commission Staff Working Paper, Annex to the Green Paper Damages actions for breach of the EC antitrust rules, (COM(2005) 672 final)*, 46 ff.

186 The ECJ clarified that point in the Manfredi decision, granting "any individual" standing. European Court of Justice, *Cases C-295/04 to C-298/04 Vincenzo Manfredi and Others v. Lloyd Adriatico Assicurazioni SpA and Others ECR I-6619.*

them,[187] other avenues of compensation could be taken. Such mechanisms can be combined under the heading of *cy pres* distribution.[188] Although not very common, the European Commission has embraced such mechanisms in special cases.[189] In addition, the national laws of Member States are familiar with concepts under which proceeds of a trial in the name of unidentified victims, such as the public as whole, are given to the state or associations to be used to protect the interest of those represented.[190] Other Member States have regulations that allow a deviation from the concept of damage awards being based on the harm caused in cases where the former may be too difficult to establish or to prove. In such cases, damages may also be based on the illegal gain the offender reaped from his law infringement.[191] In such cases, it seems the idea of deterrence, or not allowing illegal gain, takes precedence over the concept of just and full compensation of individual harm. Especially when focusing on the goal of deterrence, the possibility to use these different mechanisms may be vital. Therefore, while the traditional regulations on actions for damages will be the starting point of analysis, these other mechanisms that were developed in national Member States law will also need to be taken into consideration.

It is also quite common (at least in civil law countries), that the types of rights discussed here can be transferred to another actual or legal person.[192] In some cases, such a transfer can even be regulated to take place automatically, as is common for example often in insurance law. In other cases, owners of the right can trade it just as any other object with a certain value.[193] Such a right may then be considered to have a value in itself, independent of the original victim, so that

187 Farmer, "More Lessons from the Laboratories: Cy Pres Distributions in Parens Patriae Antitrust Actions Brought by State Attorneys General," *Fordham Law Review* 68 (1999): 361. Stuyck, et al, "An analysis and evaluation of alternative means of consumer redress other than redress through ordinary judicial proceedings Final Report," (2007). Available online at: http://ec.europa.eu/consumers/redress/reports_studies/comparative_report_en.pdf.

188 *Cy pres* constitutes a possibility to put damage awards to their "next best" use when they can not be used to compensate individual victims. An example would be awarding the damages to some agency that will use the proceeds in the general interest of the represented group, such as a charitable organisation.

189 See European Commission, *White Paper on Damages actions for breach of the EC antitrust Rules COM(2008) 165 final, SEC(2008) 404*, 20.

190 Such as the German skimming-off procedure discussed above chapter 1 section 2.3, or the Portuguese popular action, see Mulheron, "Competition Law Cases under the Opt-out Regimes of Australia, Canada and Portugal: A research paper for the Department for Business, Enterprise and Regulatory Reform," (2008), 77.

191 For example in the UK, seeOffice of Fair Trading, "*Private actions in competition law: effective redress for consumers and business, OFT Discussion Paper 916*," (April 2007), paragraph 2.11, although possibly restricted to proprietary tort cases; in Germany, §33 Abs. 3 GWB allows the estimation of the damages incurred by a plaintiff on basis of the illegal profit the defendant gained as a result of the infringement.

192 For example, in Germany §398 BGB allows for such an assignation, and although it is generally restricted to specific circumstances, it has been successfully been done in the cases brought by the Cartel Damage Claim company, see Chapter 5 section C.

193 Banks for example sell credit claims as valuable goods.

the transfer can take place through a contract that includes a payment for the transfer of the rights.[194] While this possibility may be an important concept in some group litigation mechanisms, it may not be feasible in others, as the analysis will show.

As mentioned above, there is a wide range of possibilities through which to finance such damages actions. Legal aid insurance, professional finance institutions, changes in the general regulation of court costs, and contingency fees for lawyers are only some of these. Alleviating the cost burden placed on the plaintiffs' side in one way or another will generally increase the incentives of potential plaintiffs to use the legal system to sue for damages. Nevertheless, the total effects of the different cost alleviating mechanisms are likely to differ. However, the issue of financing is not intrinsically related to group litigations. The same questions also arise with regard to traditional one-on-one litigation. The same is true for the question of how lawyers will be remunerated for their efforts in general. These matters will be taken into consideration whenever they are important to the analysis.

The prevailing method of cost and fee shifting rules, as well as rules on the discovery process, are important when looking at the efficiency of existing group litigation mechanisms. However, they may be less relevant to the specific design of a group litigation mechanism than the rules on damages or payment of lawyers, as the analysis will show.

While the existing regulations will form the starting point of the analysis, some of these regulations, as they exist in the Member States of the European Union, may have to be changed in order to make a specific form of group litigation efficient or even feasible. The analysis of the optimal group litigation will highlight these points.

C. THE ECONOMIC FRAMEWORK

1. THE RATIONALITY ASSUMPTION

Economic analysis traditionally assumes that individuals are "rational".[195] The economic definition of rationality, however, differs from the common intuitive understanding of the term in everyday life. Most economic models apply the

194 This is the approach taken by the Cartel Damage Claims Company, see Chapter 5 section C.

195 See Sen, *Rational Behaviour. The New Palgrave Dictionary of Economics.* eds. Durlauf and Blume. (2008). Available at: www.dictionaryofeconomics.com/article?id=pde2008_R000022. For a contrast of rational choice theory with insights from behavioural economics see Ulen, *Rational Choice Theory in Law and Economics.* in *Encyclopedia of Law and Economics, Volume I. The History and Methodology of Law and Economics.* eds. Bouckaert and De Geest. Cheltenham: Edward Elgar (2000), 790.

von Neumann-Morgenstern assumptions regarding individual behaviour,[196] postulating that individuals are rational maximisers of their expected utility. In that respect, utility is a measure of the relative satisfaction the decision maker will gain from a certain choice, for example the consumption of a particular good. If that level of utility is not certain *ex ante*, the decision maker can only make a choice based on the level of satisfaction she expects to derive from the choices, therefore the model deals with expected utility. The very basic assumptions concerning the rationality assumption are the following. Presented with a finite number of choices, an individual can always say whether he prefers A to B, B to A or is indifferent (completeness axiom). When the consumer prefers A to B and B to C, he also prefers A to C (transitivity axiom). The preference of one alternative over the other should not change, when an additional option is added. Overall, it is assumed that the individual will choose the most preferred option, thereby maximising her utility or welfare. This does not imply, however, that the choices made could be considered rational choices from an objective perspective.[197] Individuals can make such choices even when they are not fully informed about the actual and real alternatives; it only matters how these options are perceived.[198] Moreover, for the predictions of a certain model to hold, individuals do not even have to make these choices consciously. In fact, it is only necessary for individuals to behave as if they would follow such a rationale in aggregate. Following this standard approach in Law and Economics, the behaviour of individuals in this analysis is assumed to be rational in the economic sense.[199] This implies that individuals will consider the costs and benefits of alternative choices and choose the option that maximises their expected utility. That approach and what it entails will be explained in greater detail below.

2. THE THEORY OF OPTIMAL DETERRENCE

Economic analysis of optimal sanctions traditionally focuses on the goal of deterrence.[200] In a total (social) welfare analysis, the wealth of all individual

196 Von Neumann/ Morgenstern introduced uncertainty in the general utility analysis.

197 A very good overview over the rationality assumption, its usefullness and its justification even in light of insights from behavioural eceonomics can be found in Schäfer and Ott, *Lehrbuch der ökonomischen Analyse des Zivilrechts*, Berlin, Heidelberg, New York: Springer (2005), 58 ff; and Ulen, *Rational Choice Theory in Law and Economics*, 790.

198 Becker, "The economic way of looking at life," *Nobel Lecture, Journal of Political Economy* 101 (1993): 385 available at: http://home.uchicago.edu/~gbecker/Nobel/nobellecture.pdf.

199 In few instances also insights from behavioural approaches to Law and Economics are referred to.

200 Becker, *Law enforcement, malfeasance, and compensation of Enforces* 1. Landes, *Optimal sanctions for antitrust violations* 652, 652. Baker, *Private information and the deterrent effect of antitrust damage remedies* 385. Wils, "Optimal antitrust fines: theory and practice," *World Competition* 29 (2006): 183.

members of the society is maximised, whereas wealth distribution is irrelevant, as it has no effects on total wealth maximisation. This basic idea is closely connected to the so-called concept of Kaldor-Hicks efficiency.[201] Under this efficiency regime, changes in the system subject to the investigation are considered efficient when gains generated by the changes to some members of the affected society are larger than the losses caused to others. Using adequate mechanisms of redistribution, the winners could theoretically fully compensate the losers while total welfare would increase. If such a compensation system were used, the alterations analysed would also fulfil the requirements of Pareto efficiency,[202] in that no individual would suffer losses but at least one would be better off.

Deterrence, also called the preventive function, is a major goal of the sanctions imposed against violations of Article 101 and Article 102 TFEU.[203] The ECJ emphasised the possibilities of private actions for damages to deter infringements of competition law.[204] Also national legislation concerning damages for breaches of competition law has been drafted with the explicit aim of creating an effective private sanctioning system to increase deterrence of infringements.[205] Although the Commission and some authors argue that the foremost goal of private actions for damages is to compensate victims, i.e. corrective justice,[206] the goal of deterrence is also generally recognised as part of the functions of tort law.[207] In general, enforcement to prevent competition law infringements is a widely accepted and legitimate aim also for private enforcement.[208]

---

201 See Chapter 1, Section A 2.

202 Named after the Italian economist Vilfredo Pareto (1848–1923). A pareto improvement is said to be achieved when at least the situation of one person can be improved, without making any other individual worse off. Pareto-efficiency is achieved when no further pareto improvements are possible.

203 Krüger, *Öffentliche und private Durchsetzung des Kartellverbots von Article 81 EG,* Wiesbaden: Deutscher Universitaets-Verlag (2007), 8.

204 EJC emphazised that notion in its decision: European Court of Justice, *Case C-453/99 Courage Ltd v Bernard Crehan [2001] ECR I-6297,* no. 26 f.

205 German Bundestag, BT-Drucks. 15/3640, 35. Main goal in US antitrust:Lande, "Are Antitrust'Treble'Damages Really Single Damages?" *Ohio State Law Journal* 54 (1993): 115, 124; Easterbrook, "Predatory strategies and counterstrategies," *The University of Chicago Law Review* 48 (1981): 263, 319 (with further ref. also to court decisions in fn 126). Posner, *Antitrust Law: Economic Perspective,* Chicago, London: The University of Chicago Press (1976), 221.

206 At least now, see European Commission, *White Paper on Damages actions for breach of the EC antitrust Rules COM(2008) 165 final, SEC(2008) 404,* 3.

207 See Faure and Van Boom, *Introducing "Shifts in Compensation Between Private and Public Systems".* in *Shifts in Compensation Between Private and Public Systems.* eds. Faure and Van Boom. Wien: Springer (2007), 1, 8 f.

208 Hoseinian, "Passing-on Damages and Community Antitrust Policy – An Economic Background," *World Competition: Law and Economics Review* 28 (2005): 3, 6. Also Commission in European Commission, *White Paper on Damages actions for breach of the EC antitrust Rules COM(2008) 165 final, SEC(2008) 404,* 3, acknowledging the deterrence functions. See also Wils, *Should private antitrust enforcement be encouraged in Europe?,* 473.

2.1. *Optimal sanction*

The economic analysis of law enforcement largely rests on the economic models developed to explain the behaviour of criminals.[209] Just like the core of economic analysis, these models apply the rational choice theory. Postulating certain features of individuals' preferences,[210] the individual is assumed to maximise his or her expected utility from those preferences, under various constraints, such as limited resources. Traditionally, the economic analysis of deterrence focused on criminal law as subject. However, as private enforcement emerged as possible alternative or complement to public enforcement efforts based on criminal law, tort law became a topic of interest.[211] Criminal law is strongly connected to the principle of deterrence. Actions for damages in tort law, however, can also work as a kind of market mechanism that increases the expected costs of an offence. In that respect, they might have a deterrence effect, similar to that of criminal fines where it is more the fine that deters, than the moral connotation of a criminal sanction. Therefore, if private tort actions for damages are designed in a way to reach optimal deterrence, their impact must mirror the effect of the optimal (criminal) fine, as analysed under criminal law aspects. Therefore, the research done on the deterrence effects of criminal fines becomes relevant.

The idea to treat an individual's decision whether or not to commit an illegal act as if it were a rational decision weighing costs and benefits, is neither a completely novel, nor a very recent invention. As early as 1788, Bentham wrote about the decision of a criminal in terms of "profit of the crime" and "pain of punishment".[212] Also other classic writers, such as Beccaria and Montesquieu applied such logic to individual behaviour.[213]

The analysis of criminal behaviour became a central topic in the Law and Economics literature in the late 1970s. In his seminal work *Crime and Punishment*,[214] Gary S. Becker analysed the behaviour of a criminal as a rational

---

209 Namely the theories developed by Becker, Stigler and Landes.Becker, "Crime and Punishment: An Economic Approach," *The Journal of Political Economy* 76 (1968): 169. Stigler, "The Optimum Enforcement of Laws," *The Journal of Political Economy* 78 (1970): 526. Landes, *Optimal sanctions for antitrust violations* 652. Becker and Landes, *Essays in the Economics of Crime and Punishment,* New York: Columbia University Press (1974).

210 See the description of the rationality assumption above.

211 In the USA, only 10 percent of all antitrust cases are brought by public authorities. For recent discussions about private competition law infringements in Europe, see Van Den Bergh and Keske, "Private Enforcement of European Competition Law: Quo Vadis?" *European Review of Contract Law* 3 (2007): 468; Van Den Bergh, *European competition law and economics: a comparative perspective*, 325.

212 Bentham, *Principles of penal law*,The Works of Jeremy Benthem (1843), 399 ff.

213 Beccaria, *On Crime and Punishment. Theories of Punishment.* ed. Grupp. Bloomington: Indiana University Press (1971), 117.

214 Becker, *Crime and Punishment: An Economic Approach* 169.

decision maker, maximising his income dependent utility function. Under such assumptions, the potential criminal weighs the expected gains from committing the offence against the expected costs. The expected benefits are derived from the probability of escaping any liability times the profit or monetary equivalent of gains from the illegal conduct. The expected costs are derived from the probability of being caught and convicted times the fine or monetary equivalent of the punishment. Larger punishments or increases in the probability of being caught and convicted decrease the incentives to commit the crime,[215] whereas increasing expected benefits from the offence have opposite effects, *ceteris paribus*. Using a total welfare approach, Becker analysed which form of sanction would be socially desirable.

Becker's analysis includes two important insights for the economic analysis of deterrence. The first insight is that given positive detection costs, maximum deterrence may not be optimal, as the benefits to society resulting from deterred offences have to be balanced against the costs of enforcement. In a total welfare analysis, society should try to minimise the sum of the costs of enforcement activities and the costs borne due to remaining offences. The second insight is that from a social welfare point of view, there may be efficient violations of the law that should not be deterred. These occur when the harm done to society is less than the gain to the offender, so that the effect on total welfare is a positive one.[216]

When costs of detection and conviction are zero and the probability of being detected equals one, the optimal fine equals the total harm done to society.[217] The costs of detection and conviction include the expenditures borne by society to apprehend and convict the infringer. However, when detection and conviction is costly, while the monetary transfer of the fine from offender to society is costless, the optimal sanction should be set in a way that the amount of fine is as large as possible to allow for the minimal rate of detection. The basic arguments for this result are as follows. When imposing a fine is costless and the detection of an infringement requires expenditures, society would fare best to increase the fine as much as possible, reduce detection efforts and thereby save detection costs, while keeping the level of deterrence constant. Since the maximal level that

215 The substitutability of the probability of having to pay the fine and the amount of the fine depends on the individuals attitude towards risk. Risk-lovers would be more deterred by an increase in the probability than one in the amount of fine, while the opposite is true for risk-averse individuals. Same effect is achieved for risk-neutral persons. See *Ibidem*, 178.

216 The assumption of a social benefit from the offence was criticised for illegal conduct such as rape or murder, see e.g. Stigler, *The Optimum Enforcement of Laws* 526, 527.Polinsky and Shavell, *Public Enforcement of Law*. in *Encyclopedia of Law and Economics*. eds. Bouckaert and De Geest. Cheltenham: Edward Elgar (2000), 307. But the arguments do not relate to competition law infringements.

217 Becker, *Crime and Punishment: An Economic Approach* 169, 192.

a fine that can be set at is limited by the total wealth of the infringer, the optimal sanction consists of the total wealth of the infringer combined with the corresponding probability of detection.[218]

In the later research done in Law and Economics, different aspects of Becker's model have been investigated more thoroughly and arguments why the maximum fine may not be optimal under specific circumstances have been developed. These include criticisms that the maximum fine may be too low to efficiently deter, so that imprisonment is suggested as alternative,[219] as well as arguments connected to the idea that imposing a fine is not entirely costless.[220]

Two years after Becker's foundation laying work, Stigler 1970 introduced *marginal deterrence* into the discussion, or at least coined the term.[221] He argued that imposing the same punishment on different violations of law where the amount of resulting harm is not the same will distort the potential offender's decision whether to commit a crime that causes larger or smaller damages. One implication of marginal deterrence is that the maximum fine may not be optimal for all offences and that the penalty should rather be set in a way to resemble the amount of damages effectuated.[222] This economic argument reflects certain legal principles, such as the principle of proportionality.

In 1974, Stigler and Becker shifted their attention from setting the optimal penalty to the question of how to induce public as well as private enforcers, to perform at a high level of quality.[223] They argue that public enforcers, working on a salary basis, may fall prey to bribery or intimidation unless their salary is determined in relation to the temptation for such malfeasances. Private enforcers may avoid the pitfalls of public enforcement, when rewarded by the fine levied on, or damages paid by, the offender.[224] On the other hand, they might not as readily impose the optimal sanction as public enforcers might. As both public

---

218 Garoupa, "The Theory of Optimal Law Enforcement," *Journal of Economic Surveys* 11 (1997): 267, 268 f. Shavell, "A note on marginal deterrence," *International Review of Law and Economics* 12 (1992): 345, 346.

219 See e.g.Wils, *Is criminalization of EU competition law the answer?* 117. Möschel, *Kommentar: Erweiterter Privatrechtsschutz im Kartellrecht* 115.

220 Analysing the deterrence effect and necessity of non-monetary sanctions is Shavell, *Criminal law and the optimal use of nonmonetary sanctions as a deterrent* 1232. For an overview of models extending Beckers analysis, including positive enforcement costs, see: Garoupa, *The Theory of Optimal Law Enforcement* 267, 268 f.

221 Stigler, *The Optimum Enforcement of Laws* 526. The ideas of marginal deterrence where already presented by Montesquieu, Beccaria and Bentham, see Shavell, *A note on marginal deterrence* 345, 345.

222 Polinsky, *Public Enforcement of Law* 307, 312.

223 Becker, *Law enforcement, malfeasance, and compensation of Enforces* 1.

224 Again, these fines or damage payments would have to be adjusted for the probability of being convicted. See *Ibidem*, 14.

and private enforcement agents were not remunerated accordingly at that time in the USA, the authors conclude that performance of both enforcement entities may be enhanced compared to the applied enforcement strategies by either increasing salaries for public officials so as to protect them from bribery, or to allow private actors to engage in enforcement activities.

In 1992, Shavell extended the original analysis of marginal deterrence and concluded that the optimal sanction increases with the magnitude of harm when enforcement efforts can not be specifically tailored to the harmfulness of the act.[225] Moreover, the sanction should rise with the harmfulness of the act when the probability of apprehension falls with increasing damage caused by the illegal conduct.[226]

In addition, a great deal of research following Becker's original analysis was conducted to analyse circumstances under which the optimal fine would not be the maximum.[227] This research includes, for example, a paper by Shavell and Polinksy,[228] who evaluated the effect of different states of wealth amongst individuals with positive enforcement costs. These authors concluded that the maximum fine, which equals the total wealth of the offender, is only optimal when the probability of apprehension is independent from the level of wealth. When, on the other hand, this probability is dependent of wealth, the optimal sanction equals the harm divided by the probability of apprehension. Bebchuk and Kaplow[229] analysed the effect of imperfect information of individuals with regard to the probability of detection. They found that under such circumstances the optimal sanction would consist of a larger probability of detection and conviction, coupled with a lower fine.

Polinsky and Shavell,[230] investigated the effects of different types of enforcement costs on the level of the optimal sanction. To reach optimal deterrence, a distinction has to be made between fixed and variable enforcement costs. Whenever enforcement costs include a variable cost borne by society that

---

225 See Shavell, *A note on marginal deterrence* 345. One could argue that this will often be the case in infringements of competition law, as enforcer may not be able to concentrate their resources on the detection of those price-fixing cartels that cause the greatest damages.

226 As may be argued for the case of cartels vs other types of infringements, see report.

227 For a general overview of the numerous extensions to Becker's basic model, see Eide, *Economics of Criminal Behavior.* in *Encyclopedia of Law and Economics, Volume I. The History and Methodology of Law and Economics.* eds. Bouckaert and De Geest. Cheltenham: Edward Elgar (2000), 345.

228 Polinsky and Shavell, "A note on optimal fines when wealth varies among individuals," *The American Economic Review* 81 (1991): 618.

229 Bebchuk, "Optimal sanctions when individuals are imperfectly informed about the probability of apprehension," *The Journal of Legal Studies* 21 (1992): 365.

230 Polinsky and Shavell, "Enforcement costs and the optimal magnitude and probability of fines," *The Journal of Law & Economics* 35 (1992): 133.

depends on the number of infringements, such as costs of investigation and litigation once detection has taken place, these costs have to be placed on the infringer, each costs adjusted for the probability that in the end a fine will be imposed. If (fixed) detection costs, (variable) costs of litigation and (variable) cost of actually imposing the fine are present, that implies that the optimal sanction is set to equal the total costs imposed on society divided by the probability of detection and conviction, plus the costs of litigation adjusted for the probability that conviction will take place, and in addition the costs of imposing a fine. The general upshot of their findings is that variable enforcement costs, depending on the number of offenders, should be added on top of the penalty that equals harm divided by the probability of detection, while fixed enforcement costs should not. Under perfect circumstances, where no type I or type II errors[231] are made, society as a whole will be made better off through such an enforcement regime. There will also be no wasteful effort. An example may help to clarify this, following the analysis of Polinsky and Shavell. If total net losses caused by a detected and prosecuted offence (including enforcement costs) are 90, litigation (variable enforcement) costs are 10 and the probability of detection and conviction is 10 percent, the total award (fine) paid to the enforcer by the infringer will be 1000 (90+10 divided by 0.1). One hundred of that will compensate society for the actual harm done, which includes all resources spent on detection and conviction. Nine hundred are a pure monetary transfer between the infringer and society (from a total welfare point of view), leaving society as a whole, which includes both parties, indifferent. The design of the optimal sanction under optimal circumstances leads to the effect that the infringer will only breach competition law if his additional gain exceeds the expected 100 (1000 with a probability of 0.1) he has to pay in compensation. If the offender's gain does not exceed this amount, he is deterred and the case will not arise. The model shows how enforcers under such a system can have sufficient incentives to file suit, and that optimal deterrence could be achieved. One pitfall of this analysis is that it requires the fixed costs of detection to be set at an optimal level by the (centralised) enforcer. If this is possible, then optimal enforcement could be achieved.

Next to this so called *internalisation approach* to deterrence, which forces the potential infringer to internalise the cost imposed on society, another so called *complete deterrence theory* has also been developed.[232] The latter theory postulates that when efficient breaches, where the gain to the offender exceeds

[231] Neither false convictions nor false acquittals.

[232] See Wils, *Optimal antitrust fines: theory and practice* 183, 195 f. Hylton, "The theory of penalties and the economics of criminal law," *Review of Law And Economics* 1 (2005): 175.

the harm inflicted on society, are never possible,[233] then the optimal fine should be set at a level that exceeds the gain to the offender, so as to completely deter that behaviour. This approach has also sometimes been advocated for competition law infringements in general[234] or only for hard-core cartels.[235] In practice, so called skimming-off procedures, under which offenders have to repay the amount of illegal gain, seem to apply this concept. Nevertheless, such sanctions bear no connection to the amount of harm caused, which according to the theory of marginal deterrence can be inefficient. Moreover, simply skimming-off the illegal additional profits gained through anti-competitive behaviour does not take into account the potentially very low probability of detection. Therefore, it results in under-deterrence. The same effect occurs when these illegal gains are underestimated, so that the infringer still profits from violation of the competition regulation. It is probably for these reasons, and due to the important fact that efficient breaches are often considered a positive thing in the economic analysis, that the most commonly accepted approach to deterrence is the internalisation approach. It is that approach, which has also been frequently applied to the context of competition law infringements and which is used here.

2.2. *Optimal sanction for anticompetitive conduct*

In 1983, William Landes analysed the optimal sanction with regard to antitrust violations.[236] In line with Becker's analysis, Landes conclusion leads to an optimal sanction that imposes the net harm effectuated in society, which includes the enforcement costs per case divided by the probability of detection and conviction,[237] on the potential infringer in order to achieve deterrence. Such a sanction takes into account the fact that some anti-competitive conduct may have an overall beneficial effect on total welfare and therefore should not be deterred. Many scholars have accepted this approach.[238] In such a setting, an economic entity that contemplates engaging in an anti-competitive behaviour, like participating in a prohibited cartel agreement, can be assumed to weigh the individual (not total social) costs and benefits of such an activity against each other. The benefits can be seen in the additional profits gained by engaging in that illegal activity.[239] The costs on the other hand depend on the possibility of

---

233 Either because they naturally do not exists or because society does not allow such a weighing of gains to the offender against the damages imposed on victims.

234 Wils, *Optimal antitrust fines: theory and practice* 183.

235 Camilli, *Optimal Fines in Cartel Cases and the Actual EC Fining Policy* 575.

236 Landes, *Optimal sanctions for antitrust violations* 652.

237 *Ibidem*, 676 f.

238 See Wils, *The optimal enforcement of EC antitrust law: essays in law & economics*, The Hague: Kluwer Law International (2002), 24 f. Van Den Bergh, *European competition law and economics: a comparative perspective*, 312 f.

239 Krüger, *Öffentliche und private Durchsetzung des Kartellverbots von Article 81 EG*, 158.

being apprehended and punished and on the amount of the sanction.[240] Consequently, a rational decision maker will only engage in anti-competitive conduct, when the individual expected profits outweigh the expected costs.

When applying the described models to the field of antitrust violations, one qualification may be in order. The law against restraints of competition in Europe focuses on the firm as the target of the regulation and the one liable in actions for damages.[241] Similarly, Landes treated the firm as the decision maker in his analysis. In reality, the individuals actually deciding whether or not to enter a cartel agreement (e.g. the managers) may not be the ones who have to bear all the costs (in Europe, as opposed to the USA, only the company is fined).[242] However, in contrast to other breaches of law such as murder, it can be argued that the decision makers behind antitrust infringements do behave rationally. Often the motivation behind the decision to partake or to engage in illegal conduct will be an increase in the profit to be gained by it for the firm.[243] Non-monetary benefits and costs could also be translated into monetary terms. For example, managers, trying to impress shareholders and build a reputation are likely to be counting on a future monetary value of such a reputation in form of higher salaries. Nevertheless, costs and benefits of the contemplated offence are not fully borne by the decision maker, which gives rise to so-called *principal-agent problems*[244] and may affect the effectiveness of a sanction. A whole stream of literature is dedicated to the complex problems related to corporate liability[245] and a full application of their insights would be beyond the scope of this thesis. For the sake of this analysis, the principal agent problems between shareholders (principals) and agents (managers) and their effect on the deterrence mechanisms

240 Not explicitly taking into account other possible negative effects of a conviction, such as loss in reputation. Such effect could be theoretically included in the amount of sanction.

241 ECJ defined undertakings as one economic entity, although in reality a number of legal or actual individuals may form that entity. See European Court of Justice, *Case 170/83, Hydrotherm Gerätebau GmbH v Compact del Dott.* (1984), no. 11.

242 Van Den Bergh, *European competition law and economics: a comparative perspective*, 304.

243 Assuming that the goals of decision makers are positively correlated to the profit of the firm, such as building a positive career as manager. See also study by Feinberg, "The Enforcement and Effects of European Competition Policy: Results of a Survey of Legal Opinion," *Journal of Common Market Studies* 23 (1985): 373, 376, finding profit seeking a major cause for some EC antitrust violations.

244 Principal-agent theory (also called agency theory), refers to the relationship between an agent and his principal, where the latter delegates some tasks to the former. Problems arise, when the principal is not able to efficiently monitor the actions of the agent, who may be pursuing own interests that deviate from those of the principal. For an overview see Braun, "Principal-agent theory and research policy: an introduction," *Science & Public Policy* 30 (2003): 302; Eisenhardt, "Agency theory: An assessment and review," *The Academy of Management Review* 14 (1989): 57.

245 For an overview see Lott, *Corporate Criminal liability.* in *Encyclopedia of Law and Economics, Volume I. The History and Methodology of Law and Economics.* Eds. Bouckaert and De Geest. Cheltenham: Edward Elgar (2000), 492.

are not discussed, and the company is seen as the economic entity making the decision.[246]

This assumes a risk neutral decision maker.[247] The attitude of entities towards risk influences their welfare function, so that firms that are not risk neutral may be more or less deterred by the same sanction. Different economic models have been developed to investigate these effects, but one general conclusion shall be noted. If one accepts the following assumptions: i) the company as economic entity is risk averse (although less so with accumulated wealth – *decreasing absolute risk aversion*) ii) non-monetary costs caused by the penalty (such as reputational losses) can be translated into monetary losses and iii) there is only one sanction, the general effect of an increase of the expected penalty will be a reduction in legal offences.[248]

2.3. Optimal deterrence

The point must be repeated that optimal deterrence is not the same as maximum deterrence. Especially with regard to competition law, many activities of firms in the market will have to be thoroughly investigated to allow for an evaluation for their conformity with the law. The effects of non-hard-core agreements amongst firms, such as research and development co-operations, could be beneficial for competition, also from a consumer welfare point of view. Such benefits would be lost if there was over-deterrence, due to excessive expected penalties. Sanctions that are too high will be inefficient in several ways. First, in combination with the possibility of judicial errors[249] or unmeritous claims,[250] firms could also be deterred from engaging in a socially beneficial activity.[251] Second, when the nature of the illegal conduct has little or no relation to the amount of the penalty,

246 The way it has already been done Landes, *Optimal sanctions for antitrust violations* 652.

247 Risk neutrality of firms is a very common assumption as firms may diversify risks much better than individuals. See also Emons, *The economics of US-style contingent fees and UK-style conditional fees*, 10. Available at SSRN: http://ssrn.com/abstract=546742 or DOI: 10.2139/ssrn.546742; Souam, "Optimal antitrust policy under different regimes of fines," *International Journal of Industrial Organization* 19 (2001): 1; Kirstein, "Risk Neutrality and Strategic Insurance," *Geneva Papers on Risk and Insurance. Issues and Practice* 25 (2000): 251, 251. Available at SSRN: http://ssrn.com/abstract=21506. There may be even those that argue that cartelist may be risk-loving, see Connor, "Optimal deterrence and private international cartels," *Purdue University, Working Paper Series* (2007), 22, fn 60. Available at SSRN: http://ssrn.com/abstract=1103598. In that case, the importance of increasing the rate of detection may become all the more relevant, see fn 196 and acc text.

248 For an overview of effects of different attitudes towards risk and the general conclusion drawn from the reviewed literature on criminal behaviour see Eide, *Economics of Criminal Behavior* 345, 350.

249 Such as type I and type II errors, here are false positives relevant.

250 Which are filed to extract a settlement from defendants, despite lacking sufficient factual or legal basis.

251 See Landes, *Optimal sanctions for antitrust violations* 652, 655.

the infringer will not be inhibited from choosing the more harmful alternative.[252] Third, in as much as firms will rely on expert advice concerning the legality of their planned business transactions, excessive expected fines could result in too many resources spent on that "prevention measure".[253]

Under-deterrence takes place when the expected sanction is not large enough to make the decision maker refrain from a law infringing activity that causes more harm to society than it creates benefit. Analogue to the possible reasons for over-deterrence, under-deterrence can result because of too small expected penalties.

2.4. *Optimal enforcement*

Another important point is that enforcement costs should be minimised. The enforcement of regulations is time consuming and costly in general, but all the more so concerning complex issues such as the establishment of an infringement of competition law. The resources spent on enforcement have to be balanced against the gains to be achieved through the enforcement efforts. Optimal enforcement is achieved when the total costs of such harmful activities to society, including the costs of enforcement, are minimised.[254] This necessitates that increases in the resources spent on enforcement should be offset by a reduction in costs caused by violations. If that is not the case, over enforcement takes place, with a waste of resources. Under enforcement takes place when the costs suffered because of infringements are larger than the costs that would have to be borne to enforce the law.

2.5. *Actions for damages as deterrence tool*

Under the discussed models of optimal deterrence, the individuals decision whether or not to violate a competition law regulation depends on the expected benefits and the expected costs. Any firm committing an intentional offence is likely to expect some additional profit from the violation, or to avoid some costs otherwise incurred. These profits to the individual firm depend, amongst other factors, on the type of violation and its scope and breadth. The expected costs taken into account in the calculation are largely determined by the probability of apprehension and conviction, as well as the expected penalty. The latter parameters are those, which can be used to influence the weighing of costs and

---

252 See Stigler, *The Optimum Enforcement of Laws* 526.

253 Block, "Optimal penalties, criminal law and the control of corporate behavior," *Boston University Law Review* 71 (1991): 395, 400 ff.

254 Becker, *Crime and Punishment: An Economic Approach* 169, 181. Landes, *Optimal sanctions for antitrust violations* 652, 657. Van Den Bergh, *European competition law and economics: a comparative perspective*, 300 f.

benefits by a rational utility maximiser, by decreasing his expected utility from the offence. For actions for damages to act as deterrence mechanism, there therefore would have to be an increased probability of detection and conviction and/or an amount of penalty. Ideally, the optimal sanction and optimal deterrence could be achieved in this way.

The goal of imposing the optimal sanction, which forces the infringer to internalise all the damages caused, while enforcement costs are minimised, could theoretically be achieved through traditional individual tort claims. However, there are some obstacles to the efficiency of such tort claims. Private parties may lack necessary information and their individual incentives to discover infringements or to sue may divert from the social interest in such proceedings. Moreover, many individual suits for damages could be considered wasteful enforcement efforts, if these claims could also be as efficiently dealt with in only one costly procedure.

2.6. *Policy implications of the rational choice model*

Economic analysis using the rational utility maximising approach to discuss the behaviour of criminals has frequently been criticised. One of the most common points of critique is the assumption that a criminal will act rationally. Apart from the fact that often rationality is not understood in the economic sense, such criticism relating to the "irrationality" of offenders in the sense of emotional acts, seems to be more justified when criminal acts like assault or murder are discussed, than when economic crimes resulting from business decisions are the subject of investigation. Second, criminology, sociology and other sciences have identified a multitude of factors that influence the likelihood that an individual will commit a crime. Amongst these are peer pressure and poverty. These are factors that are excluded in this analysis, as they are probably not relevant to the decisions of companies. However, the economic analysis conducted here does not exclude other policies that may be targeted to increase education, law-abiding behaviour and moral consciousness.

An economic approach to the topic of private enforcement helps to clarify where conflicts between several simultaneously pursued goals may arise, i.e. where necessary trade offs occur. It also adds information with regard to the choice of instruments used to pursue a given goal. Moreover, it highlights the advantages and disadvantages, or costs and benefits, of specific choices in a way that can make a weighing of these more explicit and better informed.

3. OBSTACLES IN CASES OF COMPETITION LAW INFRINGEMENTS

Claims for damages under traditional tort law are likely to lead to under-deterrence and socially inefficient enforcement due to several problems connected to private litigation in cases of competition law infringements. These include the information asymmetry between victims and offenders, *rational apathy*[255] of affected parties, free riding behaviour and cost inefficiency of several proceedings. The ideal group litigation mechanisms would overcome the obstacles faced by individual tort claims.

3.1. *Information asymmetry*

It is generally true that potential plaintiffs require far greater knowledge and information with regard to the establishment of an infringement of competition law than is required in most other tort cases.[256] Private parties may lack the information and skills of public authorities in assessing a potential competition law infringement. These include for example knowledge on how to establish the relevant market, or whether price developments are caused by general economic developments in the market as opposed to being the result of an anti-competitive conduct. Private enforcement faces the problem of *asymmetric information*, where the potential defendants have a large information advantage over the potential plaintiffs. Public enforcers as well as private enforcers are faced with these obstacles, but the problems can frequently be much more severe for the latter.

The degree of information asymmetry between offenders and injured parties or enforcement agents is not uniform. Proponents of private enforcement often advance the potential information advantages other business entities operating in the affected market have over a public competition authority.[257] While a direct competitor can reasonably be presumed to have the knowledge, skills and resources to notice and combat anti-competitive conduct in many cases, this is less likely to be the case if the harmed entity is the end consumer. Consumers may lack information about the fact that harm is being done, due to the often

255 This concept, also called rational ignorance, was reportedly first developed by Anthony Downs in his seminal book *An Economic Theory of Democracy (1957)*, to explain the behaviour of voters. For a discussion of the rational apathy problem in private enforcement see Landes, *The Private Enforcement of Law* 1, 33 f.

256 Roth, *Private enforcement of European competition law – recom-mendations flowing from the German experience.* in *Private Enforcement of EC Competition Law.* ed. Basedow. Alphen aan den Rijn: Kluver Law International (2007), 61, 68.

257 Brodley, *Antitrust Standing in Private Merger Cases: Reconciling Private Incentives and Public Enforcement* 1, 35. More generally on the information advantages of private parties vis-a-vis public authorities: Shavell, "Liability for harm versus regulation of safety," *The Journal of Legal Studies* 13 (1984): 357, 360.

small but widely dispersed nature of the damages. End consumers often may not even notice a small uniform upward price movement across one industry.

Even where a potential harm may be recognised, information about the amount of, and the cause for, that harm may be lacking. Other businesses, for example direct buyers, may be expected to stay informed about the industry and the market they operate in. It may also be expected they possess sufficient knowledge about the relevant legal provisions applicable. However, few end consumers will know about competition law regulations in detail. Very few will be able to establish the relevant market, the market structure and other relevant factors to estimate whether or not a cartel is the likely cause for observed product or price alterations. Nonetheless, such skills are necessary to establish, for example, whether a perceived price increase for a particular product is the result of concerted practices of cartel members, the unilateral behaviour of a non-cartel member enjoying the benefits of the *price umbrella*[258] created by a cartel, or merely due to economic developments. Moreover, as will be discussed below, the harm done to the individual at that stage of the distribution chain can often be far too small to justify any investment in the gathering of all the necessary information. Therefore, the type of victim being inflicted with the most harm influences the degree to which asymmetric information problems occur.

The severity of asymmetric information also depends on the type of anti-competitive conduct, as well as the incentives for the offender to cure this obstruction. Cases of refusal to deal or exclusive dealing contracts convey substantial parts of necessary information to the victim. In such cases, the information about an infringement and even some of the necessary proofs are already in the hands of the victim. Manufacturer cartel agreements present a very different scenario. Detecting and proving such an infringement can be extremely complex. In some cases, these information problems can be prohibitively large.

Generally, there are two ways to overcome problems of asymmetric information. The first is to design a mechanism under which information will have to be revealed by the ones in possession of the information, or given to the less informed party by a third party. Mechanisms of this kind include notification systems, where for example cooperation agreements are made dependant on prior approval. Unfortunately, notification systems have been widely abolished. Once the decision to breach competition law has been made, offenders cannot

258 "Umbrella-effect" refers to the possibilities of cartel-outsiders in the same market to also profitably increase their prices, following the price increase of the cartel. For an example of the damages caused by umbrella-effect see Lande, "Five Myths about Antitrust Damages," *University of San Francisco Law Review* 40 (2005): 651, 654.

reasonably be compelled to divulge their anti-competitive conduct. They may be enticed to make use of leniency programs, but such tools are difficult to implement in tort actions. Nonetheless, when detection of a likely offence has taken place, specific procedural rules can make it easier for plaintiffs to gather evidence. Such solutions to asymmetric information between parties to a legal dispute are applied for example in pre-trial discovery regulations, such as those in the USA. The second way to reduce or overcome problems of asymmetric information would be to design a mechanism under which sufficient incentives to victims or third party agents are given to search for and provide the relevant information. Such incentives concerning the detection of competition law infringements are of major concern in the design of the optimal group litigation mechanism.

3.2. *Rational apathy*

Another major problem that should be overcome through the mechanism of group litigation is the rational apathy problem. It refers to situations in which it is utility maximising for an individual to decide not to invest resources into research and collecting of data, because the expected costs of doing so exceed the expected benefits.

The problem of rational apathy is relevant with regard to two aspects.[259] The first is the rational apathy that prevents individuals from investing resources in overcoming the above discussed information asymmetry. The individual harm suffered can often be so small that it is rational for the individual victim not to invest resources into research and information gathering. Rational apathy reinforcing information asymmetries is more or less persistent, depending on the type of victim and the infringement under investigation, as described above.

The second aspect of rational apathy relates to the incentives to file suit. Assuming all the necessary information is available, victims might still decide not to file suit. Again, this can be a rational choice, when the individual expected costs of a proceeding outweigh the potential gains. Just as the harm done to the individual end consumer can be too small to justify an investment in gathering of information, it can also be too small to justify investment into a costly and uncertain legal proceeding. It is important to keep in mind that competition law infringements frequently are much more complex to prove than other torts in

---

259 Both arguments have been made by several authors. See e.g. Kalven Jr, *Contemporary Function of the Class Suit, The* 684, 684 f. Schäfer, *The Bundling of Similar Interests in Litigation. The Incentives for Class Action and Legal Actions taken by Associations* 183, 184 f. Micklitz, *The Development of Collective Legal Actions in Europe, Especially in German Civil Procedure* 1473, 1476, 1482. Landes, *The Private Enforcement of Law* 1, 33 f.

general. Especially with regard to hard-core cartels, conspiring firms will be willing to invest large resources in keeping their anti-competitive conduct secret. This investment in masking conduct raises the costs of detection for the enforcer. On the other hand, when firms believe themselves to be acting in accordance with the law, detection might be easier. This is because the agreement is not being kept secret. However, in this case proving the restrictive effect on competition is likely to be a very complex and uncertain exercise. An example of such a scenario would be legal joint venture agreements, which can border on illegal cartel agreements.[260]

Moreover, an individual plaintiff suing for damages will face a defendant who is likely to be able and willing to outspend him in a legal proceeding.[261] In a perfect capital market, victims should be able to borrow money covered by the expected damage awards. If the capital market is not perfect, however, financing problems increase the rational apathy. Large commercial entities are more likely to be able to finance such a lawsuit than private end consumers are. Asymmetric spending power and resulting negotiation power between plaintiff and defendants can present a large disincentive to sue.

The incentives to sue on the side of affected firms can be less than sufficient as well. For example, in the case of firms as direct purchasers, such as retailers, the harm caused by the illegal agreement on the manufacturer's level might be passed on to the next level in the distributions chain, such as the end consumer. The less the competitive pressure on these direct purchasers, and the less price sensitive the individual demand curves faced by them are, the higher the proportion of the overcharges that can be passed on to indirect purchasers. Moreover, fear of retaliation and economic dependencies on one or more offenders can also increase the perceived costs of filing a claim for the individual firm. Their incentives to sue are therefore suboptimal from a social point of view.

These problems are exacerbated when individuals or small enterprises are more risk averse than large companies. The attitude towards risk also influences the degree of rational apathy. Risk-averse entities will be even more reluctant to

---

260 For a discussion of these problems and legal treatment see Van Den Bergh, *European competition law and economics: a comparative perspective*, 197 ff.

261 On the natural advantages of defendants in mass tort cases see Rosenberg, " The Casual Connection in Mass Exposure Cases: A Public Law Vision of the Tort System," *Harvard Law Review* 97 (1983): 849, 902 f. Coffee Jr, "The Regulation of Entrepreneurial Litigation: Balancing Fairness and Efficiency in the Large Class Action," *The University of Chicago Law Review* 54 (1987): 877, 883. On a general discussion see Hay and Rosenberg, "'Sweetheart' and 'Blackmail' Settlements in Class Actions: Reality and Remedy," *Notre Dame Law Review* 75 (2000): 1377.

engage in such exercises, as they value possible losses higher than possible gains. When more weight is placed on potential losses, any weighing of expected costs and benefits is slightly skewed towards a more negative outcome.

Solutions to rational apathy problems rest on changing the balance of costs and benefits, either by decreasing the factors that the individual incorporates on the cost side, or by increasing the benefits to be gained. The challenge for the design of group litigation is to create such effects.

3.3. *Free riding behaviour*

Another obstacle that inhibits individuals from beginning a legal procedure is the risk of so-called *free riding* behaviour, where victims have incentives to free ride on the initial investments of others. Such free riding takes place when victims stay quiescent in the hope that others may invest in costly proceedings.[262] This is beneficial for the individual remaining silent when either the outcome of that proceeding has its effect also for those who remained passive (as is the case for example with an injunction) or the evidence gathered in the first proceeding can be applied to one's own proceeding thereby reducing own costs. For these reasons, it can be profitable for private parties to delay filing their actions for damages until a public proceeding has been conducted (as follow-on actions) in which the breach of a competition law has already been established. Similarly, business entities may hope to be able to free ride on someone else's decision to file suit, when the fear of retaliation prevents the initiation of a damage claim on their own.

Whenever such free riding is possible, being the first to litigate can become a disadvantage. This can result in delayed actions or even in no actions being brought against the infringing parties.

3.4. *Total enforcement costs to society are not minimised*

Even without all the above-mentioned obstacles to private actions, individual litigation under tort law will not fulfil the criteria of optimal enforcement requiring the minimisation of total enforcement costs.

---

262 Van Den Bergh, *European competition law and economics: a comparative perspective*, 331. For free-rider problems in opt-out class actions see: Friedman, "Constrained Individualism in Group Litigation: Requiring Class Members to Make a Good Cause Showing before Opting Out of a Federal Class Action," *The Yale Law Journal* 100 (1990): 745. For an economic theory of free-rider problems in collective actions see: Stigler, "Free riders and collective action: An appendix to theories of economic regulation," *The Bell Journal of Economics and Management Science* 5 (1974): 359.

Each individual legal procedure against the same defendant for the same conduct entails at least a partial duplication of efforts and costs. Even if all the evidence gathered in the first trial is available and applicable to all the following actions, each trial will at least require time and resources spent on lawyers and court fees. These costs are only minimised when all damage claims are bundled into one procedure that clarifies the relevant factors common to all claims. Moreover, all the resources spent by several entities to detect the infringement in the first place also represent a wasteful doubling of resources.

Cost minimisation would require that the capital spent on detection as well as litigation expenditures is kept to the lowest level possible while achieving optimal deterrence. Hence, procedural efficiency is an integral part of cost minimisation.

D. SUMMARY

This chapter introduced the legal and economic framework used in the analysis of the optimal group litigation mechanism in the coming chapters. The legal framework has been less stringent than it would have been in a legal analysis. The reason for this is that many of existing rules and regulations would need to undergo change should group litigation mechanisms, which so far are not very common in the European Member States, be introduced into existing legal systems. Therefore, while taking the general legal framework as starting point, the analysis will point out which rules would need to be amended.

Having defined the most important terms and concepts, as well as having introduced the legal and economic framework, the next chapter will apply these frameworks. This will first be to generalised forms of exiting forms of group litigation as defined in this chapter. Then, the insights gained from this analysis will be used to develop another mechanism that may curb problems that remain under the known forms. This mechanism will provide an indication as to the more efficient forms of group litigation and form a kind of benchmark for the further analysis conducted in chapters 4 and 5.

CHAPTER 3
OPTIMAL GROUP LITIGATION FROM A DETERRENCE PERSPECTIVE

In this section, the framework established in the previous chapter is applied to assess the optimal design of a group litigation mechanism.[263] This section is structured as follows. First, the deterrence effects of follow-on suits are contrasted with those of stand-alone suits. Then, stylised forms of existing group litigation mechanisms, i.e. collective action and representative action, are investigated as to their effectiveness to reach the goal of optimal deterrence. In this analysis, using *backward induction*,[264] the necessary features of a group litigation mechanism that will achieve the optimal sanction are first discussed. Then, the potential of different forms of group litigation systems will be analysed with regard to optimising the probability of detection and litigation, as well as procedural efficiency. The system therefore would have to remedy the discussed pitfalls of individual litigation, namely information asymmetry, rational apathy, free riding behaviour and multiplication of litigation efforts (procedural efficiency). Moreover, its aim would be to achieve the goal of optimal deterrence while minimising total enforcement costs. The conclusion provides an overview of the findings and relates the different types of group litigation mechanisms analysed to specific types of infringements.

A. DETERRENCE EFFECT OF FOLLOW-ON SUITS VERSUS STAND-ALONE SUITS

Private claims for damages can take two different forms. They can be conducted in the aftermath of public enforcement, so called follow-on suits. Alternatively, they can take place when no public proceeding has been started, as so called stand-alone suits. If both avenues of enforcement (public and private) are taken,

---

263 As strict optimality requirements in a "first best" context might never be met to full extend, optimality is understood to refer also to optimality in a second (or third) best context.

264 Backward induction refers to the process of reasoning backwards in time, starting from the desired outcome the optimal steps that are necessary to get there are traced back to the beginning.

the timing of private enforcement becomes important to estimating its potential to deter.

In the case of private follow-on suits, public authorities have already detected the infringement. If actions for damages and/or group litigation mechanisms were restricted to follow-on suits, they could never add to the rate of detection, as follow-on cases only take place after a public investigation. When estimating their deterrence effect, therefore, the probability of being caught has to be set equal to one (certainty). Any effect on deterrence as described in the economic model above then can only lie in increasing the sanction faced by the infringer.

The optimal level of deterrence requires the optimal level for the expected penalty imposed on the infringing party, leading to neither over- nor under-deterrence. When, as in follow-on suits, the probability of detection equals one, the optimal amount of penalty would equal total loss caused to society. In the ideal case then, damages awarded in the private legal suits should not be directly established by looking at the harm done to the individual plaintiff(s), but would have to be calculated as total harm to society (including the so called *dead weight loss*).[265]

However, follow-on suits take place after a public investigation and the imposition of public fines. To ensure the total penalty imposed is at the optimal level, fines imposed in a preceding administrative proceeding by competition authorities would have to be taken into account in the private proceeding. Prior administered public fines would have to be subtracted from the damages awarded to avoid imposing a level of expected penalty that exceeds the optimal amount.[266]

The closer the level of public fines imposed on the infringer(s) is to the optimal expected sanction, the less room there will be for additional sanctions imposed by private claims for damages. The probability of detection in such a case is only related to the efforts by the public agency and not influenced by private actions. When this arguably low rate of (public) detection[267] is not adequately taken into account when the fines are calculated, the gap between the level of fines and the level of optimal sanction is greater and additional sanctions could fill a larger gap.

---

265 Dead weight loss (also *allocative inefficiency*) refers to the total social welfare loss caused by a market not being in competitive equilibrium. For a discussion see Leslie, "Antitrust Damages and Deadweight Loss," *Antitrust Bulletin* 51 (2006): 521.

266 How such downward adjustments in private suits for damages could be legally justifiable is another question, however, very much depends on the way damages will be established in court (i.e. which proxies and methods of estimation are used).

267 Estimates for the detection of cartels are roughly between 10% and 33%. Most commentators work with an assumed detection rate of about 15%. See Renda, *Making antitrust damages actions in the EU more effective. Study in support of the impact assessment of the EC White Paper on antitrust damages actions*, 96.

Consequently, private damage claims only add to deterrence if public fines are too low to deter and these private claims will capture the remainder required for reaching the optimal amount of penalty faced by the infringer. Focusing on deterrence, the only rationale for follow-on suits then would be to increase the amount of the total sanction faced by the infringer.

Before going further into the details of adequate ways to combine public fines and subsequent damage payments to reach the optimal sanction, the preceding question is, whether an upward adjustment of the insufficient penalty because of too low public fines could not be achieved in ways that are more efficient. As discussed above,[268] optimal deterrence does not mean deterrence at any cost. All other things being equal, a mechanism that is less costly in reaching a certain outcome than any other should be strictly preferred. In that respect, two separate proceedings (a private judicial proceeding following the first administrative proceeding) seems a costly way to achieve a higher or even possibly the optimal amount of penalty. Increasing the public administrative fines imposed in the first proceeding to the optimal penalty amount in the first place would be less costly and therefore more efficient.

It also has been frequently stated that the optimal monetary penalties needed for optimal deterrence, whether they are public fines alone or in combination with damage awards, can be prohibitively large.[269] Therefore, and also with respect to the above mentioned principal-agent problems between managers and shareholders,[270] several authors argue for the necessity of criminal sanctions, i.e. imprisonment of the responsible individuals.[271] However, these discussions are not part of this analysis, since criminal sanctions remain the prerogative of public authorities. Nevertheless, it could be argued that if fines at the proclaimed low level of detection need to be prohibitively large, i.e. larger than the individual wealth,[272] to reach optimal deterrence, another solution would be to focus on ways to increase the level of detection.[273] The higher the level of detection, the lower the quantum of the penalty required to achieve the optimal sanction.

268 See *section Optimal deterrence in Chapter 2.*

269 The defendant may be judgment-proof and escape (part of the) liability.

270 See *section Optimal Sanction for anti-competitive conduct* in chapter 2.

271 See for example Wils, *Is criminalization of EU competition law the answer?* 117. Möschel, *Kommentar: Erweiterter Privatrechtsschutz im Kartellrecht* 115.

272 The idea of justice expressed in the proportionality between severity of act and size of sanction should not be disturbed by the optimal sanction, which is based on actual harm caused.

273 This would also be of vital importance when additional factors, such as the *availability bias* (established in behavioural economics) taken into account. That bias reflects the notion that people base their estimate of the probability that a certain event will occur on how easy information about such an event can be brought to mind. See Korobkin and Ulen, "Law ansd Behavioral Science: Removing the Rationality Assumption from Law and Economics," *California Law Review* 88 (2000): 1051, 1087 f.

However, efforts to increase the probability of detection are costly. Therefore, the benefit of further detection efforts would have to be weighed against the costs of these efforts.[274] When the costs of increasing the probability of detection to one are larger than the resulting benefits, the optimal detection rate will remain at less than one.

The focus on increasing the detection rate has been widely acknowledged in the literature on deterrence as the major potential contribution of private enforcement to overall deterrence.[275] The problem however is that follow-on damages actions do not add to that part of the expected costs faced by the potential infringer.

In conclusion, regardless of the availability of criminal sanctions, private follow-on suits can be disregarded when looking for the optimal group litigation mechanisms from a deterrence point of view. First, they do not add anything to the probability of detection and conviction, as they only take place after a public proceeding. The rate of detection may be the crucial aspect in any enforcement activity especially when the monetary penalty needed to reach deterrence despite the low probability of exposure is likely too large. Second, if the amount of fines or sanctions imposed in the prior public proceeding are too low to efficiently deter, private follow-on actions for damages are an inefficient mechanism to increase the amount of penalty faced by the potential infringer. If necessary and feasible, such an increase should take place in the first procedure, i.e. the public enforcement, as two separate proceedings are a doubling of efforts and a waste of resources. Consequently, the subsequent analysis concerning the goal of deterrence will focus on stand-alone suits.

B. DETERRENCE EFFECTS OF STAND-ALONE SUITS WITH REGARD TO DIFFERENT TYPES OF INFRINGEMENTS

1. INTRODUCTION

Stand-alone cases, i.e. private suits where no prior public enforcement has taken place, present a different scenario. Such suits influence both the *ex ante* probability of being caught and convicted, as well as the amount of penalty faced by the potential infringer.

---

274 The same argument applies, however, to the imposition of costly non-monetary sanctions, such as imprisonment.

275 Renda, *Making antitrust damages actions in the EU more effective. Study in support of the impact assessment of the EC White Paper on antitrust damages actions*, 63.

This section examines the optimal group litigation design from a deterrence perspective in a mere theoretical sphere. In this theoretical world, few existing legal rules inhibit the options of a group litigation mechanism. It is mainly the interplay between costs and benefits that drives the litigation decision. First, consequences of the optimal sanction with regard to the way group membership is established are discussed. Then, implications for free riding and moral hazard problems, as well as for procedural efficiency follow. Finally, the interplay between the optimal sanction and settlements is sketched.

2. THE OPTIMAL SANCTION IN STAND-ALONE SUITS

2.1. *The optimal sanction and group membership*

In light of the requirements with regard to the optimal sanction from a deterrence perspective as discussed above,[276] the damages sued for in the group litigation should be based on the total damage caused to society. The optimal sanction should allow for (Kaldor-Hicks) efficient breaches, taking the probability of detection into account, and should not lead to distortions of the principles of proportionality and marginal deterrence. The total damage caused to society will include damages to victims who, in the real world, would not be in a position to provide sufficient proof of their damages. To reach optimal deterrence, this amount should be adjusted according to the probability of detection and conviction. As the offender imposes enforcement costs on society, he should incorporate these costs in his cost-benefit analysis, so that the variable enforcement costs are also imposed on him.[277] In the further analysis, it is assumed that this can and will be achieved by cost-shifting rules that impose most or all of these costs on the defendant in case he loses at trial. Therefore, for simplicity the optimal sanction will be the total damages times the inverse probability of detection and conviction.[278]

In order for the sanction imposed on the antitrust offender(s) to reach the optimal amount in a given group litigation proceeding, all losses caused to the different victims would have to be included in that very proceeding. That would require the group litigation mechanism to be of a mandatory nature.

276 See *1.3 Optimal Sanction for anti-competitive conduct* in chapter 2.

277 Polinsky, *Public Enforcement of Law* 307, 316. The incorporation of plaintiffs litigation costs may already exist in those member States that follow the British rule with regard to cost shifting.

278 The incorporation of plaintiffs litigation costs may already exist in those member States that follow the British rule with regard to cost shifting. The used simplification for the analysis does not change the main results of the analysis.

That is, members of the group should not be required to opt-in or allowed to opt-out. This is the theoretical concept that forms the basis for example for the concept of mandatory class action, as known in the USA,[279] and potentially also the underlying rationale for the Portuguese popular action.[280] Especially opt-in but also opt-out mechanisms bear the risk that not all victims will join, or that some victims may drop out of the damage action. Some may not become aware of the action, some may find the expected benefits not enough to justify the effort of informing themselves about their rights and duties of participating and therefore ignore it, and even others may deliberately decide not to be part of the group litigation as they expect to do better on their own in the wake of the group proceeding. It has been pointed out in the literature that deciding not to participate in a group litigation, but to initiate an individual proceeding, is only a viable option for those victims who have relatively large losses to sue for. Victims with small and scattered losses have no alternatives, when the expected rewards do not justify the expenses. Empirical results, though difficult to attain, seem to support that idea.[281] Moreover, opt-out rates seem to be very low on average, so that an opt-out solution may come close to a mandatory solution in reality in many cases.[282] Opt-in proceedings are likely to lead to the lowest levels of participation. Both Law and Economics literature, as well as actual experiences with forms of opt-in proceedings, corroborate this.[283]

If not all damages are sued for, the penalty imposed will fall short of the optimal sanction, leading to under-deterrence. If, on the other hand, all those victims

279 See FRCP Rule 23 (b)(1)(A); (b)(1)(B); (b)(2), although limited to specific circumstances, see Pace, "Class Actions in the United States of America: An Overview of the Process and the Empirical Literature," (2007), 11 and 15; Rowe Jr, "State and Foreign Class-Action Rules and Statutes: Differences from-and Lessons for?-Federal Rule 23," *Western State University Law Review* 35 (2007): 147, 155 f.

280 Mulheron, *Competition Law Cases under the Opt-out Regimes of Australia, Canada and Portugal: A research paper for the Department for Business, Enterprise and Regulatory Reform.*

281 See Connor, *Global price fixing* Chapter 15, 393 ff, analysing the outcome of settlements in several federal class action cases and also 417.

282 Studies of consumer cases over a period of ten years suggest an average opt-out rate of less than 0, 2%, see Eisenberg and Miller, "Role of Opt-outs and Objectors in Class Action Litigation: Theoretical and Empirical Issues, The," *Vanderbilt Law Review* 57 (2004): 1529, 1532.

283 Issacharoff and Miller, "Will Aggregate Litigation Come to Europe?" *NYU Law and Economics Research Paper No. 08-46*(2008). Available at: http://ssrn.com/abstract=1296843. Lampe and Rossman, "Procedural Approaches for Countering the Dual-Filed FLSA Collective Action and State-Law Wage Class Action," *Labor Lawyer* 20 (2004): 311, 313 f; Baetge, "National report Germany: Class Actions, Group Litigation & Other Forms of Collective Litigation," *Global Class Actions* (2007), 31. Available at http://globalclassactions.stanford.edu/PDF/Germany_National_Report.pdf; Mulheron, "Some Difficulties with Group Litigation Orders-and Why a Class Action is Superior," *Civil Justice Quarterly* 24 (2005): 40. For an example of the difficulties that an opt-in approach may entail see also the case brought by the UK consumer association WHICH?, discussed in chapter 5.

deciding not to opt-in or deciding to opt-out would indeed bring their own claims, the optimal sanction may be imposed, however at higher total costs. Moreover, in jurisdictions without strict rules of precedent, or between different jurisdictions, there may be the costs of potentially inconsistent judgments and consequent lack of clarity in the law.

In conclusion, the following statements can be made. In order to reach optimal deterrence by imposing the optimal sanction on offenders, total damages caused to society must be sued for. The optimal group litigation therefore will have to capture all harmed individuals. As neither opt-in, nor opt-out mechanisms can guarantee that all harmed individuals will be included the best mechanism seems to be a mandatory one. Overall, the optimal system would require the initiator (agent) of the group litigation to be endowed with the right to represent all harmed victims in society.[284] Moreover, the adjustment of the actual amount of harm done with the low probability of detection would require the court to be able to estimate that probability correctly and also some mechanism to circumvent legal obstacles such as the prevalent ban on overcompensation or unjust enrichment would be needed. Punitive damages or the like would have to be possible. Existing legal impediments to reaching such a solution will be discussed in chapter 4 and chapter 5.

2.2. *Reducing free riding and moral hazard problems*

Including all victims in one-procedure helps to solve the problems connected to free rider behaviour. Waiting for prior public enforcement is not an option when the group litigation mechanism is confined to stand-alone cases. Counting on some other victim to initiate proceedings is only beneficial then, when the passive group members can expect to be made at least equally well off as the initiating party.[285] Making the group membership mandatory would also overcome the disincentives of dependent business partners, who otherwise would refrain from filing suit due to fear of retaliation. End consumers would not be deterred by having to fill out forms or make initial payments in order to opt-in. Additionally, important plaintiffs with relatively large claims and sufficient individual resources to file individual claims can not opt-out to the detriment of the remaining group members. The risk that group members vital to the success of the group, for example those represented in or initiating the

---

284 Ideally, that would also include victims of the same infringement in another jurisdiction. However, cross-border solutions are not foreseen in the current European development. Compare chapter 5, section A. 1.3.7 on the U.S. nationwide class action for a brief discussion of occurring problems.

285 These questions are closely connected to the discussion about the type of agent that will represent the group. These issues are dealt with in greater detail below.

precedence case might be bought off during the proceedings or enticed to settle confidentially and exit, which would lead to under-deterrence, is avoided.[286]

2.3. *Procedural efficiency*

Looking at cost efficiency, it becomes clear that the claims for damages, as an enforcement tool imposing the optimal sanction on the infringing party or parties, should best be bundled into just one legal procedure. Having several victims claim individual damages is connected to a multiplication of efforts and a waste of resources. Court fees, lawyers and experts have to be paid several times to impose the total of the sanction. Therefore, as soon as detection has taken place, all victims should be represented in just one group litigation. Damages caused to competitors, direct and indirect purchasers, would all be dealt with in just the one legal procedure. Again, this requires the group litigation mechanisms to be of a mandatory nature, where no victim is required to opt in (as it may refrain from doing so) or allowed to opt out. Thereby the additional costs of notification and registration as they occur in opt-in and opt-out procedures can also be avoided. Also in reality, as long as the factual and legal issues are the same for the majority of the victims,[287] mandatory group litigation would generally have to be preferred from a cost perspective.

The costs analysed so far only relate to litigation expenditures. However, also the detection of an offence in the first place can be very resource demanding. These detection expenditures should be justified by the rate of detection that can be achieved. Put in another way, the optimal rate of detection should be achieved with the lowest overall burden on society. Trade offs with giving sufficient incentives for private parties to investigate potential anti-competitive conduct may be unavoidable. These aspects will be analysed thoroughly when the incentive structures of the agents are examined below.

2.4. *The optimal sanction and settlements*

Another aspect relevant to the imposition of the optimal sanction at lowest possible costs is the question of settlements.

Settlements may allow a reduction of enforcement costs by reducing resources spent on litigation. Under conditions of complete information and equal

---

286 This may be framed as a moral hazard problem. Put plainly, moral hazard arises because the acting party does not take into account the negative consequences its action has on others.

287 In the following analysis, this is assumed to be the case, as the most difficult legal issue common to all claims often will be the question of liability. Exact individual amounts of harm may be of less importance, as will be developed.

bargaining power, the settlement outcome should equal the outcome that would have resulted in a trial. When the interests of the representing party are identical to the interest of society, that settlement agreement should be the optimal sanction. Additionally, since settlements are commonly understood to require fewer resources than a court trial,[288] such a settlement would reach the desired effect at lower costs. However, when the conditions of complete information and equal bargaining power are not given, the costs to be saved by settlements compared to litigation would have to be weighted against any negative effects settlements may have on deterrence. This will be explained in more detail below.

Assuming that there is no information asymmetry, both parties have the same expectation of the outcome of the trial, both are equally risk neutral and have the same costs and resources, the settlement amount should equal that expected outcome. In this case, both parties can avoid the costs of litigation by coming to an agreement. Under such simplistic models, the adversaries will settle their dispute for the same amount as the expected trial outcome. Shavell[289] showed that a settlement is even mutually beneficial in scenarios where plaintiff and defendant have different expectations with regard to the expected outcome of the trial, as long as the sum of litigation costs to be saved exceeds the discrepancy between their expectations.

However, such models are based on strong assumptions, which may be lacking in reality. Other assumptions as to the nature and aim of the involved parties can lead to the assessment that settlement agreements bear the risk of not imposing the optimal sanction on the infringing party and thus interfere with the desired deterrence effect of claims for damages. Such assumptions include information asymmetry between the parties, different attitudes towards risk, different estimates of probabilities and strategic or opportunistic behaviour by self-interested parties.[290] These assumptions may be more realistic.

288 Gross and Syverud, "Getting to no: A study of settlement negotiations and the selection of cases for trial," *Michigan Law Review* 90 (1991): 319, 320. Shavell, "The level of litigation: Private versus social optimality of suit and of settlement," *International Review of Law & Economics* 19 (1999): 99, 100 f.

289 Shavell, "Economic analysis of litigation and the legal process," *Harvard Law School: Harvard Law School John M. Olin Center for Law, Economics and Business Discussion Paper Series, Paper 404*(2004) 9 f.

290 All possible settings can not be discussed here. For an overview of settlement models in various settings see Daughety, *Settlement.* in *Encyclopedia of Law and Economics, Volume I. The History and Methodology of Law and Economics.* eds. Bouckaert and De Geest. Cheltenham: Edward Elgar (2000), 95.

Different risk attitudes can interfere with the deterrence effect of settlements.[291] When plaintiffs are more risk averse than defendants, the bargaining power is distributed unequally, enabling the less risk averse defendant to settle for more favourable amounts. If potential offenders can count on the possibility of a settlement agreement that will be less than the expected outcome of the trial, the deterrence effect *ex ante* is diminished.

In addition, strategic behaviour of involved individuals can lead to socially inefficient settlements. Scholars repeatedly point out that while the bundling of several claims into one procedure increases the incentives to file suit, it also enhances the risk of unmeritorious cases.[292] Such frivolous suits, which are part of negative value suits (NEV),[293] are brought with the mere aim to extract a settlement from the defendant.[294] The threat of costly, publicity evoking suits could force defendants into accepting such settlement offers. These issues will be discussed in greater detail in the next section, as they may depend on the form of group litigation.

Therefore, the general assumption of settlements being a less costly mechanism to solve a dispute while reaching the same result as litigation becomes less convincing when such other factors are taken into account. Reputational losses or the economic necessity to keep certain types of information secret increase the incentives for defendants to avoid a trial, even if the allegations against them lack sufficient grounds. Other procedural rules, for example broad discovery rules[295] or possibly costly pre-trial certification procedures, strengthen these effects. Additionally, legal certainty and the development of legal rules are only facilitated when cases do go to trial. This is because most settlement agreements are not public released, which may also be an argument that needs to be taken into account by policy makers.[296]

291 *Ibidem*, 176 ff.

292 For example Hay and Rosenberg, "'Sweetheart' and 'Blackmail' Settlements in Class Actions: Reality and Remedy," *Notre Dame Law Review* 75 (2000): 1377; Rosenberg and Kozel, "Solving the Nuisance-Value Settlement Problem: Mandatory Summary Judgment," *Harvard Law and Economics Discussion Paper No. 469; Harvard Public Law Working Paper No. 90*(2004). Available online at: http://papers.ssrn.com/abstract_id=485242; Schäfer, *The Bundling of Similar Interests in Litigation. The Incentives for Class Action and Legal Actions taken by Associations* 183, 187.

293 Negative value suits are suits where the expected outcome does not justify the expected expenses for giong to trial. That can be due to the fact that the costs of suing are simply too larger, or that the probability of winning at trial is too low (for example because the case has little merits) For a model on NEV suits, see Bebchuk, *Negative Expected Value Suits.*

294 Rosenberg and Shavell, "A model in which suits are brought for their nuisance value," *International Review of Law & Economics* 5 (1985): 3.

295 As available for example in the US. For an economic analysis see *Wagener, Modelling the effect of one-way fee shifting on discovery abuse for private antitrust litigation 1887.*

296 When the relevant factors are such that settlements will generally lead to inefficient under-deterrence, policy makers could consider prohibiting settlements in such cases.

In the following analysis, settlements will generally be treated as welfare enhancing, i.e. as cost minimising, for simplicity. However, where incentives are present that may inhibit reaching the optimal settlement amount, these issues will be discussed.

C. THE OPTIMAL ENFORCEMENT AGENT

If the sanction imposed in a private action for damages is the socially optimal sanction to reach deterrence, the incentives of the acting parties leading to either too much or too little litigation become relevant. The risk of under-deterrence relates to the obstacles faced by individuals contemplating whether or not to bring an action for damages. These obstacles should ideally be overcome by the optimal group litigation mechanism. On the other hand, the mechanism should not give too large or wrong incentives, so as to avoid over-deterrence. The risk of under, but also that of over-deterrence, under which also activities are deterred which would have an overall beneficial effect for society, are both closely related to the incentives of the individual initiating and conducting the action for damages. Different entities may act as this agent and the specific issues concerning the incentive structure of each will be discussed below.

So far, the picture of one representing party (the agent) emerges, who enforces competition law on behalf of society at large, i.e., all those victims harmed by an offence, using the tool of actions for damages in a mandatory procedure to impose the optimal sanction on the violating parties. These basic principles present great similarities to the case of public enforcement. It also follows closely the general principles of optimal deterrence as laid out in the economic literature by Becker and Stigler[297], Landes and Posner[298], Shavell and Polinsky[299] and all the other works that followed. With the optimal sanction and some basic efficiency features established, the focus now turns to the incentives of the agent to act accordingly.

The optimal system should not only give optimal incentives to the agent to detect and punish anti-competitive conduct, but to also minimise the costs that activity imposes on society, including the costs of abuse of the system for personal gains. As a consequence, the optimal group litigation mechanism must exhibit features that allow for an efficient reduction of the information asymmetry problem, and an avoidance of the problems connected to free riding behaviour and rational apathy. Finally yet importantly, the design of the system should not give rise to

297 Becker, *Law enforcement, malfeasance, and compensation of Enforces* 1.

298 Landes, *The Private Enforcement of Law* 1.

299 Polinsky, *A note on optimal fines when wealth varies among individuals* 618.

principal-agent problems that distort the efficiency of the system. Focusing on the goal of deterrence, these problems, while already present between representing and represented parties, may also arise between the enforcing party as agent and society at large as principal.

Both information asymmetry and rational apathy problems are closely connected to the incentives that a specific group litigation mechanism is able to set for the initiator. The incentives of public agencies and their employees to invest in the investigation of certain incidents are explained in the Law and Economics literature using the theory of public choice.[300] Although public enforcement is not the topic of this thesis, the insights of that stream of literature may also be used in the further analysis of group actions for damages due to competition law infringement. The incentive structures of agents involved in group litigations, for example when associations act on behalf of the group, could be influenced by similar concepts, for example building or maintaining a reputation, gaining publicity or building individual careers. For, as assumed, more profit oriented purely private actors, such as firms or individuals, the incentive to sue for damages is assumed to be mainly influenced by the awards granted in court. Other possible motivations, such as revenge or the wish to altruistically contribute to the welfare of society at large are not taken into account, as it is assumed unlikely that they would be the main driving force in the majority of cases.[301] Additionally, the influence of the group litigation mechanism on the motivations to abuse the system of private claims for damages due to competition law infringements for personal gains is discussed.

The major focus of the following section will be the analysis of different agents and the particular incentive structures provided by the systems governing these agents. The analysis also follows a *backward induction* approach. Starting from the desired outcome, which is that the optimal sanction is imposed on the offender, the necessary steps leading to that outcome are traced. First, the features of the group litigation relating to the incentives and disincentives to file claim once detection has taken place are investigated. These are mainly the issues of rational apathy and free riding behaviour. Then the incentives and possibilities to detect an offence in the first place are analysed, which chiefly deal with the problem of information asymmetry and the incentives to overcome that obstacle. Lastly, also the problems that may inhibit the efficiency of the system because of inconsistent incentives of the players involved (principal-agent problems) and nuisance suits, as well as the possibility to minimise costs, are discussed.

---

300 For general insights in the theory of public choice, see Van den Hauwe, *Public Choice, Constitutional Political Economy and Law and Economics.* in *Encyclopedia of Law and Economics.* eds. Bouckaert and De Geest. Cheltenham: Edward Elgar (2000), 603.

301 Cases brought by companies in order to harm a strong competitor or cases brought in order to extract a positive settlement amount (nuisance suits) will be taken into account.

In the analysis, the question of how the optimal sanction imposed on the offender will be distributed amongst different parties will initially be left open. From a deterrence perspective, the distribution does not matter, as long as it does not benefit the infringer, and as long as it is costless. What does matter, however, is how different variations of distribution influence the players involved, therefore the discussion of the distribution issue will be developed in that respect.

1. LEAD PLAINTIFF/ ATTORNEY (COLLECTIVE ACTION)

The first possible agent acting on behalf of the collective is one member of the group.

The legislator could grant standing to one injured party to represent himself and all other victims in the position of a so-called *lead plaintiff*.[302] Any individual who has suffered harm due to a competition law infringement could hire a lawyer upon detection of the malfeasance. Ideally, this lead plaintiff would be a sophisticated player and someone frequently involved in similar proceedings. The other injured parties would be automatically members of the group, without the possibility of exempting themselves from the procedure.

In this combination, the incentives and interests of three players: society, the lead plaintiff and lawyer can conflict. Therefore, the incentives of both lawyer and lead plaintiff have to be investigated. When client's and lawyer's incentives are not completely aligned, the effects of conflicting interests can distort the efficiency of the collective action regarding deterrence. It is then relevant which interests will prevail. The same is true for the lead plaintiff acting in the interest of society.

On the other hand, while in other types of tort cases the injured party will often seek legal advice in the case of group actions it is also possible that the lawyer has incentives to approach potential clients. If that is the case, the lawyer becomes the main driving force behind the detection and litigation of offences, while the lead plaintiff may be little more than a figurehead. In that case, the possibly conflicting interests of society and the lawyers become crucial.

---

302 Term taken from the US class action concept. For an analysis of the effects of an insititutional investor as lead plaintiff in private securities litigation, see: Cox and Thomas, "Does the plaintiff matter? An empirical analysis of lead plaintiffs in securities class actions," *Columbia Law Review* 106 (2006): 1587.

1.1. Free rider problems

Free rider problems may be reduced under this type of collective action, as the mandatory nature of the mechanism includes all victims in one proceeding. Incentives to wait for a prior public proceeding that will lead to the establishment of an infringement in order to reduce costs only remain if collective actions could also be conducted as follow-on proceedings. However, in such cases, each individual still would have to weigh the risk of others filing suit first and becoming the lead plaintiff against the potential cost savings by remaining inactive and waiting for a prior public proceeding.

The crucial question is what motivation a victim has to become the lead plaintiff rather than to stay a silent group member, when the damages awarded will be distributed according to actual harm suffered later on. Becoming active would imply the spending of time and resources on the side of the initiating plaintiff. In order to provide incentives for a victim to take up that task, some additional reimbursement for these extra efforts are required. As the mandatory procedure would not allow for all parties to contract beforehand with each other, it seems that such monetary reward would need to be paid out from the total damages awarded. In the following analysis, the reward paid to lead plaintiffs will be treated as a certain share of the total damages granted to the whole pool of plaintiffs. Depending on the size of the share compared to the efforts expended by the plaintiff, it then can become more beneficial to take the role of the lead plaintiff rather than to be one of the silent group members. If the awards are not to be distributed amongst the other victims, then it is in fact only the lead plaintiff who receives some form of compensation for the suffered losses.[303] In this case, the incentive to become active would be even larger.

It may be noteworthy that when the lead plaintiff is allowed to settle the claims, there is also the possibility for the lead plaintiff to collude with the defendant(s), thereby extracting the total of damage awards, regardless of the shares the law would assign to him. If possible, this would really provide incentives to come forward and become the lead plaintiff. The reasoning for this goes as follows. Ideally, the lead plaintiff would accept only a settlement offer that equals or exceeds his expected net outcome from the trial. However, the amount the defendant(s) expect to have to pay in total exceeds that amount, as long as the lead plaintiff does not receive the total group damages. Their willingness to pay in the settlement agreement therefore is capped only by the amount that equals

303 This may be the case when total damages will be used in a cy pres mechanism, and only the lead plaintiff receives compensation and remuneration. Cy pres constitutes a possibility to put damage awards to their "next best" use when they can not be used to compensate individual victims. An example would be awarding the damages to some agency that will use the proceeds in the general interest of the represented group.

total expected damages. Within the parameters established by two amounts, the adversaries can bargain for a settlement amount that is preferred to the trial outcome by both, because litigation costs can be saved. If all the bargaining power were in the hands of the victim, he or she would settle for an amount that equals or only marginally falls short of the total damage awards. From a social point of view, this would be an efficient outcome.

On the other hand, if all the bargaining power resides with the defendant(s), the settlement amount would be only marginally larger than the expected payments made to the lead plaintiff if the case were to go to trial. In this case, there would be little incentive for an individual victim to take on the task of becoming lead plaintiff.

When it is in fact the lawyer detecting an infringement and driving the litigation, free riding behaviour would be reduced, as lawyers would only gain when they are the first to detect and prosecute. The mandatory nature of the group litigation would eliminate the free riding behaviour of lawyers bringing follow-on cases on behalf of sub groups or different classes of victims in the wake of cases unearthed by their fellow lawyers. The details of such a system and the relevant incentives structures will be discussed in depth below, where market based mechanisms are discussed.[304]

1.2. Overcoming rational apathy

It may be recalled that the individual victim will only have incentives to file suit upon detection, when the personal expected outcome at trial is as least as large as the costs of doing so. The factors that influence these variables are: the total costs of the group litigation, which the lead plaintiff may have to bear partially or totally or to pre-finance; the possibilities opened up by the group proceeding to share costs with other victims; the use of other financing mechanisms; and, ways to increase the personal outcome.

1.2.1. The total costs of litigation

One of the individuals harmed by anticompetitive conduct may be able to engage a lawyer and prosecute the claims of all other victims, including him or herself. This lead plaintiff will face many of the above discussed problems concerning traditional tort claims. Moreover, with the enactment of a group litigation mechanism, the whole procedure can become much more complex and resource demanding. For example, if not only one's own individual damages, but damages to the whole group, have to be proven. Moreover, such a group mechanism can

---

304 See section 3.

take considerably longer than traditional civil litigation. Data from the USA shows that class actions require more than four times the effort of other average civil cases.[305] In consequence, the rational apathy problem preventing the individual to start proceedings can become even more severe.

If the plaintiff only receives his actual damages as her award, the value she places on these claims is much less than the value the prosecution of these claims has for society. This is the same problem faced in traditional litigation. The incentives to file a suit in the first place may also be influenced by the fee arrangement agreed upon between lead plaintiff and legal representative. Larger fees for the attorney generally have a negative effect on the plaintiff's incentives to file suit. A plaintiff may also have to bear both his own, and the opponent's lawyer's costs, in the event the case is lost, when, as in most Member States, the English fee shifting rule is applied. Unless some additional benefits, such as compensation of expenses and an additional monetary award for becoming the lead plaintiff can be granted, the individual will tend to have even less incentives to file suit than without group litigation, as total litigation costs are likely to increase.

1.2.2. Spreading the costs

On the other hand, the use of group actions could allow the division of costs amongst all those represented. Ideally, the costs of the procedure would be spread over all the victims represented in the group litigation, thereby substantially reducing the costs each individual has to bear. However, as the optimal system has to be one of a mandatory nature, this is not a feasible solution unless the total costs of the proceeding are paid from the amount of the awarded damages and the individual lead plaintiff will bear none of the risks involved, for example costs imposed on him if the case is dismissed due to the lack of merits. It is clear that implementing such a solution would create other risks that would inhibit the efficiency of the system with regard to deterrence. For example, this may increase the risk of cases being brought before the courts with little or no merits, purely in order to extract a settlement from the defendant.

1.2.3. Using other ways of financing

Under a perfect capital market system, pre-financing of such suits would not be a problem. The claims for damages have an economic value therefore the holder of these rights should be able to borrow on the capital market against the expected

---

305 Willging, et al, "Empirical study of class actions in four federal district courts: Final report to the advisory committee on civil rules," *Washington, DC: Federal Judicial Center* (1996), 7 f. Available online at: www.fjc.gov/public/pdf.nsf/lookup/rule23.pdf/$File/rule23.pdf.

recovery of these claims.[306] While the capital market is likely to be less than perfect, other ways to shift the risk and costs may be available.

Possibilities allowing the risk of the trial, and initial expenditures to be shifted on to third parties, such as the lawyer or professional litigation funder, would greatly decrease the rational apathy problem on the side of injured parties, especially for non-commercial clients.[307] Professional funders of civil litigation already exist in a number of Member States, for example IM Litigation Funding in the UK, and Foris AG and Juratec AG in Germany, to name a few. Both mentioned alternatives would require the funder to gain compensation for the costs and risks taken, and are only likely to work when it is profitable to do so. Therefore, as seen in reality, these financiers are going to ask for a substantial share of total damage awards.

Several authors also praise the potential for contingency fees to overcome the disincentive to sue connected to the financing abilities of the plaintiff, as the lawyer bears initial expenses.[308] The possibility of reducing or shifting the risk of losing the trial because it is better distributed amongst plaintiff and lawyer in such cases also has these effects.[309] That is the case because the utility for the plaintiff will always be higher under a contingency fee contract, when she is risk averse, due to the risk-shifting feature of contingency contracts. On the other hand, as will be discussed below, contingency fee arrangements can influence the severity of principal-agent problems and the incentives to file unmeritorious suits. Other possibilities with similar effects on the rational apathy problem experienced on the injured party's side include: legal insurance schemes. specialised public financing funds or professional financers.[310] Critics of contingency fee systems often refer to such systems as methods to avoid possible negative side effects of contingency fee arrangements, i.e. principal-agent problems.[311] The potential negative effects on other factors determining the efficiency of the system must be discounted from the beneficial effects discussed here.

---

306 Schwartz, *An Economic Analysis of the Contingent Fee in Personal – Injury Litigation,* 1125, 1125. See also Landes, *The Private Enforcement of Law* 1.

307 Rubinfeld, *Contingent fees* 415, 415 f.

308 For example Gravelle, *No Win, No Fee: Some Economics of Contingent Legal Fees* 1205; Schwartz, *Economic Analysis of the Contingent Fee in Personal-Injury Litigation, An* 1125;. Rubinfeld, *Contingent fees* 415, 415f.

309 See Danzon, *Contingent Fees for Personal Injury Litigation* 213 Halpern, *Legal fees contracts and alternative cost rules: An economic analysis* 3.

310 See Office of Fair Trading, "*Private actions in competition law: effective redress for consumers and business, Recommendations by the Office of Fair Traiding*" (November 2007), nr. 5.3. Available at www.oft.gov.uk/shared_oft/ reports/comp_policy/oft916resp.pdf. See also Riley, *Damages in EC antitrust actions: who pays the piper?* 748, who propose the establishment of a contingency legal aid fund (CLAF) for cartel cases in the European context.

311 Which are discussed below.

It has to be mentioned that alternative financing systems are not only possible in any form of group litigation mechanism, but also in traditional litigation. However, both a contingency fee lawyer and professional funders will only invest resources in cases that involve sufficiently large amounts. Therefore, they might be more likely to invest in the group proceedings rather than in the individual suits that might be brought instead.

1.2.4. The lawyer as agent

The rational apathy problem concerning the lawyer is analogous to the assessment of the victims, and depends on the remuneration of the lawyer for his efforts. The remuneration may be larger under a contingency fee contract than under an hourly fee arrangement, especially when the latter is strictly regulated and capped. However, both could also be established in a way to lead to the same total amounts. What will be crucial is the effect these remuneration systems will have on the incentives of the lawyer *vis-à-vis* the incentives of society. These problems will be discussed in the section on principal-agent problems.

1.2.5. Conclusion

In conclusion it may be said that additional benefits or a reimbursement for time and effort expended on filing the suit should be granted to the lead plaintiff by allowing her to receive all, or a part, of the total damages awarded.[312] Depending on the share the plaintiff will receive, the individual assessment of whether the expected awards justify the expected expenses could be tailored towards a positive outcome. To make that positive shift, the money awarded to the lead plaintiff must at least cover the actual damages suffered, adjusted for the probability of losing at trial, and compensation for all the resources spent on and all the costs caused by the prosecution of the defendant(s).[313] Granting the lead plaintiff a share of total awards that exceeds his own actual damages would help to overcome the problem of rational apathy concerning the filing of suit persistent on the victim's side. Both end consumers and undertakings as direct victims of offences could be encouraged in these ways to bring claims. For the former, the problem of otherwise too small damages is solved. For the latter, purchasers incorporating future economic losses due to retaliation measures into their calculation could also be awarded compensation for these expected losses.[314]

---

312 The legal limits to such mechanisms will be discussed below in section C.

313 That is, when the victim is risk-neutral. The compensation would need to be higher when lead plaintiffs are risk-averse.

314 Though admittedly, this may increase the problems of nuisance suits especially in cases of competitor plaintiffs, who may stand to gain from imposing costs on their competitor.

If the lead plaintiff receives less than the total damages of the group, and the amount redistributed amongst those victims that can be identified does not amount to the full fund paid by the defendant(s), the question is raised as to what will happen to any unclaimed damages. If distribution to the victims takes place, funds may be created from which other victims able and willing to provide proof of their affiliation to the group could later receive some compensation. The remaining awards may also flow to the state or to other entities to be used for specified purposes, using the *cy pres* instrument. However, from a deterrence point of view, the subsequent distribution of the damage awards is irrelevant, as long as it does not interfere with the deterrence effect by somehow benefiting the defendant(s) or creating wrong incentives for the players involved. Distribution mechanisms that create additional costs to be borne by society will however be inefficient from a total welfare perspective.

1.3. Asymmetric information

So far, the obstacles and possible solutions connected to the filing of suits have been discussed. However, litigation can only take place once infringements have been detected. No compensation or reward is offered for any efforts spent on detection, so far.

That may not be of major importance in cases where detection is simple and consequently the problem of asymmetric information is not large. In cases where detection rates are extremely high, and no or only limited resources have to be spent on detection, special incentives for detection may be considered unnecessary. For such offences, the lead plaintiff will likely be in a good position to commence proceedings. In other cases, especially in cases of hard-core cartels, gaining knowledge about an infringement is a complex task. The type of infringement affects the potential of, and risk connected with, such an enforcement system. While horizontal cartels are covert and inherently difficult to detect, other types of infringements create far fewer problems of asymmetric information. In cases where the illegal conduct of the defendant is easy to discover, for example in types of vertical restraints, the incentives created by awarding the enforcement agent more than actual damages to overcome disincentives to invest resources in detection entails a risk of counterproductive effects, especially concerning nuisance suits. Often, the information concerning an infringement and even the necessary proof are already in the hands of the victim. Cases of abuse of a dominant position under Article 102 TFEU are also likely to be more easily observable, for example in cases of refusal to deal. Predatory pricing strategies typically harm direct competitors as well. While the practise itself is quite easily observable, the information required establish an infringement encompasses not only all the information needed to establish the dominant position of the predator, but also includes knowledge about the actual cost function of the alleged competition law infringer.[315] Competitors claiming lost profits can also appear in cases of refusal to deal. In this case, the detection rate is likely to be close to 100 percent. Here any gain to the plaintiff exceeding the actual damages caused to him would increase the risk of unmeritorious claims brought to extract a settlement despite low merits of the case, especially in cases ruled by a rule-of-reason approach or an effects based analysis. However, the detection rate in such cases should be set very high, thereby granting the plaintiff only smaller additional gains from litigation, compared to other types of offences. Over deterrence of conduct that may actually enhance total welfare is a larger risk in cases where typically competitors are the plaintiffs than in cases of cartels. In the former cases, the necessity of far reaching group litigation mechanism is also lower.

In the case of larger asymmetric information problems, victims of illegal conduct remain unlikely to invest resources to uncover such offences without providing additional awards for engaging in such activities. An example would be end consumers harmed by a price cartel where the total damages were passed on to them. That means that prosecuting victims will not only have to receive the share of total damages to compensate them for the risks and costs of litigation, but more than that to cover detection expenses.[316]

Under the collective action mechanism, both the lawyer and lead plaintiff may be given incentives to overcome the problem of asymmetric information, by granting them a larger than proportional share of the total damages. As the lead plaintiff receives a share of (or maybe even the total of) awarded damages, the amount he receives that exceeds his total costs and damages constitutes a profit that may justify initial expenditures in detection. The same argument is true for the lawyer when working on a contingency fee basis, granting also him a share of total damage awards. Obviously, the lead plaintiff will only monitor and investigate markets she is active in, and firms she is conducting business with, as personal harm is the basic requirement to become a lead plaintiff in a collective action procedure, as defined here. End consumers would cover the largest part of the market, but would also need larger compensation, as their costs of detection typically are larger than for companies. Because, just as the initial problem of asymmetric information is unequally severe depending on the type of victim, also the incentives to investigate given by the share of damages received are likely to be larger for commercial entities than for end consumers. The latter typically engages in economic exchange in a huge variety of markets and on relatively

315 On a discussion of the European approach to predatory pricing, see Van Den Bergh, *European competition law and economics: a comparative perspective*, 293.

316 Which is one of the arguments in favour for punitive or exemplary damages. They cover costs that are not compensated by compensatory damages and provide a form of reward for the plaintiff enforcing legal rules and thereby fulfilling a socially valuable task.

small scales, leading to relatively low damages. While the costs of monitoring and investigating for this affected party are considerably larger, the probabilities of finding an infringement are relatively low, due to the restriction to cases of own involvement. Risk aversion of end consumers exacerbates these problems. The share of damages received would have to be very large to justify these risky investments. For commercial entities, such as direct purchasers, granting a sufficient share of the total damages is likely to have much larger effects on the willingness to reduce existing information asymmetries. However, these entities will also be restricted to markets they conduct business in, but the information asymmetry is lower from the outset.

As already discussed, it might be that even if a collective action system is designed to grant the lead plaintiff the most active role, it is in fact the lawyer who assumes this role. An attorney would have incentives to detect anti-competitive conduct when his financial remuneration is positively impacted accordingly, for example by receiving a share of total damage awards. The lawyer could find cases in any industry and is not restricted by the necessity of his own involvement. The attorney may be in a position to specialise or focus on specific industry sectors or certain types of infringement, thereby being able to reduce investigation costs due to specialisation. In addition, infringements detected while investigating another infringement could be prosecuted. The incentives to invest resources in the uncertain endeavour of monitoring markets would be determined by the value of the share of the expected total awards in relation to the initial costs that have to be borne. Once an offence is found, victims could be approached[317] and offered to assume the role of lead plaintiff. The lawyer will also always weigh the risks and costs connected to investment in detection efforts against the potential financial rewards. Therefore, granting the lawyer only a share of the total damages caused to society (the total damages awarded in court, i.e. the optimal sanction), for example twenty or thirty percent, may lead to less detection efforts than society would like to see in certain cases.[318] A share of the total damages might well be enough to trigger some amount of investigation and litigation, but possibly not up to the amount that society at large would be willing to invest.[319]

It may be noteworthy that in these cases, in which lead plaintiff and lawyer can freely contract about the remuneration, the lawyer may end up receiving almost the total damage awards. This is because many victims may be interested in assuming the role of lead plaintiff especially when the total damage awards will

---

317 These arguments presuppose that such conduct is not prohibited. However, in many Member States lawyers are still prohibited from approaching potential clients.

318 See section 3, below, discussing the problem of adequate remuneration of the agent.

319 See the discussion of the market solution in section 3 below.

not be distributed. This gives great bargaining power to the attorney. If law does not regulate the contingency fee percentage, the attorney could contract a fee close to 100 percent of the total damage awards, minus the share reserved for the lead plaintiff by law. Other victims, that now will otherwise receive none of the damages, may even be inclined to offer part of their share as side payments to the lawyer in order to become the lead plaintiff. *De facto*, the lawyer would then be in a position to receive a sum close to total damage awards. Such a system is very likely to initiate competition amongst lawyers to invest in the detection and litigation of anti-competitive conduct. It may even be an efficient system. However, under such circumstances, it would be better to design the group litigation system accordingly and eliminate the then purely formal necessity of lead plaintiffs, which brings about costs but no additional benefits. While competition amongst several enforcers is likely to have positive effects on deterrence, some problems are also created. The effects and desirability of such a market for enforcement and possible solutions to emerging problems are discussed in section C.3. and C.4. below.

In conclusion it can be said that the degree to which asymmetric information exists depends on the type of infringement and the nature of the victim supposed to act as lead plaintiff. End consumers in cases of very small and widely spread damages will face larger costs in overcoming these obstacles, than companies harmed in other cases. Individual end consumers are likely to lack the necessary knowledge and skills to pursue a case, and are also probably only involved in very few cases (one-shot players). Moreover, it is crucial that in general the acting agent is reimbursed for detection efforts in order to provide incentives to invest resources in detection of competition law infringements.

Granting the agent only a proportional share of the total damages caused by detected infringements might give suboptimal incentives to invest in detection efforts, i.e., efforts to overcome the initial information asymmetry. Society would be better off paying the total damages to the agent but reaping the benefits of other infringements being deterred than to just suffer the losses without undertaking additional deterrence effects. Therefore, societies' and agents' interest in investing in detection efforts differ, as the latter do not take the deterrence benefits of their actions accruing to society at large into account. This problem will be discussed in greater detail below in section 3.

1.4. Principal-agent problems

As already stated, several principal-agent problems can arise in a collective action setting. When the lead plaintiff is an active player with its own interests, conflicts can arise with the interests of society and those of the lawyer. When it is the lawyer that is the active agent, and the lead plaintiff is a silent figurehead, the interests of society and the lawyer should be aligned.

Principal-agent problems in collective action settings may be increased as compared to the traditional client-lawyer relationship. It is possible that the lead plaintiff is unable or rationally unwilling to adequately monitor the lawyer. Additionally, the fact that the lawyer is representing all other possible victims that have no influence on the proceeding exacerbates the problems. Especially when the victim is not engaged in such lawsuits on a regular basis, but is only a one-shot player, the relevant abilities stemming from experience and litigation related knowledge are limited. This will often be the case when the victim in question is a private end consumer. In the case the victim is an experienced repeat player, for example someone who specialised in the detection and litigation of competition law infringements, principal-agent problems are less severe. Similarly, they are likely to be less severe in cases where undertakings are plaintiffs. The ability of such agents to monitor the lawyer's conduct, punish insufficient effort by changing lawyer, and refusing future employment, can be a sufficient counterweight to conflicting interests between client and lawyer. In the other cases, principal-agent problems could remain significant.

As noted above, a commercial client as a repeat player is likely to be in a better position to influence the legal representative's conduct than other types of potential victims of competition law infringements, such as end consumers. If the lead plaintiff is inexperienced in such endeavours, and most likely to be involved only once in such a procedure, the lawyer will often be the person who can evaluate the case and chances of success to a better degree than the client can. The lead plaintiff then is dependant upon getting correct and complete information from the lawyer, who may have incentives that deviate from those of the client.

Depending on the remuneration scheme agreed upon between client and lawyer, which can be hourly fees, contingent (conditional) fees or contingency fees, incentives of both lawyer and client, may be more or less aligned. Fee arrangements for lawyers in civil law countries are predominantly hourly fee agreements.[320] However, contingency fees, in which the lawyer receives a certain percentage of the value of the claim, or contingent or conditional fee contracts, where the financial remuneration is based on an hourly fee but is increased when the case is won, are also possible.

---

320 Stuyck, *An analysis and evaluation of alternative means of consumer redress other than redress through ordinary judicial proceedings Final Report*, 317 f.

Principal-agent problems can arise as the lawyer may have incentives to restrict the amount of effort spent on the case and consequently to advise his clients to agree upon settlement arrangements that fall short of what the plaintiff would have accepted under a complete information scenario.

Several authors compared hourly fees and contingency fees with regard to their ability to extract optimal exertion from the legal representative and found that the incentives for the lawyer to put in effort are affected by the fee arrangement. While under an hourly fee arrangement, the procedure may be artificially prolonged by the lawyer so as to increase his total remuneration, a common criticism against contingency fees is that they provide incentives to settle sooner and also for lower amounts in order to induce the defendant to settle at an early stage.[321] The ideal baseline in this analysis is found by the decision of a perfectly informed and risk neutral client able to monitor his counsellor's behaviour, who is working on an hourly fee.[322] Alternatively, it can be the effort the lawyer would exert were he to pursue the case for himself.[323] As the hourly wage is lost to the lawyer by spending time on this rather than another case and thereby constitutes his costs (*opportunity costs*), this effort equals the optimal effort the perfectly informed and risk neutral client would buy. The outcome of the case is a settlement, which is influenced by the hours spent on the case by the lawyer. The obtainable settlement amount increases with each hour, but on a decreasing scale, until a fixed maximum amount. Under such settings, the client will buy working hours of the lawyer to reach a settlement, where the client's net benefit (settlement amount minus total fees) is maximised. With a contingency fee of less than 100 percent, the attorney will spend less effort than optimal, as he bears all the costs but only receives a fraction of the additional increase in settlement amount with each hour spent on the case. If the plaintiff is risk averse, however, the loss in net settlement amount could also function as a risk premium, as gross recovery could be less than the benchmark under contingency fee arrangements.[324] Neither competitive pressure on the market for legal services nor reputation mechanism or judicial review can effectively combat this predicament.[325] On the other hand, if the client were imperfectly informed, lawyers working on an hourly fee would have incentives to prolong cases at hand, when taking on new cases is connected to some fixed costs of transition. Other

321 See Schwartz, *Economic Analysis of the Contingent Fee in Personal-Injury Litigation, An* 1125; Miller, *Some agency problems in settlement* 189; Gravelle, *No Win, No Fee: Some Economics of Contingent Legal Fees* 1205.

322 See Schwartz, *Economic Analysis of the Contingent Fee in Personal-Injury Litigation, An* 1125; Danzon, *Contingent Fees for Personal Injury Litigation* 213.

323 Schäfer, *The Bundling of Similar Interests in Litigation. The Incentives for Class Action and Legal Actions taken by Associations* 183, 194.

324 Danzon, *Contingent Fees for Personal Injury Litigation* 213, 223.

325 Schäfer, *The Bundling of Similar Interests in Litigation. The Incentives for Class Action and Legal Actions taken by Associations* 183, 194 f.

authors suggested non-linear fees as solution to principal-agent problems.[326] Their analysis suggests that, the optimal fee will be lower, the higher the expected recovery and the lower the effort needed to obtain that recoupment, as large rewards for the attorney are necessary to provide incentives to exercise effort.

Defendants may propose an inefficient settlement offer when the bargaining power is relatively concentrated on the defendant's side. Depending on the incentive structures guiding the decision making process of the lawyer, it is possible that the lawyer will collude with the defendant(s) to the detriment of his client while pursuing his own interest. If socially inefficient settlements can be beneficial for the lawyer, under-deterrence may result.

The total effect of contingency fee systems on settlement amounts depends on several other factors, so that the traditional negative view in Europe of contingency fees may not always be justified. A number of scholars[327] suggest that the opposite of traditional analysis is the case and that contingency fees may in fact reduce the incentives for lawyers to settle. That may happen for example, when the possibility of frivolous suits is taken into account.[328] Lower settlement rates and larger settlement amounts due to contingency fees also result, if the fact that once the case goes to trial, the lawyer will spend less than optimal effort on it, is adequately incorporated in the analysis.[329] Some empirical evidence, finding decreasing settlement rates and increasing settlement amounts with the instruction of a maximum cap on contingency fees strengthen these theories.[330]

Of course, lawyers' actions may be restrained by their interest in gaining or keeping a certain reputation. However, reputational issues are likely to be of less relevance when it is the lawyer who is searching for a lead plaintiff, and when the lead plaintiff typically is a one-shot player, unable to assess and monitor the lawyers' conduct. Apart from other possible motivations, such as ethical concerns and the notion of the lawyer to be part of the judicial system to promote justice, it can be assumed that a rational lawyer will estimate the benefits of accepting

326 So Hay, "Contingent fees and agency costs," *Journal of Legal Studies* 25 (1996): 503 Also e.g. Miller, *Some agency problems in settlement* 189 describing contracts in which the lawyer's percentage depends on the stage of litigation in which the suit is resolved. Also Clermont and Currivan, "Improving on the Contingent Fee," *Cornell Law Review* 63 (1977): 529 proposing contingent hourly fees combined with percentage bonuses.

327 Bebchuk and Guzman, "How Would You Like to Pay for That--The Strategic Effects of Fee Arrangements on Settlement Terms," *Harvard Negotiation Law Review* 1 (1996): 53; Polinsky and Rubinfeld, "A damage-revelation rationale for coupon remedies," *Journal of Law, Economics, and Organization* 23 (2007): 653.

328 Miceli, *Do contingent fees promote excessive litigation* 211.

329 Polinsky, *A note on settlements under the contingent fee method of compensating lawyers* 217.

330 Danzon and Lillard, "Settlement out of court: The disposition of medical malpractice claims," *Journal of Legal Studies* 12 (1983): 345.

and investing resources in a certain case brought to his attention. Most probably, these benefits are largely determined by the financial rewards for the work effort.

Solutions to the problems of adequate fee arrangements include the proposition to allow a multitude of mixed contracts, which create signalling and screening mechanisms to overcome the problems of information asymmetries between lawyer and plaintiff.[331] The idea is that lawyers of high quality will prefer contingency fee arrangements providing them with a large share, while low quality lawyers would be willing to work for lower percentage shares, maybe connected to a fixed fee. Others have suggested a hybrid contingent fee, in which the lawyer receives a fraction or maybe all of the recovery but makes a fixed side payment to the client.[332] Principal-agent conflicts between client and attorney could be overcome completely, if the lawyer would claim the total damages for his own benefit, as agent and principal become the same person. One could envision a system allowing the plaintiffs to sell their claims to the attorney, effectively increasing the contingency fee to 100 percent for a fixed side payment made from the lawyer to the victims. This could be a contractual payment made by the lawyer. However, the transaction costs of contracting with all possible victims after detection through the lawyer, existing information asymmetries, and remaining rational apathy problems, would render such a system unfeasible in most cases of infringements, where the incentives to detect are crucial. Similar solutions, which may be more efficient, will be discussed below.

Principal-agent problems are not confined to the relationship between lawyer and client. Society may also be seen as a principal, expecting the lead plaintiff or the lawyer as agent to enforce competition law for the benefit of society as a whole. In this relationship, conflicts of interests also arise. The individual incentives to sue systematically deviate from the social incentives.[333] The agent does not take any external costs, such as the costs of the judicial system, or any external benefits, such as increased deterrence, into account when deciding whether and how to pursue a claim. These additional costs and benefits, however, are borne by society, so that their interests are not aligned. These principal-agent problems could be greatly reduced if the plaintiff were to be granted the total of the damages award.[334]

In conclusion, the principal-agent problems in a collective action system can be severe. They can arise not only between lead plaintiff and lawyer, but also between agent and society. For society as the main principal with the aim of

331 See section 2.2.1.3. above.
332 Rubinfeld, *Contingent fees* 415.
333 See Shavell, *The Social versus the Private Incentive to Bring Suit in a Costly Legal System*, 333.
334 This again relates to the discussion of the optimal remuneration of agents, discussed in section 3 below.

deterrence, it might be best to grant the enforcer not only a share of total damage awards, but the whole (assuming that each litigated case and the detection efforts invested *ex ante* would have at least a marginal deterrence effect). Thereby, the incentives of society and agent would be better aligned.

1.5. Nuisance suits

The availability of a group litigation mechanism may, however, increase the risk of suits being brought against potential defendants for non-efficient reasons, such as the aim to harm a competitor or to pressure potential defendants into a settlement, even when the merits of the case are questionable.

A first risk is that competitors may strategically abuse competition law in order to harm competitors.[335] Cases of exclusionary abuses are especially prone to such strategic behaviour, as plaintiffs typically are competitors. Any increase in expected damage awards also augments the potential for abuse of competition law, as the threat of an adverse judgment becomes more severe. At the same time, the motivations to look for possibilities to abuse competition law also increase. However, in cases of exclusionary abuses or vertical restraints, the probability of detection will often be much closer to 100 percent than in cartel cases, for example, so that the increase in total damage awards due to the coupling with the inverse of the probability of detection is lower.

Another risk is that claims are being filed with the main purpose of pressuring the defendant into a settlement, even when the merits of the claim are highly disputable. The risk of such frivolous or nuisance suits has been voiced frequently in the Law and Economics literature.[336] However, not all researchers agree on the risk of such threats.[337] The Law and Economics literature has examined circumstances where plaintiffs (or their lawyers as the acting agents) have an

---

335 See Baumol and Ordover, "Use of antitrust to subvert competition," *Journal of Law & Economics* 28 (1985): 247; Breit and Elzinga, "Private antitrust enforcement: the new learning," *Journal of Law & Economics* 28 (1985): 405, 405 f.; McAfee and Vakkur, "The Strategic Abuse of the Antitrust Laws," *Journal Of Strategic Management Education* 1 (2004): 1; Crane, "The Paradox of Predatory Pricing," *Cornell Law Review* 91 (2005): 1. For an analysis of the incentives for competitors to engage in frivolous predation litigation, see Helsel, "Preventing Predatory Abuses in Litigation between Business Competitors: Focusing on a Litigant's Reasons for Initiating the Litigation to Ensure a Balance between the Constitutional Right to Petition and the Sherman Acts Guarantee of Fair Competition in Business," *Wm.& Mary L. Rev.* 36 (1994): 1135.

336 See Rosenberg, *Solving the Nuisance-Value Settlement Problem: Mandatory Summary Judgment.*Available at SSRN: http://ssrn.com/abstract=485242 or DOI: 10.2139/ssrn.485242; Bebchuk, "Suing solely to extract a settlement offer," *Journal of Legal Studies* 17 (1988): 437.

337 Silver, "'We're scared to death': Class certification and blackmail," *NYU Law Review* 78 (2003): 1357.

incentive to sue, even when the case bears no or little merits.[338] Defendants may prefer an early settlement if this costs them less than the sum of the costs of defending the case in court. The latter losses consist of the attorney's fees (the part that must be paid by the defendant irrespective of the outcome of the case), the harm to the company's reputation, and the intra-company diversion costs (costs spent on the lawsuit that cannot be used for other purposes). The size of these losses creates scope for abuses if the suing attorney can easily pressure the defendant to pay damages (parts of which are paid to him under the contingency fee arrangement), because for the company the amount of this payment is lower than the costs of defending itself in court.

A formal model of incentives to file a nuisance suit has been developed by Rosenberg and Shavell (1985). The authors show that settlement will result even when the defendant knows that the plaintiff's case is not strong enough for the plaintiff to actually want to go to trial, when the costs of a legal defence in court for the defendant outweigh the total costs of a settlement. In their analysis, the outcome depends on the assumption that filing the suit is relatively cheap, while the first response of the defendant is connected to large costs. This can be the case, when the filing a collective action by a lead plaintiff and a lawyer at relatively low costs would, for example, require the defendant to gather and provide necessary information for the initial stages for the process, such as the data necessary to identify potential other victims.[339] Further costs arise through potentially large reputational losses for example from the public notification of other victims or media coverage of a large collective action, or large costs that would have to be borne due to a reallocation of resources within the firm in the course of a trial preparation.

While the results are certainly influenced by the specific features of the US American system of class actions, empirical studies conducted in the USA do hint at existing incentives to bring meritless claims to extract a settlement offer.[340] Empirical evidence is difficult to find and results have often been

338 Rosenberg, *A model in which suits are brought for their nuisance value* 3; Katz, "The effect of frivolous lawsuits on the settlement of litigation," *International Review of Law & Economics* 10 (1990): 3; Bone, "Modeling Frivolous Suits," *University of Pennsylvania Law Review* 145 (1996): 519.

339 Bebchuk, *Negative Expected Value Suits* provides and overview of the literature.

340 Hensler et al. (2000), studied 10 cases composed of consumer class actions and mass tort class actions. Their results were ambiguous, but hinted to some problems regarding the adequacy of representation, see Hensler, et al, *Class action dilemmas: pursuing public goals for private gain,* Rand Corp (2000), Chapter 15. Also Willging et al. (1996) report mixed findings when trying to assess the frequency of strike suits. In the field of securities litigation. Willging, *Empirical study of class actions in four federal district courts: Final report to the advisory committee on civil rules*Available online at: www.fjc.gov/public/pdf.nsf/lookup/rule23.pdf/$File/rule23.pdf.

ambivalent, although in the area of securities law the existence of nuisance suit seems to have found empirical support.[341]

A certain risk of unmeritorious or frivolous suits remains whether it is a lawyer or a lead plaintiff that acts on behalf of the injured parties. However, there may be ways to curb this problem. Two possible solutions suggested in the literature are contingency fees for lawyers and cost-shifting rules.

The incentives and possibilities to file frivolous suits may be influenced by the choice of the fee agreement the lawyer works under. Several authors suggest that a lawyer working on a contingency basis can act as gatekeeper in the civil justice system while still maximising her own benefit by rejecting cases with no or little merits that the plaintiff would like to bring.[342] These effects of contingency fees have also found some support in surveys and empirical literature[343] in the USA. On the other hand, when in fact it is the plaintiff who is the better-informed party with regard to the merits of the case, allowing a multitude of mixed contracts as possibilities by which to signal lawyers' quality, will also help to overcome the problems of information asymmetries concerning the merits of the case. To enable the lawyer to distinguish strong from weak cases, he should be able to offer a multitude of different fee arrangements. In consequence, clients will signal strong cases by choosing the contracts with a low contingency fee and a mostly hourly-based payment or a fixed fee, as the need to shift risk to the lawyer is lower.[344]

Some commentators argue that a fee-shifting rule, under which the costs have to be borne by the succumbing party, could be a suitable instrument to reduce the incentives to file unmeritorious cases.[345] However, that rule only applies when the case goes to trial, and it seems unlikely that reputational losses sustained by

341 Bohn and Choi (1996), who find that most of the class actions analyzed were frivolous in nature and targeted mainly at large firms. See also Choi (2004), evaluating several studies conducted in that area and concluding that the evidence supports the existence of frivolous suits. Bohn and Choi, "Fraud in the new-issues market: Empirical evidence on securities class actions," *University of Pennsylvania Law Review* 144 (1995): 903; Choi, "Evidence on Securities Class Actions, The," *Vanderbilt Law Review* 57 (2004): 1465.

342 Dana and Speir, "Expertise and contingent fees: The role of asymmetric information in attorney compensation," *Journal of Law, Economics, and Organization* 9 (1993): 349, arguing that contingency fee systems are best when the lawyer has better information about the merits of the case than the client; see also Kritzer, *Contingency fee lawyers as gatekeepers in the civil justice system* 22.

343 *Ibidem*. For an overview on the empirical literature on contingency fees see Helland and Tabarrok, "Contingency fees, settlement delay, and low-quality litigation: Empirical evidence from two datasets," *Journal of Law, Economics, and Organization* 19 (2003): 517.

344 Rubinfeld, *Contingent fees* 415.

345 Halpern, *Legal fees contracts and alternative cost rules: An economic analysis* 3.

the defendant will also be reimbursed. Therefore, plaintiffs still might have incentives to file unmeritorious suits under such a regime.

Another argument often made, and also employed in practice, is to make the settlement subject to the judge's approval. However, such a system is inefficient in several ways. First, the judge will have to at least partially mimic the trial in order to establish whether the settlement is indeed justified or not. Second, judges are unlikely to oppose a settlement that is been promoted by both parties, especially when judges are also working under resource restraints. Last, judges may not even be involved, when the settlement is made.

In concluding it can be said that the risk of nuisance suits increases with the awards that can be gained and/or the cost that can be imposed on the opponent. Especially when competitors act as plaintiffs, caution may be warranted. However, there may be ways to curb the problem by applying adequate cost-shifting rules, or employing adequate contingency fee arrangement for lawyers to induce them to act as gatekeepers. In such cases, however, it may be that the action will actually be run by the lawyer. If this is the case, then the group litigation should be designed accordingly.

1.6. *Minimisation of costs*

Mandatory affiliation to the group ensures that all claims are dealt with in only one proceeding. Costs of litigation therefore are reduced.

However, the costs of detection might still be inefficiently high. Depending on the incentive structure created for the individual to investigate and uncover competition law infringements, efforts spent on enforcement may be more or less efficient. Granted reimbursement for the risky investment in detection, several victims and/or several lawyers may compete in the detections stage. That leads to a doubling of efforts and consequently contributes to a waste of resources for society.

In the case of lead plaintiff dominated collective actions the requirement to be a part of the group of victims in order to become a lead plaintiff channels the detection efforts of each potential victim. A waste of resources because too many enforcement agents (victims) might compete to be the first to detect and file claim then are reduced.[346] However, that is not the case when the lawyer is the driving force, where the problem of doubled efforts may be even larger. These

346 Unless anyone can invest in detection, seek out a victim and legally transfer the claims to herself with the result to become lead-plaintiff.

problems and solutions will be discussed in greater detail in the sections on market and auctions.

1.7. Conclusion

A mandatory collective action, designed to be brought by a lead plaintiff who hires an attorney, has some merits but also raises some concerns. The mandatory nature of the group litigation mechanism ensures procedural efficiency, as only one trial has to take place. Free riding incentives which otherwise might inhibit the filing of suits are also reduced, especially when the lead plaintiff is awarded more than just his actual damage. Rational apathy problems and information asymmetries, although increasing with the introduction of mandatory group litigation, can be partially overcome by compensating the lead plaintiff for his efforts and costs as well.

However, the incentives created by granting the lead plaintiff more than his share also increase the risk of unmeritorious or negative value suits. The necessity of being a victim reduces detection incentives and channels enforcement activities to parties that in some cases may not be the most suited enforcement agent, for example end consumers in cartel cases.

Moreover, the system bears risks of considerable principal-agent problems, which may inhibit its efficiency. The relationship between attorney and client depends on several factors, including the sophistication of the client and the fee contract. The interests of lawyer and client, however, can be in conflict with each other as well as those of society and solutions to these conflicts have to be found. If the system is designed with the aim to align the interests of the lead plaintiff with those of society, these problems between lawyer and lead plaintiff (and also the rest of the group) can lead to inefficient outcomes. Consequently, this can distort the deterrence effect of the group litigation mechanism. In addition, smaller groups of injured parties may be in a better position to monitor and control the lawyers' behaviour. The collective action system therefore seems less adequate for large groups of inexperienced victims. Consequently, such a system may be less suited for cartel cases than for other types of cases. Repeat player plaintiffs, such as firms frequently involved in competition lawsuits or other legal disputes, have an advantage over end consumers. Principal-agent problems between firm and lawyer, as well as problems of asymmetric information are likely to be much less severe.

Compensation for individual harm is irrelevant for the deterrence effect. Therefore, solutions that propose to eliminate principal-agent problems between client and legal representative, as well as between society and agent, by transferring the original right to the agent at the outset, thus making the agent also the principal, are preferable. Under such regimes, only the right holder's incentives should be aligned with society's interest as far as possible. Mechanisms to achieve that goal and to reduce the risk of frivolous suits will be discussed below in the section dealing with market and auctions.

2. REPRESENTATIVE ORGANISATION

Other agents that may act on behalf of all victims who have suffered harm due to anti-competitive conduct are associations. There are three different possible ways to grant associations the right to sue on behalf of victims. Bodies can be certified *ex ante*, according to specified criteria, to represent their members. Alternatively, they could be *ex ante* certified to represent the interests of a larger group, such as a consumer association representing end consumers at large. A third possibility is to allow the formation of an association on an *ad hoc* basis, to defend the interests of those harmed in a particular case at hand.

In most Member States several individuals with common interests are typically allowed to found forms of associations to achieve any legal purpose.[347] As already mentioned, this third form is less distinguishable from other forms of group litigation, as victims, lawyers or any other interested party may found an association to pursue their interests as a way to better organise and manage the suit. Moreover, the mere prospect of being able to form an *ad hoc* association once detection has taken place is unlikely to have a profound impact on the detection incentives. Founding an association is costly for just one individual and so is finding other victims to join. The obstacles are similar to those that make the more traditional form of group litigation, the joinder procedures,[348] less effective. Therefore, *ad hoc* associations seem of little value to the analysis at hand and will not be considered further.

Also *ex ante* certified associations granted standing to represent their members seem of little relevance for the creation of the best possible deterrence mechanism, since by definition not all victims will be represented. The optimal sanction could not be imposed in such a proceeding. Other mechanisms, which can achieve that goal to a larger degree, dominate this solution. Therefore, the only representative action discussed here is the one of an *ex ante* certified body granted standing to represent all victims of a competition law infringement.

347 For example the *private limited company* in England, that can be founded by one or more persons for any lawful purpose, or the *Gesellschaft mit beschraenkter Haftung* (GmbH) in Germany.

348 For more details on joinder procedures, see Chapter 2.

The agent under a representative action as defined here is an *ex ante* certified body, generally representing the interests of those who may fall prey to a competition law infringement. As already mentioned, typical associations comprised within this category would be consumer and trade organisations. As the favoured feature of the group litigation would be a mandatory form, to limit free riding problems, to minimise costs and to allow for an optimal penalty to be imposed, these associations should be certified to represent both consumers and businesses harmed alike. We would therefore be looking for a trade and consumer body, granted standing to represent all victims.[349]

As argued above, the compensation of individual victims is superseded by the need to design the group litigation mechanism in a way to achieve the interest of society at large, i.e., ensuring optimal deterrence. Therefore, conflicting interests between consumers and undertakings (traders) are relevant only as far as they distort the deterrence effect of the system.

2.1. Free riding

Incentives to free ride on prior public enforcement decisions will still persist when the action is not restricted to stand-alone claims. However just as in the case of collective actions analysed above, waiting entails the risk of not being the first to file a claim, in as much as there is competition amongst several associations. If the association is a monopolist, incentives to save large costs by concentrating on follow-on cases are large. Free riding problems therefore will remain larger when competition amongst several associations is restricted. Similarly, if several associations are granted standing only to represent their members or subgroup of victims, free riding incentives could remain large.

Therefore, overall, free riding problems in actions on behalf of all victims are largely reduced when actions are restricted to stand-alone actions and due to the fact that membership of the group represented is mandatory. This implies that once an action is filed, no other association can file suit as the group can only be represented once.

2.2. Rational apathy

The problem of rational apathy may be decreased when an association is the acting agent compared to cases brought by individual victims.

Associations are likely to be more risk-neutral than individuals, such as end consumers are, so that the risk of losing at trial will have fewer negative effects.

349 Similar to the *actio popularis*, an action brought in the general public interest, as known in Portugal, Spain or Hungary.

Another aspect to be considered is the rational apathy problem on the business' side. Whenever the filing of suit against a larger business partner entails the risk of retaliation and future losses, firms may be inclined to refrain from filing suits. Under the lead plaintiff scenario, these problems remain when the lead plaintiff is such an enterprise. In the case of associations, however, retaliation is much less likely. The association will act in its own name without the requirement of consent of one or more victims. Individual victims may not even have to appear as an opponent anywhere in the legal dispute. Especially, when the case involves a multitude of victims, retaliation against one of the victims then seems unlikely because they may not have an influence on the associations' decisions.

Pre-financing problems when capital markets are imperfect are also likely to be reduced. Associations can finance themselves through the collection of membership fees as well as through public subsidies. The larger the latter portion of their funds, and the more dependent the association from the public body, however, the more the system mirrors that of public enforcement through competition authorities. If, on the other hand, the association gets most of it funds from membership fees, the question arises as to why anyone would become a member of that association, when the benefit is spread amongst the whole of society. Of course, the advantages of membership could extend beyond the fact that the association may protect competition, as the body may also offer many different kinds of services to its members. However, a rival association offering the same package of private goods and services but without the subsidised legal assistance in the form of representative actions would be able to charge lower prices and potential members would most likely prefer to join this second association.[350] Individuals would therefore have disincentives to become members. Moreover, when associations are financed through membership fees, incentives may exist to find and prosecute only cases with high media coverage in order to attract new members. The best way for associations then would be to finance themselves through the enforcement efforts.

Regardless of the funding issue, the benefits the association will gain by prosecuting a case will have to be at least as large as the resources required to pursue it. In order to give real incentives to engage in such activities, especially when financing takes places through the rewards from enforcement efforts, the association will also have to reap some benefit on top of just breaking even.[351] Just as under the system discussed above, here the association as agent will also have to at least be compensated for all the costs incurred in the litigation process,

350 Stigler, *Free riders and collective action: An appendix to theories of economic regulation* 359, 360.

351 As described above, the idea that associations may gain in the long-run by increasing their membership is difficult to sustain, as the incentives for individual to become members and pay membership fees are not very clear.

adjusted for the probability of losing at trial.[352] Furthermore, just as above, the association may be granted a certain share of, or the total damage awards, for precisely these reasons. If the legislator would want or allow the proceeds of the litigation to be used in the interest of harmed victims, or society at large, the association might be allowed to receive the total of damage awards when used to further competition in the markets by reinvesting in further enforcement efforts. Such ideas are already applied in *cy pres* distribution mechanisms, where individual victims are assumed to benefit from the damage awards in an indirect way.

2.3. *Information asymmetry*

An association as agent[353] differs in many ways from the individual lead plaintiff and/or lawyer as agent, but there also are some basic similarities. Similar to the latter, the association as agent also needs to be provided with incentives to investigate and pursue competition law infringements. Similarly, a part or the total of the rewards granted in court could potentially be used as incentive mechanism. If the association has to finance itself entirely through the prosecution of cases, the effects would be largely similar to the ones discussed under the lead plaintiff/ lawyer scenario leaving total damage awards to the respective agent. When the association can keep a certain share of total rewards, very much like a contingency fee, the similarity to the above-discussed scenario with a silent lead plaintiff and an active lawyer is huge.

However, there also are some differences to be considered. The existing information asymmetry between the association and infringers differs from the one between victim and infringer. In general, an association will only in a very small fraction of cases, if at all, be a victim itself and thereby part of the group of injured parties. This implies that information advantages that private parties may have, as victims of an exclusionary conduct for example, are lacking for the association in the same way as for the lawyer. Unless victims notify the association of possible breaches for example exclusionary abuse of market power. The association could offer financial rewards for the information about

352 For simplicity, this is formulated as a static decision. However, long-run gains such as gained experience or reputation positively influencing the associations standing can and will be incorporated just as in any other business decision weighing costs and profits as well.

353 The association will be treated as one entity. Corporate governance or principal agent problems within the association and its employees will not be discussed here, as this would fall out of the scope of the investigation. Such a treatment is justified in the comparative exercise, as also the lawyer in the collective action may in fact be an employee of a large legal firm, so that his private gain may differ from the contingency fee.

infringements. To encourage the detection of more complex offences, however, these rewards would have to be accordingly large.

On the other hand, the association could be given a sufficiently large share of any proceeds, in order to encourage their investigation of markets, just as the lawyer as agent above. If that were the case, larger knowledge, learning effects, specialisation and economies of scale would enable the association to overcome the information asymmetry problems more efficiently than the individual plaintiff in many cases. Comparably to the lawyer as active party in a collective action, the association would be a repeat player by definition. Specialists in the relevant legal and economic fields could be hired. Also, several different associations can specialise in different industries or types of infringements. All of these advantages would place an association in a better position as agent than an individual victim might be.

To provide incentives to invest in the detection of competition law infringements, additional reimbursement for those costs incurred on top of compensation for litigation expenses will be needed. The amount of this remuneration depends on the possibility of the association to reap a profitable return on that investment.

Under a first-come, first-served condition, the possibility that remuneration will depend on the probability of success is very high when there is no, or only very limited, competitive pressure. For a monopolist, there is no risk of investing large resources in the evaluation of certain market developments and then being beaten by another entity that is quicker to start the procedure. However, the concept of a monopolist protecting competition law is not only a bit of a paradox, but also bears the risk of being very inefficient. A monopolist in markets typically is associated with supra-competitive prices, lower output and a consequent dead weight loss to society, which is inefficient from a total welfare perspective. Of course, large fixed costs and low variable costs could imply a natural monopoly.[354] However, the market characterised here is much more similar to the market concerning research and development, which is also characterised by large fixed costs and a patent right after successful innovation. Here, the market would be characterised by large fixed costs in detection and the consequent monopoly (due to the mandatory nature of the group litigation) in litigation. The relevant insights developed in innovation theory and could be applied analogously and they support the inefficiency of monopoly in dynamic markets with patent protection.[355] In such a setting, a monopolist association is likely to have only little additional impact on deterrence. Initial costs of investigating are large and

---

354 In a natural monopoly, total demand can be more efficiently be served by only one producer, for example due to economies of scale.

355 Motta, *Competition policy: theory and practice*, 55 f.

only few cases will be dealt with under budget constraints and other limited resources. These are similar to the problems that public enforcement agencies can face. This would be different only if a perfect capital market could provide virtually unlimited resources, creating incentives to invest as long as the expected net outcome is positive. Nevertheless, lack of competition allows the monopolist to carefully select and time the investigation of certain industry sectors, and the prosecution of cases. Just like a patent right holder, also the monopolist association may not be presented with the incentives to make optimal use of the rights it is endowed with.[356] In addition, a monopolist is much more likely to be captured by certain interest groups, including potential defendants, as transaction costs accompanying the capture of many different agents are much larger than transaction cost dealing with only one party.

The second alternative is to create competition amongst several similarly suited associations. In this case, the remuneration paid also has to compensate for the risk of unsuccessful investments faced by the association. The more competition there is concerning detection and prosecution of competition law infringements, the more risky the upfront investment in detection efforts becomes to these entities. Consequently, the larger the expected return on that investment must be to justify the initial expenses. Moreover, there is a problem of doubling of efforts, which constitutes a waste of resources and a loss to society as a whole.

Therefore, the association may be well suited and incentivised to overcome the problem of asymmetric information. However, this very much depends on the remuneration the association can reap from such activities. The same reasoning applies as in the case of the lawyer as agent.

2.4. Nuisance suits

In the optimal group litigation mechanism, the risk of unmeritorious suits also should be limited. However, associations may also be able to force defendant(s) into settlements, even when the case has little or no merits. In as much as incentives to do so exist, the risk of this under a representative group litigation system may be even larger than this risk under the collective action procedure. An association generally is in a better position to threaten litigation, as the financing problem is smaller. Also publicity is more easily and more extensively achieved than by a lead plaintiff and or lawyer. For an association, the probability of succeeding in these endeavours is higher than for some private individuals.

However, the incentives of associations to file nuisance suits heavily depend on the gains associations can realise through litigation and therefore on what

356 Compare section 3 below.

incentives associations are given for becoming active. These issues will be discussed in detail below.

2.5. *Principal-agent problems*

Principal-agent problems between society and association, and between association and possibly hired lawyer, may exist and cannot be overcome easily. Several authors have investigated the principal-agent problems persistent in representative actions, often in comparison with the US style class action.[357]

Typical principal-agent problems between the association and the hired lawyer could persist. The association however, as opposed to the individual victim, is a repeat player by design. This makes it a more sophisticated and experienced client, which is better able to assess and monitor the lawyers behaviour. Also the mechanisms mentioned above that could induce the lawyer to work in the interest of its client, such as building or maintaining a reputation and business relations, can work more effectively in this context. That is especially true when in-house lawyers are used, as can be assumed in this analysis.

The other principal-agent relationship of importance when looking at deterrence is the one between society as principal and association as agent. Also in this relationship, while the association acts as agent for society working on a certain remuneration schedule, society as the principal is only imperfectly informed. Principal-agent problems therefore remain.

As discussed above, especially in the case of a monopolistic association, the incentives to invest the optimal effort that the principal desires are limited.

Once detection has taken place, the association may have large incentives to avoid further costs and strike a settlement with the defendant(s). Inefficient settlements or the possibility of collusion between enforcement agent and defendants have to be minimised. Similar to the collective action, the difference between the expected net amount the defendant has to pay as result of a trial and the expected net amount the association will receive constitutes the range in which settlement negotiations can take place. However, here bargaining powers presumably are distributed more equally between the adversaries. The association is a more risk neutral repeat player and in some respects on a more equal footing

---

357 See e.g. Kalven Jr, *Contemporary Function of the Class Suit, The* 684, who compare suits brought by public bodies with class action suits; Dayagi-Epstein, "Representation of Consumer Interest By Consumer Associations-Salvation for the Masses?" *Competition Law Review* 3 (2006): 209. See also Schäfer, *The Bundling of Similar Interests in Litigation. The Incentives for Class Action and Legal Actions taken by Associations* 183, comparing class actions with suits brought by associations.

with defendant(s) than most lead plaintiffs and their lawyers in the bargaining procedure. Nevertheless, because the association bears all the costs of the proceeding and detection, while only receiving a share of total rewards, the profit maximising settlement agreement for the representative body may be below the amount required to reach optimal deterrence.

Some authors argue that principal-agent problems may be better curbed in the case of associations as representatives, precisely because the associations are repeat players, so that reputation and credibility could inhibit the representing bodies to a certain degree from pursuing only their personal interests.[358] The incentives for *moral hazard* or *shirking*[359] therefore would be reduced. On the other hand, one might argue that decisions of associations are influenced to a larger degree by possibilities to achieve publicity or other factors influencing their financing method than is the case for private individuals or individual lawyers.

However, possibilities to strengthen the position of society as principal may exist. Society, through the relevant organs, might be able to monitor and influence the association's behaviour to a certain degree. Certification, for example, could be made dependent on the past success of the association. In many Member States, standing is granted only if the association meets certain specified criteria.[360] Subsidies could also be used and made dependant on performance criteria to assure better compliance to the social goal. To produce the desired outcome, such control mechanisms would require that settlements achieved in the past be assessed as to their optimality. As the association should have gathered the relevant information to establish a breach of competition law and the amount of total damages caused, assessment might be based on the available information. However, such controls are likely to be very costly. Furthermore, as mentioned above, the larger the influence and financial support through public bodies, the more the system resembles public enforcement. The risk that the association then is influenced by certain interest groups in society and geared towards or away from certain cases is inherent in such a system.[361] The selection of markets to be

358 Dayagi-Epstein, *Representation of Consumer Interest By Consumer Associations-Salvation for the Masses?* 209, 235; Schäfer, *The Bundling of Similar Interests in Litigation. The Incentives for Class Action and Legal Actions taken by Associations* 183, 200.

359 Shirking refers to the problem that when work-effort is not easily monitored, the effort may fall short of what would otherwise be invested.

360 See for example Franke and Puttfarken, *Die Action Civile der Verbaende in Frankreich.* in *Die Buendelung gleichgerichteter Interesssen im Prozess.* eds. Basedow et al. Tübingen: Mohr Siebeck (1999), 149. Which is also the proposal by the European Commission, see European Commission, *White Paper on Damages actions for breach of the EC antitrust Rules COM(2008) 165final, SEC(2008) 404*, 4.

361 See Dayagi-Epstein, *Representation of Consumer Interest By Consumer Associations-Salvation for the Masses?* 209243 f.

investigated, or cases to be brought, could then be skewed. Generally, cases with large amount of damages and which are easier to detect are preferred by any enforcement agent that stands to gain from the damages. On the other hand, dependency on subsidies or donations can also lead to different preferences, for example combating competition law infringements in certain industry sectors only.

The only solution to eliminate any kind of principal-agent problems without the need to strengthen the clients' position by implementing costly systems of control is, again, to make the agent the principal. Only granting the association the total quantum of the damages awarded will give the association the correct incentives to reach efficient settlements for its own sake, and thereby align interests of society and association. The prospect of such immense financial rewards would lead to tough competition amongst associations, provided that there are many certified associations. Auctions could be used to decide, which association would be allowed to pursue the claim. This option will be discussed in the section C.4. below.

2.6. *Minimisation of enforcement costs*

Litigation costs can be greatly reduced in a mandatory representative action, similar to the collective action discussed above. However, costs of detection may not be minimised.

When there is competition amongst associations concerning the detection of offences, total enforcement costs are probably not minimised. Overlaps in detection efforts are highly likely. Several entities will use a lot of resources to scan markets and investigate undertakings' conduct. Often these entities would be searching in the same market, collecting information and assessing the legality of specific behaviours. These losses associated with the doubling of effort to society increase with the number of competing associations in the market for detection.

2.7. *Conclusion*

From a deterrence perspective, representative actions have little advantages over collective actions in general. Competition amongst several entities is necessary in order to minimise free riding problems. Rational apathy problems are less severe than in the case of collective actions. In addition, while problems of information asymmetry may initially be larger than under collective actions in some cases (those where private information is easily available and the lead plaintiff acts as agent), in others it may be more easily overcome. Compared to collective actions brought by an aggrieved victim of exclusionary abuse of a dominant position, these advantages are likely to be much smaller, and may even be outweighed by possibly larger information problem faced by the association. This in turn may lead to a dependence on the assistance of the victims to identify or pursue a claim. On the other hand, advantages over lead plaintiffs as one-shot players reduce the obstacles faced in detection of other types of infringements, such as cartels.

The risk of unmeritorious suits may remain significant. In order to become active, associations have to have an independent interest in detection and litigation. Indirect incentives, such as the possibility to increase its member base may induce unmeritorious litigation when the costs of doing so are smaller than the expected gain. Granting the association a share of the rewards on the other hand can also increase the risk of unmeritorious suits.

In addition, principal-agent problems can remain significant. Compared to collective actions brought by an end consumer, the representative body has several advantages as repeat player. When principal-agent problems between lead plaintiff and lawyer are severe, the association may be a better principal to control the agent. However, principal-agent problems between society and association may remain, when adequate solutions to these problems are missing. One solution could be, to allow the association to retain the total of damage awards to finance further enforcement activities.

Overall, representative actions brought by associations might be more effective than collective actions when rational apathy, information asymmetry and principal-agent problems between individual victim and lawyer are large. Such will be the case for example in cartel cases with widespread but small individual damages. Conversely where rational apathy, information asymmetry and principal-agent problems are initially small, which is the case when undertakings are the victims of an offence, for example of an exclusionary conduct, collective action may allow for more efficient use of private information advantages.

The right system of representative actions necessitates competition amongst several associations, which ideally should be entitled to represent all victims of a certain competition law offence. Allowing society to benefit from the competition amongst enforcers while avoiding unnecessary waste of resources is a challenge that occurs also in other areas, such as intellectual property. Solutions to these challenges and the remaining problems of unmeritorious suits and principal-agent problems between association and society are discussed below, when the mechanism of competition of several enforcers, its advantages and disadvantages is discussed.[362]

---

362 See sections 3 and 4 below.

3. THE MARKET BASED SOLUTION

This section briefly sketches the general idea behind a market for enforcement. The benefits and problems of such a mechanism will be discussed in greater detail in the next steps, including possible solutions to the pitfalls. This discussion will gradually lead to a refined version of the general concept of a market for enforcement.

The idea of enforcement directed through market mechanisms was already being discussed by Becker and Stigler as early as 1974.[363] According to these authors, by using market mechanisms, incentives to detect violations and to bring suit would increase, while free competition amongst a number of enforcement firms will reduce enforcement costs.[364] The main idea is to align the interest of lawyers as agents, and society as principals, by assigning the rights to claim damages to the agent *ex ante*, thereby making the interests of society directly those of the agent.

In the real world, the Cartel Damage Claim[365]company and professional litigation investors are proof that, at least the litigation of (through public authorities) detected infringements is treated as a financial investment decision by some entities. Although it may sound strange to some ears, particularly European ones, that lawyers or other entities may treat litigation as an investment opportunity, this idea has always been an argument in discussions about the contingency fee system in the USA, describing lawyers as the *entrepreneurial lawyer.*[366] If it were not for the requirement that victims are included in the group litigation action automatically (mandatory), enforcement agents such as the Cartel Damage Claim company could compete on not only the detection of infringements, but also the consequent representation of victims in front of a court as well. Depending on the system, victims could choose, who may represent them[367] or whom to sell their claims to. Therefore, the injured parties would be in control to accept the best deals offered to them. That presupposes, however, that victims are sophisticated and not rationally apathetic. Studies conducted in the USA find that opt-out rates are extremely low, indicating that injured

---

363 See Becker, *Law enforcement, malfeasance, and compensation of Enforces* 1.

364 *Ibidem*14 f.

365 Cartel Damage Claim company – bought claims of 29 victims of a German cement cartel in the wake of a public investigation.

366 Silver, *Class Actions – Representative Proceedings.* in *Encyclopedia of Law and Economics, Volume I. The History and Methodology of Law and Economics.* eds. Bouckaert and De Geest. Cheltenham: Edward Elgar (2000), 194, 200. See also Miller, *Some agency problems in settlement* 189, 213; Coffee Jr, "Understanding the Plaintiff's Attorney: The Implications of Economic Theory for Private Enforcement of Law through Class and Derivative Actions," *Columbia Law Review* 86 (1986): 669.

367 Either working on an hourly fee or a contingency basis.

individuals do not in fact search for better options.[368] Of course, if not all injured parties would choose the same agent, several trials dealing with different bundles of claims would be possible. As argued above however, such a solution would not lead to procedural efficiency. Moreover, defendants could use the system to their advantage by striking early deals with the most important victims or groups to the detriment of other cases. In addition, whenever the agents would be working on any form of fee basis principal-agent problems would arise, further compromising the efficiency of the system.

For the optimal market idea, it is important in this respect to keep in mind that deterrence only requires the violator to pay for the impairment caused to society. No further requirement is made to the distribution of this payment except that the infringer may not be among those who benefit from it. In consequence, the monetary awards granted in court could remain with the entity filing the claim, when deterrence is the only goal.[369] If only a certain percentage of the total award is used to reimburse the agent, the incentives structures would be largely similar to those described above when analysing the incentives of a lawyer working on a contingency fee basis.[370] One of the major problems in the group litigation forms discussed above are exactly these principal-agent problems, which occur between the representing party and the lawyer, but also between the society and the representing party. As far as the representing party's interests do not equal those of society, inefficient deterrence may result. These problems arise, when lawyers or associations acting as agents have their own interests and motivation to pursue competition law infringement that differ from those of society – which, following the deterrence approach, is the prevention of the harm caused by infringements of competition law.

In general, society would be willing to incur costs of detection and prevention almost equal to the total harm avoided (which should include harm avoided by deterring other offences) and still be better off. Meanwhile individuals, lawyers and associations are only willing to invest up to their own benefits to be gained.[371] Therefore, society can have a larger interest in the prosecution also of

---

368 Eisenberg and Miller (2004), found an average of 0.6% opt-out rate. Eisenberg, *Role of Opt-outs and Objectors in Class Action Litigation: Theoretical and Empirical Issues, The* 1529available at SSRN: http://ssrn.com/abstract=528146.

369 This concept relates very much to the discussion of efficient assignment of property rights in the Law and Economics literature (for an introduction and overview see Bouckaert, *Original assignment of private property. Encyclopedia of Law and Economics.* 1999). However, the agent could not only be granted the rights, but they could also be transferred from the victim to the agent.

370 See arguments made concerning effects of contingency fees on settlement and meritless claims above.

371 Compare Shavell, *Social versus the Private Incentive to Bring Suit in a Costly Legal System, The* 333.

small individual damages, than the individual right holder can. Again, one often cited solution to these problems would be to unite the interests of agent and principal into one single entity, for example by transferring the dispersed rights to claim damages (which in the hands of the original right holders may have no actual value) as a bundle to the agent (in who's hands the claims may actually be valuable).[372] This might in essence require the agent to be able to receive the total of the optimal sanction amount awarded as compensation for his efforts.

The question to be solved is whether granting the agent a share of the optimal sanction (total damages awarded in trial, with the adequate multiplier in place to impose the optimal sanction) would give sufficient, or even efficient, incentives to engage in detection efforts to an adequate amount. If not, would granting the total amount to the agent be necessary to induce investments closer or equal to the investments society would regard as optimal. The optimal investment in detection would be up to the point were total marginal costs of enforcement would equal total marginal benefit. To answer that question, however, further research is needed to identify the functions of the costs of detection activities and the benefits resulting from these activities, which would also entail the knowledge about the value of losses caused by violations of competition law, as well as deterrence rates. Moreover, systematic relationships between these relevant values would need to be established. However, a few tentative thoughts may be provided here.

The benefits of society gained by the detection of competition law infringements need to be known, in order to be able to compare the total benefits of one detected infringements against the relevant costs. Measuring deterrence is, however, very difficult. Nevertheless, it seems that methods are being developed to provide estimates, and they are already sometimes being employed. For example, the European Commission and the Office of Fair Trading (OFT) in the UK have both published estimates about avoided future losses due to the detection and ending of certain infringements. Neelie Kroes, European Commissioner for Competition, has stated that there have been: "Direct consumer savings of at least €8bn in 2008, which compares favourably to our operating costs of around €100 million. And this does not even begin to take into account the indirect benefits of deterrence."[373] Also the OFT calculated the benefits of ending of two offences against competition law to have avoided losses to consumers of a total of £ 90 million.[374] Therefore, at least estimates of the value of future losses otherwise

---

372 See Wagner, *Kollektiver Rechtsschutz – Regelungsbedarf bei Massen- und Streuschäden*, 41.

373 Neelie Kroes, "Introductory Speech, ICN Seminar on Competition Agency Effectiveness, Summary report, Brussels, January 2009", 7. Available at www.icn-zurich.org/Downloads/Materials/ICN_CPIWG_Report-for-OIB.pdf.

374 Office of Fair Trading, *Private actions in competition law: effective redress for consumers and business, OFT Discussion Paper 916*, 6.

caused by detected offences do exist. Moreover, approximations on the deterrence effects are also being generated. A study conducted for the OFT delivered estimates about how many infringements were abandoned or significantly altered due to the detection of one infringement of the same kind.[375] Their conservative estimates were as follows: for cartels the ratio was between 5 and 16 to one, for commercial agreements between 7 and 29 to one and for abuses between 4 and 10 to one.[376] Therefore, one detected and ended infringement does not only avoid future losses caused by that particular infringement, which in some cases may be larger that the losses caused up to the time of detection, but in particular it creates considerable cost savings due to the deterrence of other offences. Considering these values, the tentative thoughts would be as follows.

If one detected cartel infringement would only save society in total five times as much damages as the detected one already caused (as damage awards are based only on already caused damages),[377] the deterrence benefit to society would be five times the actual damages. Assuming the market for enforcement would help to raise detection rates for cartels only to 25 percent,[378] the optimal sanction would result in four times the actual damages, which is less than the benefits created to society, so that society would have a net gain when the payment to the enforcer is deducted. The difference becomes much greater, when the detection and deterrence rate, as well as the value of losses avoided, would indeed be larger. For a detection rate of 33.33 percent and a deterrence rate of 10, for example, the net benefit to society would be at least seven times the actual damages. If the agent were to receive the whole optimal sanction, that remuneration (the four or three times the actually caused damages) would include a large risk premium for having taken on the highly risky and uncertain task of investing in enforcement activities. Whether or not the resulting investment decision made by the enforcement agent would result in the optimal, under or over investment of

375 Deloitte & Touche LLP, "The deterrence effect of competition enforcement by the OFT," *OFFICE OF FAIR TRADING* (Nov 2007)A report prepared for the OFT by Deloitte, November 2007, OFT962.

376 The range is due to the results of questionnaires answered by legal professionals (lower bound) and companies (upper bound), *Ibidem* 8 f.

377 That would mean that the other deterred cartels in average only would have caused losses of the same amount as the detected cartel did until it was detected. However, the deterred cartels may also have lasted much longer and at least therefore also cause considerably larger damages.

378 Assuming public detection efforts remain constant, this could be a tentative estimate. The argument here is that the discussed system would fare better than existing systems and the optimal sanction, i.e. a larger damage multipler, would be imposed, so that detection rates should be increased considerably. Renda, *Making antitrust damages actions in the EU more effective. Study in support of the impact assessment of the EC White Paper on antitrust damages actions*, 73 and 101 ff, provide an overview over estimates of current detection rates and the impact private actions for damages may have on these. Based on their overview, their assumed detection rates for cartels are 20% in the US and 15 in the EU, (page 72), which could be increased in Europe up to 25% by the enhancement of private enforcement (page 103).

resources cannot be deduced from these figures. However, it seems, especially when the net benefits to society are considerably larger, that more detailed and elaborated research may show that providing the enforcement agent with the total of the optimal sanction would at least not lead to over investment in enforcement activities. Also taking the benefit-cost ratio provided by the Commission into account, it seems as if there might be room for further, total welfare increasing investment in enforcement activities. If, on the other hand, the optimal sanction would induce enforcement agents to invest too much into detection efforts, providing the agent with only an adequate share would then make it possible to set up a fund with the other share, which then might be used in one way or another to compensate victims.[379] Further developments in the next years might provide knowledge about the amount of remuneration necessary to at least induce some investment in private detection activities, when it happens that also stand alone actions will be brought.

Despite the question of the optimal reward for the agent, such a theoretical mechanism does not work when the legal system in question prohibits the transfer of such rights. In the USA, for example, already the alienability of legal claims is strictly restrained.[380] In most European States, rights can be transferred, especially those that are largely independent of the original owner where the right was generated. In the case of widely dispersed and small damages, where the individual's rights are more or less only theoretical present, governments of Member States have already considered alternatives to traditional damage claims.[381] The actual legal possibilities of such reassignment transfers may be another question. Nevertheless, here it suffices to say that until recently, many victims of offences were not granted standing to sue under their national competition laws, so that a legal transfer in any form of these non-existing rights would not have been necessary and that the granting of these rights to indirect purchasers is still debated in some countries. In addition, the transfer of personal rights generally is not only a theoretical possibility.

Once the transfer of rights were installed, or adequate standing provided to the agent, the total of the damage awards could remain with the agent bringing the claim, thereby aligning his interests with those of society. Transferring the damage claims to the agent should cause great incentives to a large number of parties to spend resources into matching specialisation, as well as detection and prosecution of infringements. Given the large damages caused to society by

379 Which, when costly, would be inefficient from a deterrence perspective, but might greate other benefits to compensate these costs (i.e. increasing compensatory justice or the like).

380 See (also for an economic analysis) Abramowicz, "On the Alienability of Legal Claims," *The Yale Law Journal* 114 (2004): 697.

381 For example skimming-off procedures, see Deutscher Bundestag (German Parliament), *Entwurf eines Gesetzes gegen den unlauteren Wettbewerb (UWG), BT-Drucks. 15/1487.*

many violations of competition law, the number of entities closely observing the firms conduct in the market could at least initially become sufficiently large. Investing in the detection and conviction of competition law infringements could become a very profitable business. The result could be a market for enforcement.

To avoid several litigations of the same infringements, a mechanism is needed to ensure that only one costly proceeding will take place. Giving the right to proceed to trial or to pursue the case any further could be given on a first-come, first-served basis. Anyone finding an infringement could be granted the rights to pursue the case when he is the first to register that infringement with an established registry. That eliminates the problems of several trials and part of the resources wasted due to doubling of efforts connected to it. However, there are also some problems connected to such a system, as it creates a *race to court*. These effects will be discussed in greater detail in the following analysis.

For the individual enforcer, such private enforcement equals a financial investment into a risky business transaction. Similar to research and development activities, large upfront investments are required, and the return on these investments is connected to large uncertainties. Private information, where it exists, could be put into use in two ways. In some cases, the victims themselves would be encouraged to file suit. In others, the enforcers offer rewards for the information brought to their attention. As long as the expected profits outweigh the costs, economic entities should find it profitable to enter such a market. Risk-neutral agents should be more inclined to do so than risk-averse agents, so that larger and diversified firms should develop.

To investigate certain effects of competition between several enforcement agents, one might start with the perfect competitive market. Other possibilities, such as a market of diversified products, will be discussed later. Such a market would require all private enforcers (P.E.s) to be of a symmetrical nature. That implies that they all have the same costs functions, the same information and the same probability of success. Ideally, entry into that market of enforcement of competition law should be costless. Naturally, when such a system is introduced, some parties may have a competitive advantage over others, such as lawyers and professional entities over laymen. However, just as in any other market, too, no one possesses all the necessary skills, so that all have to incur entry costs at some point in time.

Investment in such endeavours entails many uncertainties. P.E.s will only invest resources in detection efforts, if the expected awards (which as the optimal sanction equal the total damages to society caused by the detected infringement, times the inverse of the probability of detection) exceed those costs. The individual probability of finding a violation, the probability of being the first to file claim, and the probability of prevailing in trial, flow into their calculation as well. This is because under the portrayed circumstances, only one plaintiff can reap the rewards of his efforts, while all others will strike out. Consequently, private actors will also have to include the probability of being the first to file claim into their cost-benefit calculation.

In such a market, if it is a perfect competitive market, the probability of getting caught faced by the violator increases with each additional entry, as more resources in total are spent on detection efforts. As assumed, these additional costs should have the desired effect, and some potential infringers will be deterred from their anti-competitive conduct. Those missing infringements in turn should reduce the probability for each P.E. to spot an offence. Alternatively, to still find an infringement, more costs have to be borne. These effects reduce the expected return on investment, depending on the number of competing P.E.s. Each entry of a newcomer reduces the overall probability of success of all P.E.s in the market. The risk of losing the race to be the first diminishes the expected return on investment for the individual investor, analogous to the patent race problem in the area of intellectual property protection.[382] At some point, another entry will reduce total rewards below costs, deterring that entry. Just as proclaimed by the theoretic concept of the market in perfect competition, a certain number of entities will then remain in the market and earn a normal return on investment. Competitive pressure in the market should also, according to general economic theory, lead to the development of the most cost efficient methods to detect and prosecute infringements.

The existence and the level of that equilibrium depend on several factors. The higher the costs of enforcement compared to the damages awarded, and the lower the individual's probability of success, the less lucrative the investment in enforcement is. If that is the case, the market should consist of fewer participants.

If enforcers are indeed not of a symmetrical nature, another market structure could instead develop. This could be more a market of differentiated products. The participants in the market could develop specific skills to investigate selected industry sectors, certain types of markets, or different types of infringements. Such a development may have an effect on the specific features of the equilibrium, but the other features of the market would remain the same. Some firms may

382 Compare:Abramowicz, "The Uneasy Case For Patent Races over Auctions," *Stanford Law Review* 60 (2007): 803, 812 f. For an overview on patent races see: Dasgupta and Stiglitz, "Uncertainty, industrial structure, and the speed of R&D," *The Bell Journal of Economics* (1980): 1.

also specialise in detection, and after having secured the rights to the claims, sell them to firms specialising in further analysis of the cases and prosecution. As there already are some professions that focus on the economic analysis of markets or on the solution of legal disputes, such a division of labour could be relevant, particularly in the early stages of such a market system. A further specialisation may be between P.E.s who concentrate on the detection, and firms or lawyers that specialise in the litigation of offences. Once a P.E. has secured the rights, he may sell or licence them to a more efficient firm (specialised in litigation rather than detection).

The number of infringements is not fixed but changes over time. New infringements occur, old ones cease to exist. This remains true even when the optimal sanction leads to optimal deterrence. As the costs of enforcement will be weighed against the benefits in terms of deterrence, it would most likely not be optimal to deter all and every infringement. As a consequence, there would always remain a certain set of offences.[383] In addition, the fact that infringements that are not subject to a *per se* prohibition but more to a rule of reason approach[384] leads to a probability of detection and conviction that will be lower than 1, meaning that the market for enforcement will remain attractive for enforcement businesses.

3.1. *Free riding*

Mandatory affiliation to the group of represented victims eliminates free riding incentives for the individual victims. Therefore, free riding could only be a problem in the arena of the P.E.s.

With regard to free riding at the detection stage, P.E.s cannot free ride on each other, as long as the first one to file suit or to register the infringement is the only beneficiary. In addition, incentives to await a prior public enforcement, when follow-on suits are allowed, are reduced, as the economic risk of not being the first is likely to outweigh any possible cost savings. Time is of essence in such a setting and free riding will be significantly diminished.

Free riding could take place when one infringement makes the detection of others easier (as the path-dependency argument states).[385] The detection and

383 This would all the more be true for less theoretical and more practical approaches. Even the most generous assumption of possible increases in detection rates due additional private enforcement remain far from full detection. See Renda, *Making antitrust damages actions in the EU more effective. Study in support of the impact assessment of the EC White Paper on antitrust damages actions*, 71 ff.

384 See Chapter 2 on the types of infringements.

385 Competition authorities often detect infringements while already investigating another offence in the same market.

subsequent prosecution of one infringement can provide information that facilitates the detection of another infringement in the same market. In as much as that is a reliable feature, enforcers could still have an incentive to wait for others to make the first step. This could allow them to focus their research efforts on more profitable targets. However, the first one to detect an infringement will probably have an advantage over his competitors in detecting the next infringements, as he is the first to have relevant information discovered in the first infringement. Therefore, there is little scope for free riding after all.

Free riding could also still occur after detection has taken place and the cases have been registered. Depending on the specific requirements to be met to file or register such claims, it could be possible that several infringements against competition law by the same defendant(s) are registered by different P.E.s. If they are related, as can be the case for example with price maintenance in the downstream market and a cartel in the upstream market, evidence collected in one trial could reduce the resources necessary to pursue the other offence. Then one P.E. might prefer the other P.E. to proceed to trial first, leading to delayed or no action. Such free riding may be curbed, however, with an adequate definition of the scope of the rights that can be registered, so that there is as little overlap as possible.

Overall, with strong competition in the market for enforcement, free riding behaviour is kept to a minimum.

3.2. *Rational apathy*

Rational apathy on behalf of the victims is overcome, as it is the agent, or P.E. that becomes active, suing for the total of damages caused to society. However, some rational apathy may remain even on the P.E.'s side. Having to provide evidence for total harm caused to society undoubtedly does put a great burden on the enforcer and the proceedings are very costly in consequence. This is true for all of the above-discussed agents. This is all the more so in cases that are not subject to a *per se* prohibition. In cases of a *per se* prohibition large returns on investment in some cases, for example large cartels, would likely justify virtually any expenses necessary to provide proof of liability and damages in front of court. Once detection has taken place, any calculation weighing the costs of litigation against the expected rewards should turn out in favour of litigation. Nevertheless, in other cases, for example cases of vertical restraints, the expected rewards may not trigger large investments in litigation or detection, especially when the issue of whether or not the behaviour constitutes an infringement is highly debatable in court.

The market idea as structured so far would provide large incentives to invest in both detection and litigation of competition law offences, as the agent becomes a professional investor or enforcer, weighing the costs of enforcement against the expected benefits. However, not all types of infringements may seem equally attractive as investment opportunities.

3.3. *Information asymmetry*

Unfortunately, it is not only the incentives to litigate that matter in determining deterrence effects. In addition, a major point of consideration are the incentives to invest in the detection itself. The type of infringement is likely to have an impact on these decisions.

As described above, the information costs of getting the necessary information, knowledge and data can be immense, especially for those who are not already specialised in competition law and the underlying economic theories. The detection of an infringement requires many resources to be spent on scanning the developments in markets, conduct of firms, and keeping up to date with legal developments, while success is uncertain. To compensate for these costs and risks, a large benefit is necessary.

In the case of a market for enforcement, however, the agent enforcer would be placed in the position to weigh the costs and benefits of investing in detection, in a manner that is more aligned with the aims of society. The expected awards from such investments would justify investment in detection (and litigation) up to the amount that society would be willing to incur in order to avoid the losses caused by infringements.

3.4. *Nuisance suits*

Nuisance or frivolous suits can be brought for a number of reasons. Whenever costs can be imposed on potential defendants that would exceed a certain settlement amount, defendants may prefer to settle the case, even when it has little or no merits. As discussed earlier, such costs can be caused by losses in reputation or internal reallocation of resources necessary for the defence against such a claim in court. These incentives to bring frivolous suits remain, also under a market scheme.

As has been investigated and pointed out in the Law and Economics literature, awards that exceed the actual harm suffered by victims and thereby impose a windfall on the plaintiff and create incentives to file unmeritorious suits.[386] This

386 See discussion on incentives to file unmeritous suits above.

is especially the case in non-cartel cases. The immense awards that could be granted can outbalance the minimal probability of winning the case at trial. For such reasons, in the USA, where treble damages are awarded in antitrust cases, scholars suggested the actual damages be decoupled from the remaining part.[387] However, that has to be balanced against a reduction in incentives to litigate.

The here envisioned system of first-come, first-served, could encourage the filing of cases where the merits have not yet been established. If defendants have to react already to the first filing, costs are imposed on them arbitrarily. Therefore, the ability to abuse such a system depends highly on the way the first filing will be regulated, i.e., what requirements have to be fulfilled. Moreover, the concern about nuisance suits would be larger in cases where competitors to the proclaimed offender act as P.E.

It is possible that the combination of market ideas with auction mechanisms could counter the incentives and possibilities to file unmeritorious suits. These mechanisms will be analysed in detail later.

As already described above, applying the fee-shifting rule predominant in Europe, which forces the losing party to reimburse the prevailing party for their legal expenses, also can have a dampening effect on the possibility of such suits. However, it may not be able to counter it completely on its own.[388]

3.5. *Minimisation of enforcement costs*

As with the other systems, the mandatory property of group litigation enables costs savings for society, when the optimal sanction is imposed on infringing parties in only one costly proceeding. Through this process, litigation costs could be minimised.

On the other hand, costs of detection also have to be considered. Following the analyses by Polinsky and Shavell, and Landes,[389] the optimal sanction includes only variable enforcement costs, such as costs of litigation and gathering of evidence once detection has taken place. Costs of detection, the costs associated with screening of markets, are fixed costs and only enter the optimal sanction

387 Polinsky, *Detrebling Versus Decoupling Antitrust Damages: Lessons from the Theory of Enforcement* 1231; McAfee, *Private v. public antitrust enforcement: A strategic analysis* 1863.

388 Generally increased incentives to sue: Wagener, *Modelling the effect of one-way fee shifting on discovery abuse for private antitrust litigation* 1887. American Rule spurs frivolous suits:Feuerstein, *Two-Way Fee Shifting on Summary Judgment or Dismissal: An Equitable Deterrent to Unmeritorious Lawsuits* 125, 128. Some supporting empirical evidence is provided by Snyder, *The English rule for allocating legal costs: evidence confronts theory* 345.

389 Polinsky, *Enforcement costs and the optimal magnitude and probability of fines* 133; Landes, *Optimal sanctions for antitrust violations* 652.

through their impact on the probability of detection faced *ex ante* by the infringer. These costs of detection, and accordingly the probability of detection, have to be set at an optimal level. In their model, Polinsky and Shavell leave it to the public enforcement agency (or government) as a monopolist to set these costs at the optimal level. Under the envisaged system of competition amongst several enforcement agents in an investment market, however, these costs are the sum of individual investment decisions rather than the decision of a centralised authority.

Under the portrayed circumstances, many enforcers may like to investigate and prosecute anti-competitive conducts. The problem with the first-come, first-served scenario is that, similar to the problems connected to patent races, many enforcers may be spending resources to detect an infringement in the same market, but they may not be the first. All costs spent on the detection of the same infringement are wasteful and a loss to society. Solutions to that complication have been discussed also in other areas of law, which may also be applicable here.

In the stream of literature concerning economic analysis of patent rights, such problems have been studied as *patent races*. Patent race models typically also rely on a winner-takes-all contest.[390] Several competitors try to be the first to complete a certain innovation and secure the patent rights on it. As only one can succeed in getting the patent, resources of the competitors spent could be considered a waste to society from a total welfare perspective. The literature is divided into two groups. Some authors proclaim the inefficiency of patent races due to such duplication of efforts.[391] Others argue that the race leads to offsetting benefits, such as more innovations in aggregate.[392] While an increased number of total innovations may offset the waste of resources to society in patent races, in this application the benefits could be seen in the increased deterrence effect due to larger detection rates. It is possible that these avoided losses to society outweigh the inefficiently large costs of detection. Moreover, the simplest models of patent races and the race to be first to file a claim might not be entirely analogous. In the case of fixed screening costs and variable litigation costs, the fixed costs spent by competitors on investigating the same market cannot be said to be a complete duplication of efforts. This is different compared to those models of a patent race, where there is only one firm that innovates in the end and

390 Fullerton, et al, "Using auctions to reward tournament winners: Theory and experimental investigations," *Rand Journal of Economics* 33 (2002): 62, 64 f.

391 Duffy, "Rethinking the prospect theory of patents," *University of Chicago Law Review* 71 (2004): 439.

392 Scotchmer, *Incentives to Innovate.* in *The New Palgrave Dictionary of Economics and the Law.* ed. Newman. London: Macmillan (1998), 273, 273 ff;.Merges and Nelson, "On the complex economics of patent scope," *Columbia Law Review* 90 (1990): 839, 908.

achieves the patent while all the other resources are lost. Other patent race models might be more applicable, particularly those in which the Research and Development (R&D) investments by other competitors are not completely wasted but may lead to different types of innovations. The first entity to detect a certain infringement is not going to make the detection costs spent by his competitors redundant altogether. This is because the resources invested in screening the market in question may well lead to the detection of other infringements.

To limit the losses to society, commentators propose letting firms secure the patents as early as possible.[393] Likewise, enforcement agents should then be allowed to file an initial claim as early as possible, to secure the rights of representation. Thereby other enforcers would cease to spend resources on the investigation of the same case, while the detector would be protected from the free riding behaviour of other enforcers. As mentioned above, the right balance concerning the requirements to file suit, has to be found between allowing early filing and avoiding meritless claims.

Alternative mechanisms could also be considered. The state could reimburse the enforcement agent for their efforts and resources spent. The reimbursement for efforts rather than only for successful efforts can lead to inefficient investment in detection efforts, as such a system borders on a system with public enforcement agencies with agents working on a certain salary scheme.[394] Therefore, that alternative will not be discussed here in greater detail.

To avoid large a waste of resources due to duplication of detection efforts, one might also divide the totality of competition law infringements into certain sectors, for example, certain industry sectors in specified geographical markets. Rights to investigate these sectors and litigate the resulting cases could then be granted to only one enforcement agent each, similar to license agreements. As the possible returns on investment in these sectors are unknown to the regulator as well as the agents, a suitable way to determine which area should be given to which agent and at what price has to be employed. For such reasons, auctions could be held, in which the right to detect and litigate are granted to the highest bidder. That option will be discussed in the section C. 4 of this chapter.

---

393 See Abramowicz, *The Uneasy Case For Patent Races over Auctions* 803, 806 f. Filing claims relatively early is also a concept used when after filing pre-trial discovery procedures are held before the actual trial begins.

394 Becker, *Law enforcement, malfeasance, and compensation of Enforces* 1 and the discussion in Chapter 2, section C.2.1.

3.6. *Principal-agent problems*

The relevant principal-agent relationship in the market scenario is that between society and the enforcement agent. The risk that enforcement agencies collude with defendants and not invest optimal efforts will be minimised, when the interests of agent and society are completely aligned.

Once the enforcer has secured the right to proceed to trial, he may strike a deal with the defendant to settle the claim. Nevertheless, the settlement amount acceptable for the enforcer agent will generally equal the expected trial awards.[395] On basis of the theories described above,[396] granting the agent 100 percent of the awards should then lead to low settlement rates but large settlement awards. This would diminish the risk of both unmeritorious suits and inefficiently low settlement agreements.

However, principal-agent problems may not be overcome completely, even if the enforcer agents are allowed to keep the total of damage rewards and therefore work on a 100 percent contingency fee scheme. Some differences in interest may nevertheless remain. Society will prefer to tailor detection efforts and consequent deterrence effects to those infringements that lead to the largest damages. Generally, the individual P.E. would also pursue this aim. The enforcer may also have other incentives, however. His decision on who to pursue may also be based also on a minimisation of costs and/or risks, rather than a maximisation of rewards. Even when assuming symmetric enforcers, the selection of subjects to be investigated and that of cases to be prosecuted is likely to be skewed. To save on investment costs, the first detection will take place with the most easily detectable types of infringement, and only later issues that are more complex will be tackled. Nevertheless, these deviations from society's interest should be lower, compared to the other alternative mechanisms discussed above.

Another problem is moral hazard. Similar to the situation in patent rights, allowing the filing of a claim (granting the patent) at an early stage may lead to the decision that litigation (or development of the patented invention) is not worthwhile after all or that it may be profitable to wait. Once detection has taken place and the rights have been secured, the enforcers could have an incentive to prolong the time until litigation begins. In particular, this will be the case, when damages awarded include interest rates, so that the damages to be compensated are calculated from the moment of the harmful act until the resolution of the

---

395 See theory on optimal settlements, discussed under 2.1.3.2 above.

396 See section 2.1.3.2 above.

case. This is the case in most Member States.[397] However, such risk can be considered minimal, as it can be expected that defendants will abandon their anti-competitive conduct once it has been spotted and officially noted. Other reasons to wait might be more probable. Much more important is the risk that it may in fact be the defendants themselves securing the rights and postponing or over all preventing litigation of the case. Therefore, a group of defendants should be excluded from having standing. Additionally, to avoid any risk that rights are secured but never tried, additional regulations could be enacted to make sure that once the detection is official, litigation has to follow within a given time period. If not, the case should be given to other enforcement agencies willing to start proceeding.

Nevertheless, even if litigation after a certain amount of time is mandatory and defendants are officially excluded from the process, the problem remains that defendants may unofficially become the active participants. Defendants may be seeking or providing an enforcement agent that will file suit and immediately settle the case for a symbolic amount. Deterrence would be severely impeded that way. One way to combat that problem would be, again, to make the settlements dependant on courts approval. However, that would entail increased costs, as courts would still have to examine all the evidence to be able to assess the adequacy of the settlement amount. Prohibition of settlements could avoid these problems, but comes at the cost that total enforcement costs will not be minimised. One way to avoid that possibility for defendants is to separate detection from litigation and to hold auctions for the litigation procedure. This mechanism will be discussed in Section C. 4. below.

3.7. Conclusion

Under such a market system, free riding and rational apathy will be minimised. Problems of asymmetric information will likely be overcome to a larger degree in some cases compared to collective actions and the system of representative actions, too. Generally, cost efficiency would be also in the interest of the enforcer agent and the incorporation of all damages in one procedure should lead to procedural efficiency. This could be a very efficient mechanism especially in those cases, where the damages are spread amongst a very large population of victims, rational apathy is large, and information asymmetry is severe. This may be less the case concerning types of infringements that mainly harm other companies. However, some problems will still have to be dealt with.

---

[397] Renda, *Making antitrust damages actions in the EU more effective. Study in support of the impact assessment of the EC White Paper on antitrust damages actions*, 436 f.

Risks of frivolous suits can remain. To curb these, attention has to be paid to the way the filing of suits to secure the rights is regulated. The requirements would have to be broad enough to allow an early filing, to minimise the costs associated to doubling of efforts. On the other hand, the requirements should be strict enough to avoid completely meritless claims, filed solely with the purpose to secure potentially existing rights or to pressure defendants into settlements. Another option to curb these problems could be additional auction mechanisms.

Another disadvantage of such as system is the competitive waste of resources that also occurs in the area of R&D under patent rights. The legislator could decide to regulate the market, but that would distort the market forces and lead to other problems. With regard to the goal of minimisation of enforcement costs, there will likely remain some waste of resources in such a system. This waste could only be avoided if there was a monopolist conducting the detection and prosecution, like a competition authority. However, that, as discussed above, would open the door to other problems, which can inhibit the efficiency of the enforcement system. In addition, the individual incentives to invest in enforcement may be sub-optimal. Effects of such an enforcement monopoly will be relevant below, when auction mechanisms before detection are described, as the auction winner will be a monopolist within the licensed area.

A major risk in such a system relates to the possibilities of collusion between enforcement agents and offenders. Defendants could search for an enforcement agent to strike a settlement even before their infringement is discovered. That way, infringers could buy their freedom from prosecution at very low stakes. Deterrence would not be achieved. One way to solve this problem (and potentially others) would be to compel the enforcer who secured the rights of representation to make an upfront payment according to the expected value of the claims, which he then can only recoup when he actually prosecutes the case. This upfront payment should be large enough to avoid any profitable buy off possibilities for the defendant, in which defendant and enforcer collude. To efficiently receive information about the value of the claims and the consequent amount of up front payment, auctions could be held. This is analysed below.

4. DETERMINING THE AGENT: AUCTION MECHANISMS

When total damage rewards remain with the enforcer, because either the claims were transferred to him, or because some other legal instrument is employed to come to the same effect, such as *cy pres* distribution, auction mechanisms may be employed to either replace or amend the enforcement market solution investigated above.

Auctions may be employed at two stages of the enforcement activities, before and after detection. Auctions held before detection resemble ideas voiced in the area of patent rights, where they are discussed as possible solutions to the problem of double efforts in patent races.[398] Auctions held after detection has taken place have been advocated as solutions to principal-agent problems in group litigation mechanisms.[399] Both auction systems could be employed to complement any of the above discussed systems as a device to establish the agent in particular cases, whenever competition between enforcement agents arise.

Another distinction to be made would be whether the action itself is subject to the auction, so that the representing agent becomes the owner of the action, or whether it is only the right to represent the aggrieved victims. The latter types of auctions have in fact already been employed to establish the legal counsel in group litigation, for example in the USA.[400] However, as in the market mechanism, the action winner is considered to be granted the total damage awards granted in court in general.[401]

4.1. *Auctions before detection*

Auctions before the detection stage could be held to sell the rights of investigating specified sectors for a limited time. These rights to investigate would have to be clearly defined in order to avoid resources wasted on litigation between different right holders. Then it would be possible to "licence"[402] these rights to enforcement agents. As the value of these licences is initially unknown to the agents as well as to the licensor (society), the most efficient way to discover that information would be to hold auctions for these licences. That way, the licensees (enforcement agents) determine the price for the licences. Under this type of auction, the agent becomes the owner of the actions. The proceeds of the auction might theoretically also be used to set up funds to compensate victims or to use in a *cy pres* distribution. However, that will be less relevant from a deterrence point of view, as long as offenders will not profit from that redistribution.

---

398 See Abramowicz, *The Uneasy Case For Patent Races over Auctions* 803.

399 Macey and Miller, "Auctioning Class Action and Derivative Suits: A Rejoinder," *Northwestern University Law Review* 87 (1992): 458; Rosenberg and Sullivan, "Coordinating Private Class Action and Public Agency Enforcement of Antitrust Law," *Journal of Competition Law and Economics* 2 (2006): 159.

400 Critical on the U.S. experience:Fisch, "Lawyers on the Auction Block: Evaluating the Selection of Class Counsel by Auction," *Columbia Law Review* 102 (2002): 650.

401 The proceeds of the auction could theoretically be used to compensate victims directly or indirectly. However, any distribution mechanism that will create additional costs could be avoided from a deterrence point of view, as it has no effect on the prevention of competition law infringements.

402 See Stein and Harel, "Law & Economics at the Animal Farm: Offering a New Solution to the Class Action Agency Problem," *Working Paper Series*, 17. Available at SSRN: http://ssrn.com/abstract=271431. The authors discuss this solution as Franchising of Law-Enforcement.

The specific design of the auction depends on the particularities of the market and has to be constructed with great care. A whole stream of literature is dedicated to the analysis of the optimal design of auctioning mechanisms under specific circumstances.[403] Some of the major problems faced by auction designers are risks of collusion and predation or entry deterrence.[404] While general concepts of auctions exist, for example ascending, descending or sealed bids, a multitude of variations are possible. Different mechanisms can be combined in several stages, or additional regulations can be used. When deciding upon an auction system, the auctioneer has to tailor the auction mechanisms to the specific features of the subject at hand.

Following the idea of a sealed-bid first-price auction here, licensing the enforcement activities through auction could take place as follows. In the auction, agents will place bids to be able to investigate and prosecute infringements in a specific area according to their estimates of their individual probability of detection and the harm caused by the infringements. Each participant would have to assess the expected damage awards that can be earned in that particular market segment and his individual costs of detection and litigation. When deciding upon the bid, each will have to weigh larger expected profit margins against the possibility that someone else places a higher bid. Although each bidder would like to keep his bid as low as possible in order to maximise the net expected profit, placing low bids decreases the probability of winning the auction. More efficient enforcers, which have lower costs, will be able to place higher bids than less efficient competitors can, so that licences will be granted to more efficient enforcers. The proceeds of the auction may be used to set up funds to be used to compensate victims of infringements.[405]

If the rights to investigate and litigate go to the highest bidder, the risk associated with the detection and prosecution are placed on that party. Risk-averse agents are therefore less likely to participate in such endeavours than risk neutral or risk loving agents.

In addition, potential defendants could place a bid in the auction. In case all defendants in one market would be able overcome collective action problems and jointly win the bid, they in effect would compensate society. It seems that any auction where potential defendants participate should result in large bids, as

403 For an overview seeKlemperer, "Auction theory: A guide to the literature," *Journal of Economic Surveys* 13 (1999): 227.

404 See Klemperer, "What really matters in auction design," *Journal of Economic Perspectives* 16 (2002): 169.

405 Though these redistribution issues matter less from a deterrence perspective, as long as they do not benefit the offender and do not distort the incentive structures connected to the deterrence based enforcement mechanisms.

participation of those potentially violating the law should be a good indicator that there is something to detect and litigate. However, when in civil litigation the multiplier to total damages given by the probability of detection will be in place, this option will be less attractive to the potential offenders.

The effectiveness of such a system greatly depends on the way the auction is organised. Obviously, the auction mechanism has to be designed in a way that effectively prohibits any form of bid rigging[406] and assures as many competitive bids as possible. Moreover, the auction design has to incorporate circumstances relating to the auction, such as the likely number and distribution of bidders.[407] Under circumstances of perfect information, perfect capital markets and perfect competition, winning bids should equal the optimal expected damage awards, placed by the most cost efficient enforcer.

4.1.1. Free riding

Under such a scenario, free riding behaviour is eliminated, as no agent can expect to be able to free ride on some other entities efforts. A necessary requirement is, however, that the rights to be auctioned are adequately defined.

4.1.2. Rational apathy

Generally, rational apathy concerning the weighing of litigation costs and expected damage awards should not be relevant under such a system. Rational apathy on the side of victims as represented entities is avoided by the mandatory group affiliation. The agents are motivated by expected profits.

A crucial aspect in this set up, however, is that the auction participants will have to have substantial financial resources in order to be able to place and pay the winning bid.[408] In an ideal world, firms should have access to virtually unlimited funding in the perfect credit markets.[409] In less perfect circumstances, the ability

406 Bid rigging refers to a collusive behaviour by competitors in auction like setting. Competitiors come to an agreement of who should win the auction, while the non-winning parties place bids only for appearance sake.

407 For a description of more or less successful auctions and analysis of the mistakes made see:*Ibidem*.

408 Very rough estimates of cartels operating in Europe for example place the total social losses caused between € 25 billion and € 69 billion, see Renda, *Making antitrust damages actions in the EU more effective. Study in support of the impact assessment of the EC White Paper on antitrust damages actions*, 110 f.

409 Assumptions of a perfect financial or credit market: No arbitrage opportunities, no transaction costs, no taxes, and no restrictions on short selling. Lending rates equal borrowing rates. All securities are perfectly divisible. See Franke et al, *Statistics of financial markets: an introduction*, Berlin: Springer (2008), 11.

to place and pay bids could be severely hampered, and only very few undertakings may be able to participate in the auction. However, it may also be possible to postpone the actual payment of the bid until the "license" to investigate expires. In case the expected profit was realised, the enforcer has the relevant amounts at his disposal. If the bid was overly optimistic, the winner could be held liable for the rest of the bid.[410]

Another aspect of such a system in a less than perfect world also includes the constantly changing circumstances in the market. This implies that the value of the rights bought at the auction changes over time, as markets evolve. The probabilities of certain states of the market to be investigated reduce the expected return on investment and in consequence, also the amount participants are willing to bid in the auction.

Again, enforcement efforts would be a large investment under uncertainty for the enforcer, which will only be undertaken if a sufficient return on investment is expected. In the other systems discussed above, the enforcer was able to earn a profit from either a share or the total of damage awards. Such amounts can be substantial. Expected profits for the auction winner are determined by the difference between bid, the costs of detection and litigation or settlement, and the expected damage awards. It is questionable whether the prospect of profits determined that way would suffice to induce sufficient, or even efficient, investment in these enforcement efforts.[411]

Rational apathy on the side of individuals as enforcers is likely not to be overcome by such a system and to remain large. Especially risk averse agents with limited financial resources will not embark on such highly risky investment opportunities. The necessity to compete for licences and pay the licence fee greatly reduces the incentives to invest compared to the market solution.

4.1.3. Asymmetric information

The problem of asymmetric information is slightly different in this scenario than in the group litigation mechanisms discussed above. Also here, information about particular infringements is missing from the outset, therefore the general statistical distributions of infringements and the damages caused become very important. Estimates of these values are inherently difficult, but attempts have

410 Similar proposal has been made by Harel and Stein, who propose a fee-forfeiture in auctions for class action litigation. See: Stein, *Law & Economics at the Animal Farm: Offering a New Solution to the Class Action Agency Problem*, 33. Available at: http://ssrn.com/abstract=271431.

411 See the discussion about the remuneration of P.E.'s in the enforcement market above.

frequently been made.[412] Some markets are likely to be more prone to certain types of infringements than others are. Damages caused can also depend on the type of market in question.[413] Theoretically, also competition authorities working under budget constraints and under pressure to show results should be capable of making similar estimates in order to decide which markets to focus their efforts on. If such a system were in place for a longer time, experience might also provide some data that could be used. In this respect, comparisons with legal systems in which private enforcement of competition law infringements has been in place for some time, such as the USA, might also be helpful.

However, compared to the other systems described above, the licence mechanism hinders efficient specialisation in overcoming asymmetric information. When the licence is defined as applying to a certain market segment, for example, very different types of infringements may appear in that market segment, so that the licensee can not specialise on, for example, the detection of cartel infringements rather than that of abuses of dominant positions. Compared to the market mechanism, specialisation is hampered.

4.1.4. Nuisance suits

The risk of unmeritorious suits to be brought is likely to remain significant under these circumstances. The agents investigating certain areas have had to incur large upfront costs or liabilities to obtain the licences. The pressure to at least recapture these costs is likely to increase the already existing incentives to file suits with little or no merits, to force potential defendants into settlement agreements whenever there is a possibility to do so.

4.1.5. Principal-agent problems

The risk of under-deterrence because the winner might collude with potential defendants once the auction process is completed is minimised. Whoever wins the bid has to at least recoup the amount of his bid and will not accept settlement offers below that amount.

---

412 For a summary and overview see: Renda, *Making antitrust damages actions in the EU more effective. Study in support of the impact assessment of the EC White Paper on antitrust damages actions*, 71 ff.

413 Empirical evidence found connections between size of overcharge and industry. See Bolotova, "Cartel overcharges: An empirical analysis," *Journal of Economic Behavior and Organization* 70 (2009): 321; Renda, *Making antitrust damages actions in the EU more effective. Study in support of the impact assessment of the EC White Paper on antitrust damages actions.Connor, Optimal deterrence and private international cartels.* Available at: http://ssrn.com/abstract=787927.

In the best possible auction with numerous bidders, the winning bid would equal all expected damage awards[414] that could have been litigated for. Therefore, if the auctioning system is optimally designed, competition amongst bidders should prevent the defendants from being able to buy their freedom from competition for an inefficiently low amount.

It should also be possible that some offenders join forces in the auction to place a bid for the market section they operate in. Winning the auction would relieve them for the assigned period of the risk of detection of any anti-competitive behaviour. Nevertheless, defendant(s) would have to place the highest bid to win the auction and that forces the winner to either actually pay the expected collectible damage awards upfront or to pay after the license expires. This leads to an imposition of the damages done to society on the defendant(s) in any case without the requirement for litigation.

It could also happen that a small share of the firms in that particular industry sector join forces in a consortium to win the auction. In such a case, highly informed and interested parties will enforce the competition law in that industry, controlling the conduct of other firms outside the consortium.

When agents place bids according to the total expected damage awards of the auctioned sector, and litigate the detected infringements to recoup their bid, principal-agent problems are minimised. The interests of society as principal and enforcement agent are aligned to a great extent through the auction mechanism.

4.1.6. Minimisation of costs

Procedural efficiency is guaranteed by the mandatory inclusion of all possible claims into just one proceeding. Moreover, detection and litigation efforts will be distributed more efficiently. Enforcers that are more efficient will be in a better position to win the auctions than less efficient enforcers. After the auction takes place, the auction winner will have large incentives to keep the costs of detection and litigation as low as possible as well, while still achieving the aimed at profit. The actual detection and litigation efforts therefore should be efficient.

On the other hand, while at first glance such an auction may be a remedy for allocative inefficiency due to a doubling of efforts,[415] one also has to take into account that enforcement agents will all have to invest large resources on the

414 To be more precise: the expected damage awards as estimated by the highest bidder.

415 Classical problem in the case of patent races, see Perry and Vincent, "The Optimal Timing of Procurement Decisions and Patent Allocations," *International Economic Review* 43 (2002): 1035.

gathering of relevant information in order to be able to place an adequate bid. To establish the value of the rights to investigate a certain market share for a limited time, information about the likelihood of infringements, the probability of being able to detect different infringements, and the amount of damages caused is needed. The more accurate firms want to be in their estimation, the higher the social losses will be due to a doubling of efforts preceding the auction. Moreover, the auction process itself can be very costly, which adds to total enforcement costs.

4.1.7. Conclusion

A major advantage of a system complemented by auctions as described above is that auctions overcome the principal-agent problems between society and the agent. Incentives to collude with the defendants and to agree on inefficiently low settlements are lacking. In case the defendants wanted to buy their freedom from prosecution through a settlement with the auction winner, they will at least have to compensate the enforcer for the bid paid at the auction. The enforcement agent would demand at least the expected share of the bid and consequently the expected damages (as evaluated by him) caused by each defendant. The defendants as well as the enforcer would therefore theoretically settle on the expected amount of damages that would result were the case(s) brought to trial. Such settlements would be efficient from a social and deterrence point of view.[416] Also free riding behaviour is avoided and procedural efficiency is achieved. Detection and enforcement efforts would be channelled to the most efficient enforcement agent.

However, the auction mechanism also imposes a lot of costs on society. These costs comprise the cost of the auction itself as well as all resources spent by competing bidders when estimating adequate bids. Moreover, the increased incentives to file suits with little merits bear the risk of inefficient use of resources and of over-deterrence. Moreover, smaller possible profits compared to the market mechanism, combined with the huge obstacle of adequate funding because a perfect capital market is lacking and the complexity of the licensing mechanisms, further decreases the efficiency of such a system. Overall, this system seems not to be an attractive or even feasible solution, especially not for risk-averse individuals or agents with limited resources.

4.2. Auctions after detection

Auctions may also be held at a later stage, when detection has already taken place, to cure some of the problems found in the other litigation systems

416 See discussion on merits of settlements above.

discussed above.[417] This section therefore deals with a variation of these systems, rather than a substitute. However, as the optimal collective action as well as the optimal representative actions will end up at the market solution, the auction discussed here takes the market solution as starting point. These auctions can be combined with collective and representative actions, as well as the more general market approach. It then needs to be investigated how introducing a second step, the auction after detection, alters the incentive structures of these described mechanisms.

Once detection of a competition law infringement has taken place and the rights have been established (registered), an auction system may be used to organise the litigation of the claims. The auction model effectively splits the enforcement market into two markets in which entities compete with each other. In the first market, *detectors* compete on the detection of an offence. In the second stage, *litigators* compete in auctions for the right to litigate the arising damages claims due to competition law infringements. Detectors would be compensated for their efforts through the auction proceeds, so that in effect the total damage awards would be split between litigators and detectors, incorporating the costs and risks borne by each party. The litigator will take his costs, risks and expected profit into account when placing the (winning) bid, so that the detector would be compensated accordingly.

Just as in the other type of auction described above, the litigant considering placing a bid in the auction to represent the total group of victims will have to weigh the costs of litigation and the connected risks of loosing at trial against the expected awards. Placing his bid, he will further have to carefully balance the probability of placing a non-winning bid, because it is too low, against the reduction of his expected profit margin. As opposed to the system discussed above, however, the information necessary to establish the value of the detected case is already present and could be made available to all participants. Under these circumstances, the costs to be incurred to place a bid are considerably smaller and competition amongst several bidders is focused on efficiency in litigation.

If the litigator does not succeed in obtaining the ownership of the claim, the auction could nevertheless be conducted to establish only the right to litigate. As mentioned above, such auctions have already been employed in practice. The litigators competing in the auction could place a bid according to their estimate

417 This approach could be said to mirror the so called two-tier patent system, in which a registered idea is sold at auction to be developed by another entity. See Bar-Gill and Parchomovsky, "A marketplace for Ideas?" *Texas Law Review* 84 (2005): 395, 417 f.

of the damage awards, according to their fee, or both. Harel and Stein[418] discussed such systems and argued that a bid on the amount to be sued for would be part of the optimal system. The litigator would be bound by that amount and lose his fee in case his bid was "unreasonably optimistic".[419] Together with a ban on settlements yielding an amount below the winning bid, the authors argue that most problems with existing auctioning mechanisms (and general principal-agent problems in class actions) could be overcome that way.

Another alternative would be the auction of the action itself, so that the litigator succeeds in obtaining ownership. In that scenario, the detection agency can be reimbursed for the invested resources through the auction proceeds. Under perfect circumstances, the winning bid would equal the net expected damage awards from litigation. In order to give the right incentives to detection agents, these proceeds would have to go to the detector, net a return on investment for the litigator.

4.2.1. Free riding

Free riding behaviour in such a setting is not profitable for either detectors or litigants. Detectors trying to free ride in any way on other detectors' efforts risk not being the first to secure the rights and therefore forfeit remuneration for their costs through the auction proceeds. Litigators are unable to free ride as their right to litigate is established only in the auction.

4.2.2. Rational apathy

Whoever detected the infringement and filed suit already has already established the right to represent the total of victims. Be it the market, collective actions or representative actions, the rational apathy of the individual victim to file suit would be at least reduced if not overcome.

Rational apathy concerning agents' incentives to file suit under this system would be rational apathy concerning participation in the auction. The profit to be gained depends on several factors, including the amount of and nature of competing bidders, as well as the risk of loosing at trial. Greater competition should increase the amount of the winning bid, thereby reducing the winners' profit. Litigants that are more efficient should be able to place higher bids. Riskier cases should yield smaller auction proceeds than more straightforward ones.

---

418 Stein, *Law & Economics at the Animal Farm: Offering a New Solution to the Class Action Agency Problem*available at: http://ssrn.com/abstract=271431.

419 *Ibidem*, 33.

Of course, the financing problem is the same as in the previously discussed auction system. However, the amount of financial resources needed is considerably smaller in this scenario, though still very large in total amounts. The specific design of the auction has an influence on the degree of the financing problem. Again, actual payment of the bid could be postponed until the trial has ended.

Under most ideal circumstances, winning bidders would be able to earn a normal return on their investment. However, the final proceed of the auction also depends on the bidders' attitudes towards risk and their adequate estimation of the relevant parameters. As together with the transfer of the rights,[420] also the remaining risk connected to the prosecution of the claims is passed on to the successful bidder, the payment made to the detector will be less than the total and the winning bidder could earn a potential profit. This resembles auction ideas that already have been employed in the USA. Incentives to participate in such auctions are dependant on the potential profits litigators may gain. As these are taken away from detectors, ideally the potential profits for litigators reflect the costs and risks connected to the litigation. In this scenario, the detector does not have to bear these, so that the incentives are only distributed amongst two parties instead of one enforcement agent.

However, with regard to optimal deterrence of competition law infringements, the incentives for detection are also highly relevant. In the Law and Economics literature, this issue has generally not been a focal point. Instead, the majority of the contributions have focused on the US style class action with a lawyer working on a contingency fee basis as starting point, and the alignment of interests between lawyer and victims as goal. In the scheme discussed here, two parties form the private enforcement agent: detector and litigator. The first has incentives to invest in detection according to the group litigation scheme in place. If it is a market for enforcement, the incentives are similar to those under the market mechanism. He does not receive the total of expected damage awards, but he also does not bear the risk and costs that are connected to the litigation. The litigator does not invest in detection, but only in the litigation. His incentives are influenced by the prospect of profit that can be obtained when the bid is less than the actual damages awarded.

In the second stage auction model, the detector could and should be reimbursed through the proceeds of the auction. In a perfectly designed auctioning system under perfect information, the winning bid should equal the expected proceeds of the trial, minus litigation costs and normal return on investment. Granting

420 Either the right to represent or the rights to claim damages.

the detection agency a certain share or all of the proceeds would then give incentives for detection as analysed in the different systems above.

4.2.3. Asymmetric information

Asymmetric information could be overcome according to the underlying scheme in which the detector operates. The litigator may still face some information problem when investigating the potential value of the bid. However, depending on the way the filing is regulated, the detector will have already discovered most of the relevant information.

4.2.4. Nuisance suits

Auctioning the rights to litigate a detected infringement greatly reduces the possibilities to file meritless suits. At least initial information on the case at hand has to be provided to conduct the auction and will be made public to (at least) the potential auction participants in the process. The auctioneer could resemble a control mechanism weeding out cases with little or no merits, allowing only those cases to proceed that pass a preliminary revision. If the filing of such a suit will only be made public after it has been decided to take the case to such an auction mechanism, then the threat of filing a suit in order to extract a settlement even though the case has little merits is also made less credible and the costs for the potential defendant could be reduced. Nuisance suits may be eliminated completely when litigation is made mandatory.

4.2.5. Principal-agent problems

The effectiveness of such a system to overcome principal-agent problems between representing and represented parties by aligning the interest of both and eliminating incentives to strike inefficient settlements seems quite straight forward.

Auctions have been frequently discussed in the Law and Economics literature as solutions to the perceived principal-agent problems between representing party (mostly a lawyer conducting a class action) and the injured parties.[421] The basic effect of auctioning claims to competing lawyers is to unite lawyers and claimants interests, as plaintiffs are compensated from the proceeds of the auction and the lawyer winning the bid will succeed to the rights of the plaintiffs. An alternative

---

421 See Schäfer, *The Bundling of Similar Interests in Litigation. The Incentives for Class Action and Legal Actions taken by Associations* 183; Rosenberg, *Coordinating Private Class Action and Public Agency Enforcement of Antitrust Law* 159; Macey, *Auctioning Class Action and Derivative Suits: A Rejoinder* 458.

proposed in the literature is to auction only the right to represent the victims, leaving their rights intact and their compensation dependant not on the auction proceeds but the outcome of the trial. In this scenario, the right to represent the class is auctioned to the bidder with the highest expected recovery. In case the lawyer fails to recover that amount later, she will lose her (contingency) fee in case her bid was unreasonably optimistic. Settlements yielding less than the proposed recovery for claimants would be prohibited. With these three mechanisms at work, the principal-agent problems would be solved efficiently, while the interests of the claimants would be appropriately protected.[422]

The second step auction compels the litigating agent to at least recoup the winning bid from the defendants. That greatly reduces principal-agent problems between society and agent.[423]

4.2.6. Minimisation of costs

Again, when bidders assess the value of the claims to be auctioned, which includes the assessment of the total damages caused, the *ex ante* probability that this infringement will be detected, and the probability of winning the suit, all bidders invest resources. This doubling of efforts seems unavoidable, but it presumably is much less than in other scenarios. In this case, only one specific infringement has to be investigated and depending on the requirements to be fulfilled by the detector to register the claims, a lot of necessary information may already be available.

However, the doubling of efforts that takes place at the detection stage still persists. As argued above, this may be a waste for society that could be outweighed by the benefits of increased deterrence.

One has to bear in mind that auctions are costly. Not only to the ones investing resources in research to calculate their optimal bid, but also the procedure itself generates costs that must be borne by society, on top of the detection and litigation costs. However, the total costs to society have to be weighed against the reduction in losses caused by principal-agent problems and inefficient group litigation mechanisms that insufficiently deter violations of competition law.

---

422 Stein, *Law & Economics at the Animal Farm: Offering a New Solution to the Class Action Agency Problem*. Available at: http://ssrn.com/abstract=271431.

423 For a brief discussion of whether or in how far such a mechanisms could be incorporated into legal systems of Member States, see the legal obstacles discussed in chapter 4, section C.

4.2.7. Conclusion

Auctions held before the litigation stage have a number of advantages over the other individual systems discussed above. Free riding behaviour, the risk of frivolous suits and principal-agent problems are minimised. The problems of individual rational apathy concerning the filing of suits or investing in detection efforts (overcoming information asymmetry) are also reduced in those cases where they are large. However, such a system creates additional costs, on top of unavoidable double effort costs, and may not lead to the socially optimal investment in these detection and litigation efforts. Moreover, adequate funding mechanisms for auction participants as well as detectors are needed. Of vital importance is also the requirement that the auction mechanism is carefully designed to fit the specific circumstances.

Nevertheless, auctions after detection seem to be a viable and quite efficient way to curb principal-agent problems, which can persist in any of the above discussed group litigation mechanisms. Moreover, risks of unmeritorious claims are largely reduced, if not eliminated by establishing another control instance. Incentives to participate in the litigation auction are provided through the profit that litigators are able to secure for themselves in the winning bid. The more competition in the auction, the smaller that profit is likely to be. The incentives to detect for the detector remain dependant on the remuneration the detector can expect from the auction proceeds. These would not be total damage awards, but, depending on the complexity of litigation and its riskiness, more or less close to that amount.

A two-stage model with market for enforcement in the first stage, and an auction for litigation in the second stage, is likely to be the most beneficial in cases of widespread and small individual damages caused by competition law infringements. This will be the case, for example, when end consumers suffer losses due to a price cartel where all losses where passed on to them.

D. CONCLUSIONS

The introduction of group litigation mechanisms for damages actions based on competition law into existing legal systems brings about the potential to overcome some obstacles that exist to individual claims for damages. On the other hand, other problems might be made more severe or created by such a legal change. It is therefore necessary to carefully examine the goal to be achieved with such a mechanism and to intelligently design the system in a way that it achieves the given goal in the most efficient way. A cost benefit analysis as conducted here, even if only qualitative and not quantitative statements are possible, provides necessary information to legislators in order to make adequate choices.

The legal aim of introducing group litigation mechanisms in this analysis is assumed to be only that of deterrence of anti-competitive conduct. Compensation of individual harm is only a matter of redistribution from an economic point of view. Admittedly, the goals of enforcement of competition law and its enforcement are numerous, including compensatory justice. However, just as aiming with one arrow at several targets simultaneously is a challenge, the different goals pursued by the introduction of group litigation mechanisms may be in conflict with each other. For example, pursuing optimal deterrence comes at the costs that compensatory justice for individual victims may not be achieved at the same time. The policy makers and legislators then have to decide which goal is given preference over others, and has to be aware of the fact that the pursuit of one goal may come at costs with regard to the degree to which other goals can be achieved.

Breaches of competition law affect various types of victims to larger or lesser degrees and pose more or less specific obstacles to individual claims for damages. Consequently, the different forms of group litigation are also more or less suited to overcome the specific problems at hand. The main reasons for these differences are asymmetric information problems and the possibilities of the victim or agent in question to overcome these, as well as the severity of principal-agent problems between the various affected entities (victims, agents and society at large).

To provide a quick summary, table 1 below shows the efficiency of different group actions in cases of infringements causing small and widely spread individual damages.[424] The forms of group litigation compared are collective actions with a lead plaintiff as main actor, representative actions brought by associations and the combined market/auction-after-detection solution. The degree to which problems remain, relative to the other options, are indicated by – signs, ranging from 0 (problems are largely reduced) to – – – (problems remain large).

[424] The table can only depict a very rough comparison. For detailed discussions of the issues involved please see the relevant text above.

Table 1

Remaining problems with regard to:	*Lead plaintiff collective action*	*Representative action*	*Market & Auction after detection*
Free riding	0 / – *(mandatory group, but: incentives to become lead plaintiff?)*	0 *(mandatory group, no free riding)*	0 *(mandatory group, no free riding)*
Rational apathy	– – *(lead plaintiff bears costs and risks of initiating collective action, compares individual benefits with costs of litigation)*	– *(association compares total damages with costs of litigation, but: what are incentives?)*	0 *(compares total damages with costs, business like investment decision)*
Information asymmetry	– – – *(initial problems are large, little incentives to invest resources to overcome these problems)*	– – *(better abilities to overcome asymmetry, due to expertise, learning effects, etc.)*	– *(most incentives to overcome, specialised in overcoming these problems)*
Nuisance suits	– *(collective action increases potential costs that may be imposed on defendant, individual gains might be increased)*	– – *(larger threat potential than individual(s) in collective action))*	0 / – *(can be reduced in auctions)*
Principal-Agent Problems	– – – *(lead-plaintiff is one-shot player, problems remain between client(s) and lawyer as well as plaintiff and society)*	– – *(association is repeat-player, more options to curb these problems, remaining agency problems between society and associations)*	– *(agents are repeat players, incentives are better aligned with those of society)*
Minimisation of costs	0 / – *(mandatory group, little doubling of efforts, also because of little incentives to invest)*	– – *(mandatory group, but competition between several associations leads to doubling of efforts)*	– *(mandatory group, most efficient detectors and litigators, but race to detect)*

Collective actions initiated by a lead plaintiff in competition law cases claiming damages seem to be less efficient in those types of infringements, where especially end consumers are affected. Such a system requires the largest participation of the victims, who as end consumers might not be adequately equipped. Such a system would fare better in cases where only few firms are affected, for example in cases of abuse. The harmed undertakings are likely to be more sophisticated, experienced and repeat players. However, the necessity for group litigation mechanisms to foster actions for damages due to competition law infringements is less obvious in cases where only one or few sophisticated victims, such as firms, suffer relatively large damages. In such cases, the added benefits of group litigation compared to individual litigation might be only small and possibly outweighed by the increased complexity and costs compared to individual litigation and the risk of unmeritorious suits.

When the collective action is in fact run by the lawyer, the whole group litigation should be designed accordingly, as the lawyer will be acting as an entrepreneur. As has been argued, the lawyer as enforcement agent could be an efficient mechanism, especially in cases where obstacles to individual litigation are large, when that form of group litigation is designed in a way that actually introduces the market of enforcement.

Similar to the results of the analysis concerning collective actions run by a lawyer, adequately designed representative actions seem to be more suited in cases where a large number of victims is affected, especially when they consist of mainly end consumers. When the consequences of a competition law infringement are typically spread over a large group of various victims, the obstacles to detection and litigation faced by individual victims are more severe. Therefore, mechanisms that create incentives for an agent to act on behalf of society at large become more attractive. Allowing the benefits of competition between different associations and especially providing adequate incentives to detect and prosecute infringements again pushes the representative action in the direction of a market of enforcement agents in such cases. Just as is the case for collective actions, representative actions also seem less needed, when the number of victims is small, individual damages are large and the victims tend to be sophisticated players.

When individual damages are very small and widely spread amongst a large number of victims, mechanisms that turn the detection and litigation into an actual investment decisions seem to be most efficient, thereby inducing a market based enforcement of competition law. That is particularly the case when auction mechanisms are employed, in order to secure that the optimal (or best possible) sanction will be imposed on the infringer. The use of the market-based mechanism combined with auction mechanisms seems to be most efficient way to align the interest of society as principal and those of its private enforcement agents. Auctions also provide solutions to curb remaining problems in collective and representative actions, when several enforcement agents compete.

It cannot be neglected that legal restrictions as they exist in the area of tort law, constitutional law or other regulations might severely inhibit the efficiencies of all of the above systems. These limitations will be discussed in the following chapters. However, the insights developed in this chapter provide several layers of vital information for legislators contemplating to design group litigation mechanisms. First, when deviations from the most efficient system, as developed here, are made, for example the selection of an opt-out rather than a mandatory system in cases of small and widely spread damages, the analysis conducted here will answer the question, at what costs these deviations will have to be made. Hence, justification of these choices will have to make sure that the gains realised by that choice at least compensate for these costs. Second, the analysis also highlights necessary trade-offs that occur within the design of a specific mechanism, for example between incentivising litigation and avoiding nuisance suits, so that additional safeguards may be established. These theoretical results should therefore also be very valuable in the real world. Moreover, comparison with the mechanism developed here allows for a better assessment of existing systems.

CHAPTER 4
THE EUROPEAN WAY AHEAD

In this chapter, the proposals made by the European Commission are analysed with regard to their potential to reach their different goals. In the first part of the chapter, a short overview is given of the way ahead as envisaged by the Commission. In the second part, the proposed mechanisms are analysed with regard to their ability to achieve the goal of enforcement, i.e., deterrence, using the insights gained in the previous chapter. The focus remains on the group litigation mechanisms, but other mechanisms that strengthen or weaken some of the potentials of the group litigation will also be taken into account. In the third part, legal obstacles regarding the introduction of the optimal deterrence mechanism as they may exist are discussed. Lastly, other aims of the reform and the degree to which those might be realised are also discussed. The last two parts provide some general, though sometimes critical, ideas concerning the justification of the Commission's decision.

A. THE WAY AHEAD AS PAINTED IN THE WHITE PAPER[425]

Vigorous competition in an open internal market provides the best guarantee that European companies will increase their productivity and innovative potential. Competition law enforcement is therefore a key element of the "Lisbon strategy" which aims at making the economy of the European Union grow and create employment for Europe's citizens.

Facilitating damages claims for breaches of the antitrust rules will not only strengthen the enforcement of competition law, but will also make it easier for consumers and firms who have suffered damage from an infringement of competition law rules to recover their losses from the infringer. […] (European Commission, Background to the Green and White Paper)[426]

---

425 Although expected already in spring of 2009, unfortunately the Directive following the White Paper did not materialise while the work on this thesis was still conducted.

426 See http://ec.europa.eu/competition/antitrust/actionsdamages/index.html.

While the major aim of the planned reform remained a bit of a mystery after the Green Paper, the Commission has clarified this point in the following White Paper. With the adaptation of the White Paper, the primary focus of enhancing enforcement of competition law through private actions for damages now seems to have been placed on full compensation of victims of competition law infringements. "All victims" should be "fully compensated".[427] Deterrence has been degraded to being a side effect, albeit a welcomed one. In its Impact Assessment Report, the Commission addressed again the "clear deficit in terms of corrective justice"[428] with regard to the current redress mechanisms in cases of antitrust damages in the Member States and the expectation that effective mechanisms will "create additional deterrence".[429] The major aim of the discussed and proposed changes in procedural rules and other regulations seems to be to overcome these deficits, in order to ensure effective compensation of victims of competition law infringements. However, whether this goal should always take clear precedence over the goal of deterrence has not been clarified.

In this section, only a quick overview over the proposed legal changes is given. The effects of these proposals are discussed in greater detail when the White Paper is assessed with regard to its potential to achieve deterrence or other goals.

The most important proposal in the White Paper to this research was the introduction of several group litigation mechanisms. In particular, the Commission proposed the following group litigation mechanisms as complements:[430]

> *"representative actions, which are brought by qualified entities, such as consumer associations, state bodies or trade associations, on behalf of identified or, in rather restricted cases, identifiable victims. These entities are either (i) officially designated in advance or (ii) certified on an ad hoc basis by a Member State for a particular antitrust infringement to bring an action on behalf of some or all of their members"*
>
> *"opt-in collective actions, in which victims expressly decide to combine their individual claims for harm they suffered into one single action."*

Next to these, a number of additional mechanisms are proposed, to facilitate the bringing of actions for damages due to competition law infringements. With

427 European Commission, *White Paper on Damages actions for breach of the EC antitrust Rules COM(2008) 165 final, SEC(2008) 404*White Paper, 2 f.

428 European Commission, "Commission Staff Working Document, Accompanying document to the White Paper on Damages actions for breach of the EC antitrust rules, Impact Assessment, {COM (2008) 165 final} {SEC(2008) 404} {SEC(2008) 406}," (2008), 13.

429 *Ibidem*, 13, 22, 23.

430 European Commission, *White Paper on Damages actions for breach of the EC antitrust Rules COM(2008) 165 final, SEC(2008) 404*, 4.

regard to standing, the Commission has opted for allowing also indirect purchaser standing. The passing-on defence, with the burden of proof resting on the defendant, is being allowed and a presumption of full passing-on should be established in cases brought by indirect purchasers. National courts are advised to employ mechanisms to avoid a double indemnification of the same harm, which may result from such presumptions. Disclosure *inter partes* should be ensured at a minimum, in line with existing legal procedures in many Member States. Final decisions taken by public bodies should be made binding for national courts dealing with follow-on actions for damages. Once an infringement has been proven, the defendant can only escape liability when able to prove that the breach of competition law was the consequence of an *excusable error*. Therefore, fault does not need to be established by the plaintiffs. With regard to the calculation of damages, the Commission offered to publish non-binding guidelines on simplified methods, or approximate methods to establish the amount of harm. Some minimum requirements concerning limitation periods are also proposed. Accordingly, limitation periods for continuous or repeated infringements should not start before the day the infringement ceases and before the victim can reasonably be expected to have knowledge about the harm.[431] For follow-on actions, a new limitation period should be set to at least two years after public authorities have taken a final decision concerning the infringement. In addition, the Member States are encouraged to re-evaluate their cost and fee shifting rules. In particular, court fees should be set "in an appropriate manner".[432] Further, mechanisms to enhance settlements should be installed and in certain circumstances it should be possible to alleviate the potential financial burden on plaintiffs by reducing their liability for the defendants' costs even if their claim is unsuccessful. A last thought is given to the interaction of private claims for damages with public leniency programmes. The leniency applicant should be given protection through a non-disclosure rule concerning all corporate statements made by the applicant. Further protection is not proposed, yet, but opened for discussion.

B. EVALUATION OF THE PROPOSED MECHANISMS WITH REGARD TO DETERRENCE

From its selected options, the Commission expects, next to enhanced compensation of victims, also an increase in "deterrence rates".[433] Despite the

431 The latter requirement might be in need of further qualification, as in some cases an individual indirect purchaser may hardly ever be reasonably expected to gain knowledge about the harm, until some third party informs him or her.

432 *Ibidem*, no. 2.8., 9 f.

433 European Commission, *Commission Staff Working Document, Accompanying document to the White Paper on Damages actions for breach of the EC antitrust rules, Impact Assessment, {COM (2008) 165 final} {SEC(2008) 404} {SEC(2008) 406}*, 58.

problem that the achievement of these two goals sometimes may be in conflict with each other, deterrence as well as compensatory justice can only be increased in as much as the proposed systems have the potential to overcome the problems faced by plaintiffs in individual litigation. The first issues to be analysed in this section are therefore the degrees to which obstacles to individual private litigation can be mitigated or overcome. In the second part, the question whether the amount of damages awarded will suffice to reach the optimal sanction is discussed. In the third section, the potential to reduce costs imposed on society is analysed. The fourth section provides a summary of the findings.

The analysis therefore draws on the insights gained in the previous chapter and thus analyses, how well the proposed mechanisms will fare with regard to deterrence, which is one of the goals pursued by the European Commission. The previous analysis focussed on stand-alone actions, while the European Commission proposal also allows for follow-on actions.[434] However, that analysis can still be applied for two reasons: first, it can serve to analyse the efficiency of the proposals with regard to the (also wanted) stand-alone actions. Second, the inefficiencies discovered in the previous analysis can also be used to identify inefficiencies with regard to follow-on actions.

1. OVERCOMING EXISTING OBSTACLES TO PRIVATE LITIGATION

1.1. *Free rider problems*

Free rider problems may persist despite the proposed group litigation mechanisms. The system as proposed by the European Commission envisions collective opt-in actions, representative actions by *ex ante* certified associations and by *ad hoc* certified associations, as complements.[435] Along side these mechanisms, traditional litigation will persist unaltered, as the individual plaintiffs will not be deprived of their right to bring claims for damages on their own.[436] This, combined with the system inherent feature that in most cases each form of group litigation will capture only a sub-group of the total group of victims, enables free riding incentives and possibilities to remain.

Given the complexity connected to the establishment of competition law infringements, individual victims may decide to wait for others to litigate

434 European Commission, *Commission Staff Working Paper accompanying the White Paper on Damages actions for breach of the EC antitrust rules*, no. 21, 11 f.

435 *Ibidem*, no. 59 f, 21 f.

436 *Ibidem*, no. 61, 21 f.

whenever possible. This may be either individual suits, collective actions or associations stepping in and bringing the first suit. The judgment, alongside the information made public in the first claim can in some cases greatly reduce the burden on the individual plaintiff. While the judgements in prior actions for damages might not be binding for the court in all cases, they could at least be invoked as evidence.[437] Therefore, especially in complex cases, where a lot of investment into the legal claim is required, individuals may still hesitate to take action.

Associations may have incentives to free ride for similar reasons. As all the proposed systems are considered to be complements, different representative bodies, for example trade and consumer associations, or associations representing different subgroups, may hope to be able to free ride on the efforts of another. This is predicted to be especially likely in those cases where all the plaintiffs will be identified and the total of awards eventually distributed. That is because, depending on the regulation on how the associations will be remunerated for their expenses, the incentives to become active may be very limited in the first place.

Depending on the specific regulations enacted, discovery rules may decrease the possibilities to free ride on efforts spent on prior litigation by other agents. When, due to the confidential nature of relevant information, public access to vital evidence gathered in one proceeding is limited or evidence is only indirectly produced,[438] important information might not be disclosed to other parties. Albeit, such limitations run counter the Commission's plans to alleviate the burden for potential plaintiffs.

The incentives to free ride may be further mitigated if there is effective competition between several bodies or collective actions and when the representative agent has some personal interest in litigating the case. Theoretically, the complementary nature of the proposed mechanisms, together with the requirement to avoid double indemnification of specific harms,[439] could induce competition between different representing agents. This may be especially so, when double compensation is to be avoided on a first come, first served, basis. Under such circumstances, an entity generally interested in being able to prosecute a specific case on behalf of a defined group could, in theory, face the

437 *Ibidem*, no. 225, 68 and fn 118.

438 The Commission discussed both of these possibilities to reduce the scope of disclosure, see European Commission, *Commission Staff Working Document, Accompanying document to the White Paper on Damages actions for breach of the EC antitrust rules, Impact Assessment, {COM (2008) 165 final} {SEC(2008) 404} {SEC(2008) 406}*, no. 117, 36.

439 European Commission, *Commission Staff Working Paper accompanying the White Paper on Damages actions for breach of the EC antitrust rules*, 22, no. 61.

risk that all members or a subgroup of the group might be represented in another group litigation which is initiated at an earlier stage. If that happens, the association might forego all or part of the benefit it was hoping to reap from pursuing the case. This would greatly reduce the incentives to free ride. Any benefits that might be gained by waiting for other actions to provide necessary information would have to be weighed against the risk that the group members would all or in part be represented in another proceeding. However, the actual possibilities for competition are limited. The first obstacle to effective competition would be specific regulations envisioned for the group litigation mechanisms. *Ex ante* certified entities might stand to gain the most from prosecuting cases, especially when the damages sued for are those of unidentified victims, and will be awarded to the entity in way of *cy pres* to be used in the further interests of those represented. On the other hand, these bodies shall be subject to specific verification requirements,[440] which confines the number of designated bodies and consequently greatly reduces possible competition amongst them.[441] *Ad hoc* certified bodies, established with the aim of protecting a specific interest, may only represent their members. Therefore, the options for competition are severely limited. It may be that after one *ad hoc* certified body has been established, another may try to get sufficient members to join and to be certified as well. These options, however, will not lead to real competitive pressure.

A lack of sufficient funding further decreases the possibilities for competition. This is especially so when associations are self-financing though membership fees. Additionally, it is also the case when their certification requires them to meet a certain threshold of members, in which case they will need to develop a considerable membership base. Only few consumer organisations or associations actually reach large numbers of membership.[442] Therefore, competition between different associations on a national level is, and will be, limited.

Competition on an international level is likely to be even less feasible. Organising an association that represents members located in different Member States is likely to be a very complex task. Moreover, it is envisaged certification requirements will be established through national law. Therefore, it seems that certified bodies, such as consumer associations or trade associations, are and shall remain, limited to representing the interests of national consumers or

---

440 *Ibidem*, 19.

441 Experience from the UK for example show, that the certification requirements can lead to very, very small numbers of certified bodies. In fact, in the UK, only one consumer association was certified to bring actions for damages before the CAT. See section B in Chapter 5.

442 Some Member States regulate a minimum member base for certain certifications. The UK consumer association *Which?* for example is one of the largest and most active in Europe and still only a small fraction of UK population is covered. Dayagi-Epstein, *Representation of Consumer Interest By Consumer Associations-Salvation for the Masses?* 209, 224 ff.

industries. Though there will be several associations within the European Union, competition amongst them will nevertheless be severely restricted. The prospect for competition between representative actions and collective actions also seems to be limited. As individuals will always retain the possibility to enforce their rights themselves, the filing of suit through an association seems not to foreclose the possibilities for individuals to opt-out, for example by leaving the association, and starting their own proceedings at a later stage.

Very important in this respect are the inadequate levels of self-interests that representative agents (associations or the lead plaintiff/lawyer duo) may have to initiate cases. This depends on how inducements for the agents are regulated. When associations in representative actions stand to gain from the litigation only indirectly, for example through increased popularity, possibly leading to a larger income in membership fees or subsidies in the future, the cases that associations will be willing to take and compete on are severely restricted. For opt-in collective actions, the stimulus for active competition is even less. When being the lead plaintiff is not connected to some additional benefits on top of receiving the individual damages awarded in court, it would be preferable for each potential lead plaintiff if someone else expends the effort.

Incentives to free ride on decisions by any competition authority can be assumed to remain significant, due to the complexity of competition cases. Limited budgets may well lead to a focus in the litigation efforts of both private individuals and associations, using the group litigation mechanism on follow-on actions. The proposed rules on the binding effects of competition authorities, the possible usage of prior judgements as evidence and the extended limitation periods facilitate the bringing of follow-on actions.[443] That in turn increases the incentives to free ride on public enforcement efforts rather than to initiate stand-alone cases.

It therefore is likely that free riding behaviour will remain significant and lead to a focus on follow-on rather than stand-alone actions. Even in such cases, however, the risk that only a fraction of these cases will be initiated seems to be high. Much depends on the approach the legislator will take on issues of the remuneration and incentive schemes for associations and lead plaintiffs or lawyers alike.

---

443 See proposals on Limitation periods, Binding effect of NCA decisions and indication of usage of prior judgements as evidence, European Commission, *White Paper on Damages actions for breach of the EC antitrust Rules COM(2008) 165final, SEC(2008) 404*, 8 f and 5f, and no. 225 at 68, respectively.

1.2. *Overcoming rational apathy*

Additionally, rational apathy on the side of the victims is likely to remain significant. While opt-in collective actions might enable the individual plaintiff to gain information about other similarly suited victims, the plaintiff initiating the suit remains uncertain about how many of the informed victims will decide to opt-in after being informed about the suit. Opting-in still requires efforts by the individual, who has to gather information and possibly also to provide evidence. Depending on the specifics of the case at hand, the rate of others opting-in may be very small. The initiating plaintiff then faces the risk of solely having to bear the costs of a litigation that is more complex, time consuming and expensive than a traditional trial. This is especially the case, when, in order to protect the interests of the represented claimants, similar regulation will be enacted as has been in a number of countries that already have experience with collective or class action mechanisms. With some variations, typical criteria for the admissibility of such class action proceedings include: numerousity of claimants; a preliminary investigation into the merits of the claims; commonality of claims; and, adequate representation.[444] All of these requirements make the proceeding more complex and costly for the initiating defendant, due to the fact that it has to be evaluated by court whether they are sufficiently met. Other issues increase the cost risk faced by the potential plaintiff as well. One issue is the costs that have to be incurred because of the nature of the proceedings as group litigation, such as the costs of notifying other victims. Also the rebuttable presumption of full pass-on of overcharges in price fixing cases, as proposed by the Commission, can have a negative effect on indirect purchaser claims. The information of passing-on rates is likely not to be in the hands of the defendants, but in the hand of the direct purchasers. As third party to the proceeding, these are more protected and would have to be heard in the event the defendants achieve a disclosure order.[445] That also complicates the procedure and therefore increases the costs faced by the potential plaintiff in case he loses and has to bear the costs of the proceedings.[446]

Of course, when a large number of claimants can be found and opt-in, the costs can then be split amongst a large number of participants. Therefore, individual costs will be reduced. Another possibility would be to let the costs be borne by professional litigation funders. However, such professional funders are likely to be more interested in cases with large values, this could be at risk if only few victims decide to opt-in, especially when the individual values of the claims are

444 Mulheron, *The class action in common law legal systems: a comparative perspective*, Portland: Hart publishing (2004), part 11.

445 European Commission, *Commission Staff Working Paper accompanying the White Paper on Damages actions for breach of the EC antitrust rules*, no. 122 f, 38.

446 As is common in the EU Member States, applying the British or European cost shifting rule.

low. Experience in the UK showed, that opt-in rates varied enormously.[447] This is likely to reduce the willingness of professional funders to invest before the opt-in stage has been completed. The named plaintiff and/or his lawyer might have better access to such third party funding when a sufficient number of victims have been contacted earlier and have declared their willingness to opt-in. That again can be a time consuming and expensive task. Another cost-adding factor may be the lawyer's fees. This will particularly be the case if they increase with the stakes in the proceeding, as they may do either because of the way lawyer's fees are regulated, or because the workload increases.

On the other hand, when the plaintiff pondering whether to initiate such a suit already has information about the number of other victims and their willingness to participate in the suit, the system might work well. However, in such cases where the number of victims is not too large, joinder procedures might also be feasible and the additional costs created by filing several claims[448] might be offset by the cost savings due to the less stringent requirement tests in a certification proceeding.

If the system is able to encourage a representative association to become active and bear the costs and risks on behalf of individual victims, then the problems related to the rational apathy of individuals causing them to refrain from filing a suit due to the possible financial risks may be reduced. Associations on the other hand may not have large incentives to become active from the outset. Detection and establishment of anti-competitive conduct is a difficult task. One way or another, associations would have to stand to gain from such activities, otherwise their level of activity may remain suboptimally low. This largely depends on the way they will be reimbursed for their services. However, such reimbursement schedules need to be designed very cautiously, as not to encourage abuse.

Overall, the rational apathy problem cannot be overcome efficiently through the mechanisms proposed by the European Commission. While the rational apathy of individual victims may be reduced when an agent becomes active representing them, the incentives for the possible agents to become active remain suboptimal with regard to the rational apathy concerning litigation.

447 As reported in Final Report for the Civil Justice Council, "'Improving Access to Justice through Collective Actions', Developing a More Efficient and Effective Procedure for Collective Actions," (2008), 100.

448 Which may even be avoided when the plaintiffs decide to assign their claims to one of them, who then would litigate all claims in one proceeding (joinder of claims).

1.3. *Asymmetric information*

As discussed above, asymmetric information problems can be an immense obstacle to litigation concerning the breach of competition law. In particular, end consumers harmed in large numbers, but on very small individual scales, are very likely to face these problems.

Surely, an opt-in collective action might make it possible for one aggrieved victim to inform others. Once the claim has been filed, notification of other victims has to take place in order to give them the opportunity to opt-in. Thereby, victims who might have been ignorant of the fact that they were harmed could be made aware, as well as becoming informed about the cause of their damages. Such systems would work best in cases where the lead plaintiff has the relevant information about harm, causes and potential other victims readily available. Such cases might arise in the context of exclusionary abuses or vertical restraints, for example. The contractual relationship or the failure to contract are obvious to the lead plaintiff, so the cause for the resulting harm is easily established. The lead plaintiff might also know other potential victims, those operating in the same market as the lead plaintiff. Even if the other victims for some reason are not in a position to recognise the harm and cause, the lead plaintiff can initiate proceedings and thereby inform others. Similarly, representative actions may cure the lack of information on the victims' side, once they have detected an infringement and started proceeding.

However, the question remains how these patrons, be it individuals or associations, will be encouraged to overcome the asymmetric information problems they are facing. In cases where the information about the infringement is easily obtainable, for example in cases of vertical restraints or refusal to deal, the problem is less significant. Typically, the number of aggrieved victims is relatively small and the information of the harm and its cause is transmitted directly from the infringer to the victim. However, in such cases the added value of utilising a group litigation mechanism compared to traditional individual litigation or joinder procedures may also be limited. That is because the problem of asymmetric information, one of the major obstacles to be overcome, is limited by nature, so that there is less need for a group litigation mechanism. Especially, when the lead plaintiff is in a similar position as the rest of the group, so that actually all members would have virtually equal access to information and resources. Such cases may arise in vertical restrictions with contractual limitations on the retailer, for example.

The problem of asymmetric information is much larger in the case of covert infringements causing losses to a large number of victims, who might remain unaware of the harm and its cause. In such cases, the potential for group litigation mechanisms to install agents acting on behalf of victims that are in a better position to overcome the lack of information is largest. However, these agents will have to be adequately incentivised, and it is questionable whether the proposed representative action or the collective action is going to have such effects on lawyers, potential lead plaintiffs, or associations. The lead plaintiff, initiating a collective opt-in action can only start proceeding once he has been harmed and is aware of the amount of harm and the causes. Lawyers and associations however, will typically not be harmed themselves. For these agents, the information asymmetry is at least as large, if not larger in some cases, than for the individual victims. The comparative advantage these agents can have over the individual victims arises in their specialisation into overcoming these information asymmetries that is possible on their side. In order to overcome these asymmetries, incentives will be needed to give the agents a personal benefit from curing the lack of information. Detection of competition law infringements is a complex task, which typically requires more knowledge and resources than, for example, a case concerning product liability or disputes with travel agencies. It is questionable, whether hourly fee arrangements for lawyers or the prospective larger membership base for associations will grant sufficient benefits for these agents to become active in solving the considerably large information problem. Moreover, lawyers in many Member States are prohibited from advertising, so that their possibilities to contact potential victims are severely inhibited. Under the current proposals discussed here, the question of how to adequately incentivise associations has not been addressed.

Of course, in follow-on actions, much of the missing information regarding the law violation and the infringing parties will be made available by the public authorities. If private actions for damages will only take place in such cases, the proposed group litigation mechanisms add little to remedy the remaining problems of asymmetric information. The question in such cases remains, who will be aware of this discovered and published information and who stands to gain sufficiently enough to act on that information.

Overall, the problems of asymmetric information remain significant. The group litigation mechanism, as proposed, grants few incentives to overcome that problem. When drafting the regulations concerning group litigation mechanisms, Member States should pay attention to the question of incentives. This question has not been dealt with sufficiently thus far. Both associations and individuals will still have great incentives to limit their activity in bringing stand-alone actions to only those cases where information asymmetry is not present to any significant extent, evidence is easily acquired and the illegality of the conduct is quite unambiguous. In short, to cases where obstacles also to traditional individual litigation are very small. Stand-alone actions therefore will only take place in a limited number of cases, most likely those where the problem of asymmetric information is small from the outset. Therefore, the effect of these measures on detection rates of infringements is likely to remain extremely limited.

1.4. Principal-agent problems

In opt-in collective actions, principal-agent problems between the victims and the legal representative, the lawyer, could increase slightly compared to the individual client-lawyer relationship as it exists in individual trials. The less those victims that opt-in are involved in the process, the less influence they can exert on the lawyer. It could happen that only the lead-plaintiff has an impact on the way the case is handled. This very much depends on how exactly the opt-in collective action is going to be designed. When victims are not parties in the proceedings themselves, but are also bound by settlement decisions taken by the lead plaintiff/lawyer duo, principal-agent problems could be more severe than when victims are involved in the proceeding and can decide upon settlement offers themselves. The lead plaintiff himself may not be adequately trained to monitor and assess the lawyer's conduct. Even if the lead plaintiff is a sophisticated client, the mere requirement of similarity of claims to be bundled into one proceeding cannot guarantee that the lead plaintiff will have exactly the same preferences as other victims in the collective action. Attitudes towards risk as well as the nature and importance of the relationship between the plaintiffs and the defendant(s) can differ. For example, some victims may have made specific investments in reliance of their relationship with the defendant and depend heavily on the business relationship with the defendant, meanwhile others may have sufficient alternatives. On top of this, the lawyer himself may have interests that slightly differ from those of the group. The fee schedule may have an important role in that respect.[449] Regardless of the way the fee system is construed, it is the lawyer putting effort into the case. He therefore has to evaluate the reimbursement he obtains for expending these efforts also with regard to possible alternative uses of his resources and their reimbursement.

Similar problems between association and represented victims may persist in the case of representative actions. Though the association is probably a more sophisticated client in the lawyer-client relationship than individual plaintiffs the association may nevertheless pursue its own interests by initiating a certain case, which may or may not coincide with the interests of those represented. Here, it is the association that bears the risks and costs of the proceeding, and on top of that, possibly the costs of distributing any damages awards. Limited budgets would compel associations to choose between different cases and their

449 See Chapter 3, 2.2.1.5 for a more detailed discussion.

efforts and persistence in pursuing them. These choices can be influenced by various factors such as the media attention connected to certain but not other cases, the possibilities to make use of professional litigation funders, the number of members affected, or the degree of harm caused.

These problems have been analysed above[450] and in the legal and economic literature to a great extent. The requirement of representativeness of the lead plaintiff is one of the elements considered as capable of mitigating against these problems. Therefore, it has been applied in many countries that have introduced collective actions. It has to be noted that there will always be a conflict between the goal of securing the representativeness of the lead plaintiff and the effectiveness of group litigation mechanisms. As has been the experience in the UK[451] with the representative rule under the Civil Procedure Rule,[452] the introduction of too narrow a definition of required "same interest" can render the procedure ineffective. Moreover, that requirement alone will not solve the problem sufficiently and will be irrelevant in the case of representative actions. Other solutions discussed to solve the problem in both collective and representative actions include: judicial review of settlements and lawyers fees, or even auctioning the action or rights to represent. However, the European Commission has only foreseen mechanisms to facilitate settlements, but no solutions to the principal-agent problem have been proposed.

More important than principal-agent problems between the representing parties and individual victims from a deterrence point of view, however, is the principal-agent relationship between society and the active parties. Society would prefer resources to be spent on deterring those infringements that cause the largest total losses to society. The agents however may prefer to concentrate their activities on other sets of cases, for example cases where the facts are clear and evidence is easily obtainable, or, due to the specific construction of the group litigation mechanisms, where identification and notification of victims is a simple task and therefore less costly. Society might also prefer investment be made into the pursuit of stand-alone cases, especially when increasing detection would lead to larger deterrence effects as the increase in sanction may have,[453] whereas the agents are likely to prefer follow-on actions to save on costs. All these principal–agent problems relate to the different incentives of private parties to sue, compared to the social optimum.

---

450 See Chapter 3.

451 Final Report for the Civil Justice Council, "'Improving Access to Justice through Collective Actions', Developing a More Efficient and Effective Procedure for Collective Actions," (2008), 70 ff.

452 See Chapter 5, under section B.1.

453 As is suggested by the availability bias as researched in the behavioural economics, sociology and criminology.

The designs of the proposed group litigation mechanisms are constructed with the main aim of compensating victims. Therefore, the prior discussed conflicting interests between society and agents concerning deterrence effects are less relevant. However, the conflicts between victims and their representatives will remain unsolved also when compensation for victims is pursued. If Member States have to implement these group litigation mechanisms, they should incorporate possible solutions to mitigate principal-agent problems, because these are likely to be even more severe when the aim is that of deterrence.

2. REACHING THE OPTIMAL SANCTION

Establishing a system that includes the losses of all victims will coincide with the goal of establishing the total harm caused to society by an antitrust-infringement, as basis for the optimal sanction. However, the optimal sanction may never be achieved in the proposed systems. This is not only because that amount will still have to be adjusted for the low probability of detection and conviction. In this section, a closer look is taken at the potential of the proposed mechanisms to reach the optimal sanction.

With regard to the amount of damages, several issues become relevant: whether aggregate damages may be sued for and awarded to the group as a whole, how damages are to be calculated, whether exemplary damages will be used, and how many individual damages will be included in the proceeding.

The first issue is the question as to what kind of damages are going to be awarded. On the one hand, the Commission states that victims should not receive more than the total actual harm.[454] According to the ECJ[455] this includes both actual loss (*damnum emergens*) and lost profits (*lucrum cessans*). Additionally, damage amounts awarded in group litigation actions should "correspond to the harm suffered by those included or represented".[456] This would require total damages to be established on the basis only of the harm caused to those victims represented and sufficient proof of these damages in order to avoid over- or under-compensation, which would exclude some of the victims harmed by the infringement.

---

454 European Commission, *Commission Staff Working Document, Accompanying document to the White Paper on Damages actions for breach of the EC antitrust rules, Impact Assessment, {COM (2008) 165 final} {SEC(2008) 404} {SEC(2008) 406}*, 23.

455 European Court of Justice, *Cases C-295/04 to C-298/04 Vincenzo Manfredi and Others v. Lloyd Adriatico Assicurazioni SpA and Others ECR I-6619*, no. 95.

456 European Commission, *Commission Staff Working Paper accompanying the White Paper on Damages actions for breach of the EC antitrust rules*, 21.

On the other hand, the Commission also recognises that there are no Community principles prohibiting victims from receiving more than their actual damages, even if it may constitute an unjust enrichment.[457] On the contrary, the Commission stresses the point that in the *Manfredi* judgement the ECJ dealt with damages awarded in excess of actual damages suffered in an "enabling"[458] way. It is also acknowledged that victims might need further incentives than mere compensation of actual harm in order to bring action for damages, so that the Commission foresees changes in the definition of damages if experience should show a need for such additional incentives.[459] These deliberations are a departure from the principle of just and full compensation of individual harm, which would be welcomed from a deterrence perspective.

Apart from the discussion of whether supra-compensatory damage awards could be available in cases of competition law infringements or not, a second issue relates to the calculation of damages. That also has an impact on whether victims will receive full, and not more than, compensation for the factual loss suffered and naturally also on the degree of deterrence effects. In that respect, the Commission again argues that the requirement of precise quantification of the amount of harm suffered may not stand in the way of awarding damages, due to the principle of effectiveness.[460] It is submitted that calculating damages in a way to neither under- nor over-compensate victims may be "arguably a practically impossible or excessively difficult" exercise.[461] For such reasons, the Commission considers simplifying the calculation of harm in accordance with the legal principle of *ex aequo et bono* (according to the right and good). The explicitly proposed options include: an *a priori* assumption of harm in price fixing cases as that of average overcharges;[462] the rebuttable assumption that damages were fully passed-on to indirect purchaser plaintiffs;[463] and the illegal gain as basis for calculating the damage in those cases where the exact calculation of harm would be too complex, for example in representative actions, where the victims neither need to be identified, nor be directly compensated.[464] From a deterrence perspective, any approximation mechanism can lead to both over- and under-compensation of individual victims, as well as to under-deterrence for some cases and over-deterrence for others, since the sanction has no systematic relation to the harm caused.[465]

---

457 *Ibidem*, 57 f.
458 *Ibidem*, no. 191, 58.
459 *Ibidem*, no. 195, 59.
460 *Ibidem*, no. 197, 60.
461 *Ibidem*, no. 198, 60.
462 *Ibidem*, no. 200, 60.
463 *Ibidem*, no. 219, 66.
464 *Ibidem*, no. 194, 59.
465 See the discussion on the optimal sanction in chapter 2 section C.

Whether punitive damages are available or not, as long as damages are based on individual harm, opt-in collective actions will increase the potential sanction faced by infringers only in as much as it encourages those plaintiffs to become active or involved who otherwise would have remained silent, for example due to rational apathy or asymmetric information problems. The same is true for representative actions where the number of victims represented depends on membership. Associations will in many cases only represent a sub-group of all harmed individuals. However, as opt-in or membership based mechanisms are likely to lead to less than full participation of all potential claimants, the amount of damages, when calculated only on basis of the harm done to those that opt-in, will also remain too low to efficiently deter. This is true even in those cases where all aggrieved parties will opt-in, since other types of losses, for example those caused by the dead weight loss, will still not be recoverable.

A further difficulty related to the amount of damages awarded relates to the concept of passing-on defence in direct purchaser claims and the rebuttable presumption of full passing on of overcharges in the case of end consumer claims. This is discussed in more detail below. These rebuttable assumptions entail the risk of the same damages being claimed by different plaintiffs in parallel or subsequent proceedings. The Commission encourages national courts to take measures to prevent any "under or overcompensation"[466] in such cases. In some cases, the passing-on defence will be a fairly simple mechanism to apply, for example in cases where cost-plus contracts or other forms of fixed mark up contracts exist between the direct purchaser and the original seller. There, the passing-on is easily established and is likely to be invoked by the defendant. In other cases, however, this may not be the case. From a deterrence perspective, the potential double compensation of harm is not very problematic in itself. Any doubling of damage awards would, in the deterrence model, equal actual harm and a probability of detection and conviction of 50 percent, which is very high. However, these measures could also have a negative impact on other issues, which will be discussed below.[467] Moreover, there will be no legal certainty and no systematic relationship between harm caused, probability of detection, and the sanction imposed. This reduces the deterrent effect of "double damages" and may distort the potential infringers decisions ex ante.

Another problem might arise with regard to the proposed assumptions on passing-on rates. Under the proposed regimes, defendants and direct purchasers might have incentives to collude to the detriment of indirect purchasers. A defendant facing subsequent actions for damages, one brought by direct

466 *Ibidem*, no. 128, 69.
467 See directly below.

purchasers and another by indirect purchasers, might try to collude with the direct purchasers. This will be an especially attractive option when the judgement in that case is either directly binding or can be used as evidence in the rebuttal of the assumption of full passing-on in the claim of indirect purchasers. Both, defendants and direct purchasers, will have incentives to reach a verdict stating that there was no passing-on. The defendant then will be able to rebut the presumption favouring the indirect purchasers in subsequent indirect purchaser claims. If plaintiffs then are unable to rebut the rebuttal, the defendant can save additional costs of litigation and possible exposure to media attention. For the direct purchaser, this outcome amounts to enrichment in the amount of the actual passed on overcharges. This additional profit could be, of course indirectly and hidden, be split between defendant and direct purchaser. This would decrease any deterrence effect of the proposed mechanisms. On top of that, the loosing parties would be the very ones the Commission tries to favour – the end consumer. A solution to this risk would be to exclude prior judgments as either binding or as *prima facie* evidence. However, that again would jeopardise some of the major aims of the reform, including facilitating access to evidence, procedural efficiency and legal consistency.

In summary, the optimal sanction will most likely not be reached. The awarded damages under the proposed systems risk remaining insufficiently low for several reasons. These include: the lack of adjustment of the damages for the probability of detection; the related issue of unavailability of exemplary damages; the requirement to base the calculation of damages on the individual harm suffered and proven; and the necessity to avoid overcompensation. However, much depends on the way damages are to be calculated in the end and the mechanisms the courts will apply to avoid double indemnification of a particular harm. Unless a different way to assess damages is introduced which captures the missing parts of the optimal sanction, i.e., the deadweight loss and the adjustment for the probability of being caught and convicted, the non-participating victims and the probability of detection, the amount of damages will not reach optimal deterrence levels. This is particularly true for stand-alone actions. In case of follow-on actions, the sanction includes the fine imposed in the preceding public proceeding and the amount of damages awarded in the follow-on action. The optimal sanction could nevertheless only be reached in a fraction of cases, if at all, and only by coincidence.

3. MINIMISATION OF COSTS

In general, the costs imposed on society are likely to increase under a group litigation system. A proclaimed cost saving found in the comparison of the procedural costs under group litigation and individual procedures initiated by all group members relies on the assumption that all victims would have initiated individual claims absent the group proceeding. However, this will seldom be the case, especially since the reform is based on the finding that hardly any cases have been brought.[468] Therefore, when more cases are brought before the courts due to infringement of competition law, also the system costs will rise.[469] Apart from that, the reform will also have an impact on other costs. These will be discussed in this section. The minimisation of costs incorporates several issues. The first relates to the costs imposed on society through abuses of the system. These costs will be discussed in the first part. The second part will analyse the potential to reach procedural efficiency with the proposed mechanisms. A last factor, which could also be classified as costs imposed on society includes the negative impacts the envisioned system may have on the efficiency of leniency programs.

3.1. Minimising the risk of nuisance suits

Abuse of the possibility to litigate could impose large costs on society. Some cases could be brought with the sole aim to extract a settlement, others with the aim to increase the defendant's costs.

Taking into account that the outcome of a trial might not always be certain, potential defendants face a large risk when threatened with a trial, even if the estimated chances of winning the case are large. The costs faced when the judgement does turn out to be in favour of the plaintiffs can be enormous. This encourages settlement of cases, even if the probability of winning the case is relatively large, i.e., when the plaintiffs' case has relatively little merits. In addition, the concept of joint liability puts a lot of pressure on the party being the defendant. In cases of several firms being jointly responsible for a breach of competition law, for example in cartel cases, the plaintiffs can choose one of the defendants and claim the total damages from him. The defendant can then, at a later stage, take redress from his partners. However, this will entail further costly proceedings and also includes the risk that some of the other parties may be judgement proof, leaving the main defendant with the costs of paying the damage awards.

---

468 See the results of the Ashurst Study.Waelbroeck, *Study on the Conditions for Claims for Damages in Case of Infringement of EC Competition Rules: Comparative Report, Open Procedure COMP/2003/A1/22, Ashurst Study for Directorate General Competition of the EU Commission*, London, England.

469 Unless the courts so far have been paid, but without having enough work load. In that case, when the work load increases but no further working hours or other costs have to be paid, the costs will remain the same. However, that seems to be fairly unlikely.

The risk of unmeritous suits being brought by or on behalf of end consumers is likely to be only marginally influenced through the introduction of opt-in collective actions in the way envisioned. Cases with little or no merit are strongest when the group of represented victims is large. Also media attention can have an impact. Larger media attention can damage the defendant(s) reputation to a larger degree. Compared to individual litigation, both threats are more credible in an opt-in collective action. However, proceedings initiated by one of the victims might not result in a great number of others opting-in. The represented group is subject to the risk of remaining relatively small. Under such circumstances, media attention given to the potential case might be limited as well. Similar effects arise with regard to representative actions brought by associations, with the variation that associations through representative actions might be able to put more pressure on the defendant than individuals can in a collective action. Associations can represent larger groups and have a large advantage with regard to generating publicity over individuals.

As all group litigation mechanisms are supposed to be complements, the defendant(s) might still fear any publicity concerning a potentially illegal conduct, as other group litigations, or their threat, might follow, and therefore be willing to settle quickly. The Commission opposed the introduction of very low discovery thresholds as well as a shift of burden of proof, as it recognised the related potential for abuse.[470] As alternative, the Commission proposed a minimum level *inter partes* disclosure,[471] subject to a careful proportionality test balancing the interest of defendants and plaintiffs.[472] However, the envisioned facilitation of access to evidence may still enable plaintiffs to threaten defendants with a costly disclosure procedure. The detailed proposal by the Commission reads:

> *"As a minimum standard of disclosure in actions for antitrust damages, national courts should under specific conditions have the power to order disclosure inter partes of precise categories of information or evidence relevant to the claim.*
> *Conditions for a disclosure order in actions for antitrust damages should include that (a) the claimant has asserted all the facts and offered all those means of evidence that are reasonably known and available to him, provided that they show plausible grounds to suspect that he suffered harm through the infringement of competition rules by the defendant; (b) he has shown to the satisfaction of the court that he is unable, applying all efforts that can reasonably be expected, to assert the specific facts or to produce the evidence for which disclosure is envisaged; (c) he has specified sufficiently precise categories of information or evidence to be disclosed, and (d) the court is satisfied that*

470 European Commission, *Commission Staff Working Paper accompanying the White Paper on Damages actions for breach of the EC antitrust rules*, no. 91 f, 29 f.
471 *Ibidem*, nr. 93 f, 30 f.
472 *Ibidem*, nr. 100–109, 31 f.

the envisaged disclosure measure is relevant to the case as well as necessary and proportional in scope."[473]

Much will depend on the courts' definitions of what can be "reasonably expected" of the plaintiff and what "sufficiently precise specification of categories of information" is. With regard to that, however, the Commission states that "the claimant cannot be expected to demonstrate any elevated degree of probability that his claim is funded".[474] Especially in stand-alone litigation, courts may take that severe limitation on the plaintiffs' side into account, thereby possibly encouraging cases to be brought despite their having limited merits. Then there is scope for abusive claims, brought in order to extract a settlement offer from defendants that wish to avoid relatively broad discovery orders issued by the court. Severe sanctioning of the non disclosure of requested evidence and new mechanisms to preserve evidence, through regulations enabling public or private seizure could further boost the pressure on defendants to avoid the discovery stage.

The same is true for the presumption of full passing-on in indirect purchasers' claims, which the defendant must rebut. This rebuttal would probably require him to ask for a disclosure order against the indirect purchasers, which are the parties most likely to be in possession of the relevant evidence. As third parties, however, these are more protected than the direct parties to the proceeding,[475] which increases the risk that the defendant may not be able to rebut the assumption and even if, only at larger costs.

A general reduction of court fees and the proposed introduction of special cost rules that would alleviate the plaintiff from having to bear the defendants costs if the action was unsuccessful would make bringing cases with little merits or "blackmail suits" more profitable in general as well.[476]

The Commission also encourages the Member States to create settlement mechanisms to reduce costs. If there is an incentive for defendants and direct purchasers to collude as described above,[477] then the parties could pursue a judgement when settlements would not provide evidence to be used by the defendant in a subsequent claim brought by indirect purchasers. That would make the envisioned settlement mechanisms unattractive to the parties and reduce the number of settled cases.

---

473 *Ibidem*, nr. 109, 34.
474 *Ibidem*, nr. 102, p. 32.
475 *Ibidem*, no. 122 f, 38.
476 *Ibidem*, no. 261 f, 79.
477 See section on the sanction above.

The undifferentiated approach to actions for damages, which fails to distinguish between the different types of infringements and different types of victims, might also increase the possibilities for competitors to strategically abuse the judicial system. The "competitor plaintiff" has substantial motivation to initiate also cases with low merits, to protect himself from competitive pressure, and/or to raise his rivals' costs. Civil litigation cases concerning vertical restraints or abuse of dominant position may, contrary to the findings of the Ashurst Study[478] already be being widely used by (more or less) aggrieved companies. At least, the German Federal Competition Authority contradicted the Ashurst Study by pointing out that in Germany in the year 2004 alone, 240 cases applying competition law rules were brought by companies. In 174 of these companies were using competition law as a shield, for example claiming nullity of anti-competitive contracts.[479] This could be argued to demonstrate that the obstacles for companies against using competition law when it is to their advantage are not as large as may have been suspected. Any facilitation of private claims for damages increases the risk that firms will take advantage of these possibilities where possible. The added value of group litigation mechanisms in cases where the group of aggrieved parties is very small and necessary data is readily available then has to be weighed against the increased risk of abuses in such cases.

Summarising, the proposed group litigation mechanisms have the potential to increase the scope for abusive claims from the plaintiffs' side compared to the traditional two-party proceedings. Taken as a whole, however, the proposals in the White Paper are likely to increase the incentives to file unmeritous suits only to a small degree when enacted. That fact might be contributed less to the efficiency of the system and more to the system inherent preference of victims and representatives to focus on follow-on actions rather than stand-alone cases.

3.2. *Reaching procedural efficiency*

Procedural efficiency relates to the potentials of group litigation mechanisms to reduce the cost of proceedings compared to several individual litigations, from a society point of view. Bundling several claims into one procedure allows for the realisation of economies of scale, for example with regard to the costs of court or legal representatives. In addition, costs for the individual plaintiff can be reduced when these are split amongst a number of claimants and the defendant can also

---

478 Ashurst Study, Waelbroeck, *Study on the Conditions for Claims for Damages in Case of Infringement of EC Competition Rules: Comparative Report, Open Procedure COMP/2003/A1/22, Ashurst Study for Directorate General Competition of the EU Commission*, London, England.

479 Bundeskartellamt, "Private Kartellrechtsdurchsetzung, Stand, Probleme, Perspektiven – Diskussionspapier," (2005), 4. Available at: www.bundeskartellamt.de/wDeutsch/download/pdf/Diskussionsbeitraege/05_Proftag.pdf.

save on costs when defence has only to take place once for all claims. However, the full potential for that procedural efficiency will not be reached through the proposed mechanisms for several reasons.

The proposed devices to foster actions for damages in cases of infringements of Article 101 and Article 102 TFEU will apply to "any individual",[480] including indirect purchasers. The Commission therefore decided not to follow proposals to limit standing in actions for damages to direct purchasers. Theoretically, that would open the door to the possibility to include all victims of breaches of competition law in one group litigation, thereby reaching the greatest procedural efficiency. However, the specific design of the proposed group litigations will not allow for that possibility to be realised in practice.

Opt-in collective or representative actions allow for the realisation of some economies of scale in the judicial process, compared to several individual cases. Although the action itself may be more expensive than one individual trial, the sum of several individual trials held otherwise could outweigh these costs. However, these improvements compared to traditional means of litigation will presumably be relatively small. This is because an opt-in collective action is generally more attractive for plaintiffs in cases where the group of victims is small and the facts of the case are quite clear, as identification of victims and individual harms are less complex in these cases.[481]

In representative actions brought by associations on behalf of their members, the group of represented parties will also fall short of encompassing all victims in most cases. Some victims can never fulfil the requirement of proving their damages, some victims may have interests converse to those represented by the association, and not all victims with similar or identical interest might be members of the association in question. Several associations can represent several subgroups of victims. For example, indirect purchaser and direct purchaser could never be included into one group, as the former are granted the rebuttable assumption that all overcharges were fully passed on,[482] which runs exactly counter of the claims the direct purchasers would bring. This requirement *de facto* excludes direct purchaser and indirect purchaser claims being brought in the same proceeding.

480 In line with ECJ *Courage* and *Manfredi*, see European Commission, *Commission Staff Working Paper accompanying the White Paper on Damages actions for breach of the EC antitrust rules*, 15, 61.

481 Unless adequately remunerated for their efforts, also lawyers will have little incentives to step in and become active. See discussion in Chapter 3 and above, and the problems in Germany with the KapMuG, discussed in Chapter 5.

482 European Commission, *White Paper on Damages actions for breach of the EC antitrust Rules COM(2008) 165 final, SEC(2008) 404*, 8.

The concept of several group litigation mechanisms and individual trials as complements further reduces the economies of scale that can be realised. Incentives to free ride on prior decisions could lead to several trials even if all victims could theoretically be included in one proceeding. In theory, courts would be able to consolidate parallel actions brought by or on behalf of plaintiffs at different stages of the distribution chain, if several actions are brought simultaneously. However, the burden on the courts may become immense in such cases. The reason for this is the solution the Commission proposed with regard to passing-on of overcharges, which will make it unfeasible to include all victims in one proceeding. Moreover, it will be in the interests of parties not to bring suits simultaneously in order to be able to free ride on the efforts of another party.

The Commission did not follow proposals of commentators on the Green Paper that advocated a prohibition on the passing-on defence.[483] Therefore, defendants can rebut the harm as calculated by direct purchasers, if part of that harm has been passed on. Evidence necessary to prove and calculate the amount of passing-on will typically be in the hands of the direct purchasers, but may be extracted by court order in the proceeding. On the other hand, the Commission opts for a rebuttable presumption of full passing-on of overcharges in cases brought by indirect purchasers. Again, the evidence needed by the defendant is likely to be in the hand of direct purchasers, not parties to the proceeding. Standards regarding the disclosure order in these cases are set higher and the third parties would have a right to be heard in the proceeding.[484] This adds to the complexity of the proceeding in general and the costs of the proceeding for the defendants in particular. If separate actions could be joined into one in which direct as well as indirect purchasers claim to have suffered the full amount of passing-on, the proposed solution seems to be to leave it for the court to establish who actually suffered which part of the harm.[485] Under such conflicting interests of the parties, however, it seems unlikely that it would be possible to join actions under national laws requiring a certain similarity or alignment of claims.

Overall, procedural efficiency is not realised to the full extent that is theoretically possible. Not all victims can be included in just one proceeding, and the complementary nature of all proposed group litigation mechanisms and the

483 See for example:Bulst, "(Comments on the Green Paper) Damages Actions for breach of EC Antitrust Rules," (2006) 3 f; The European Consumers' Association (BEUC), "Damages Actions for breach of EC anti-trust rules: BEUC position on the Commission`s Green Paper," (2006), 5 f; Max Planck Institute for Intellectual Property, Competition and Tax Law, "Comments of the Max Planck Institute for Intellectual Property, Competition and Tax Law (Munich) on the DC Competition Green Paper of December 2005," (2006), 2.

484 European Commission, *Commission Staff Working Paper accompanying the White Paper on Damages actions for breach of the EC antitrust rules*, no. 122 f, 38.

485 *Ibidem*, no. 222, 68.

traditional ways of redress, can lead to a number of proceedings arising from the same infringement. The procedure will become more complex, not only because of any safeguards installed related to the certification of group litigation, but also because the courts are advised to avoid double jeopardy for the defendant concerning the particular harm caused. Depending on the mechanisms designed to avoid such problems, overall procedural efficiency may be even more severely hampered.

3.3. *Interaction with leniency programs*

The Commission has recognised the need to investigate the effects of private actions for damages on public leniency programs. In the White Paper, protection of leniency applicants is only granted with regard to the disclosure or reproduction of information submitted to public authorities in the application process for immunity.[486] Further considerations concerning the limitation of civil liability of the applicants *vis-à-vis* the victims or with regard to joint liability are discussed, but no definite proposal is given yet.

The evidence provided by the leniency applicant will be protected, but the decision taken by the authority will have binding effect. Therefore, evidence concerning the illegality of the conduct is not necessary in a follow-on group litigation. The leniency applicant therefore still risks being held liable, under the joint liability approach, for all the harm caused, not only to his direct contract partners but also to plaintiffs. This is likely to have a negative impact on the willingness of infringers to come forward and apply for leniency. As the leniency programs have been considered successful in destabilising cartels, the deterrence effect of leniency programs will be reduced. It is questionable, whether the increased litigation for damages can compensate these losses to society efficiently.

4. CONCLUSION

The proposal of the European Commission fails to realise all the potential group litigation mechanisms could have with regard to deterrence. In their proposals, free riding behaviour between different agents is not completely eliminated and large incentives to free ride on prior public investments in investigation and prosecution remain. The problem of asymmetric information also remains significant with regard to opt-in collective actions. In cases, where lack of information is most prominent, opt-in collective actions will most likely be

486 European Commission, *White Paper on Damages actions for breach of the EC antitrust Rules COM(2008) 165 final, SEC(2008) 404*, no. 285 f, 84 f.

seldom used. In such cases, representative actions might have more potential to overcome these problems, however the incentives for the representative agents may be insufficient to realise these potentials. The amount of sanction necessary to efficiently deter anti-competitive behaviour can hardly be reached. The focus on compensating individual harm severely hinders possibilities to adjust damages awards accordingly. Principal-agent problems are not solved satisfactorily. The optimal behaviour from a total social welfare point of view does not coincide with the incentives schemes created for the agents and the victims. In addition, principal-agent problems between agents and victims will remain. The risk of unmeritous suits is not severely increased, just as the incentives to sue in general are not. Finally yet importantly, one of the most prominent potentials of group litigation mechanisms, procedural efficiency, is not realised to its full extent.

Overall, the proposed mechanisms are not designed to efficiently increase deterrence in any meaningful way. This may be justified by legal restraints as they exist and the desire to necessitate as little change in the existing legal systems of the Member States as possible.[487] Another justification may be the pursuit of goals other than deterrence. Then the question remains, whether these other goals the Commission is pursuing will be reached sufficiently to offset the costs of failure to enhance deterrence and the costs brought about by the introduction of these mechanisms.

C. LEGAL OBSTACLES CREATED BY TORT LAW AND OTHER AREAS OF LAW

In addition to the pursuit of differing goals, the legal limitations that currently exist in the Member States of the European Union may provide justification for the European Commission's deviation from the optimal group litigation structure. First, legal rules as commonly found in the Member States may make it impossible to achieve the optimal sanction in actions for damages. Second, there might be constitutional and other restraints on the possibility to introduce mandatory affiliation to the group of represented victims and possibly even opt-out solutions. Third, regulations and general concepts of legal systems can inhibit the possibilities to grant enforcement agents part of or even the total of damage

---

487 It may also be considered to be too costly to change specific regulations. This could be framed as harmonisation costs, which will not be explicitly discussed here. For a detailed analysis of the harmonisation costs with regard to the main features of private enforcement of competition law see Renda, *Making antitrust damages actions in the EU more effective. Study in support of the impact assessment of the EC White Paper on antitrust damages actions*, incorporating these costs.

awards in order to grant incentives to engage in detection and/or litigation. These three issues will be discussed in this section.[488]

This section draws on, *inter alia*, the national comments on the White Paper of several Member States, literature of a legal comparative nature, as well as on the consensus reached and ideas developed by the European Group on Tort Law.

1. LIMITATIONS CONCERNING THE OPTIMAL SANCTION

In order to reach the optimal sanction, damages have to be calculated in a more abstract way than the sum of exact individual losses as proven in court. They also will have to be amended by punitive or exemplary damages of some sort. This may be in conflict with long standing legal traditions in many Member States.

The general principle in most Member States still remains that of exact damages. A general and widely applied principle of tort law is that of *restitutio ad integrum*.[489] The basic idea is to restore the victim to the position he would have been in had the damaging event never occurred, in as far as monetary compensation can achieve that. The focus therefore in most Member States is on the injury suffered by the victims. Consequently, harm is typically established according to the (in German) so called *Differenzmethode*, which is the difference between state the victim finds itself in after the event and the state victim would be in had the event not occurred.[490] Thus, damages have to be substantiated and proven on an individual basis, even when bundling measures are used.[491]

488 Without claiming completeness.

489 Office of Fair Trading, *Private actions in competition law: effective redress for consumers and business, OFT Discussion Paper 916*, 7; Comparing UK and France, noting the general principle is restitutio ad integrum: Hill, "Litigation and Negligence: A Comparative Study," *Oxford Journal of Legal Studies* 6 (1986): 183; Quarta, "Recognition and Enforcement of US Punitive Damages Awards in Continental Europe: The Italian Supreme Court's Veto," *Hastings International and Comparative Law Review* 31 (2008): 753; Magnus, *Unification of tort law: Damages, Principles of European Tort Law*, 188.; Renda, *Making antitrust damages actions in the EU more effective. Study in support of the impact assessment of the EC White Paper on antitrust damages actions*, 236; European Group on Tort Law, *Principles of European tort law: text and commentary*, Wein, New York: Springer (2005), Article 10:101.

490 See Clark et al, "Study on the conditions of claims for damages in case of infringement of EC competition rules-Analysis of economic models for the calculation of damages," (2004). Available at: http://ec.europa.eu/competition/antitrust/actionsdamages/economic_clean_en.pdf; European Group on Tort Law, *Principles of European tort law: text and commentary*, Article 2:101.

491 Federal Ministry of Economics and Technology, et al, "Comments of the Federal Ministry of Economics and Technology, the Federal Ministry of Justice, the Federal Ministry of Food, Agriculture and Consumer Protection and the Bundeskartellamt on the EU Commission's White Paper on "Damages actions for breach of the EC antitrust rules," (2008), 5. Deutscher Bundesrat, "Comments of the German Federal Council (Stellungnahme des Deutschen

Therefore, a plaintiff has to substantiate his claim that he incurred damages as a general rule.

Where this kind of evidence is necessary, harm caused to some types of victims by anti-competitive behaviour may never be considered. These are the victims, for example, that would have gained consumer surplus by an exchange with the offender, had he offered his products at competitive prices. However, where general provisions allow a deviation from the general principles that a specific form of proof for the harm caused has to be provided, it might be possible to also include these victims. Such exemptions are described, for example, as general principles by the European Group on Tort Law, in cases where providing sufficient proof would be too difficult or too costly.[492] European Member States have similar regulations in place that allow a separation of the individual amount of harm suffered and the granted damage awards.[493]

While the idea of an abstract calculation of damages seems to be obviously in conflict with principles of just compensation applied in the Member States, it may not be as clear-cut in every and all cases. In fact, some Member States already allow more abstract definitions of damages in some specific instances. Provisions that allow for the disgorgement of (illegally gained) profits are an exception from the general principle of strictly harm based damage awards.[494] Under such regulations, the awards granted to the plaintiff are in fact not connected to the actual damages suffered. However, the proceeds of such proceedings do not always flow to the plaintiff. Under some regulations, the disgorged profits go to the Treasury, while the plaintiff can only expect to be reimbursed for his costs.[495] A few examples may suffice here. Establishing the illegal gain is recognised as a way to calculate the harm caused, for example in Par. 97 I UrhG (*Copyright Act*) Germany, and under the concept of restitutionary damages in the UK. In Hungary, even a legal presumption concerning the

Bundesrats) (2008), BR-Drucksache 248/08," (2008), 4. Both sources available at; http://ec.europa.eu/comm/competition/antitrust/actionsdamages/white_paper_comments.html.

492 European Group on Tort Law, *Principles of European tort law: text and commentary*, Article 2:105. Such deliberations also led the European Commission to issue a call for a tender to conduct a study on quantification methods for damages caused by competition law infringements, see http://ec.europa.eu/dgs/competition/proposals2/2008a510_tender_specifications.pdf.

493 In the UK, exemplary damages can be awarded in cases, where the profit aimed at by the defendant exceeds the amount recoverable by the plaintiff. Also, restitutionary damages are possible, when other remedies are considered inadequate. In Germany, §33 Abs. 3 GWB allows the damages to be based on the illegal gain, explicitly because of the difficulties to estimate individual harm in cases of competition law infringements. See chapter 5, sections B 1.2.1 and C 1.3.1 respectively.

494 Also called restitutionary damages.

495 See for example regulations under German law against unfair competition practices (UWG, par. 10).

damages in hard-core cartels has been debated, regulating the damages to be a 10 percent market price increase.[496] The Commission also proposes similar presumptions, when overcharges are assumed to have been entirely passed on in cases claimants are indirect purchasers and damages are to be presumed to be average overcharges in price fixing cartel cases.[497] Whether all these rules have to be seen as very specific and restricted exceptions proving the general rule or might be taken as hints to the fact that the general rule itself has to be interpreted less strict than traditionally presumed, is a subject to be clarified in legal disputes and analysis.

The Commission stretches the point that exact calculation of damages may be too complex to ensure the possibility to exercise the rights for damages and that the principle of exact damages shall not conflict with the principle of effectiveness.[498] Moreover, the envisioned possibility in exceptional cases to sue on behalf of victims, who will not be identified either before or during the proceeding,[499] necessitates a less rigid approach to the calculation of damages. It remains to be seen, if the Commission includes suggestions on this subject in the expected non-binding guidance on the calculation of damages.[500]

A closely linked issue is that of exemplary damages. According to the minimum standard of European law,[501] at least compensation of the actual losses (damnum emergens), lost profits (lucrum cessans) and interest are granted. Punitive damages, however, or any other form of damage awards that exceed the calculated harm, are foreign to a great number of Member States as general principle. However, in order to be able to adjust the damages for the probability of detection, such a legal instrument would be necessary.

Only few countries of the European Union allow a departure from that concept in the form of punitive or exemplary damages (Cyprus, Ireland and UK),[502]

---

496 Competition Law Research Centre (Hungary), "Comments on the White Paper," 6. Available at; http://ec.europa.eu/comm/competition/antitrust/actionsdamages/white_paper_comments.html.

497 European Commission, *Commission Staff Working Paper accompanying the White Paper on Damages actions for breach of the EC antitrust rules*, 67, nr. 220, 60.

498 *Ibidem*, 58, nr. 192.

499 See *Ibidem*, 19, footnote 30 and acc. Text.

500 See Oxera and Komninos, "Quantifying antitrust damages – Towards non-binding guidance for courts," (2009), a study prepared for the European Commission in preparation of the guidance on calculation of damages, in which the authors describe a variety of tools to be used for estimated damages depending on the specifics of the case at hand.

501 As recognised by the ECJ in *Manfredi,European Court of Justice, Cases C-295/04 to C-298/04 Vincenzo Manfredi and Others v. Lloyd Adriatico Assicurazioni SpA and Others ECR I-6619.*

502 Renda, *Making antitrust damages actions in the EU more effective. Study in support of the impact assessment of the EC White Paper on antitrust damages actions*, 424.

although they are not commonly used.[503] Where such damages are available, they are considered to fulfil functions of punishment as well as deterrence.[504] In most member States, however, such punitive damages are considered to be against public policy (*ordre public*)[505] and the monopoly of the state concerning sanctions[506] as general principles. For similar reasons, for example, Italian[507] and German[508] courts rejected the enforcement of US punitive damage awards. Again, however, the legal landscape in the Member States is not as strict as it may seem at first glance. In 2001, the Spanish Supreme Court recognised a USA judgment including punitive damages.[509] The court argued that deviations from the principle of mere compensation are not uncommon in the legal system and the judgement not contrary to public policy. Forms of damages that have no connection to the actual harm suffered or such with the declared goal of deterrence or sanctioning function have also been applied in Germany.[510] In copyright law,[511] infringement of personal rights,[512] and (in accordance with European law) in cases of gender discrimination in employment issues[513] the

---

503 *Waelbroeck, Study on the Conditions for Claims for Damages in Case of Infringement of EC Competition Rules: Comparative Report, Open Procedure COMP/2003/A1/22, Ashurst Study for Directorate General Competition of the EU Commission, London, England,* 84.

504 See for example:The Law Commission, "Sixth Programme of Law Reform: Damages, LAW COM No.247, 1997," (1997) 5. Available at: www.lawcom.gov.uk/docs/lc247.pdf; The Law Reform Commission, "Report on Aggravated, Exemplary and Restitutionary Damages," *Modern Law Review* (2000), 5. Available at: www.lawreform.ie/publications/data/lrc107/lrc_107.html.

505 Renda, *Making antitrust damages actions in the EU more effective. Study in support of the impact assessment of the EC White Paper on antitrust damages actions,* 236; Möschel, *Kommentar: Erweiterter Privatrechtsschutz im Kartellrecht* 115, 115.

506 Joint Working Party of the Bars and Law Societies of the United Kingdom ("JWP"), *Response to the Commission White Paper on Damages Actions for Breach of the EC Competition Rules,* 3. Available at: http://ec.europa.eu/comm/competition/antitrust/actionsdamages/white_paper_comments.html. For Germany see: Federal Court of Justice (BGH), *Decision of Federal Court of Justice (BGH) 4th June, 1992, BGHZ (4th June, 1992 - IX 149/91)* (1992)118, 312, 344.

507 The Italian Supreme Court, *Corte di Cassazione, 1183/2007* (2007)n. 1183, 19 January 2007.

508 Topic of the Federal Court of Justice (BGH), *Decision of Federal Court of Justice (BGH) 4th June, 1992, BGHZ (4th June, 1992 - IX 149/91)* 312.

509 Jablonski, "Translation and Comment: Enforcing US Punitive Damages Awards in Foreign Courts-A Recent Case in the Supreme Court of Spain," *The Journal of Law and Commerce* 24 (2004): 225, 242.

510 Discussing and proposing supra-compensatory damages in competition cases, see:German Monopolies Commission, *Das allgemeine Wettbewerbsrecht in der Siebten GWB-Novelle, Sondergutachten der Monopolkommission gemäß, §44 Abs. 1 Satz 4 GWB* 40 ff. For a comparison between US and Germany, see: Behr, "Punitive Damages in America and German Law-Tendencies towards Approximation of Apparently Irreconcilable Concepts," *Chicago-Kent Law Review* 78 (2003): 105.

511 §97 I *Urheberrechtsgesetz* UrhG (Copyright Act).

512 In the judgement BGH, *Caroline of Monaco BGHZ (15th November, 1994 - VI 56/94)* (1994)128, 1 ff, the German Federal Court (BGH) pointed to the necessity of damage awards to be large enough to deter.

513 Allgemeines Gleichbehandlungsgesetz AGG (Equal Treatment Act). (2006),§15 (1) 1, (2) 1. That law, was the consequence of Directives 76/207/EEC, 2000/43/EC, 2000/78/EC.

preventive and sanctioning functions of damages have been recognised. It also seems that the principle of monopoly of sanctioning of the state is at least generally interpreted as not to extend to contractual sanctions, which are privately imposed sanctions.

The implementation or recognition of exemplary damages awards is generally debated. In the regulation *Council Regulation 864/2007, On the Law Applicable to Non-Contractual Obligations* (Rome II),[514] as well as the *Council Regulation (EC) 44/2001*[515] an explicit exemption was made for cases where non-compensatory damages are regarded as conflicting with the public policy. The question of exemplary damages was also addressed in the *Manfredi* judgment by Advocate General Geelhoed who was of the opinion it would be best to leave such decisions to the national legislators.[516] The Commission's opinion is that the concept of punitive damages is not considered to be against the *acquis communautaire*[517] and that Community law does not exclude the possibility that victims are better off after the claim has been brought.[518]

Overall, also here exemptions from the general rule can be found and might hint towards possible solutions to the perceived impossibility of the desired rules concerning the optimal group litigation mechanism.

2. LIMITATIONS CONCERNING MANDATORY GROUP LITIGATION

Apart from the difficulties in establishing damages, which may require each individual and his damages to be identified, other legal restrictions to mandatory group litigation may exist.

Accordingly, damages are awarded for material as well as immaterial losses. The expressive aim is to ensure deterrence effect of those damages, see European Court of Justice, *Sabine von Colson and Elisabeth Kamann v Land Nordrhein-Westfalen, Case – 14/83* (1984).

514 Par. 32: *Considerations of public interest justify giving the courts of the Member States the possibility, in exceptional circumstances, of applying exceptions based on public policy and overriding mandatory provisions. In particular, the application of a provision of the law designated by this Regulation which would have the effect of causing non-compensatory exemplary or punitive damages of an excessive nature to be awarded may, depending on the circumstances of the case and the legal order of the Member State of the court seised, be regarded as being contrary to the public policy (ordre public) of the forum.*

515 Par. 34 (1): *A judgment shall not be recognized: (1) if such a recognition is manifestly contrary to public policy in the Member State in which recognition is sought* […].

516 *Manfredi, European Court of Justice, Cases C-295/04 to C-298/04 Vincenzo Manfredi and Others v. Lloyd Adriatico Assicurazioni SpA and Others ECR I-6619.*

517 European Commission, *Commission Staff Working Paper accompanying the White Paper on Damages actions for breach of the EC antitrust rules*, {COM(2008) 165 final} {SEC (2008) 405}, 57 f, no. 190.

518 *Ibidem*, 58, no. 192, 64, no. 211.

Already the opt-out solution for group litigation in Europe has been frequently rejected by commentators on constitutional grounds, as they may conflict with principles of due process as well as the right for a day in court if not all victims are adequately notified of and included in the proceedings.[519] In a mandatory group litigation that covers all victims, including those who refrained from purchasing the good or service in question, victims will generally not participate in the proceedings. Conflicts with constitutional and human rights might make the implementation of such a system impossible.

However, some legal concepts exist that might be interpreted as mirroring a mandatory group litigation.[520] In Spain, representative consumer associations are granted standing to represent unidentified victims and claim for their damages.[521] However, only positive judgements are binding and victims are left to execute the judgement themselves. A similar approach is taken in actions brought in the public interest, such as the popular action in Portugal.[522] In addition, in cases of widely dispersed and small damages, where the individual's rights could be considered to be only theoretically present, the governments of Member States have already considered alternatives to traditional damage claims, proposing the introduction of skimming-off procedures.[523] Such mechanisms may be especially relevant in cartel cases where the group of end consumers bears most or all of the total damage. If the legal systems of the Member States allow such mechanisms, either because the public interest is concerned or individuals will be unable in practice to exercise their rights, there possibly might be room also for a mandatory group litigation system. Moreover, when individual damages are too small to justify litigation or will not be even discovered in the

---

519 See R. Nordh, "Group Actions – The Swedish Experience" 2 June 2005). Available at: www.courdecassation.fr/formation_br_4/2005_2033/intervention_m._nordh_anglais_8144.html; Micklitz, *The Development of Collective Legal Actions in Europe, Especially in German Civil Procedure* 1473, 1494, 1499. Possible conflicts with Article 6 ECHR are also seen byJoint Working Party of the Bars and Law Societies of the United Kingdom ("JWP"), *Response to the Commission White Paper on Damages Actions for Breach of the EC Competition Rules*, 5, footnote 5 and acc. text. Available at: http://ec.europa.eu/comm/competition/antitrust/actionsdamages/white_paper_comments.html.

520 Although they may not exclude individual rights to claim for damages, as would be the case in the optimal deterrence regime developed here.

521 Article 11 LEC (Spanish Civil Procedure Act) 1/2000.

522 Law 83/95 and Article 26-A Portuguese Procedure Code, see Bonelli Erede Pappalardo, Bredin Prat, Hengeler Mueller, Slaughter and May and Uría Menéndez, "Damages Actions for Breach of the EC Antitrust Rules, Comments on the Commission's White Paper," (30 June 2008), 13.
Available at: http://ec.europa.eu/comm/competition/antitrust/actionsdamages/white_paper_comments.html.

523 For example German skimming-off procedures under §10 UWG-Gesetz gegenden den unlauteren Wettbewerb (Act against unfair competition) in cases of dispersed damages (Streuschaeden), see Deutscher Bundestag (German Parliament), *Entwurf eines Gesetzes gegen den unlauteren Wettbewerb (UWG), BT-Drucks. 15/1487.*

first place, one may argue that the right of having the "day in court" would remain nothing but an empty shell.

Apart from constitutional and human rights concerns, the incorporation of all victims of a certain infringement into one group could also be rendered impossible when strict laws are enacted that require the members of the group to have essentially identical subject matter.[524] The same is true with regulations that limit standing in representative actions to associations representing their members or only a subgroup of the potential victims. Such limitations are common in the Member States with regard to actions brought by associations[525] and have also been followed by the Commission in its White Paper.

3. LIMITATIONS CONCERNING THE POSSIBILITIES TO REWARD ENFORCERS

As has been pointed out in all forms of group litigation mechanisms, providing the representative with less than the total damages is likely to give rise to principal-agent problems between society and agent and therefore to interfere with the deterrence goal. To align the interests of society, which wishes the optimal sanction to be imposed on the infringing parties, with those of the representative agent, the latter would have to be granted the total optimal sanction.

Providing the agent or the litigant with the total of damages awarded also raises legal concerns. Depending on interpretation, the agent either succeeds the victims in the rights to damages, works on a 100 percent contingency fee basis, or is awarded the damages by way of *cy pres*. All of these concepts are not very common in the Member States.

3.1. Transfer of rights

The contractual transfer or the right to claim damages seems to be largely unproblematic in most Member States. A right can be transferred by either contractual relationship or a juridical act.[526] In general concepts of subrogation (as they exist) the direct contract between injured parties and representative might not even be necessary when the third party (representative) performs the obligations of the debtor.[527] Such transfers are already used in the case of the

---

524 For example required in Germany for joinder procedures in the ZPO §59 ff.

525 For example in Germany, industry associations are restricted to representing their members, while in the Netherlands the Dutch Consumentenbond can represent only consumers.

526 European Group on Tort Law, *Principles of European tort law: text and commentary*5:101 ff.

527 Compare, *Study Group on a European Civil Code in co-authorship with the Research Group on EC Private Law, Book III: Obligations and corresponding rights. Principles, Definitions and*

Cartel Damage Claim company.[528] Whether such transfers can take place without compensation for the original right holder, however, is questionable. The damage claims being assets of economic value, transfers without compensation might be in conflict with fundamental property rights.[529] The value of the claims in the hands of the individual victims might be disputed, however, when the rights would or could not be enforced anyway, and are negligible on an individual basis.[530]

In theory, the representative could succeed the victims in the role of right holder, so that the rights have to be transferred in one way or another. While transferring of claims typically takes place in contractual relationships, it can also be regulated by law or follow a judicial order.[531] Such a transfer can also follow widely accepted legal mechanisms, under which a party who fulfils a legal obligation of another party (debtor) to the benefit of the creditor, succeeds in the role of creditor. In the case of group litigation mechanisms, such a transfer could occur when the agent would make an upfront payment to the victims, fulfilling the expected obligations of the defendant(s). This could be the case, were the victims to be compensated by auction proceeds in the case of auctions for litigation, which will be discussed below. However, that would inhibit the efficiency of such systems with regard to deterrence. The transfer might possibly also be achieved by court decision, when the agent acting on behalf of victim would register the claims in cases where the individuals would not file suit themselves. Then, it may not even be necessary to transfer the rights from the individual right holder in those cases, where individual effectuation of these rights will not take place in any case. For example, in case of damages that fail to reach a certain amount, victims may not be granted standing in court anyhow. There are also estimates, which amounts of damages are too low for individuals to pursue their rights for damages.[532] In these cases, the rights to claim damages may remain with the victims, who will not effectuate them. Then, its seems, there should be fewer problems with granting standing to the agent as well for the

Model Rules of European Private Law, Draft Common Frame of Reference (DCFR) Interim Outline Edition. 141, 154 f., Par. 2:101: Performance by a third person. Available at: http://webh01.ua.ac.be/storme/DCFRInterim.pdf.

528 See the discussion of the Cartel Damage Claim Company at 2.2.3.2 above, and below.

529 As garanteed by Article 71 (1) EU Charter of Fundamental Rights.

530 See also Landes, *The Private Enforcement of Law* 1, 33 f., arguing that the assignment of property rights of legal claims on a first-come first-serve basis might be sensible in cases where enforcement costs are relatively large compared to the individual claim value.

531 For actual selling of damage claims see CDC. On the legal possibilities of transferal see section C.

532 In Germany, that amount is estimated to be between 25 and 75 Euro.Micklitz and Stadler, *Das Verbandsklagerecht in der Informations-und Dienstleistungsgesellschaft,* (2005), 1323; Säcker, *Die Einordnung der Verbandsklage in das System des Privatrechts,*CH Beck (2006), 50.

same amounts, acting on behalf of total society, even if that standing would not be based on the same legal right.[533]

Nevertheless, the transfer of rights to the agents might be too difficult to implement into existing legal systems.

3.2. *Contingency fee of 100 percent*

The representative or agent could also be instituted as mandated to represent the rights of the victims, as is done for example with associations in injunction procedures. As remuneration for his effort, the agent could also be working on a 100 percent contingency basis. However, the view on contingency fees in the Member States differs from country to country, and has been subject to recent changes. While most Member States have a ban on contingency fees, Belgium, the Netherlands and the UK have had recent debates on the subject. In Germany, contingent as well as contingency fees were prohibited for a long time.[534] However, the Federal Constitutional Court just declared the complete ban on contingency fees unconstitutional, if access to justice is hampered.[535] In Italy, the government just recently abolished the ban.[536] However, even if the contingency fee is prohibited, there might be legal ways to come to the same result de *facto*. While in Germany the ban on contingency fee was not questioned by the German Federal Constitutional Court, yet, a group of lawyers decided to found a company (in Belgium) to buy the claims of victims of a German Concrete Cartel, which had been fined by the German Federal Competition Authority. In the contractual transfer of the rights, the Cartel Damage Claim company receives 20 percent of the total rewards.[537] This amounts to a *de facto* contingency fee. However, a contingency fee arrangement still presupposes a contract between the original right holder and the agent, which is impossible in practice between agent and all represented victims of a particular competition law infringement. That solution may therefore also be very difficult to implement.

---

533 Such arguments are also made by Wagner, *Kollektiver Rechtsschutz – Regelungsbedarf bei Massen- und Streuschäden* 41, 75;Micklitz and Stadler, *Leistungsklagen von Verbänden.* in *Das Verbandsklagerecht in der Informations- und Dienstleistungsgesellschaft.* eds. Micklitz andStadler. (2005), 1309, regarding claims brought by associations, 1339 ff.

534 Both contingency fees and conditional fees were prohibited under section 49b of the Old German Act on Lawyers' Remuneration (Rechtsanwaltsvergütungsgesetz).

535 See in the matter BverfG, 1 BvR 2576/04 2006, Bundesverfassungsgericht – Pressestelle, *Pressemitteilung Nr. 27/2007 vom 7. März 2007, Zum Beschluss vom 12. Dezember 2006 – 1 BvR 2576/04 (press release 27/2007)* (2007),, available at www.bundesverfassungsgericht.de/ en/ press/bvg07–027.html.

536 The Italian government also removed the prohibition of the *pactum quota litis* with the recent decree 223/06.

537 See www.carteldamageclaims.com/presse/CompetitionLaw360_080707.pdf.

3.3. *Cy pres distribution*

If the *cy pres* mechanism of compensating the victims can be employed, the enforcement agent can theoretically be granted the proceeds to continue his mandate as enforcement agent to the benefit of society. The *cy pres* mechanism requires that the awards be used to further the interests of those represented. That indirect benefit to all victims could be found in the increased deterrence and future persecution of competition law infringements. However, *cy pres* seems to be much less feasible in case one of the victims is in fact the agent, as for example the lead plaintiff. That a private individual could be held responsible for such investments in the public good is debatable. Nevertheless, when the agent is a company or association with the aim to persecute competition law infringements, *cy pres* distribution might well be an option. Especially in those cases, where group litigation promises the largest benefits and the individual victims are least likely to ever have brought actions, which are probably cartel cases with end consumers as the victims. Therefore, from the discussed three alternatives, this mechanism might even be a feasible way to achieve the desired incentives for the agents.

D. OTHER SPECIFIC AIMS OF THE COMMISSION AND THEIR REALISATION

As has been pointed out already, the Commission made clear in the White Paper, that the overriding goal of the reforms was not deterrence, but compensatory justice. Whether the mechanisms will lead to efficient compensatory justice is not easy to establish. This is because compensatory justice is not clearly defined and the value society places on an increase in compensatory justice for a certain number of victims of competition law infringements is difficult to measure.[538] However, a tentative discussion is possible, as to what degree the aim of full compensation to all victims is reached.[539] Thereby potential pitfalls and costs can be identified, using the insights gained in the analysis on the deterrence effects. That exercise will be done in this section.

---

538 It might also be noteworthy at this point to mention that the focus on justice and compensations deliberations by policy makers has been extensively analyised and criticised by Kaplow and Shavell, as it may make individuals often worse off than policies established under a welfare approach, see Kaplow and Shavell, *Fairness versus Welfare,*Harvard University Press (2002).

539 The Commission wants to introduce measures that insure that "**all victims** of infringements of EC competition law **have access to effective redress mechanisms so that they can be fully compensated** for the harm they suffered" European Commission, *White Paper on Damages actions for breach of the EC antitrust Rules COM(2008) 165 final, SEC(2008) 404*, 2 f.

1. THE GOAL OF COMPENSATORY JUSTICE

Corrective justice for the "greatest possible number of victims"[540] is the primary objective the Commission pursues, apparently not only in the area of competition law.

Compensation of individual harm is not a typical goal in the economic analysis of law based on a total welfare analysis. The mere redistribution of wealth, *ceteris paribus*, amongst different members of the society does not have an impact on total welfare. However, economic analysis focused on deterrence can also inform the deliberation of compensatory justice. One crucial factor made clear in the deterrence analysis above is that that both, deterrence and compensation, will only be achieved in as much as actions for damages will be encouraged. Moreover, that goal will be pursued at costs that have to be borne by society, independent of the specific aim. With regard to the goal of compensatory justice, whether or not the costs will be justified depends on how much corrective justice will in fact be achieved and the value society attaches to compensatory justice. Quantifying the value of compensatory or corrective justice to society is a difficult task. However, at least some remarks might be made with regard to the potential of the proposed mechanisms to reach the goal of full compensation of all victims. As both requirements: "full compensation" and "all victims," may not be met simultaneously, the analysis will first deal with the first and then the second requirement individually.

1.1. Full compensation

Full compensation requires the compensation of total harm, including lost profits and interest. As such, the Commission aims at providing full compensation. However, several features of the proposed and discussed mechanisms may be in conflict with that aim.

There are a number of obvious deviations from the goal of full compensation. The explicitly proposed possibility to use *cy pres* distribution mechanisms in those few cases, where individual victims may not or only very difficultly be identified, is one example. The indirect use of the damage awards to the benefit of certain groups of society will most likely not lead to full compensation of individual borne harm. The use of the damages awarded will only indirectly benefit the victims. Moreover, some members of the society will benefit from *cy pres* distribution that never incurred a loss due to the infringement. In such

540 European Commission, *Commission Staff Working Document, Accompanying document to the White Paper on Damages actions for breach of the EC antitrust rules, Impact Assessment, {COM (2008) 165 final} {SEC(2008) 404} {SEC(2008) 406}*, 65 f.

cases, it seems, the focus is shifted away from the goal of individual compensation towards other legal concepts and principles, such as punishment of the breach of law, the disgorgement of ill-gotten gains and possibly even deterrence.

A second, very obvious deviation is constituted by any deliberations on facilitating the way damages could be calculated. Using already existing mechanisms in the Member States, such as establishing the damages as the amount of illegal gain and the proposal to use ex ante fixed amounts in cases of price overcharges deviate from the principle of compensation of actual harm. Such tools, though certainly a way to reduce expenses and efforts necessary to establish the amount of harm, would make full compensation of actually suffered harm, while avoiding unjust enrichment, a matter of chance. Both mechanisms bear no relation to the actual harm suffered. The same is true for the *a priori* assumption of full passing-on in cases brought on behalf of indirect purchasers. It is undoubtedly true, that the exact calculation of individual damages may be too complex in some cases, so that other mechanisms may be more feasible. Again, this waters down the principle of just and full compensation of incurred losses to the victims.

Full compensation is also hampered by incentives of the agents acting as representatives, which do not coincide with those of the victims, especially in the area of settlement negotiations. Whenever representative associations or the named plaintiff and or his lawyer stand to gain something on their own behalf, may it be cost savings or direct additional financial benefits, from settling also for less than the actual amount of harm, full compensation will not be reached. Therefore, the principal-agent problems between the victims and their representatives are crucial. However, they are not entirely overcome by the proposed mechanisms.

Overall, the goal of full compensation of victims cannot be fully reached. At best, it seems, something will be taken from the infringer and something will be given to some of the victims. Too many trade-offs are necessary, including the trade-off between full compensation and incentives for the agents, as well as a trade off between too high costs and the degree to which the goals can be achieved.

1.2. All victims

The question of whether all victims will receive at least some partial compensation depends on two issues. One concerns the potential of all victims being included in proceedings and the other the incentives to initiate such proceedings.

Without going into detail, it is clear that those victims bearing the losses that constitute the total welfare loss (dead weight loss) will not receive any compensation unless they stand to gain from *cy pres* distribution by chance.

Additionally, the proposed group litigation mechanisms are designed in a way as to always include only a subset of the victims. Direct and indirect purchasers will have to be represented in different proceedings. Members of one consumer association will not be included in the proceeding initiated by another. In that respect, it must be noted that the envisioned collective action and representative actions are likely to be more of use to victims that have relatively large claims and/or are part of a stronger interest group. On top of that, the selection of cases to be pursued is skewed, depending on the own incentives of the agents, be it lawyer, named plaintiff or association, to become active. Larger claim values will ease the opt-in collective action proceeding and cause larger publicity also in representative actions. Media attention is also more likely to be given to members of some certain interest groups than to others. While the individual victims may stand to gain the most in such cases, that is not necessarily true for the whole society. Cases with widely dispersed damages of low individual value are likely to remain unattractive for the agents, event though the total harm caused to society may be immense. Only if all subgroups will in the end have their own proceeding, will the number of victims receiving at least partial compensation not fall short of all those, who might have been granted compensation in court. For that, sufficient incentives must be created for all those agents to actually initiate proceedings, which is likely not to be the case.[541]

All those who might in the end be represented in either a collective action or a representative action will also only receive some damage awards, when cases will be initiated. As most of the cases will be follow-on cases, the probability of getting some form of collective redress will be equal to the probability of detection and conviction of infringers by the public authorities at best. The number of potential stand-alone cases will not increase that probability significantly. It has to be weighed against the public proceedings, which will not be followed by actions for damages, as there may be some stand-alone cases, but also some public proceedings without follow-on litigation. Follow-on cases are likely to be less than 100 percent, because of difficulties of proving harm, lack of sufficient funding for the proceedings, lack of own incentives of the agents to pursue that particular case, and other conceivable reasons.

On the whole therefore, only a subset of all victims harmed by a competition law infringement will receive some form of compensation under the envisioned system.

[541] See chapter 3.

1.3. *Conclusions*

The goal of full compensation of all victims as compensatory justice cannot be achieved by the proposed mechanisms. Feasibility necessitates trade-offs already between the two subsets of that goal, i.e., between full compensation and the compensation of all victims. On top of that, compensatory justice in general has to be compromised to make the litigation system workable. Therefore, the proposed solutions can only be seen as some compromise between conflicting goals and the result of inability to rank the pursued goals strictly and explicitly.

2. INTERMEDIARY GOALS

Next to the overriding goal of compensation of victims of a competition law infringement and the welcomed side effect of increased deterrence, the Commission mentioned some related considerations and aims of the proposed reform steps. In this part, a quick look is taken at the degree to which these goals may be achieved.

2.1. *Reducing the difference between small damages and large individual costs*[542]

The goal of reducing the difference between small damages and large individual costs relates to the litigation costs. In economic terms, this goal seems to address the problem of rational apathy, where the victim weighing the potential benefits of litigating the case against the costs of doing so finds it better to refrain from filing suit. However, the presented group litigation mechanisms on their own are unlikely to be the best tools to achieve such goals, if they were chosen as the ones to pursue. Numerous alternatives exist, all with their own benefits and possible problems. Amongst these alternatives are reduced or waived court fees, special small claims procedures, contingency fee regulations for lawyers, and different types of legal insurances, all of which reduce the individual costs. On the other hand, awarding punitive damages could increase the otherwise too small damage awards, also forming an alternative.

Opt-in collective actions are not a first choice tool to reach such a shift in the individual cost-benefit ratio regarding the incentives to claim damages. As has been stated above, the procedure in itself will be more costly than traditional litigation and the possibility to share the costs depends on the willingness of other victims to opt-in. However, these need to be identified and contacted in

[542] European Commission, *Commission Staff Working Paper accompanying the White Paper on Damages actions for breach of the EC antitrust rules*, 15 ff.

order to do so, which increases the costs and consequently the risks of the victim trying to initiate the case. Considering the additional problems created through the introduction of collective actions, it is far from certain that they would constitute a better solution to the problem of rational apathy than other alternatives, which relate to the adequate financing of civil litigation proceedings.[543]

Representative actions also do not necessarily diminish the costs and compensation ratio in themselves. By being able to bundle a large number of claims into one proceeding, the association may be enabled to realise some economies of scale. However, again the costs of the proceeding will be larger than under traditional litigation. That is all the more so, when the costs of preparing and prosecuting a case increase exponentially with the stake of the claim. On top of these costs, also costs connected to the notification of victims and the distribution of the damages awarded in court must be included in the calculation. It should also be noted that these costs in some cases might even outweigh the damages awarded.[544] Most importantly, the costs are not borne by the parties supposed to receive the damage awards, so that in fact one party (the victims) receives damage awards and has no costs, while the other (the association) only has costs and no awards *per se*.

2.2. *Fostering stand-alone as well as follow-on actions*[545]

Despite the stated intent to foster not only follow-on but also stand-alone actions, the above conducted analysis suggests that the incentives to bring stand-alone actions are very limited. So far, the Commission has not developed specific incentives schemes for parties that are or might become involved to invest resources in the detection of competition law infringements. Stand-alone cases are therefore only likely when the detection is very simple and most of the relevant information for filing suit is readily available. In these circumstances, it is also likely that the aggrieved victims would have brought damages actions even without group litigation mechanisms.

---

543 For an overview and a discussion of different funding alternatives in the UK, see Lord Justice Jackson, "Review of Civil Litigation Costs,Preliminary Report by Lord Justice Jackson, part 4 chapter 12, The Funding of Civil Litigation," (2009), available at: www.judiciary.gov.uk/about_judiciary/cost-review/docs-prelim-report/part4.pdf. Discussion conflicts between plaintiff, lawyer and professional litigation funder, see Waye, "Conflicts of Interests between Claimholders, Lawyers and Litigation Entrepreneurs," *Bond Law Review* 19 (2007): 9.

544 See Wagner, *Kollektiver Rechtsschutz – Regelungsbedarf bei Massen- und Streuschäden* 41, 75; Farmer, *More Lessons from the Laboratories: Cy Pres Distributions in Parens Patriae Antitrust Actions Brought by State Attorneys General* 361, 399 f; Eichholtz, *Die US-amerikanische Class Action und ihre deutschen Funktionsäquivalente*, 299.

545 See European Commission, *Commission Staff Working Paper accompanying the White Paper on Damages actions for breach of the EC antitrust rules*, no. 1, 7.

2.3. *Preserving competition in the internal market (deterrence)*

All arguments under the heading of "preservation of competition" are related to the goal of deterrence.

The preservation of competition is done through the deterrence of anti-competitive conduct. Therefore, little can be added here and the reader is referred to the analysis in chapter 3 and the one above in this chapter.

A few comments could be in order, however, with regard to the comments of the Commission, that neither consumers nor competitors should bear the costs of illegal anti-competitive conduct. So far, the focus has not been on the protection of competitors, probably rightfully so, as possibilities for competitors to file suit against each other have to be treated very carefully. On the other hand, focusing merely on the consumers may lead to systems that force the competitors and other market participants to bear the costs of an infringement.

3. CONCLUSION

The goal of corrective justice for aggrieved parties in cases of illegal anti-competitive conduct is not reached to the full extent. Consistently, choices have to be made concerning trade-offs between just compensation and the incentives for active parties or the costs involved. Exact establishment of harm can be too complex and hinder potential plaintiffs in exercising their rights. Some claims may never be adjudicated, so that *cy pres* distribution mechanisms might be an option. Throughout the initiatives, however, one central problem seems to be too little addressed, whether looking at deterrence or at compensatory justice as goal: the incentives of parties to become active. Without adequate incentive schemes, the effect of all mechanisms will be severely hampered. On top of that, none of the intermediary goals discussed are reached to substantial extents.

E. GENERAL ASSESSMENT

After taking a look at the potentials of the planned group litigation mechanisms, including the other legal reform proposals, to reach the proclaimed purposes, it becomes clear that the proposed mechanisms fall short of their potential. Neither compensatory justice nor deterrence are reached to their full extent. Moreover, these goals do not seem to be pursued in a strict and consequent manner. Trade-offs with feasibility or costs can explain these deviations from the set goals only to a certain degree. The question arises whether there exists some justification outside the analysis that may be responsible for some of the choices made. This section provides a few thoughts on this subject, without the claim of completeness.

There are many possible explanations for the Commission's choice of avenue. Most likely, a combination of several or all forms the real driving force, though it is not possible to identify the bundle exactly. One of the potentially most influential reasons may have been that, irrespective of the legal discussion about whether the Commission has the mandate to impose such regulations on the Member States, the Commission had to take into account the legal and cultural traditions of the Member States. Otherwise, the opposition to such changes would likely be large. Therefore, an acceptable compromise has to be found, if at least some progress is desired. Economically, that could be framed as *harmonisation costs*. Mandating the introduction of legal rules that do not fit into the general concepts of the legal systems in the Member States would lead to very large costs of harmonisation, especially when the introduction of new codes on civil procedure concerning competition law infringements would spill over to other areas of law. During the initial consultation stages, where comments on the Green Paper were invited, it also became clear that there exists a wide spread and profound European prejudice against the US American class action, with its "bounty hunting" or "ambulance chasing" lawyers and an overly litigious culture.[546] Such a system therefore was to be avoided in Europe, according to many commentators on the Green Paper and the Commission itself.[547] Opposition to the introduction of a system that would capture a majority of the US American class action features was likely to be very strong. However, as has also been pointed out by commentators abroad,[548] the question remains whether

546 To demonstrate the wide spread of such colourful assessments, see for example Schnell, "Class Action Madness in Europe – a Call for a More Balanced Debate," *European Competition Law Review* 28 (2007): 617, 617; Kroes, "left cowboy hat at home", Speech March 9, 2006. Kroes, "More private antitrust enforcement through better access to damages: an invitation for an open debate," *Opening Speech at the Conference 'Private Enforcement in EC Competition Law: The Green Paper on Damages Actions'* (9 March 2006); "litigation culture"Hodges, "Competition enforcement, regulation and civil justice: what is the case?" *Common Market Law Review* 43 (2006): 1381, 1398; "ambulance chasing laywers" Kroes, *More private antitrust enforcement through better access to damages: an invitation for an open debate.*

547 Associazione fra le società italiane per azioni, "Comments on the Green Paper on damages actions for breach of the EC antitrust rules," (2006), available at http://ec.europa.eu/competition/antitrust/actionsdamages/files_green_paper_comments/assonime.pdf; CEFIC, European Chemical Industry Council, "The comments of the chemical industry on the commission GREEN PAPER on damages actions for breach of EC Antitrust rules," *CEFIC*(12 Apr 2006) www.cefic.org/Files/Publications/comments.pdf; International Chamber of Commerce (ICC), "ICC Comments on the Commission's Green Paper on damages actions for breach of the EC antitrust rules," http://ec.europa.eu/competition/antitrust/actionsdamages/files_green_paper_comments/icc.pdf.

548 Issacharoff, *Will Aggregate Litigation Come to Europe?*. Available at: http://ssrn.com/abstract=1296843.

with the aim to introduce a very European group litigation mechanism the European Commission has not "thrown out the baby with the bath water". Despite the justifications given for the choices made, there might still be room for improvement.

First of all, the goal that was to be achieved with private enforcement of competition law seems to have changes from a focus on deterrence[549] to a combination of deterrence and compensation[550] to a full focus on compensatory justice.[551] That shift in focus may well be an extreme expression of the shift in European competition law in general, away from a total welfare perspective and towards a consumer welfare oriented approach. The Commission was frequently reprehended by commentators abroad, who claimed that the focus on consumer protection was lacking.[552] Obviously, the choice of the major goal of the reform largely influences the methods to be employed and the variables to be taken into account. It should be made clear, however, that the typical argument used in the discussion by practitioners and theorists alike, which is that the pursuit of compensatory justice also adds to deterrence, conceals the fact that focusing on the one goal comes at a cost – the cost that the other goal is not achieved as well as it might have been. Moreover, to allow for transparent decision making and a higher quality in the debates and discussions, definitions of concepts like consumer welfare and corrective justice would be needed just as much as a ranking of different goals.

Another point strongly emphasised by the Commission is the need to preserve a strong and effective public enforcement system.[553] The Commission did not want to enhance private enforcement in a way that it might work as a substitute to public enforcement. It was stressed, that the aim of private enforcement was considered to be different to that of public enforcement. A focus on compensation for victims achieved through follow-on actions would have been a consequent result. However, it seems that that approach was not followed through completely

549 See Mario Monti, "Private litigation as a key complement to public enforcement of competition rules and the first conclusions on the implementation of the new Merger Regulation" Brussels, 2004), where compensation is considered a positive side-effect.

550 See Kroes, *Enhancing Actions for Damages for Breach of Competition Rules in Europe, SPEECH/05/533*, where "a strong deterrent effect" and "benefits for the functioning of the market and the competitiveness of the economy" are mentioned as the acknowledged benefits, while compensation of victims is considered second addition "there is more to private enforcement than optimising the impact of competition policy".

551 See Kroes, *Consumers at the heart of EU Competition Policy SPEECH/08/212*, dealing with compensation of harmed consumers, where deterrence is reduced to "obvious deterrent effects we cannot put a price on".

552 See Fox, "'We Protect Competition, You Protect Competitors'," *World Competition* 26 (2003): 149.

553 European Commission, *Commission Staff Working Paper accompanying the White Paper on Damages actions for breach of the EC antitrust rules*, no. 17, 11.

either, especially since the first group of cases under which private enforcement of competition law may act as a complement to public enforcement mentioned was stand-alone cases.[554] The group litigation systems and all the other proposed mechanisms to enhance private enforcement could have been more specifically tailored to these types of actions and the general reference in the discussion to stand-alone actions and the enhanced deterrence effects could and should have been skipped entirely.

Therefore, even though the Commission may have several justifications for their choices, such as legal limitations or other goals pursued, the whole analysis and discussion of private enforcement of European competition law could be improved if such restrictions were to be made explicit. Under the same heading, a clear statement of the goals to be achieved and their relative importance, as well as a definition of the relevant concepts used would be needed.

554 *Ibidem*, no. 21, 11 f.

CHAPTER 5
COMPARISON AND ANALYSIS OF SELECTED LEGAL SYSTEMS

This chapter examines forms of group litigation developed in three selected countries: the United States of America (USA), the United Kingdom (UK),[555] and Germany. The focus is on those mechanisms that are, or may be, applied in the case of competition law infringements.

The selection of these countries was motivated by the following facts. The US American system is one of the most prominent group litigation mechanisms world wide, it is considered a prime example of group or collective action,[556] and is also the mostly widely used. Moreover, most of the insights concerning the effects and efficiency of issues concerning group litigation have been developed in the USA. Therefore, it seems absolutely necessary to investigate this form of bundling similar interest into one proceeding, even though the European Member States profess that they do not want to copy that system. The UK was selected because, while also a common law system as is the USA, it is also close to the European civil law countries in some areas. Therefore, it is an interesting intermediate between continental civil law and the USA. The UK developed a different set of mechanisms that have been applied for some time and are now being assessed and possibly altered. The experience of the UK, and the perceived advantages and disadvantages of different mechanisms, can provide very valuable insights for future group litigation designs for other European Member States. Germany was selected as representing one of the more traditional civil law countries, where, so far, only few cautious steps have been taken in developing new forms of group litigations. The German resistance and scepticism towards other types of aggregate litigation, especially the US American-style class actions, can be considered to be very large.

After its description, each system will be assessed with regard to its potential to reach optimal deterrence, using the insights gained in chapter 3. Because the

555 The UK will be used here as only comprising England and Wales.

556 German commentators used the term "Paradebeispiel", see Beuchler, *Länderbericht Vereinigte Staaten.* in *Das Verbandsklagerecht in der Informations- und Dienstleistungsgesellschaft.* eds. Micklitz andStadler. Münster: Landwirtschaftsverlag (2005), 941, 953.

overall effect of a specific group litigation mechanism depends also on other regulations beyond the mere design of the group litigation mechanism, such as rules on fees and cost shifting or rules on damages, a selection of other relevant issues deemed as most important will also be presented.

In the conclusions, a final comparison between the systems will be made and possible policy implications will be drawn.

A. UNITED STATES OF AMERICA

In the USA, as a Federal State System, Federal Regulation concerning class actions exists next to regulations in the 50 individual States. As the comparison between USA and EU competition law is made at the federal level in this thesis, many USA States' regulations mirror the Federal Regulation[557] and the trend set in the *Class Action Fairness Act 2005* (CAFA) was towards more federalisation of class actions, in this section the focus will be also on the Federal System. Within that choice, also more emphasis is placed on class actions, rather than on other procedures like joinders, and furthermore on class actions seeking monetary relief. These types of actions in the realm of private enforcement seem to account for the vast majority of private enforcement cases in the USA.[558]

1. THE US FEDERAL LEGAL SYSTEM

1.1. Joinder and consolidation

Joinder and consolidations are, as in many countries, also part of the *Federal Rules of Civil Procedure* (FRCP) in the USA. Rule 69(a) of the FRCP on permissive joinder of parties allows plaintiffs to join in one action "if they assert any right to relief jointly, severally, or in the alternative in respect of or arising out of the same transaction, occurrence, or series of transactions or occurrences and if any question of law or fact common to all these persons will arise in the action."

Likewise, consolidation regulation exists. Rule 42(a) of the FRCP allows courts to order joint hearings or trials in cases where common questions arise in separate actions before the court.

---

557 Although there can be differences in substantive law as well as the application of regulation in the courts. For an overview seePace, *Class Actions in the United States of America: An Overview of the Process and the Empirical Literature*. http://globalclassactions.stanford.edu/PDF/USA__National_Report.pdf.

558 See Lande and Davis, "Benefits from Private Antitrust Enforcement: An Analysis of Forty Cases," *University of San Francisco Law Review* 42 (2008): 879, 901.

These regulations mirror very similar regulations in most countries also in European Member States.[559] However, these mechanisms are of much less importance in reality than the class action mechanism discussed below.

1.2. *The class action*

The most prominent example of group litigation is the US American class action under the Federal Rule of Civil Procedure 23 (FRCP 23). This rule also applies to class actions in antitrust cases. There are two basic forms of class actions regulated under that rule. Generally speaking, the first is a mandatory class action and the second an opt-out class action. This distinction is presented here, even though a specific class action can be based on a number of grounds for certification and liability issues. For example, it is possible to seek injunctive relief and (punitive) damages at the same time or sub-classes of one case may be based on different rules.

Rule 23(b)(1) and (2) apply to mandatory class actions, which are applied when separate actions would risk inconsistent adjudications or conflict with the interest of other class members on the one hand, and when the adequate remedy for the class as a whole would be injunctive relief or a declaratory judgement, on the other hand. In cases, where the limited funds of the defendant(s) might risk access to justice for future plaintiffs, a class action claiming damages can also be taken under Rule 23(b)(1).

Rule 23(b)(3) is the more common opt-out class action, also called *common -question class action*, which can also be brought as action for damages. Rule 23 requires that for such an action to take place, it must be superior to any other available method (FRCP 23(b)(3)) and therefore forms a kind of superiority test. This needed superiority also refers to joinder or consolidation procedures. The opt-out class action is the most widely known US American class action; nevertheless, opt-in procedures are also possible.[560] Another exception, where the default rule for the class action is one of opt-in, can be found in the *Federal Fair Labor Standard Act*, for example.[561]

559 These procedures are very similar to the procedures also common in Civil Law countries. SeePace, *Class Actions in the United States of America: An Overview of the Process and the Empirical Literature*26 ff. Available at: http://globalclassactions.stanford.edu/PDF/USA__National_Report.pdf.

560 Willging et al report 3 cases found in the Georgetown study that required opt-in procedures,Willging, *Empirical study of class actions in four federal district courts: Final report to the advisory committee on civil rules*, 54. Available online at: www.fjc.gov/public/pdf.nsf/lookup/rule23.pdf/$File/rule23.pdf.

561 United States Code, 29 U.S.C. Par. 216 (b) (2000). For a discussion see also: Lampe, *Procedural Approaches for Countering the Dual-Filed FLSA Collective Action and State-Law Wage Class Action* 311.

In order to be certified, a class action must fulfil a number of requirements. These are: numerousity of claims; commonality of issues; typicality of the representative parties; and, adequacy of representation. Definability is also considered to be an implicit requirement[562] and refers to the necessity of the class being sufficiently identifiable. Numerousity of claims under federal regulation does not prescribe a minimum number of parties or claims, but the general practice seems to be a comparison with a number of claims that could still make a mere joinder of claims feasible.[563] Commonality of issues refers to the requirement that legal or factual issues that are common to all represented parties should predominate the questions of law or facts that only are relevant in the individual claims (FRCP 23(b)(3)). However, restricting the class action to certain issues is also allowed by law (FRCP 23(c)(4)), although the exact relationship between issue-classing and the requirement of predominance of common issues seems to be debated at Federal Appellate Courts.[564] Typicality means that the claims or defences of the party that represents the class have to be typical of the claims or defences of those represented (FRCP 23(a)(3)). With regard to adequacy of representation, the federal regulation applies to lawyer and lead plaintiff simultaneously and requires that "the representative parties will fairly and adequately protect the interests of the class" (FRCP 23(a)(4)). A preliminary inquiry into the merits of the cases is not mandated, and the US Supreme Court held that the certification of an action as class action does not require such an exercise[565], however rulings on dispositive motions before certification are possible.[566]

Certification of the class, if it fulfils all the necessary requirements, takes place after motions already have been filed and decided upon and a preliminary discovery has taken place. If the class is not a mandatory class falling under FRCP 23(b)(1) and (2), where notification may take place but is not required by law, the class members have to be notified in a next step. The court then has to order a notification of the potential class members, using "the best notice that is practicable under the circumstances, including individual notice to all members who can be identified through reasonable effort" (FRCP 23(c)(2)(B)). The law also establishes some minimum requirements to the form of notices, which have to be submitted "in plain, easily understood language"[567] and also to the content,

---

562 Rowe Jr, *State and Foreign Class-Action Rules and Statutes: Differences from – and Lessons for? – Federal Rule 23* 147, 152 ff.

563 Pace, *Class Actions in the United States of America: An Overview of the Process and the Empirical Literature*6; Sergius Koku, "An analysis and the effects of class-action lawsuits," *Journal of Business Research* 59 (2006): 508, 510; Rowe Jr, *State and Foreign Class-Action Rules and Statutes: Differences from – and Lessons for? – Federal Rule 23* 147, 153.

564 *Ibidem*, 161.

565 U.S. Supreme Court, *Eisen v. Carlisle & Jacquelin, 417 U.S. 156* (1974), 174 (1974).

566 Rowe Jr, *State and Foreign Class-Action Rules and Statutes: Differences from – and Lessons for? – Federal Rule 23* 147,160.

567 FRCP 23(c)(2)(B).

having to state the nature of the action, the binding effect of such action and how and when victims can opt-out. The impracticability of other alternatives, such as individual letters to all victims, which need to be identified beforehand, sometimes can lead to notification through newspaper or magazine advertisements. Even if notification takes place through letters to the individual class members, information of all those represented can not be guaranteed, as only those identified will receive such notice and sometimes the letter sent may go unnoticed by or not even reach the recipient.

When the class is certified, the court also has to appoint the class counsel and, in cases where there are several applicants for that position, to decide on which counsel would best be able to represent the class.[568] In recent years, courts have increasingly used auction mechanisms to determine the best suited class counsel when one had to be chosen out of a number of competitors.[569]

During the procedure, the court may also make use of several orders, so as to protect the represented class members or to manage the procedure in an efficient way. Amongst the possibilities to protect silent class members is the option that the court may order further notice to be given to inform them about the steps in the action, proposed extent of the judgment, a possibility to notify the court about inadequate representation, or to grant intervention possibilities.[570]

Settlements are generally dependant on courts approval (FRCP 23(e)). In case of a class action under Rule 23(b)(3) FRCP, the court may make approval dependant on a second stage opt-out possibility for the class members (FRCP 23(e)(4)). However, that rule is reported to have been applied only in a very limited number of cases.[571]

1.3. Other relevant issues

1.3.1. Rules on damages

With regard to antitrust damages, Section 4 of the *Clayton Antitrust Act* provides a special feature for antitrust litigation, as it states that any injured party shall recover treble the actual damages suffered.[572] Whether this mandatory trebling

568 FRCP. 23(g).

569 One of the more prominent examples was the class action against the auction houses Christie's and Sotheby's, see U.S. District Courts, *In re Auction Houses Antitrust Litigation, 164 F. Supp. 2d 345 (S.D.N.Y. 2001)* (2001).

570 FRCP 23(d)(1)(B).

571 Rowe Jr, *State and Foreign Class-Action Rules and Statutes: Differences from – and Lessons for? – Federal Rule 23* 147, 167 f – possibly because both class counsel and defendant have incentives to argue against such opt-out at that stage.

572 United States Code. 15 U.S.C. Par. 15 (1994).

is to be interpreted as mandatory punitive damages or as mandatory remedial damages, seems to be a matter of dispute in the courts as well as the literature, though it may be of less importance with regard to its deterrence effects.

Pre-judgment interest is generally not granted. Although Section 4 of the Clayton Act provides that a court may award prejudgment interest in antitrust cases for the period between the filing of the complaint and judgment, if such an award is considered "just in the circumstances", it seems that such interest has been hardly ever granted.[573] For such interest to be granted, only three factors shall be taken into account by the court: intentional delay caused by one of the parties by making assertions or filing motions lacking in merit or otherwise acting in bad faith, breach of regulations that provides for sanctions due to dilatory behaviour or expeditious proceedings and conduct of one of the parties with the major aim to delay the proceedings or to increase the costs.[574] Because of the lack of pre-judgment interest, the US American treble damages may be closer to actual damages with interest than to threefold the sustained damage.[575] It may also be noteworthy that de-trebling for successful leniency applicants was introduced in the *Antitrust Criminal Penalty Enhancement and Reform Act 2004*.[576]

When not all class members can be identified, or not all of them are willing or able to collect their damages after the procedure (which may be subject to submission of claim forms and supporting materials), *cy pres* and *fluid recovery* class recoveries are possible.[577] Under the *cy pres* mechanism, the class recovery fund will not be distributed amongst the class members, but put to its next best use, for example given to an organisation that works in the interest of those represented. Under fluid recovery it may be decided, that instead of compensation, other mechanisms may be used, for example a general price reduction for the defendant's product for a certain time of period. Both mechanisms can be also employed, when individual compensation is regarded as too costly or unfeasible.

As regulation seems to be missing, the Federal Courts have discretion with regard to the use of left over funds, which they have been using in a variety of

573 Lande, *Are Antitrust'Treble'Damages Really Single Damages?* 115.

574 United States Code. 15 U.S.C. Par. 15 (a).

575 In fact, Lande (1993) calculates the real multiplier from a defendants (deterrence) point of view to be only between 0, 35 and 2,01 instead of 3, for business plaintiffs around 1 and for consumer plaintiffs to be between 0,64 and 1,32. See *Ibidem*.

576 For a discussion see Randall, "Does De-Trebling Sacrifice Recoverability of Antitrust Awards," *Yale J.on Reg.* 23 (2006): 311.

577 Shepherd, "Damage Distribution in Class Actions: The Cy Pres Remedy," *University of Chicago Law Review* 39 (1971): 448. For a discussion of fluid recovery (*cy pres* distribution) as one form of nonpecuniary settlements, seeMiller and Singer, "Nonpecuniary Class Action Settlements," *Law and Contemporary Problems* 60 (1997): 97, 154.

ways.[578] It seems that the use of unclaimed funds is sometimes not even decided upon or supervised by judges.

1.3.2. Costs, fees and cost-shifting rules

Generally, the so called American rule (as opposed to the British or European rule) applies with regard to cost-shifting, which postulates that each party bears her own costs.

However, there are some exceptions to this rule. One relates to the settlement possibility. Under the offer of judgement rule, the plaintiff that declines an offer made by its opponent prior to the trial risks having to face the defendants litigation costs that result later in the trial, when the judgment rendered turns out to be not more favourable than the settlement would have been (FRCP 68(d)).

Another exception specifically for antitrust litigation is regulated in Section 4 of the Clayton Act. Under this rule, the successful plaintiff can recover treble damages, as well as attorneys' fees and costs. The United States Code (15 U.S.C.) §15 states that the plaintiff "shall recover threefold the damages by him sustained, and the cost of suit, including a reasonable attorney's fee." This is in fact a one-way fee-shifting rule that does not foresee the same rule for the defendant in general. The downsides and upsides of such a rule have been heavily debated in the literature.[579] It seems plausible that such a one-way fee-shifting rule encourages plaintiffs to file suit in general. That includes also cases involving small stakes, a low probability of winning or large expected litigation costs. At the same time, it increases the costs imposed on defendants, and may thereby add to deterrence. Higher expected trial costs for the defendant may also encourage defendants to reach settlement agreements. This could be a more ambivalent effect, when nuisance suits are a possibility.

---

578 Rowe Jr, *State and Foreign Class-Action Rules and Statutes: Differences from – and Lessons for? – Federal Rule 23* 147, 170 ff.

579 Arguing for a shift from the American to the British Rule: Polinsky and Rubinfeld, "Optimal awards and penalties when the probability of prevailing varies among plaintiffs," *The Rand Journal of Economics* 27 (1996): 269. Available at SSRN: http://ssrn.com/abstract=567; analysing the incentives to file unmeritous suits: Bebchuk and Chang, "Analysis of Fee Shifting Based on the Margin of Victory: On Frivolous Suits, Meritorious Suits, and the Role of Rule 11, An," *Journal of Legal Studies* 25 (1996): 371; modelling the effects of cost shifting rules on with regard to (inter alia) settlement offers:Gravelle, "The efficiency implications of cost-shifting rules," *International Review of Law & Economics* 13 (1993): 3; see also Kaplow, "Shifting plaintiffs' fees versus increasing damage awards," *The Rand Journal of Economics* 24 (1993): 625.

A very common fee schedule in the US is the so-called contingency fee arrangement. Under a contingency fee contract, the lawyer agrees on pre-financing the litigation against a certain percentage of the recovery. Thereby at least large parts of the costs and risks connected to a trial are shifted from the plaintiff to the lawyer. As such, agreements between counsel and individual class members are not possible ex ante in class actions, the courts developed the so-called common fund doctrine, which mirrors the contingency fee contract.[580] Under this principle, class counsel will be rewarded from the common class fund, the recovery for the class as a whole, as it is regarded fair and adequate that all those represented in and benefiting from the class action would also participate in the costs of the litigation. The contingency fee arrangement seems to have worked as an effective alternative to other mechanisms of financing of litigation, such as legal aid and legal insurance, so that these alternatives did not develop to such an extend that can be found in other jurisdictions without such fee arrangements.[581]

In the case of antitrust litigation, however, a cost-shifting rule is applied. 15 U.S.C. (Clayton Act) §26 states "in any action under this section in which the plaintiff substantially prevails, the court shall award the cost of suit, including a reasonable attorney's fee, to such plaintiff". What is to be considered reasonable fees will have to be determined by the judge. In cost-shifting cases, such as antitrust cases, judges can also apply the so-called "loadstar" method to determine lawyers' fees to be reimbursed by the defendant. Under this approach, the lawyer will receive remuneration based on an hourly fee, which will be adjusted by a multiplier reflecting the complexity of the class action in question and the service rendered to the class.[582] However, it seems that *de facto* contingency fees are the prevailing method for lawyers' remuneration.

In a settlement, class counsel and defendant may agree upon the structure and amount of lawyers' payment, for example whether the fee will be a percentage of the total amount to be paid to the class or whether lawyers and court fees will be paid on top. Though subject to courts approval,[583] the fee arrangement may be very often approved by courts, especially when defendant and lawyer jointly

---

580 See for exampleU.S. Supreme Court, *Sprague v. Ticonic National Bank 307 U.S. 161,167* (1939); and U.S. Supreme Court, *Trustees v. Greenough (1882) 105 U.S. 527* (1882).

581 Kilian, "Alternatives to Public Provision: The Role of Legal Expenses Insurance in Broadening Access to Justice: The German Experience," *Journal of Law and Society* 30 (2003): 31, 36 f.

582 Pace, *Class Actions in the United States of America: An Overview of the Process and the Empirical Literature* 42. Available at: http://globalclassactions.stanford.edu/PDF/USA__National_Report.pdf.

583 Polverino and Cengiz, "A Class Action Model for Antitrust Damages Litigation in the European Union," *World Comeptition* 30 (2007): 479,486.

argue the adequacy and fairness of their agreement including attorney's fees and when no class member comes forward to object.[584]

Empirical literature has found that class action contingency fees for lawyers have tended to be somewhere between 18 percent and 30 percent of the recovery, i.e., the class fund. Eisenberg and Miller found a mean of close to 22 percent, while Willging *et al* found values between 24 percent and 30 percent of total recovery amount as attorneys' fees.[585]

1.3.3. Passing-on defence

Arguing that indirect purchasers may refrain from filing suit, so that the efficiency of private enforcement would be in danger, and the estimation of passing on amounts would be a complex burden on the courts, standing to sue has been restricted by the US Supreme Court to direct purchasers in the famous decision *Illinois Brick v. Illinois*.[586] This decision was a consequence of the equally famous Supreme Courts decision of 1968, *Hannover-Shoe*,[587] in which the court decided that the passing on defence was not available under federal law. Though continuously discussed and sometimes heavily criticised,[588] these rules are still in place on the federal level. However, a large number of States allowed the passing on defence under their State antitrust laws.

1.3.4. Disclosure rules

The Federal Rules on Civil Procedure provide for generally wide discovery possibilities, compared to common discovery procedures in civil law countries. FRCP 26(a), regulates that the lawyers on both sides, within short time after the pleading, must disclose "all documents, data compilations, and tangible things" in their possession, without a request from the other side. This also includes "a copy of, or a description by category and location of, all documents, electronically stored information, and tangible things that are in the possession, custody, or

---

584 See also the discussion on judges approval of settlement agreements below.

585 See Eisenberg, et al, "Attorneys Fees in Class Action Settlements: An Empirical Study," *Journal of Empirical Legal Studies* 1 (2004): 27, 27;Willging, *Empirical study of class actions in four federal district courts: Final report to the advisory committee on civil rules*. Available online at: www.fjc.gov/public/pdf.nsf/lookup/rule23.pdf/$File/rule23.pdf.

586 U.S. Supreme Court, *Illinois Brick Co. v. Illinois, 431 U.S. 720.*

587 U.S. Supreme Court, *Hanover Shoe, Inc. v. United Shoe Machinery Corp., 392 U.S. 481.*

588 Instead of many, Critical:Harris and Sullivan, "Passing on the Monopoly Overcharge: A Comprehensive Policy Analysis," *University of Pennsylvania Law Review* 128 (1979): 269. Supporting:Landes, *Should Indirect Purchasers Have Standing to Sue under the Antitrust Laws – An Economic Analysis of the Rule of Illinois Brick* 602. For an overview see Richman and Murray, "Rebuilding Illinois Brick: A Functionalist Approach to the Indirect Purchaser Rule," *Southern California Law Review* 81 (2007): 69.

control of the party and that the disclosing party may use to support its claims or defences, unless solely for impeachment" (FRCP 26 b) and depositions of witnesses, interrogations, even before the facts of the case have been tried. Non-compliance with these discovery rules can result in serious punishments. Next to reimbursement of the opposing party's costs, the judge may also rule that certain evidence is no longer admissible or even draw adverse conclusions from the failure to provide the required information.[589]

It is quite possible that broad discovery rules have an impact on the effectiveness of the group litigation mechanism, by shifting costs and risks of evidence production away from plaintiffs and more towards defendants. While therefore the initial problems of asymmetric information and/or rational apathy may be reduced, the scope for nuisance suits might be augmented by the same token.[590]

1.3.5. Role of judges

Judges in civil law countries are generally perceived to have a much more active role in the litigation process than they typically have in common law countries, such as the USA.[591] In the USA, the opposing lawyers are the main players presenting evidence and questioning witnesses, while the judge retains a position as manager of the case or referee between the opposing parties.[592] Therefore, in civil law countries the judge has a larger influence on the scope and form of the litigation process than in the USA.

It may be possible, that the more active role of judges in civil law countries may have slight advantages in controlling the development of a group litigation suit and maybe even to curb some of the problems arising, for example, from principal-agent problems between represented and representing parties.

589 SeeAmerican Bar Association, Chicago, US (ABA), "ABA Comments on the Commission's Green Paper on damages actions for breach of the EC antitrust rules,",5. Available online at http://ec.europa.eu/comm/competition/antitrust/actionsdamages/files_green_paper_comments/ aba.pdf.

590 See for example Wagener, *Modelling the effect of one-way fee shifting on discovery abuse for private antitrust litigation* 1887,1898 f, analysing the effect of other procedural rules on discovery abuses. A critical discussion on the merits of the arguments for existing abuses in the US is provided in:Burroughs, "Mythed It Again: The Myth of Discovery Abuse and Federal Rule of Civil Procedure 26 (b)(1)," *McGeorge Law Review* 33 (2001): 75.

591 Final Report for the Civil Justice Council, *"Improving Access to Justice through Collective Actions", Developing a More Efficient and Effective Procedure for Collective Actions* 40. Available at: www.civiljusticecouncil.gov.uk/files/Improving_Access_to_Justice_through_Collective_Actions.pdf.

592 Apple and Deyling, *A primer on the civil-law system,*Federal Judicial Center (1995), 37. Available at: www.fjc.gov/public/pdf.nsf/lookup/civillaw.pdf/$file/civillaw.pdf.

1.3.6. Jury trials

One of the large differences between civil law and common law countries is the right to a jury trial in civil litigation cases.[593] In the USA, that right is embedded in the Seventh Amendment to the Federal Constitution. "In Suits at common law, where the value in controversy shall exceed twenty dollars, the right of trial by jury shall be preserved, and no fact tried by a jury shall be otherwise re-examined in any Court of the United States, than according to the rules of common law".[594] Actual and punitive damages are considered legal remedies, for which cases the right for a jury trial is generally applicable.[595]

Consequently, under FRCP 38(b), any party may demand a trial by jury of any issue triable of right by a jury. In antitrust cases, the requirement of a minimum amount of controversy of $20 is likely to be met in most cases. If the parties do not demand a jury trial, a bench trial will result, unless the judge himself orders a trail by jury (FRCP 39(b)).

It is questionable and highly debated whether a jury consisting of a representative sample of the whole society would be able to adequately understand and assess the factual and legal questions brought up in a competition infringement case, which are likely to be very complex in many cases.[596] For example, plaintiff's lawyers in Canada consider antitrust cases as too complex to be heard by a jury.[597] However, the generally perceived biases and shortcomings of jury trials are not always supported by empirical findings. Some research suggests that juries do not fare as badly as is often common prejudice.[598]

While the benefits or disadvantages of jury trials are disputed in the USA and in other countries, specifically in complex issues like antitrust cases, it seems that the number of cases that actually reach the trial stage and therefore the decision by a jury in the USA is relatively small.

---

593 In Member States of the European Union largely abandoned, jury trials are sometimes still possible, mostly restricted to criminal cases. See e.g. the *Geschworenengericht* in Austria.

594 The United States Bill of Rights, Seventh Amendment.

595 See eg.United States Court of Appeals, *8th Circuit, No. 96-2925 Kampa vs White Consolidated Industries, Inc.* Explaining the rules for determining whether there is a right to a jury trial in a federal civil case: Wright and Williams, "Remember the Alamo: The Seventh Amendment of the United States Constitution, the Doctrine of Incorporation, and State Caps on Jury Awards," *South Texas Law Review* 45 (2003): 449.

596 For a discussion see Crane, "Antitrust Antifederalism," *California Law Review* 96 (2008): 1, 33.

597 Nicholson and Hersh, *Canada.* in *Private Antitrust Litigation 2007 – In 19 Jurisdictions Worldwide.* ed. Mobley. Global Competition Review (2007), 13.

598 See Clermont and Eisenberg, "Trial by jury or judge: Transcending empiricism," *Cornell Law Review* 77 (1991): 1124;Vidmar, "The American Civil Jury for Auslander (Foreigners)," *Duke Journal of Comparative & International Law* 13 (2003): 95.

Crane reports that in fact only 77 of 3,766 private antitrust cases filed between 2001 and 2005 went to trial in the end. Of these only 45 cases were tried in front of juries.[599] Consistent figures can be found also for the year 2005, in which of a total of 707 terminated federal antitrust cases only 12 cases reached a trial and of those, only 9 were jury trials.[600]

So the overall effect of that specific feature of US American antitrust litigation may be relatively minor, at least at trial stage. However, it may be that the availability of jury trials may influence the opponents bargaining powers or strategies in settlement negotiations. It could be that large company defendants are strongly opposed to jury trials, when they perceive juries as generally more plaintiff friendly, even when that belief is not supported by empirical evidence.

1.3.7. Multiple nationwide class actions

In the USA, defendants can face problems that may also occur in cases of internationally operating defendants in the EU, having to defend themselves against multiple group litigations that may include the same plaintiffs in different States. In the USA, a nation wide operating defendant may face several class actions in several states, all trying to certify nation wide classes. These cases arising in different courts cannot currently be consolidated.[601]

Inefficiencies arise through the connected doubling of efforts and the possibility of defendants to choose a suitable plaintiffs counsel to strike a beneficial settlement agreement. Moreover, a consistent adjudication and the development of the law are at risk in such cases. This may have a negative impact on the deterrence function of such cases, especially when they provide an opportunity for defendants to undergo forum shopping, and form a kind of menu of plaintiffs and lawyers amongst which to choose the most favourable from.

599 Crane, *Antitrust Antifederalism* 1, 35, fn 140, basing the statistics on data collected from the annual reports of the administrative offices of the U.S. courts, available at www.uscourts.gov. Also Connor and Helmers report that the great majority of private antitrust suits are settled. Of 36 international cartels convicted in the United States during 1990–2003 only 5 cases went to trial. See Connor and Helmers, "Statistics on Modern Private International Cartels, 1990–2005, AAI Working Paper No. 07–01," *The American Antitrust Institute* (2007). Available at SSRN: http://ssrn.com/abstract=944039.

600 See Crane, "Antitrust Modesty," *Michigan Law Review* 105 (2006): 1193. The statistics reported by Crane come fromU.S. District Courts, *Table C-4, U.S. District Courts – Civil Cases Terminated, by Nature of Suit and Action Taken, during the 12-Month Period Ending September 30, 2005* (2005), www.uscourts.gov/judbus2005/appendices/c4.pdf (last visit: October 12, 2007). See also, for 2006, www.uscourts.gov/judbus2006/contents.html. (last visit: October 12, 2007).

601 Alexander, "An introduction to class action procedure, available at www.law.duke.edu/grouplit/papers/classactionalexander.pdf," *Online* (2000), 21.

2. DETERRENCE EFFECTS

Private enforcement of antitrust laws plays an important role in the USA. Recent studies report that damage awards granted in civil litigation represent a major share of the penalties imposed on competition law infringers.[602] Surprisingly, stand-alone suits seem to be a large part of this litigation activity that by no means is marked overwhelmingly by follow-on actions. In fact, empirical studies conducted for the time between 1973 and 1983 found that up to 91 percent of private antitrust cases were stand-alone suits.[603] Only 20 percent of cases concerning horizontal antitrust infringements were follow-on suits.[604] Also today, in the large majority of private US American cases, the avenue chosen in antitrust litigation is that of a class action.[605]

2.1. *Joinder and consolidation procedure*

These mechanisms are based on individual claims being filed by plaintiffs. As such, they generally are not able to overcome problems of individual suits. Rational apathy may be reduced when an individual cost reduction is possible under certain circumstances. For example, when the costs of the trial can be divided between several plaintiffs and the joinder does not lead to a more complex and costly trial. However, information asymmetry and free riding behaviour cannot be cured by this mechanism. Additionally, procedural efficiency cannot be achieved when a small number of plaintiffs join in an action against a defendant, whose anti-competitive behaviour leads to damages for a large number of injured parties, who may bring individual suits or form other joinders.

2.2. *Class actions*

The number of antitrust class actions has been on the rise since 1997.[606] One of the reasons for the success of class actions mentioned by American commentators

---

602 Connor, *Global price fixing*, 109.

603 See Kauper, *An Inquiry into the Efficiency of Private Antitrust Enforcement: Follow-on and Independently Initiated Cases Compared*, 1163, 1180. See also Lande, *Benefits from Private Antitrust Enforcement: An Analysis of Forty Cases* 879, 890 f, stating the majority of damage awards was recovered came from stand-alone actions.

604 See Kauper, *An Inquiry into the Efficiency of Private Antitrust Enforcement: Follow-on and Independently Initiated Cases Compared*, 1163, 1180.

605 Emanuelson, et al, "More of the same: growth in private antitrust litigation and cutbacks by the US Supreme Court," *The Antitrust Review of the Americas* (2009), 1. Available at: www.howrey.com/files/News/3efcfaf9-bf96-44ee-afe8-c2ff63e38fdc/Presentation/NewsAttachment/9a415689-9d64-4c61-b096-dfd4ee74cdf6/US%20Private%20Enforcement%2019.pdf.

606 Issacharoff, *Will Aggregate Litigation Come to Europe?*; Emanuelson, *More of the same: growth in private antitrust litigation and cutbacks by the US Supreme Court*, 1.

is the existence of entrepreneurial lawyers.[607] Other features of private antitrust litigation as described above, including the contingency fee for lawyers, are seen to have helped the perceived success of the class action regime in the USA as well.[608] Therefore, though applicable at least in part also to joinder procedures, these will be discussed here in combination with the class action mechanism, as this is the most prominent and debated group litigation mechanism in the US American private antitrust litigation.

One-way fee shifting greatly reduces the financial risks that potential plaintiffs face in litigation, especially when coupled with a contingency fee arrangement, under which the lawyer pre-finances the litigation. While this combined effect will influence the private cost-benefit analysis concerning the filing of a suit and therefore reduce the problem of rational apathy in those cases where it exists, it also creates an increased risk of unmeritous cases being brought. The plaintiff can become risk free under the applied cost-shifting rule. It would then rest on the lawyer as investor of the litigation to act as a gatekeeper and to select only cases with sufficient merits. However, the pre-trial discovery following a relatively uncomplicated and unsubstantiated first filing of a claim can impose substantial costs on the defendant or the first filing of the case may trigger follow-on cases. This increases the defendant's willingness to settle also cases with little merits, to avoid these other costs. Therefore, the lawyer may also be willing to take on cases with little merits but with a potential for an early settlement.

As far as procedural efficiency is concerned, the great number of class members represented in class actions greatly reduces the costs per case compared to individual suits brought by all members of the class. However, Willging *et al*[609] also found in their study that the vast majority of federal class action required significantly more time and resources than non-class cases. These additional costs would have to be taken into account when determining the procedural efficiency overall.

Settlements in class actions are dependant on judge's approval.[610] While this sometimes has been regarded also in the literature as a safeguard against unfair settlements or settlements that are more beneficial to the lawyers than to class

607 Alexander, *An introduction to class action procedure,* available at www.law.duke.edu/grouplit/papers/classactionalexander.pdf, 26; Issacharoff, *Will Aggregate Litigation Come to Europe?*

608 Alexander, *An introduction to class action procedure,* available at www.law.duke.edu/grouplit/papers/classactionalexander.pdf, 26.

609 Willging, *Empirical study of class actions in four federal district courts: Final report to the advisory committee on civil rules.* Available online at: www.fjc.gov/public/pdf.nsf/lookup/rule23.pdf/$File/rule23.pdf.

610 Pace, *Class Actions in the United States of America: An Overview of the Process and the Empirical Literature* 41. http://globalclassactions.stanford.edu/PDF/USA__National_Report.pdf.

members, its efficiency might be questioned in reality. Judges may be reluctant to re-open a case that could be closed with the settlement, when their time and resources are limited. Moreover, in cases where the settlement is already agreed upon and filed for approval together with the claims and motion for class certification, which can happen as well, judges will not have been presented the facts and expert testimonies they might have seen at trial. Under such circumstances, it will be difficult also for generally well-informed and specialised judges to judge the adequacy of the settlement agreement. Some empirical findings may provide substance to such criticism. Willging *et al*[611] found in their study on class actions that in fact 90 percent of settlements are approved by the courts, even when class members object to the terms of the settlement.

Contingency fee arrangements are seen as providing large incentives for lawyers to specialise in class action litigation, as collected fees can be substantial.[612] However, these fee arrangements can also give rise to principal-agent problems, as discussed in detail in chapter 3.[613] The incentives for lawyers to investigate and to litigate against competition law infringements will always deviate from the social interest in doing so, as lawyers receive only a fraction of the total damages caused to society and do not take the benefits accruing from deterrence effects to society at large into account.

Overall, as far as the deterrence effect is measurable or can be estimated,[614] even the US American private enforcement system seems to fall short of optimal deterrence effects. Connor[615] reports that damages awarded are low compared to the overcharges brought about in price fixing cases and too low compared to the optimal level of deterrence needed when the low probability of being caught is taken into account. He estimates that the real sanctions/real damages ratios in the USA for the "harshly punished"[616] vitamin cartels were only about 26 percent, of which 7.5 percent were imposed by the government.[617] The deterrence effect of the US American system may well be larger compared to the 4.2 percent real sanction/real damages ratios that the EU penalty achieved, if one can extrapolate from these findings. However, attempts to analyse the deterrence

611 Willging, *Empirical study of class actions in four federal district courts: Final report to the advisory committee on civil rules*. Available online at: www.fjc.gov/public/pdf.nsf/lookup/rule23.pdf/$File/rule23.pdf.

612 Alexander, *An introduction to class action procedure*, available at www.law.duke.edu/grouplit/papers/classactionalexander.pdf, 12.

613 See section on collective action in Chapter 3.

614 A good overview of methods and results in determining deterrence effects can be found in Gordon and Squires, "The Deterrent Effect of UK Competition Enforcement," *The Economist* 156 (2008): 411.

615 Connor, *Global price fixing*, 410 ff.

616 *Ibidem*, 424.

617 *Ibidem*, figure 16.3, 430.

effect focusing on detection rates also seem to point to a larger effectiveness of the US American system compared to the existing European systems, as it constitutes a combination of public and private enforcement, with the majority of cases being brought by the latter enforcement agent.[618] While not perfect and leading to optimal deterrence, the US American system at least seems to have an advantage over the currently dominant systems in the European Union.

B. UNITED KINGDOM

The system of the United Kingdom (UK),[619] though also a common law system as the legal system of the USA, has developed their own unique procedures to bundle similar interests into one proceeding. Its experience and the current discussion in the UK about future reforms of these systems can provide useful insights for other countries contemplating the design and implementation of new forms of group litigation.

1. THE LEGAL SYSTEM

1.1. Forms of group litigation mechanisms in competition law infringements

Generally, actions seeking the establishment of a competition law infringement and resulting compensation for damages can be brought by any harmed individual in front of the ordinary English courts.[620] In addition, any person who has suffered loss as a result of an infringement may institute a claim for damages before the Competition Appeal Tribunal (CAT), when public authorities have found an infringement of competition law.

The procedure before the ordinary English courts is governed by the general Rules on Civil Procedure (CPR). Therefore, the general CPR are applicable and consequently so are the mechanisms for bundling similar interest into one proceeding that are laid down or applied therein. These mechanisms will be presented shortly under the heading "Litigation before ordinary courts". As part of the general CPR, the management powers of the Court also extend to handing

618 See Renda, *Making antitrust damages actions in the EU more effective. Study in support of the impact assessment of the EC White Paper on antitrust damages actions*, 70 ff.

619 The UK will be understood in this text as comprising England and Wales. Scotland has not introduced a group litigation mechanism, see Hodges, "Country Report: England and Wales," (2007), 1. http://globalclassactions.stanford.edu/PDF/England_Legislation.pdf.

620 Cumming et al, *Civil Procedure Used for Enforcement of EC Competition Law by the English, French and German Civil Courts*, Alphen aan de Rijn: Kluwer Law International (2007), 14.

down a group litigation order (GLO). This particular group litigation mechanism will be discussed in greater detail below.

The individualised follow-on proceedings before the CAT are of lesser importance, when looking at group litigation mechanisms, as is done here. Therefore, the focus will be placed on a special representative follow-on action, which can be brought by designated bodies on behalf of consumers. This representative action was particularly designed for cases of competition law infringements and enacted 2003. This mechanism will be described and discussed last.

1.1.1. Litigation before ordinary courts

As is the case in many other countries, those in the UK are also long familiar with traditional mechanisms to bundle claims, such as joinder, consolidation and even test cases. A special representative rule, which may have been akin to collective action mechanisms, has also existed for a long time. However, it was very rarely used. Additionally, attempts to increase representative actions by associations have been made in several areas of law. These mechanisms will be described only briefly in this section.

1.1.1.1. Joinder, consolidation and single trial of multiple actions

As is common in most countries, courts in the UK also have the power to consolidate any number of individual proceedings into one, resulting in only one large claim being brought against a defendant (CPR 3.1. (2)). Similarly, the court may order several claims to be tried at one proceeding, without consolidating them, thereby leaving the individual claims intact (CPR 3.1. (2) h).

In addition, several actions claiming damages due to the same competition law infringement with the same or similar issues brought before the Competition Appeal Tribunal (CAT) can be consolidated or heard at the same trial by power of the Tribunal.[621]

These mechanisms are similar to the ones used in the USA, discussed above. Their effects have been analysed above, so that further analysis here will be refrained from.[622]

621 Competition Appeal Tribunal, Rules 2003, para 17 (1).
622 USA in this section B 1.1.1.1 and in Chapter 2, A 1.1.

1.1.1.2. Test cases

Test case procedures have been employed for a long time in the UK as a mechanism to efficiently deal with cases that involve multiple plaintiffs, without a specific statutory provision for it (except for test case procedures employed within the Group Litigation Order, discussed below). The court, within its role of managing the litigation, has the power to stay individual claims, which raise a number of common issues, and only prosecute one or a limited number of cases that entail these common issues (CPR 3.1 (2) f). The outcomes of these prosecuted test cases are binding via and within the limitations of the precedence rule.[623] The selection of a case or cases to be the test case is not regulated and up to the courts discretion, which led to numerous selection criteria.[624]

However, test case procedures still require plaintiffs to file suit on an individual basis and also to litigate the individual issues or at least file claims once the common issues are decided upon in the test case procedure. This mechanism therefore lacks efficiency and the barriers for prospective plaintiffs to come forward remain unsolved.[625]

Overall, the test case procedure mirrors test case procedures in other jurisdictions, for example the German test case procedure (KapMuG, discussed below) and generally exhibits the features that are used here to define a test case procedure.[626]

1.1.1.3. Representative rule

The representative rule (regulated in CPR 19.6) establishes a form of collective action mechanism, under which one named plaintiff (or defendant) can file (or defend) an action on his own behalf and on behalf of a represented class, when they share the same interests. The court may also order that an action be continued under the representative rule. Contrary to the consolidation procedures, the represented class members do not themselves become party to the litigation, but are bound by the outcome, unless the court rules otherwise (CPR 19.6(4)). The possibility for the court to rule on the binding effect of the outcome of such an action reduces the certainty for plaintiffs and defendants with regard to the actual size of the group, as the court may make the binding

---

623 Final Report for the Civil Justice Council, "Improving Access to Justice through Collective Actions", *Developing a More Efficient and Effective Procedure for Collective Actions*, 25 f.

624 Gibbons, "Group Litigation, Class Actions and Lord Woolf's Three Objectives – A Critical Analysis," *Civil Justice Quarterly* 27 (2008): 208, 231 f.

625 Final Report for the Civil Justice Council, "Improving Access to Justice through Collective Actions", *Developing a More Efficient and Effective Procedure for Collective Actions* 84.

626 See chapter 2 A 1.1.

effect on represented parties dependant on certain circumstances or requirements.

The requirement of the same interest has traditionally been interpreted very narrowly and understood as entailing i) a common interest, arising, for example, from the *same* contract; ii) a common complaint; and iii) a remedy other than damages, that benefits all represented.[627] Later judgments tried to establish a more flexible interpretation, also allowing damages as remedy and widening the very narrow definition of the same interest requirement.[628] One recent case under that rule was *Emerald Supplies &ANR / British Airways*,[629] following the commencement of investigation by the European Commission of several airlines in 2006. The plaintiffs tried to bring a case against British Airways for price fixing and market sharing agreements on their own behalf as well as on behalf of other direct or indirect purchasers of airfreight services. The court ruled that as the interests of those parties that should be represented could not be considered to be in line, the case could not be brought under rule 19.6 CPR.[630] However, the court pointed to the GLO procedure as alternative.

However, despite the fact that this mechanism has been in existence for over 100 years and several attempts were made to apply this rule and to make it more flexible with regard to the two requirements, the representative rule nevertheless has not been used to any significant extent, mainly because of the generally strict interpretation of the requirements, especially the requirement of the *same* interest.[631]

1.1.2. Group litigation orders

The group litigation mechanism in the UK that attracted the most interest in the literature and debate concerned with group litigation mechanisms, is the

627 This interpretation was established in judgements rendered as early as 1901 and 1919. See Final Report for the Civil Justice Council, "Improving Access to Justice through Collective Actions", *Developing a More Efficient and Effective Procedure for Collective Actions,* 34.

628 For a discussion of the representative rule and its development see Mulheron, "From representative rule to class action: steps rather than leaps," *Civil Justice Quarterly* 24 (2005): 424.

629 High Court of England and Wales, *Emerald Supplies Ltd v British Airways plc [2009] EWHC 741 (Ch); [2009] WLR (D) 136* (2009).

630 Dawes, "The English High Court strikes out a representative claim brought on behalf of "all other direct or indirect purchasers of air freight services", refusing to stretch the scope of the English civil procedure rules in order to encourage the bringing of private damages actions (Emerald Supplies & ANR / British Airways), No 26352," *e-Competitions* (Jun 2009).

631 See Final Report for the Civil Justice Council, *"Improving Access to Justice through Collective Actions", Developing a More Efficient and Effective Procedure for Collective Actions,* 34 f.; Hodges, *Country Report: England and Wales,* 2 f. http://globalclassactions.stanford.edu/PDF/England_Legislation.pdf.

so-called Group Litigation Order (GLO). The GLO was introduced in 2000 and is regulated in the Civil Procedure Rules (CPR) 19.10 – 19.15. It was part of a general reform of the Civil Procedure under Lord Woolf and heavily relies on general principles established at that time for all types of civil litigation.[632] The perceived inefficiencies with regard to case management that the other existing forms of bundling similar interests into one proceeding (test cases, consolidation and actions under the representative rule) exhibited especially in cases with many plaintiffs, led to the need for an efficient mechanisms to deal with large scale multiparty litigation.[633]

The main feature of this system is that it is to be understood as a case management procedure, intended to provide an efficient mechanism to manage multiple individual claims, rather than a new form of civil procedure. Judges facing multi-party claims already were applying similar mechanisms.[634] In the general reform of civil proceeding, the judge was sought to become an actively involved case manager, to allow for a (cost) efficient and just dealing with cases. Saving expenses and a dealing with cases in a way that is proportionate to (amongst others) the amount of money involved were explicitly laid down as explanation for a just dealing with cases in CPR 1.1(2).

Each plaintiff must still file its own claim, which is connected to a fee.[635] When a GLO is established, these claims have to be entered into a group register, established for that GLO (CPR 19.11). The court may determine, upon application or on its own initiative, whether GLO procedure will be applied, when a number of claims giving "rise to common or related issues of fact or law" (CPR 19.10) exist or are presumed to exist. In an application for a GLO procedure, a summary of the nature of litigation, the number of claims already filed and the likely number of parties involved, the common issues of fact and law likely to arise and whether subgroups with regard to any matters may exist must be provided.[636]

A GLO must fulfil a number of requirements to be certified.[637] The two most important ones are: numerousity of claims and commonality of interests (CPR 19.10. and 19.11). CPR 19.11 states that a GLO may be ordered "where there are or are likely to be a number of claims giving rise to the GLO issues", while CPR

632 See *Ibidem*, 2 f. http://globalclassactions.stanford.edu/PDF/England_Legislation.pdf, 11.

633 Final Report for the Civil Justice Council, *"Improving Access to Justice through Collective Actions", Developing a More Efficient and Effective Procedure for Collective Actions*, 2008, 28.

634 Hodges, *Country Report: England and Wales*, 2 f. http://globalclassactions.stanford.edu/PDF/England_Legislation.pdf, 11.

635 Gibbons, *Group Litigation, Class Actions and Lord Woolf's Three Objectives – A Critical Analysis* 208, 220.

636 Practice Direction 19 B – Group Litigation, 3.2.

637 See Mulheron, "Reform of collective redress in England and Wales," *CIVIL JUSTICE COUNCIL*(2008), 2008, 15. www.civiljusticecouncil.gov.uk/files/collective_redress.pdf.

19.19 defines GLO issues as "common or related issues of fact or law". Predominance of common over individual issues is not a formal requirement, however, sometimes a *de facto* predominance test has been applied when determining the effective approach to deal with certain cases.[638] Next to these requirements, the GLO procedure has to follow the general principles of civil procedure, which would demand suitability of the GLO procedure as a way to deal justly with cases (CPR 1.1(1)) and superiority over other litigation mechanisms (Practice Directive 19 B – Group Litigation, 2.3). Moreover, the GLO must be permitted, after consultation, by the Lord Chief Justice (Queen's Bench Division), the Vice Chancellor (Chancellor Division) or the Head of Civil Justice (Country Court) (PD 19 B 3.3). In the order, directions for the establishment of a register must be made, a court must be selected and also the GLO issues to identify claims that are to be treated under the GLO have to be specified (CPR 19.11(2)).

The mechanisms to establish the group of represented seems to be one that lies somewhere between test case and opt-in procedures. Claimants that are or whish to be represented in the GLO procedure need to be entered into the register established through the GLO. As lawyers are not generally prohibited from advertising, it is possible for them to inform and seek out potential group members to be represented.[639] Therefore, also lawyers may be the actual initiators and actors in the GLO. However, extensive advertising by lawyers can also have negative effects, as it may find courts disapproval and possibly some of the costs incurred might be considered as unreasonable and unnecessary.[640]

The court can specify the details to be given in the statement necessary in order for a plaintiff to be entered into the register. This may require plaintiffs to file their own proceedings with all the costs involved, but the court may also exempt plaintiffs from any costs and just allow them to enter the register.[641] It is also possible that, in order to verify the plaintiffs' right to join the GLO, the court orders that special evidence or documentation to be provided upon application.[642] Cut off dates for the entry can also be given, after which claims can only be added with special permission (CPR 19.13. (e)). However, plaintiffs can also opt-out by applying for a removal of their claim from the group register (CPR 19.14).

The judge's discretionary power in effectively managing the case also extends to the determination of the lawyer(s) to represent the GLO issues (CPR 19.13). In practice, it seems, the lawyers tended to come to an agreement amongst

638 Hodges, *Country Report: England and Wales*, 17 and 22.
639 *Ibidem*, 14.
640 Mulheron, *Reform of collective redress in England and Wales*, 2008, 27.
641 Hodges, *Country Report: England and Wales*, 18.
642 *Ibidem*, 18.

themselves, possibly mediated by the Law Society (bar association), on which lawyer or which group of lawyers will represent the GLO issues in court.

The court can also decide that one or more claims of the group have to proceed as test cases (CPR19.13.(b)). It seems that this approach has been widely used, especially in product liability cases.[643] This system then mirrors the classical test case procedure, as defined here.

Whether the GLO is conducted as test case or not, any judgment or order given binds all members of the group and the judge may also decide upon the binding effects for future claims that will be entered in the register (CPR 19.12(1)).

The court cannot estimate an aggregate amount of damages.[644] Each plaintiff has to prove his or her damages individually and these issues have to be decided upon on an individual basis, so that only in settlement agreements, a lump sum payment to be divided between the group members may be possible.

One particular feature of the civil proceedings that should also be mentioned is, that a viability test, some form of cost-benefit weighing, evolved especially in the group litigation and has also been introduced in the CPR, which asks courts to consider whether the costs of taking a certain steps will be justified by the resulting benefits (CPR 1.4(h)). This, however, does not seem to be a strict weighing of costs of litigation against the damage awards, as the application in cases shows.[645]

1.1.3. Actions for damages before the Competition Appeal Tribunal

In addition, any person who has suffered loss as a result of an infringement may institute a claim for damages before the Competition Appeal Tribunal (CAT), when an infringement of competition law has been found by the European Commission, the Office of Fair Trading (OFT) or the CAT (*Competition Act 1998* (CA), s47A & B).

---

643 Gibbons, *Group Litigation, Class Actions and Lord Woolf's Three Objectives - A Critical Analysis* 208, 233; Final Report for the Civil Justice Council, "Improving Access to Justice through Collective Actions", *Developing a More Efficient and Effective Procedure for Collective Actions* 87; Hodges, *Country Report: England and Wales*, 16.

644 Which is exactly one of the recommendations (rec 7) of the report to the Lord Chancellor, see Final Report for the Civil Justice Council, "Improving Access to Justice through Collective Actions", *Developing a More Efficient and Effective Procedure for Collective Actions*, 165.

645 In the GLO case Judge Macduff, *Dawson & Others v. First Choice Holidays & Flights Limited* (2007), the court found it appropriate at a certain point of the trial to cap future expenses of the opposing parties to a total of £430,000, while total damages where estimated to be around £400,000. The plaintiffs legal representation had estimated the future expenses at £720,000. See Hodges, *Country Report: England and Wales*, 29.

1.1.3.1. Individual actions for damages before CAT

The restriction of private actions for damages before the CAT to only follow-on actions was introduced in the *Enterprise Act 2002*, which became active in 2003. In the 5 years after that provision, a total of only 8 follow-on actions for damages had been commenced (one by the designated consumer association *Which?*, which will be discussed below), although the sum of OFT and European Commission decisions was much larger (15 infringements finally established by the OFT (or CAT) alone in the years 2003–2006).[646]

The filing of such a damage claim before the CAT requires the plaintiff also to include in the claim form a "concise statement of the relevant facts" (CAT R 32(3)(a)) and calculation and proof of the harm caused. Such "front-loading" has been considered as barrier to filing claims on an individual basis as well as claims brought by consumer associations.[647]

1.1.3.2. Follow-on representative action

In several areas of law, the UK introduced the possibility for designated bodies to bring representative actions. For example, in the area of misleading advertising, unfair terms in consumer contracts, and consumer law, designated bodies may bring actions for injunctions or enforcement orders against infringers. Typically, the available remedy is restricted to injunctions or enforcement orders, which order the defendant to cease a certain conduct. In the area of consumer protection, the representative action may be brought to enforce a certain consumer protection regulation, so that the remedy typically is an injunction.[648] There are only few exemptions, the most important of which for our purposes is the follow-on representative action in the area of competition law.

The *Enterprise Act 2002* introduced two possibilities for initiatives due to competition law infringements. The first was the so-called "super-complaint" (see Enterprise Act 2002), under which a designated consumer body may bring a complaint to the OFT, to which the OFT must respond within 90 days.

The second, and important one, was a special procedure for actions for damages due to competition law infringements, which has come into force in 2003 in Section 47B of the *Competition Act 1998* (CA). Under this regime, an *ex ante* specified body may bring representative actions on behalf of two or more harmed consumers. Harm caused to a business is not covered by that provision.

---

646 Mulheron, *Reform of collective redress in England and Wales*, 50 ff.

647 See the discussion of the case brought by the consumer body *Which?* discussed below.

648 See Hodges, *Country Report: England and Wales*, 26 and elsewhere.

This representative action before the CAT is limited to follow-on actions as well, as an anti-competitive infringement must be established prior to the proceeding (CA s 47 A (5)). This establishment can only be done by public authorities, such as the OFT, the CAT or the European Commission.

The associations applying for specification need to meet a number of criteria, including impartiality, integrity, independence and proof that they act in the interest of the consumers.[649] The Secretary of State decides over specification. As the only (until 2009) specified body was the consumer organisation *Which?*, designated in 2005, the mechanism was *de facto* only available since 2005.

Represented parties have to give their explicit consent in order to be represented in the proceeding. The commencement for such a proceeding requires the filing of the claims on behalf of the consumers by the designated body according to the general rules (CAT R 32)[650], and in addition the names and addresses of those represented, their written consent to being represented and clarification whether all named individuals are consumers within the purpose of section 47B of the *Competition Act 1998* (CAT R 33).

Damages are awarded on an individual basis, unless the designated body and all individuals represented are in agreement that the total be paid to the designated body, which then will take on the task of distribution.[651]

While the individuals represented are protected against an adverse cost ruling in case the claims would be unsuccessful, as these can not be enforced against them (*Enterprise Act 2002*, 4, cl. 7) the designated body to bring such an action faces the risk having to bear the defendants costs under the British cost rule that is applied.

Also the CAT R define a "justly" dealing with cases, mirroring the general CPR, as, amongst others, dealing with a case in ways which are proportionate to the amount of money involved (CAT R 44(2)(c)) and saving expenses (CAT R 44(2)(b)). Therefore, also the CAT may apply a certain viability test.

The experience in the one case brought under this procedure showed that the filing of such a claim is connected to substantial upfront efforts by the designated bodies, as the claim forms have to state succinct statements of the facts and legal issues of the case, as well as the amount of damages sued for. All these statements

---

649 Secretary of State, *Claims of behalf of consumers, guidance for prospective specified bodies*, www.berr.gov.uk/files/file11957.pdf.

650 See The Competition Appeal Tribunal Rules. (2003). Available at: www.opsi.gov.uk/si/si2003/20031372.htm.

651 Hodges, *Country Report: England and Wales*, 10.

have to be supported by documents, which also have to be added to the claim form. This approach to representative action can be considered an opt-in solution connected to substantial front-loading.[652]

1.2. *Other relevant issues*

1.2.1. Rules on damages

In principle, it seems, the UK also follows the common concept of compensation of actual harm caused in cases of actions for damages. As opposed to many civil law Member States, however, the UK is familiar with exemplary or punitive damages.

The general rules on damages restrict the application of punitive or exemplary damage awards to very specific circumstances, for example when the defendant aimed at making a profit that exceeds the generally recoverable damage amount by the plaintiff.[653] This requirement could be fulfilled in a number of cases of antitrust infringements. However, there seems to be no established case law yet on whether exemplary damages can be generally awarded in damages actions due to breach of either national competition law or European competition law.[654] It seems that at least in follow-on cases, exemplary damages may not be available. In the *Devenish* case, where a number of direct purchasers of the vitamin cartels filed claims for damages after the European Commission had already imposed a fine on the defendants, the High Court restricted the availability of exemplary damages to stand-alone cases.[655] The court reasoned that, based on the *ne bis in idem* principle, exemplary damages could not be awarded in cases where the defendants already were subject to a fine with regard to the same conduct.[656]

In the same ruling, the court established that in antitrust cases restitutionary awards would not be available and that damage awards based on the illegal gain of the infringer would generally be only appropriate where compensatory

---

652 See the discussion of the case brought by the consumer association *Which?* below.

653 See The Law Commission, *Sixth Programme of Law Reform: Damages, LAW COM No.247, 1997*, 1. Available at www.lawcom.gov.uk/docs/lc247.pdf.

654 Simmons, "Damages for economic loss: Questions of procedure," *Competition Appeals Tribunal* (2007), 17. Availabe at: www.courdecassation.fr/colloques_activites_formation_4/2007_2254/economic_loss_10397.html?idprec=9489.

655 High Court of England and Wales, *Devenish Nutrition Ltd v Sanofi-Aventis SA (France) and others [2007] EWHC 2394* (2008).

656 The judgment was upheld by the England and Wales Court of Appeal (UK), *Devenish Nutrition Ltd v Sanofi-Aventis SA (France) and others [2008] EWCA Civ 1086; [2008] WLR (D) 317* (2008).

damages would not be the adequate remedy for the claimants.[657] It seems that this point touched upon the issue of passing-on, as the claimant may have passed part of the excessive prices on to its purchasers, so that restitutionary damages may have made the claimant in fact better off than he would have been absent the competition law infringement. However, the Court of Appeal did not want to address the passing-on defence explicitly.[658]

Aggregate damage awards are also not available, yet. As is common also in civil law countries, for example Germany, the individual damages have to be assessed and proven. The Civil Justice Council has, however, made arguments for the introduction of aggregate damages in group litigation proceedings as part of its reform proposal concerning access to justice.[659]

1.2.2. Costs, fees and cost-shifting rules

The general provision on cost shifting in the UK is the loser pays principle (the so-called British, Continental or European Rule). This rule is also applied in the case of a consumer association under the representative follow-on action, but is not enforceable against the individuals represented in that proceeding. Cost recoveries, however, are made dependant on reasonableness.[660]

In the GLO, the cost-shifting rule also applies to the plaintiffs that entered the register. The costs there are divided into individual and generic costs. The latter are born by agreement by the group jointly and typically also include the costs of a test case.[661] Potential plaintiffs therefore face the risk of having to bear the defendants litigation costs, when the case is lost, while having possibly very limited influence on the proceeding itself.

It is necessary to guarantee the possible payment of defendants costs in case of an adverse judgment, so that it is required from plaintiffs for any type of litigation to acquire an After the Event Insurance (ATE insurance), when Legal Expense Insurance (LEI), also called Before-the-Event Insurance, is not obtainable.[662] As LEIs may not cover tort cases, getting ATE insurance may be necessary especially in group litigation. However, applying for such insurance in a group litigation

---

[657] Mcdougall and Verzariu, "Vitamins Litigation: Unavailability of Exemplary Damages, Restitutionary Damages and Account of Profits in Private Competition Law Claims," *European Competition Law Review* 29 (2008): 181. High Court of England and Wales, *Devenish Nutrition Ltd v Sanofi-Aventis SA (France) and others [2007] EWHC 2394.*

[658] *Ibidem*, no. 91.

[659] Final Report for the Civil Justice Council, "Improving Access to Justice through Collective Actions", *Developing a More Efficient and Effective Procedure for Collective Actions,* 165.

[660] Hodges, *Country Report: England and Wales*, 28 f.

[661] *Ibidem*, 19 f.

[662] *Ibidem*, 22 and 26 f.

mechanism may also be extremely costly and complex. Insurers are likely to require a detailed risk assessment of the case, which in a group litigation may sometimes be a very complex task. Insurance premiums for ATE insurance seem often to be larger than reasonable in group litigation,[663] and as only a reasonable premium may be recovered from unsuccessful defendants, the prospective plaintiffs will face additional costs.

Contingency fees as in the USA are not available in England. However, conditional fee arrangements are possible, regulated in the Conditional Fee Arrangements Regulations (CFAR)[664] and the Conditional Fee Arrangements Orders (CFAO).[665] These agreements consist of a no-win-no-fee arrangement, coupled with the possibility to increase lawyers' fees up to 100 percent in case of a success (CFAO 2000). Just as with the cost-shifting of reasonable costs in general, the court will decide, what percentage increase is considered reasonable and therefore recoverable.[666]

Further different mechanisms to finance litigation exist. Legal aid is available and relatively well funded.[667] The Legal Services Commission (LSC) provides funds for high cost litigation, but the annual budget for such expenditures is capped (at currently £ 3 million).[668] Three criteria should be met in order to qualify for such legal aid: a public interest in the case, it must be affordable and the case must exhibit sufficient merits.[669] Applying for such funding therefore seems to entail a certain level of efforts to be devoted to providing the LSC with adequate and sufficient material to apply these tests. Generally, the LSC considered funding common interest litigation over individual litigation, as the latter can be financed through LEIs.[670] Overall, the legal aid system is much

663 *Ibidem*, 28.

664 Conditional Fee Arrangements Regulations (2000). Available at www.opsi.gov.uk/si/si2000/20000692.htm.

665 Conditional Fee Arrangements Order. (2000).Available at www.opsi.gov.uk/si/si2000/20000823.htm.

666 Cumming, *Civil Procedure Used for Enforcement of EC Competition Law by the English, French and German Civil Courts*, 60 ff.

667 See European Commission for the Efficiency of Justice (CEPEJ), "European JudicialSystems 2002, Facts and figures on the basis of a survey conducted in 40 Council of Europe Member States," (2002), 19 ff. Available at: http://siteresources.worldbank.org/intlawjustinst/Resources/CEPEJreport.pdf; European Commission for the Efficiency of Justice (CEPEJ), "European JudicialSystems 2006, Facts and figures on the basis of a survey conducted in 40 Council of Europe Member States," (2006) 6. Available at: www.coe.int/t/dghl/cooperation/cepej/evaluation/2006/Report2006resume_en.pdf.

668 Legal Services Commission, *Access to Justice Act 1999, The funding code*www.legalsevices.gov.uk/civil/guidance/funding_code.asp.

669 Hodges, *Country Report: England and Wales*, 27.

670 *Ibidem*, 2, ff.

more predominant in the UK, compared to Germany.[671] However, the strong reliance on legal aid may not come without problems and costs, especially in group litigation cases.[672] The industry of professional litigation funders is developing in the UK, as in many other European jurisdictions, as well.[673]

The judge in a GLO also has the discretionary power to review, upon objection of a party, and to cap costs when necessary, with the effect that a maximum amount of recoverable costs is established.[674] While this may help to avoid unnecessary spending of the parties, it also increases the uncertainty of plaintiff's lawyers, concerning their remuneration for their efforts and litigation expenditure in general.

1.2.3. Passing-on defence

The concept of a passing-on defence is a matter of discussion in the UK, as it is in Germany and other European Member States. In the UK, it also depends also whether the damages to be sued for due to competition law infringements are considered to be based on the right of restitution, under which a passing-on defence would not be possible.[675] The OFT, in its discussion paper concerning private actions for damages in competition cases argued that representative actions should also be available on behalf of consumers.[676]

So far, no judgment has been rendered concerning the issue.[677] The issue was raised in the case *BCL OLD Co and others v Aventis SA* and others before the CAT and mentioned as a "novel and important issue".[678] However, the case settled before the CAT could rule on these issues.

---

671 Kilian, *Alternatives to Public Provision: The Role of Legal Expenses Insurance in Broadening Access to Justice: The German Experience* 31, 40f.

672 Discussing moral hazard problems and inefficiencies is Collins, "Public Funding of Class Actions and the Experience with English Group Proceedings," *Manitoba Law Journal* 31 (2005): 211.

673 Mulheron and Cashman, "Third party funding: A changing landscape," *Civil Justice Quarterly* 27 (2008): 312.

674 Gibbons, *Group Litigation, Class Actions and Lord Woolf's Three Objectives – A Critical Analysis* 208, 236 ff.

675 Röhling, *Die passing-on defence im deutschen Recht.* in *Festschrift für Ulrich Huber zum siebzigsten Geburtstag.* eds. Baums et al. Tübingen: Mohr Siebeck (2006), 1117, 1234.

676 Office of Fair Trading, *Private actions in competition law: effective redress for consumers and business, OFT Discussion Paper 916*, 15. www.oft.gov.uk/shared_oft/reports/comp_policy/oft916.pdf.

677 Farrell and Ince, *UK: Private Enforcement.* THE 2009 EUROPEAN ANTITRUST REVIEW – a GLOBAL COMPETITION REVIEW SPECIAL REPORT. *Global Competition Review* (2009).

678 United Kingdom Competition Appeals Tribunal, *BCL Old Co Ltd & Ors v Aventis SA & Ors, Court of Appeal – United Kingdom Competition Appeals Tribunal, January 28, 2005* (2005), 14 f.

1.2.4. Disclosure rules

The UK has, compared to other European countries, wider disclosure provisions.[679] Also compared to the US American disclosure mechanisms, the CPR provide for a more encompassing obligation to list all relevant information the party is aware off, including information in the hands of third parties (CPR 31.10(9); 43(2)) or such information that may adversely affect the parties own case (CPR 31.6). Within the process of litigation, the discovery process, relevant documents on which the parties intend to rely on have to be listed and to be disclosed upon request of the opposing party, unless the opposing party has legal rights or duties to refuse the disclosure (CPR 31.3(1)).

Pre-action disclosure orders can also be given by the court on application of a prospective party to the proceeding, when a number of requirements are met (CPR 31.16). The requirements include the desirability of such advance disclosure to dispose of the proceeding or to save on costs. However, in the order, the court must specify the documents or group of documents to be disclosed (CPR 31.16.(4)).

De facto, the scope of disclosure is often determined in negotiation processes between the opposing parties, in so-called preliminary meetings.[680] Because this may be a disadvantage for one party when large information asymmetries exist, as may often be the case in competition law cases, the judge in CAT procedures is supposed to take a more proactive approach in the preliminary stage to ensure a better balance of powers of the opposing parties.[681]

1.2.5. The role of judges

Especially since the reform of civil procedure, the judge is expected to play an active, interventionist, managerial role in a civil proceeding. Special re-education of judges and lawyers has taken place and the approach seems to have been widely accepted.[682]

---

679 Reported by theOffice of Fair Trading, *Private actions in competition law: effective redress for consumers and business, OFT Discussion Paper 916*, 33; Ashurst Study,Waelbroeck, *Study on the Conditions for Claims for Damages in Case of Infringement of EC Competition Rules: Comparative Report, Open Procedure COMP/2003/A1/22, Ashurst Study for Directorate General Competition of the EU Commission, London, England*, 61; Farrell, *UK: Private Enforcement*.

680 Renda, *Making antitrust damages actions in the EU more effective. Study in support of the impact assessment of the EC White Paper on antitrust damages actions*, 355 f.

681 CAT R 20 (1).

682 Hodges, *Country Report: England and Wales*, 12.

As such, the judge has much more influence on the way the proceeding is conducted than its US American counterpart does. Thereby, the more actively involved judge may also have some more possibilities to potentially curb problems occurring in group litigation, for example due to principal-agent problems.

2. DETERRENCE EFFECTS

In this section, some observations made concerning the deterrence effects of group litigation mechanisms in the UK will be discussed, concentrating on the two most relevant and most discussed features, the GLO and the representative follow-on actions in the area of competition law. Overall, the number of UK and European competition law litigation cases solved in court in the UK since 1970 seems to have been not more than 90. However, this figure may leave out a larger number of settlements.[683]

2.1. Group litigation order in general

The GLO procedure is a case management tool and remains closer to joinder procedure (or test case procedure) than to a collective opt-in action, as claims will remain intact and only during proceeding be (partially) be treated in aggregate. It is questionable, if this mechanism helped to bring forward claims, that otherwise would not have been brought. While even proponents of the GLO state that some issues remain to be solved,[684] critical voices brought forward a number of facts and discussion points that severely question the efficiency of the GLO mechanism in its current form.

One crucial point of criticism is the opt-in approach.[685] Opt-in rates reported in a survey showed that the rates of the 97 cases dealt with in one form of group proceeding or another,[686] varied enormously (between less than one and up to 90 percent) and only achieve an average of 50 percent.[687] The survey presented

683 Reported and settlements discussed byRodger, "Private Enforcement of Competition Law: The Hidden Story," *European Competition Law Review* (2008), pp.96–116, p96.

684 Hodges, *Country Report: England and Wales* 31.

685 See Mulheron, *Some Difficulties with Group Litigation Orders – and Why a Class Action is Superior* 40; Gibbons, *Group Litigation, Class Actions and Lord Woolf's Three Objectives – A Critical Analysis* 208, 220f; Final Report for the Civil Justice Council, "Improving Access to Justice through Collective Actions", *Developing a More Efficient and Effective Procedure for Collective Actions.*

686 This not only includes GLo procedures, but also other group management proceeding agreements made in court.

687 Mulheron, *Reform of collective redress in England and Wales*, 16 ff.

several major reasons for low opt-in rates.[688] First, the large number of potential group members to be identified at the outset of the action. Second, the low expected damage recovery per individual. Third, the existence of actual or merely perceived barriers to opting-in by individuals, such as economic or social reasons, for example having to bear also a share of the common costs on top of the individual costs, having too small individual damages, assuming better outcomes in individual trials or scepticism towards the "class action" process or the other class members. Similarly, participation rate for some exemplary cases found in European Member States, was established as being less than one percent.[689]

Low opt-in rates can have a number of adverse effects. In case the court applies a stricter cost-benefit analysis early on in the proceeding, when not all potential group members have opted in yet, the costs of the proceedings could be found as not being justified by the total of damages to be recovered.[690] As has been discussed in chapter 3, low opt-in rates of harmed parties also lead to inefficient proceedings and/or too little sanctions for reaching optimal deterrence.

Another crucial aspect, which could render the procedure inefficient, is the question how such litigation can be financed. It is recognised by critics and proponents of the GLO alike, that the funding issue still needs to be solved or at least improved.[691] As described above, the insurance system is a complex one in the UK and insurance for group proceedings may be difficult and/or costly to obtain. Moreover, applying for legal aid via the LSC can take a lot of time and resources and still not be granted at the end, which could create disincentives to start proceedings. Lack of funding, however, will always severely inhibit the efficiency of a group litigation mechanism, and thereby reduce deterrence effects of available civil litigation procedures.

The applied cost-shifting rule of loser pays may help to reduce the amount of unmeritous claims being brought, as plaintiffs face the risk of having to pay defendants litigation costs. However, some experience in the UK shows that cases with little or no merits are still brought. Especially in product liability cases, plaintiffs seem to have lost in most cases and only few cases were settled. Commentators claimed that defendants went to trial in these cases because of the strong belief that the cases brought against them had little or no merits.[692]

---

688 *Ibidem*, 24, 33 f.

689 *Ibidem*,154.

690 Gibbons, *Group Litigation, Class Actions and Lord Woolf's Three Objectives – A Critical Analysis* 208, 221 f.

691 Mulheron, *Reform of collective redress in England and Wales*, 72 ff; Hodges, *Country Report: England and Wales*, 83.

692 *Ibidem*, 3 f.

Another case commentators and the court judged as speculative was a GLO run by lawyers as the first GLO under a contingency fee arrangement, in the course of Tobacco litigations.[693] While only anecdotal evidence, such cases at least highlight the remaining possibility of abuse.

Settlements are not subject to judge's supervision. This increases the risk that settlement agreements may fall short of the optimal amount necessary to influence (potential) defendant's behaviour. Especially, as the individual in the GLO may have very little influence on the proceeding, despite the fact of having enough interest to file a claim or at least go through the procedure of applying for entry into the GLO register. As has been stated, full information of individuals represented in the GLO, which would be necessary in order to exert control, may be desirable, but might be "simply not compatible with efficient management and resolution of a case within sensible price constraints".[694] It is therefore likely that these procedures are more under the control of the selected lawyers, than that of the individuals. That is particularly likely to be the case, when the GLO is continued as test case procedure. This entails the risk of all the consequences discussed above.[695]

The great flexibility and discretionary power that is given to judges in general and particularly in the GLO may allow courts in multi-party cases to apply the most appropriate management mechanism on a case-by-case basis, however it also introduces a great element of uncertainty for actual and potential parties involved.

Lawyers may not have sufficient incentives to bring cases, where the actual costs of filing and trying the case are large. First, there is a risk that these costs may be considered unreasonable by the judge at one point and the recoverable fees could be reduced to a certain amount. Second, the conditional fee, capped at a maximum of a 100 percent success fee, may not achieve sufficient incentives to take on such high cost and high risk tasks.[696] That is all the more true, when

693 Gibbons, *Group Litigation, Class Actions and Lord Woolf's Three Objectives – A Critical Analysis* 208, 225.

694 Hodges, *Country Report: England and Wales*, 24.

695 See Chapter 3, Section C 1.4 on the principal-agent problems between lawyer and clients under the collective action model.

696 For formal models comparing contingent contingency fee arrangements and the resulting incentives for lawyers with regard to litigation expenditure, see Hyde, "Conditional versus contingent fees: Litigation expenditure incentives," *International Review of Law & Economics* 26 (2006): 180; Emons, *The economics of US-style contingent fees and UK-style conditional fees.* Both works hint to principal-agent problems also being present in UK-style contingent fees and possibly even larger than under the US contingency fee system.

lawyers should also be incentivised to discover breaches of competition law and therefore be the actual enforcement agent.[697]

All of these effects reduce the efficiency of the GLO with regard to deterrence. And indeed, commentators concluded that the GLO procedure had no influence on defendants conduct.[698] It is not surprising, that reform proposals are being discussed.

As far as actual experience is concerned, the theoretical effects may be supported by empirical findings. From 2000 until 2009, there have been a total of 70 group proceedings registered as GLO.[699] Of the first 62 cases, the largest part of claims dealt with issues of care home or child abuses and the next largest part with environmental issues.[700] The total number of multi-party cases brought has gone down constantly and considerably, which is claimed to be an effect of increased public investigations in the beginning, especially in the area of care home or child abuses.[701] Similar developments can be seen in the number of GLO's. While in 2001 and 2002, 18 and 11 cases were brought, respectively, the numbers declined to 6.75 cases per year on average in the following years, and there were only 4 cases in 2007 and 3 in 2008.[702]

2.2. *Actions for damages due to competition law infringements*

As has been mentioned above, and noted by the OFT, consumer compensation in cases of breaches of competition law has been extremely limited so far, despite the legal possibilities to obtain damages. Consumers had, according to the OFT, obtained "virtually no redress".[703] The actual deterrence effect of these avenues to sue for damages is consequently likely to be only very limited as well. Indeed, surveys conducted in an attempt to estimate the deterrence effect of the OFTs enforcement activities revealed that private actions for damages are still seen as relatively irrelevant regarding their influence on companies conduct.[704] These studies conducted for a report for the OFT in 2007, which used questionnaires

---

697 See chapter 3, section C 1 on collective action.

698 Hodges, *Country Report: England and Wales*, 35.

699 See the list maintained by her Majesty's Court Service, available at: www.hmcourts-service.gov.uk/cms/150.htm.

700 Mulheron, *Reform of collective redress in England and Wales*, 9 ff.

701 As reported by the LSC, see *Ibidem*, 2008, 74. Its likely that also the number of GLO's was affected by that development.

702 See the list maintained by her Majesty's Court Service, available at: www.hmcourts-service.gov.uk/cms/150.htm.

703 Office of Fair Trading, *Private actions in competition law: effective redress for consumers and business, OFT Discussion Paper 916*, 11.

704 Deloitte & Touche LLP, *The deterrence effect of competition enforcement by the OFT* 77 f. Available at: www.oft.gov.uk/shared_oft/reports/Evaluating-OFTs-work/oft962.pdf.

send to companies, showed a lack of interest of harmed companies to bring damages claims despite the legal possibilities to do so. Amongst the reasons for not bringing an action despite being harmed by anti-competitive conduct were the bad expected cost/damage award ratio, the time to be spend on litigation, the importance of the business relationship with the potential defendants, lack of sufficient evidence and that there were no prior decisions by the OFT for commencing a follow-on action.[705]

Follow-on representative actions have been used only once by the only designated body so far, the consumer organisation *Which?*, in the case of the football T-shirt price fixing of manufacturers and distributors.[706] *Which?* had originally asked for exemplary damages. However, the ruling by the High Court in 2007 stated that exemplary damages cannot be recovered when a public body has already fined the defendant and that restitutionary damages cannot be granted in competition law cases.[707] This put the case at serious risk, greatly diminishing the value of the case. Although the potential group of represented encompassed thousands of consumers of these T-Shirts, and *Which?* launched considerable media campaigns, the number of harmed individuals that opted-in was very low (in the end only 144 consumers were named in the action). The small number of participating consumers, coupled with the ban on exemplary and restitutionary damages and the low value of individual damages (about £ 20 each) would have run the risk of making the case fail the viability test if continued in court. Ultimately, the case was settled between the parties through an agreement that the defendants would reimburse the named consumers in the representative action and offer other victims a free mug or T-Shirt or optionally £ 10, upon proof of a purchase of one of the T-Shirts in question in one of their stores. After this case, *Which?* publicly announced that it was not to bring any more actions of this kind in the future.[708]

As this case may demonstrate, problems with the representative follow-on procedure are connected to the limitations of the opt-in feature and the important problem of funding and risk bearing. Though only one proceeding has taken place, it can be assumed that the opt-in limitations experienced in the GLO may also apply to the representative follow-on action. Under both procedures, identifying and gathering potential plaintiffs prior to or early on in the process of filing the claim are costly and time-consuming exercises. A potential viability test or cost capping orders by the judge could have a great

---

705 *Ibidem* 77 ff.

706 Farrell, *UK: Private Enforcement.*

707 High Court of England and Wales, *Devenish Nutrition Ltd v Sanofi-Aventis SA (France) and others [2007] EWHC 2394.*

708 Final Report for the Civil Justice Council, "Improving Access to Justice through Collective Actions", *Developing a More Efficient and Effective Procedure for Collective Actions* 141.

influence on the selection of cases brought under both regimes, so that cases with small individual damages might not be brought.

Under the representative follow-on action, the designated body bears the risks and costs of such an action. When such designated bodies are charity organisations and dependant on donations, the funds available for such (potentially extremely costly) actions are extremely limited. Under the GLO, application for necessary insurance for litigation may be *de facto* unavailable.

The lack of exemplary or punitive damages in these proceedings further decreases the deterrence effect, when the total of damages sued for are less than the actual damages caused and the fines imposed in the prior public proceeding are not large enough to cover the remainder of the optimal sanction.

The restriction for competition law infringement cases brought before the CAT to follow-on cases reduces the potential for deterrence effects of private actions for damages. The same is true for the restriction of representative actions to consumer protection cases, which exempts a number of harmed parties, such as small or medium enterprises or any consumer in a business relationship with the defendant(s).

Overall, the experience in the UK seems to have been that the currently available mechanisms of group litigation are still far from achieving the goals they were set up to meet. The OFT recommended already in 2007 that representative bodies should also be allowed to bring stand-alone cases on behalf of consumers as well as business.[709] Moreover, it also suggested that the opt-in regulation could be broadened to allow judges also to pursue a trial on an opt-out basis, where it is deemed appropriate.[710] The above-mentioned findings on the efficiency of private competition law enforcement with regard to its deterrence effects support such calls for changes. Recent discussions and reform proposals therefore aim at widening the scope of existing group litigation procedures and at introducing new procedures, in particular opt-out mechanisms, mechanisms to include business in representative actions and the possibility for aggregate damage awards.[711]

---

709 Office of Fair Trading, *Private actions in competition law: effective redress for consumers and business, Recommendations by the Office of Fair Traiding* 04.10.2009, 12. www.oft.gov.uk/shared_oft/reports/comp_policy/oft916resp.pdf.

710 *Ibidem*, 26 f.

711 See Final Report for the Civil Justice Council, "Improving Access to Justice through Collective Actions", *Developing a More Efficient and Effective Procedure for Collective Actions*; Mulheron, *Reform of collective redress in England and Wales*.

C. GERMANY

As opposed to the assessment of the Ashurst study[712], several commentators stated that private enforcement of competition law had already been heavily used even before the German competition law (*Gesetz gegen Wettbewerbs-beschränkungen*, GWB)[713] had been reformed in 2005. Basing their assessment on the statistics collected by the German Federal Competition Authority (FCA), they report that in the time between 2002 and 2006 about 900 cases where registered dealing with violations of antitrust law.[714] While this has been seen as proof that private enforcement is already sufficiently developed, it has to be noted that these cases where typically cases brought by firms due to vertical agreements, abusive practices or discrimination against dependent companies, while hard-core cartels where not often alleged.[715] Taking into account issues like the problems connected to the treatment of the passing-on defence before (and after) the reform,[716] it is unlikely that this amount of litigation reached the full potential even the old regulations would have provided for. The detailed assessment of the efficiency of the now existing regulations will be done below.

1. THE LEGAL SYSTEM

1.1. Test case procedures (Kapitalanleger-Musterverfahrensgesetz)

Though not applicable in cases of competition law infringements today, the test case procedure in the area of capital market litigation (KapMuG) that came into force 2005 should be mentioned here as well for three reasons. First, because the test case procedure under the KapMuG is the most innovative approach to collective actions in Germany at the moment.[717] Second, the legislator provided this mechanism in order to overcome some of the problems that are also relevant for a group litigation mechanism in anti-trust cases, such as procedural inefficiency and the problem of rational apathy due to a disparity between costs

712 Waelbroeck, *Study on the Conditions for Claims for Damages in Case of Infringement of EC Competition Rules: Comparative Report, Open Procedure COMP/2003/A1/22, Ashurst Study for Directorate General Competition of the EU Commission, London, England.*

713 The analysis of the German competition law will be restricted to the law against restrictions of competition (GWB), excluding the law against unfair competition (Gesetz gegen unlauteren Wettbewerb, UWG) unless noted otherwise.

714 Böge, *Up and Running, or is it? Private enforcement-the Situation in Germany and Policy Perspectives* 197, 197; Bundeskartellamt, *Private Kartellrechtsdurchsetzung, Stand, Probleme, Perspektiven – Diskussionspapier*, 4. Available at: www.bundeskartellamt.de/wDeutsch/download/pdf/Diskussionsbeitraege/05_Proftag.pdf.

715 *Ibidem*, 4.

716 See the discussion of the passing-on defence issue in Germany below.

717 For the development and a description see Stürner, "Model case proceedings in the Capital Markets," *Civil Justice Quarterly* 26 (2007): 250.

and damages in cases of small and dispersed damages.[718] The experience with this form of litigation may provide valuable insights when contemplating the introduction of this mechanism also in competition law. Third, this procedure was designed as an experiment running for five years until 2010 and if the experiment is considered a success, an integration of that procedure into the general rules of civil litigation *Zivilprozessordnung* (ZPO) is proposed.[719] When that happens, this mechanism would also apply to civil litigation in competition law cases.

The procedure begins with individual actions for performance, including actions for damages, filed before the Regional Court *(Landgericht)*, which has jurisdiction in the region in which the defendant has his registered office. In these individual claims, also a motion for a test case declaration (*Musterfeststellungsantrag*) has to be filed. In that motion, the plaintiff has to describe the legal or factual questions to be answered in the test case declaration and to show that these questions are relevant for other similarly suited cases.[720] Test case declaration motions are published in a registry, §2KapMuG, and the individual procedures are halted, §3 KapMuG. Once a minimum of ten such motions in similarly suited cases are registered in the registry, the Regional Court rules upon which questions are to be sent to the Higher Regional Court *(Oberlandesgericht)* to be decided upon in a test case trial, §4 KapMuG.

The trial of the test case itself takes place before the Higher Regional Court. Once the test case procedure has been published in the register, all cases that may be affected by the test case declaratory judgment are halted, irrespective of whether a motion for a test case declaratory judgment has been made in the individual trial or not, §7 Abs. 1 KapMuG.[721] The selection of a test case plaintiff is done by the court, taking into account the value of the plaintiffs claims or an agreement amongst the plaintiffs on a test plaintiff (§8 Abs. 3 KapMuG). The plaintiffs not chosen to be the test case plaintiff are included as third party plaintiffs. The ruling is binding on all courts in which the individual cases have been filed and

---

718 See Deutscher Bundestag (German Parliament), *Entwurf eines Gesetzes zur Einführung von Kapitalanleger-Musterverfahren, BT-Drucks. 15/5091* (2005). available at http://dip21.bundestag.de/dip21/btd/15/050/1505091.pdf.

719 Stürner, *Model case proceedings in the Capital Markets* 250, 265 f.; Deutscher Bundestag, Beschlussempfehlung und Bericht des Rechtsausschusses (6. Ausschuss) zu dem Gesetzentwurf der Bundesregierung- Drucksache 15/5091, BT-Drucks. 15/5695, 22.

720 Deutscher Bundestag (German Parliament), *Entwurf eines Gesetzes zur Einführung von Kapitalanleger-Musterverfahren, BT-Drucks. 15/5091* 20 ff.

721 However, in a recent decision the Federal Court of Justice (BGH) ruled, that a halting of a procedure where no test case motion could have been filed, is not legitimate. It thereby rejected the wide interpretation of that rule of the Regional Court, see *BGH, 16.06.2009, case no XI ZB 33/08*. (2009).

will be continued after the declaratory judgment in the test case procedure, as far as it is relevant for the ruling of these courts, §7 Abs. 1 KapMuG.

Once the test case declaration has been issued, the individual trials are continued and the individual issues like damages and causation are decided upon.

As a consequence of the individual claims remaining intact, settlements can only be agreed upon concordantly, requiring the consent of every individual plaintiff and defendant (§14(3) KapMuG).

For the test case procedure, no additional court or lawyers fees arise (§17 KapMuG). However, the costs, for example expert fees, are borne jointly and divided between the plaintiffs on a *pro rata* basis (§17 KapMuG).

1.2. Group litigation in competition law

Germany reformed its competition law (GWB) also to facilitate private damages claims. One of the major legal disincentives to bring actions for damages due to competition law infringements was abandoned in that reform. The so-called principle of *Schutzgesetzverletzung* (breach of a law intended to protect other individual's rights) previously required parties to have incurred harmed caused by the breach of a legal rule designed to protect them. In restrictive interpretations by courts, the breach of competition law only gave rise to compensation rights, when the infringing act was particularly aimed at harming the claimants. With the reform, §33(1) GWB now allows for damage claims by competitors or other market participants, as far as they are (directly) affected by the infringement.[722] Moreover, §33(4) GWB made prior decisions by national public competition authorities or the European Commission binding for courts in cases of §33 and §34 a GWB and thereby facilitated follow-on claims for damages or skimming-off procedures.[723]

All actions brought before the court due to competition law infringements (either national or European competition law) have to be filed at the general courts for civil litigation, the Regional Courts (*Landesgerichte*), though there dealt with either by trade chambers of the court or assigned to a Regional Court determined to be a court for competition cases (*Kartellgericht*).[724] As these are courts for civil

722 The requirement to be directly affected will be discussed below together with the passing-on defense.

723 Though verbally restricted to actions for damages, legal scholars regard the binding effect to also apply to representative actions for injunctions. See Halfmeier, *Popularklagen im Privatrecht: zugleich ein Beitrag zur Theorie der Verbandsklage*, Tübingen: Mohr Siebeck (2006), 139.

724 Bechtold, *Kartellgesetz: Gesetz gegen Wettbewerbsbeschränkungen: Kommentar*, München: CH Beck (2008), 614 f.

litigation matters, the general rules for civil litigation apply unless some special regulation takes precedence.

It may be noteworthy, that the German FCA has to be informed about all civil litigation concerning competition law infringements, including Article 101 and 102 TFEU and may decide to participate and get involved in civil proceedings (§90 GWB).

1.2.1. Joinder, consolidation and assignation

As far as the general rules on civil litigation are applicable, the traditional forms of bundling similar interests into one proceeding in Germany are joinder (§§59 and 60 ZPO) and consolidation procedures (§147 ZPO). Under both mechanisms, each plaintiff has to file an individual claim, which may be bundled later on. Even under joinder procedures, it is not necessary that the plaintiffs will all use the same legal representative and all issues of individual cases will be dealt with and decided upon in the joint proceeding. As these procedures have been discussed already above, the analysis will focus on other mechanisms to bundle similar claims into one proceeding.

It would also be possible for a number of claimants to assign their claim to just one plaintiff (§398 *Bürgerliches Gesetzbuch* BGB), however, this mechanism has rarely been used.[725] One notable application of this concept are the cases the Carted Damage Claims company (CDC) acquired from victims of cartels, which will be discussed in detail below.

1.2.2. Representative injunction actions

Representative actions for injunction are possible to be brought by specified associations under §33(2) GWB (*Unterlassungssanspruch*) in cases of breach of the GWB or EU competition law. Associations that are granted standing have to foster and protect trade issues and to represent firms, that offer "the same or similar products or services on the same market" (§33(2) GWB). Moreover, to have standing, the association must have a substantial number of affected firms as members.[726] This limits standing to associations representing the interests of competitors of an infringer and reduces possibilities for other trade associations

725 Schilken, *Der Zweck des Zivilprozesses und der kollektive Rechtsschutz. Kollektiver Rechtsschutz im Zivilprozess.* ed. Meller-Hannich. Baden-Baden: Nomos (2008), 21, 42.

726 *Ibidem*, Bechtold, *Kartellgesetz: Gesetz gegen Wettbewerbsbeschränkungen: Kommentar*, §33, 303, rn16.

to become active on behalf of other market participants. The legal literature considers this limitation as an oversight on behalf of the legislator.[727]

Consumer associations, though discussed in the legislative process, were expressively not included in the new GWB.[728] They also do not fall under the current definition of associations that can be granted standing.

This form of representative action under §33 GWB has hardly ever been applied, so that legal literature and jurisprudence on the topic, as well as conclusive experience are lacking.

1.2.3. Representative actions for (restitutionary) damages: Skimming-off procedures

Associations founded to foster or protect trade and industrial interests can also initiate skimming-off actions under §34a GWB. The competition law infringements causing the activity have to be done intentionally and affect a large number of parties (in the sense of widely dispersed and scattered damages).[729] These widely dispersed effects are considered to only exist in cases, where harmed individuals are not expected to enforce their own rights on a larger scale.[730] As the FCA has the same possibilities to employ skimming-off procedures, the standing for associations is subsidiary to the activities of the FCA. Only if the latter does not pursue that particular infringement is it possible for associations to file such actions.

The proceeds from the trial flow to the State and do not remain with the association. This has been heavily criticised already during the legislative process, as incentives for associations to invest resources in such activities can be expected to be of very limited nature.[731] Also this type of action has not been applied, yet.

---

727 Seeliger, *Kollektiver Rechtsschutz im Kartell- und Wettbewerbsrecht.* in Kollektiver Rechtsschutz im Zivilprozess. ed. Meller-Hannich. Baden-Baden: Nomos (2008), 73, 83; Halfmeier, *Popularklagen im Privatrecht: zugleich ein Beitrag zur Theorie der Verbandsklage*, 135.

728 However, these associations might still have the possibility to sue for an injunction in cases of breaches of competition law on basis of the law against unfair competition (§3 UWG), which may also apply.

729 Bechtold, *Kartellgesetz: Gesetz gegen Wettbewerbsbeschränkungen: Kommentar*, §34, rn 3 f, 319; German Monopolies Commission, *Das allgemeine Wettbewerbsrecht in der Siebten GWB-Novelle, Sondergutachten der Monopolkommission gemäß, §44 Abs. 1 Satz 4 GWB*, p.47. www.monopolkommission.de/sg_41/text_s41.pdf.

730 {{390 Bechtold, Rainer 2008}}, §34, rn 4, 319.

731 *Ibidem* 51; Hehne, et al, *Die Eignung des deutschen Zivilprozessrechts zur Durchsetzung des europäischen Kartellrechts im Lichte der 7. GWB-Novelle.* in *Das europäische Kartellrecht nach der Vo 1/03 im Wechselverhältnis von Europäischem Recht und Innerstaatlichem Verfahrensrecht.* eds. Tietje andBlau. Berlin: Berliner Wissenschafts-Verlag (2005), 86.

1.2.4. Assignation as special case: The Cartel Damage Claims company

Assignation is a possibility to assign claims to another party that then succeeds in the rights, which is very common in many civil law countries.[732] While this principle does not in itself form a real group litigation mechanism, it has been successfully applied in Germany recently and shall therefore be discussed here.

The Cartel Damage Claims company,[733] although a company established under Belgian law, shall be discussed here for three reasons. First, the company was (at least co-) founded by two German lawyers. Their "circumvention" of the ban on contingency fees and the general legality of their approach were strongly debated in Germany. Second, their first case was brought against a German cement cartel, discovered and fined by the German FCA, in front of a German court. Last, this case is greatly influencing the development of private antitrust litigation in Germany, as it raised many relevant questions that at least have to be ruled on now, establishing new case law.

In 2005, the Cartel Damage Claims company (CDC) was founded under Belgian law, with the company statutes of enforcing damages claims due to competition law infringements. The company acquired the damage claims of 29 companies harmed by a German cement cartel, which had been investigated and fined by the FCA earlier on and claimed the damages before the court in Düsseldorf, Germany on its own behalf. This approach was heavily discussed and sometimes its legality disputed in the literature and the print media, sometimes viewed as a way to circumvent the ban on contingency fees and collective actions in Germany.[734] However, the court ruled in 2007 that that claim was admissible, as the CDC had become the owner of the claims in accordance with §398 BGB.[735] The German Federal Court of Justice upheld this ruling in 2009.[736] The case still continues.

Since then, the CDC became active in further cases. In March 2009, CDC filed an action for damages, again in Germany, due to a European hydrogen peroxide cartel, which had been investigated and fined by the European Commission.[737]

---

732 This principle is also used, for example, in the Austrian form of representative action by associations.

733 Most of the information about what CDC is and how works can be found on their internet page www.carteldamageclaims.com/.

734 See e.g.Haucap and Stühmeier, "Wie hoch sind durch Kartelle verursachte Schäden: Anworten aus Sicht der Wirtschaftstheorie," *Wirtschaft und Wettbewerb* 58 (2008): 413, 413.

735 LG Düsseldorf, *21.2.2007 - 34 O (Kart) 14705* (2007), 847–849.

736 *BGH, Beschluss vom 7. April 2009 - KZR 42/08* (2009).

737 European Commission, *Case COMP/F/C.38.620 - Hydrogen Peroxide and perborate* (2009), available at http://ec.europa.eu/competition/antitrust/cases/decisions/38620/en.pdf.

This time, 32 companies harmed by the cartel assigned their claims to CDC, which consequently filed the claims on its own behalf.

The CDC acquires the claims as valuable property from the original right holders against a certain amount that could be a percentage of the discovery. As a financing option, the CDC uses their earnings from past cases to pre-finance future litigations, but also uses external professional litigation founders and investors.[738] Thereby, the CDC bears the risks and costs of litigation and not the original claim holders. As a return on investment, the CDC keeps a percentage of the damages awarded. This indeed resembles the contingency fee arrangement known in the USA and, until recently, strictly banned in Germany. It is now only available in very specific circumstances.[739]

1.3. Other relevant issues

1.3.1. Rules on damages

Exemplary or punitive damages, as well as damages multipliers, like double damages, have been discussed,[740] but have never found their way into regulation. In general, damages are only awarded up to the degree of actual harm suffered, according to the so-called *Differenzhypothese.* The principle of *Differenzhypothese* refers to the assessment of damages on basis of a comparison of the current state the victim (or the victim's wealth) is in and the state the victim (or the victim's wealth) would have been in, had the damaging event never happened. This form of assessment of damages consequently includes also interest or lost profit.

Interest on the damages is generally available and granted from the date where the damage occurred, §33(3) GWB. The amount of interest is calculated according to the general rules of laid down in §288 and 289 German Civil Code (*Bürgerliches Gesetz Buch*, BGB).

Due to the difficulties in assessing the amount of the damages, §33(3) GWB allows the estimation of the damages incurred by a plaintiff, also on the basis of the illegal profit the defendant gained as a result of the infringement. The latter amount is then presumed to equal the damages incurred by the opposing party, but this presumption can be disputed. Overall, the plaintiff might only have to provide an estimate of damages, for example a certain range with a minimum

---

738 Www.carteldamageclaims.com/english/case_funding_engl.htm.

739 The change in the ban on contingency fees will be discussed below.

740 Supporting double damages:German Monopolies Commission, *Das allgemeine Wettbewerbsrecht in der Siebten GWB-Novelle, Sondergutachten der Monopolkommission gemäß, §44 Abs. 1 Satz 4 GWB* 28.

amount.[741] However, the plaintiff does not have a free choice between the methods of estimation, rather, the illegal gain is one possibility to estimate damages in cases, where other mechanisms fail or are too difficult.[742]

1.3.2. Costs, fees and cost-shifting rules

Court fees as well as lawyers' (hourly) fees in Germany are strictly regulated, for example, lawyers' fees are determined according to the German Statute on Attorneys Fees (*Rechtsanwaltsvergütungsgesetzes*, RVG). These fees increase with the value of the claim (*Streitwert*) in each case, but on a decreasing scale. This may give lawyers an incentive to avoid, whenever possible, a bundling of similar interests in one case, where the value of the claims would then be aggregated, as the sum of fees assessed on the individual value would be larger than the fee assessed on bases of the aggregate value.[743] Freedom of contract does allow lawyers and clients to agree to larger payments. However, these agreed fees are not subject to the cost-shifting rule, so that the plaintiff will have to pay these additional sums in any case from his own expenses, even if he wins. However, when plaintiffs are using legal insurance to finance their litigation, the regulated fees for lawyers become *de facto* binding, as insurances will only cover these expenses.

Contingency and conditional fees had been banned in Germany until recently, and now are only available in a very restrictive set of circumstances. The Federal Constitutional Court (*Bundesverfassungsgericht*) ruled in 2006, that a general ban of contingency fees was against the Constitution, when it was the only way for an aggrieved party to gain access to justice.[744] The legislator therefore changed the rules of the RVG accordingly in 2008, particularly §4 a, on contingent fees.[745] However, the conditional fee arrangement or contingency fee arrangement can only be agreed upon when the financial circumstances of the plaintiff are dire enough to allow such an agreement. Nevertheless, other costs, such as court costs or the costs of the opposing party in case the trial is lost, remain with the client. Moreover, the lawyer may not pre-finance the litigation, §49 B II (*Bundesrechtsanwaltsordnung*, BRAO). As such, the effect will be

741 Mühlbach and Rinne, *Germany: Private Antitrust Litigation* THE 2009 EUROPEAN ANTITRUST REVIEW – *A Global Competition Review Special Report*. Global Competition Review (2009), where the court acknowledged the damage estimates of the plaintiff (which happens to be CDC).

742 Bechtold, *Kartellgesetz: Gesetz gegen Wettbewerbsbeschränkungen: Kommentar*, §33, rn 28.

743 Such arguments have been made also with regard to the KapMuG, discussed above.

744 BVerfG, (Bundesverfassungsgericht – Federal Constitutional Court), *Beschluss vom 12. Dezember 2006 – 1 BvR 2576/04*.

745 For a discussion of this new rule and its interpretation seeKilian, "Das Gesetz zur Neuregelung des Verbots der Vereinbarung von Erfolgshonoraren," *Neue Juristische Wochenschrift* 61 (2008): 1905.

different to those arising from the contingency fee arrangements in the USA *per se*. It remains to be seen, if many plaintiffs will fulfil these strict requirements in the future and what impact on litigation this new regulation can have.

Germany, however, has legal aid and legal insurance systems. Legal aid, however, seems to be the less favourable alternative, being subject to a stringent test of the available means of the applicant, so that it is not very often and not to large extents granted.[746] The German legal expense insurance market, however, is the largest in Europe.[747] Legal expense insurance, on the other hand, while significantly used,[748] does not cover all risks. Given a lack of non-commercial,[749] private litigation for damages due to competition law in Germany so far, damages actions for breaches of competition law may not be explicitly excluded, yet. However, given the large risks and uncertainties involved, it seems likely that such risks may not be insurable in Germany at reasonable rates.[750]

The general cost-shifting rule applied in Germany is the so-called British or European rule, under which the succumbing party has to bear the costs of the proceeding and the lawyers' fees of the opposing party. However, §89 GWB provides the possibilities for parties to apply to the court for a one-way fee reduction in cases on basis of §33 or §34 a GWB, when the financial strain would otherwise be too large. In such a cost protection order, the court can diminish the value of the claim for the party requesting such an order. Thereby, the court and lawyers fees will be calculated on basis of the lower claim value for the party protected by that order. However, if the party subject to such a cost protection order prevails at trial, the succumbing party will have to bear the court costs and lawyers fees as calculated on basis of the full value of the claim. The non-protected party will also remain liable for the costs not recoverable from the cost-protected opponent even when it prevails.[751] Notice, that at least in such cases, lawyers will earn more in case the party they represent wins as compared to when their party looses at trial, introducing a contingent element into the lawyers' remuneration.

---

746 An exeption is the area of family law, typically not covered by legal insurance. SeeKilian, *Alternatives to Public Provision: The Role of Legal Expenses Insurance in Broadening Access to Justice: The German Experience* 31, 43 f.

747 Kilian and Regan, "Legal expenses insurance and legal aid – two sides of the same coin? The experience from Germany and Sweden," *International Journal of the Legal Profession* 11 (2004): 233, 237.

748 Kilian, *Alternatives to Public Provision: The Role of Legal Expenses Insurance in Broadening Access to Justice: The German Experience* 31, 38, estimates that 42% of German households hold legal expense insurance.

749 Legal expense insurance for commercial disputes is not offered in germany, see *Ibidem*, 36.

750 That was also a problem encoutered in the UK concerning insurance in GLO cases, see section B 1.2.2 above.

751 Cumming, *Civil Procedure Used for Enforcement of EC Competition Law by the English, French and German Civil Courts*, 274 f.

1.3.3. Passing-on defence: an open question in Germany

The passing-on defence was, prior to the reform, sometimes assessed by the court at the stage dealing with the accruement of damage. When passing-on was established, courts could dismiss the case on the basis that the existence of damages had not been proven.[752] Other courts and voices in the legal literature considered the passing-on of damages as part of the establishment of the amount of harm, at which offsetting benefits would have to be taken into account, according to the so-called principle of *Vorteilsausgleich*.[753]

The new regulation unfortunately is not clear on the subject. §33(3) GWB now states, that "When a service or product is purchased at too high prices, the damage is not already excluded, because the service or product was sold on."[754] This formulation has opened the door to further discussions and has not added to legal clarity.[755] Some consider this regulation as an exclusion of a passing-on defence, possibly with the necessity to restrict standing to direct purchasers.[756] Others argue, the exclusion is only directed at a general passing-on defence, used as an argument to deny already the rise of damages and thereby the grounds for the claim. The new regulation should instead be read as dealing with the burden of proof. While under the general assessment of damages (following the *Differenzhypothese*) the plaintiff has to provide proof of the amount of harm he incurred, this new regulation would shift the burden of proof with regard to passed-on overcharges on the defendant.[757] The passing-on defence then could still be applied under the principle of *Vorteilsausgleich*, taking offsetting benefits

752 LG Mannheim, *11.07.2003 – 7 O 326/02*; Seeliger, *Kollektiver Rechtsschutz im Kartell- und Wettbewerbsrecht* 73, 80.

753 LG Dortmund, "1.4.2004, 13 O 55/02 (Kart)"; Emmerich, *§33 GWB. Wettbewerbsrecht*. eds. Immenga andMestmäcker. (2007), rn 53.

754 Translation by the author. Original text: *Wird eine Ware oder Dienstleistung zu einem überteuerten Preis bezogen, so ist der Schaden nicht deshalb ausgeschlossen, weil die Ware oder Dienstleistung weiterveräußert wurde* (§33(3) GWB).

755 Wagner, "Schadensersatz bei Kartelldelikten," *German Working Papers in Law and Economics* 2007 (2007): 18, 22 ff.

756 Bechtold, *Kartellgesetz: Gesetz gegen Wettbewerbsbeschränkungen: Kommentar*, §33 rn 23, 26; 305 f.; German Monopolies Commission, *Das allgemeine Wettbewerbsrecht in der Siebten GWB-Novelle, Sondergutachten der Monopolkommission gemäß, §44 Abs. 1 Satz 4 GWB* 35; Andrelang, "Damages for the Infringement of Article 81 EC by Cartel Agreements According to sec. 33 (3) GWB The Changes of Law Concerning" Protective Law" Requirement and the" Passing-On" Defence," *World Competition* 30 (2007): 573, 583 ff.

757 Wissenbach, *Schadenersatzklagen gegen Kartellmitglieder*. in *Beiträge zum transnationalen Wirtschaftsrecht*. eds. Tietje et al. (2006), 21, 21, Böge, *Up and Running, or is it? Private enforcement-the Situation in Germany and Policy Perspectives* 197 199. See also Bundestag, "Beschlussempfehlung und Bericht des Ausschusses für Wirtschaft und Arbeit zu dem Gesetzentwurf der Bundesregierung: Drucksache 15/3640, Entwurf eines Siebten Gesetzes zur Änderung des Gesetzes gegen Wettbewerbsbeschränkungen, BT-Drucks. 15/5049," *Bundestags-Drucksache* 15 (2005): 5049, 49. Avaiable at: http://dip21.bundestag.de/dip21/btd/15/050/1505049.pdf.

into account when assessing the amount of damages.[758] However, this approach has already been rejected by some commentators in cases of passing-on of damages onto third parties in general, as the required direct causal link between the harming event (here the cartel prices) and the resulting benefits (the passing-on of overcharges) is considered absent.[759] It is very interesting that the majority of commentators even seem to reject that possibility to apply the *Vorteilsausgleichung* because of the preventative function of tort law, which would be at risk if indirect purchasers would not file claims.[760]

In the preamble, the legislator left the final solution to the case law, but so far, no judgment has brought clarity regarding this subject.

1.3.4. Disclosure rules

A general discovery process separated from the trial does not exist in Germany and suggestions to introduce pre-trial discovery procedures are rejected in the literature.[761]

As in many civil law countries, claims being filed need to be sufficiently substantiated by the plaintiff to allow for a preliminary robustness assessment of the case by the judge.[762]

Discovery of further evidence takes place during the proceeding. Concerning the procedural rules on discovery in trial, each party has to present evidence for the facts presented. The court may order a party, upon request of the other party, to provide certain and specified evidence, §142 ZPO. Such an order can also be given against third parties, which may hold relevant documents. §422 ZPO states that the opposing party has to provide the documents requested by the other party, as long as the rules of private law provide the right for such a request. These discovery rights in Germany are generally based on substantive law. For example, §810 BGB states that anyone may request the presentation of a document from another party, if she has a legal interest in the document. Though not explicitly regulated, information asymmetry should also be taken into

758 Bundeskartellamt, *Private Kartellrechtsdurchsetzung, Stand, Probleme, Perspektiven – Diskussionspapier*, 12; Mühlbach, *Germany: Private Antitrust Litigation*.

759 Roth, *§33 GWB*. in *Frankfurter Kommentar zum Kartellrecht*. ed. Helmuth. Köln: O. Schmidt (2001), no. 145 ff.

760 Kersting, "Perspectives for Private Enforcement in European Antitrust Law (Perspektiven der privaten Rechtsdurchsetzung im Kartellrecht)," *Zeitschrift für Wettbewerbsrecht (ZWeR) – Journal of Competition Law-Heft* (2008): 252, 257, with references.

761 Böge, *Up and Running, or is it? Private enforcement-the Situation in Germany and Policy Perspectives* 197, 202.

762 Renda, *Making antitrust damages actions in the EU more effective. Study in support of the impact assessment of the EC White Paper on antitrust damages actions*, 348.

consideration. The German Federal Supreme Court has stated that the party not bearing the burden of proof can be expected to cooperate in clarifying the facts.[763]

1.3.5. The role of judges

The judge in a German civil trial takes a much more active approach, than is common in the USA. It is the judge that questions witnesses and even has certain obligations to protect the right of the parties presenting their case before him. Under §139 ZPO, the judge has to discuss the issues of facts and law with the parties, ensure that all relevant points are commented on by the parties and may even point out relevant facts, which a party may have overlooked.

Again, as such, the more active civil law judge may be better suited to influence the group litigation proceeding than its counterpart in the USA.

2. DETERRENCE EFFECTS

The discussion of the deterrence effects of the German procedures will focus only on the most relevant mechanisms, representative skimming-off procedures, the Cartel Damage Claim company model and the test case procedures under KapMuG.

2.1. Representative skimming-off procedures

The experience in Germany with skimming-off procedures in competition cases is quickly subsumed – it does not exist. As of 2008, no such case has been brought, not even as follow-on claim.[764] It is reasonable to expect that also the deterrence effect of this mechanism can only be marginal. It is probable, that the lack of such actions is a result of the specific design of this mechanism. While the specified body does bear all the costs and risks connected of such an action, the proceeds in case the trial is won will go to the state treasury. Moreover, the potential to gain otherwise, for example by attracting a larger member base and thereby increase the revenue from membership fees, is also limited, as such actions do not provide direct benefits to the members. The indirect effect, i.e.,

763 See, e.g. BGH, *Decision of September 30, 2003 (file No. X ZR 114/00)* (2003), 335, 336. In this context see also the new version of §142 of the ZPO (German Civil Code of Procedure) which came into effect on January 1, 2002 and provides for a possibility to order the presentation of files which are (probably) in the possession of a party to a lawsuit.

764 CDC, "Comments on the European Commission's White Paper on Damages actions for breach of EC antitrust rules,", no. 17. Available at: http://ec.europa.eu/competition/antitrust/actionsdamages/white_paper_comments/cdc_en.pdf.

protection through increased deterrence, may be too hard to sell to potential members.

Given budget constraints of associations and the complexity of competition cases even as follow-on cases, it is very unlikely that the mechanism as it stands will ever create a significant amount of civil litigation.

2.2. *The Cartel Damage Claim company model*

The Cartel Damage Claim company is surely an innovative and interesting approach, which potentially can, compared to traditional litigation, partially reduce rational apathy problems, free riding behaviour and principal-agent problems, and lead to more procedural efficiency.

However, the limits of such an approach with regard to the goal of deterrence are also quite straightforward. One of the major downsides is to be found in large transaction costs. While high value cases with a small number of direct purchasers as victims can be profitable investments for such companies, such companies will most likely not take on cases with small and widely dispersed damages. The costs of finding and contracting with a sufficient number of victims are likely to outweigh the potential profit to be earned, especially when the law allowing assignation of claims is very restrictive and entails a number of requirements and safeguards.

Moreover, even when competition should arise in this new market for cartel damage litigation,[765] it is very probably that litigation companies would always rather pursue follow-on cases rather than stand-alone cases, as these require considerable less investment and risks than stand-alone cases. That remains true even when, like the CDC, firms would offer their own version of leniency programs for cartel members that provide necessary information and proof.[766] Unless otherwise regulated, cartel members are separately and jointly liable, so that one cartel member can be sued for the total amount and then can take redress on the other members. As a result, no reduction in actual liability is granted for a cartel member that comes forward. Consequently, such leniency programs are likely to have only small impacts. The effect of such an approach on the level of detection in turn will also be very limited or non-existent. However, it is discussed and may be possible under current legal regimes, to reduce the actual liability of the cartel member that provides useful information to the plaintiffs, as this could be interpreted as partial reparation.

---

765 As may well be the case, as US firms start to enter the European market.
766 Www.carteldamageclaims.com/english/leniency_plus_engl.htm.

From a deterrence perspective, not only the impact on the rate of detection will be limited, but also the sanction that can be imposed on the infringer will fall short of the optimal sanction for several reasons. The fact that some harm caused to society by competition law infringements has no victims eligible to claim damages, such as the dead weight loss, already reduces the potential sanction to be imposed below the optimal sanction. Even if all the eligible victims of a cartel infringement could be found and their claims bought without incurring any transaction costs, the fact that the profit to be earned by this activity will only be a percentage of the sum of damages also only grant incentives to invest in that activity up to a certain degree, and not correspond to the interest society as whole would have in that activity. Investment in that activity will consequently be lower than the optimal investment from a society point of view. This problem is the same problems that can occur under the contingency fee arrangement in the USA.

2.3. *Test case procedures akin to the KapMuG*

The test cases procedure, if applied in its current form also in competition law cases, is also likely to fall short of the optimal deterrence level. First of all, the fact that each plaintiff still has to file an individual suit has a number of restricting effects on this form of group litigation compared to other alternatives. The rational apathy problem, as far as present, will not be overcome by this mechanism to a large degree. While the test case procedure allows the plaintiffs to share the costs concerning the trial over the common issues, all remaining issues that were not part of the test case declaration have to be tried individually at own costs and risks. The potential cost reduction for the individual plaintiff also has to be weighed against the reduced possibilities to influence the test case trial.

A legally problematic point, but positive from a deterrence perspective, is the fact that all potential plaintiffs could be *de facto* forced to claim their damages and then possibly join the test case trial, when a test case procedure has begun, due to the regulation on limitation periods. The publication of the test case procedure may be considered to be the date at which harmed individuals could be reasonably expected to have become aware of the damaging conduct, so that the relatively short limitation period of one year would begin to run (according to §46 BörsG).[767] This effect would largely reduce incentives to free ride on other plaintiff's efforts.[768]

---

767 Schneider, "Auf dem Weg zu Securities Class Actions in Deutschland?-Auswirkungen des KapMuG auf die Praxis kapitalmarktrechtlicher Streitigkeiten," *Betriebsberater (BB)* 60 (2005): 2249, BB 2005, 2249, 2256.

768 This effect would have been even more efficient when the BGH would not have ruled that cases without a legitimate possibility for a motion for test case procedure could not be

Moreover, lawyers are given adverse incentives that inhibit the full potential of the test case procedure. As the test case trial itself does not entail any additional payment for the lawyers, these may well have incentives to maximise their fees by influencing the choice of test case plaintiff to their favour. Possibilities to do so are given by the fact that the court may chose the plaintiff with the largest case value and that the test case trial can be commenced as soon as ten motions for a test case declaration are registered. Under these circumstances, lawyers may try to secure ten plaintiffs early on and promote the largest value case as test case procedure, as their fees in the test case trial will be determined on basis of the test case value. This in turn may lead to a run-to-court amongst the plaintiffs' lawyers. Otherwise, lawyers will have little incentives to take on the complex and difficult test case, without additional remuneration. Moreover, they may prefer to pursue the cases on an individual level, rather than to employ test case or joinder procedures, due to the design of the fees, which can be larger being a sum of individual fees than one fee based on the sum of the claim values.[769]

D. CONCLUSION

In comparing the three described legal systems of the United States, the United Kingdom and Germany, certain trends seem to emerge. While Germany seems to be the most traditional system, only reluctantly, it seems, deviating from traditional forms of two party litigation, the UK seems to have made a larger development in that direction in the near past. Therefore, the experience made in the UK is very valuable to other European countries. However, even though the UK introduced developments with regard to group litigation much earlier than Germany for example, it seems that the current situation is only an intermediary step. As their different types of group litigation have not in general been considered as a great success, the voices arguing for reform are proposing changes towards a system that uses more of the US American features. This development should be of great interest to all Member States considering the introduction of a group litigation mechanism in competition law cases.

While the US American system itself maybe less than perfect considering deterrence, from the presented legal systems here it seems to be the most widely used and potentially most effective. Arguably, features of the US American system, such as opt-out class actions, may come at costs that are not included in this analysis, such as the often cited guaranteed right to a day in court or due process, which society may or may not give a value of its own – even if it may not

involved in a specific test case proceeding, so that a wider spectrum of plaintiffs against the same defendant could have been included.

769 That is due to the fee structure under which fees increase with the claim values but on a decreasing scale.

be reasonably exercisable in reality. However, whatever the arguments for a deviation from a system that would reach a higher, or the highest, degree of deterrence are, their value to society should always and explicitly be weighted against the costs that lesser degrees of deterrence would impose on society.

The experiences in the UK and Germany clearly show that especially representative actions lack real efficiency when the incentive structure guiding the decisions of an association are disregarded. Costly and risky proceedings may be taken on occasionally, but the system inherent disincentives for associations gaining little from such activities compared to the costs involved mirrors the rational apathy problem encountered in traditional individual suits.

Mechanisms designed merely to make cases manageable that involve a large number of claimants also miss the point when having the goal of deterrence, as they do not eliminate the individuals' incentives to remain rationally apathic or to free ride. Principal-agent problems can persist as well, as can be seen for example regarding the lawyers' incentives in the German test case procedure. Managing mechanisms are valid in those cases, where the obstacles to individual litigation by companies or private individuals are only small from the outset. However, even in such cases they do not lead to procedural efficiency.

Procedural efficiency can only be fully reached when all victims can be joined in one proceeding. Therefore, neither the opt-out class action procedure of the USA, the opt-in GLO procedure of the UK, nor the joinder/test case procedures of Germany can reach full procedural efficiency. However, the degrees to which procedural efficiency can be reached runs in the opposite order, with the USA being followed by the UK and Germany last.

Overall, for both collective and representative actions, one cannot escape realising one crucial point. The incentives given to the agents of society, may they be lawyers or associations, cannot be disregarded. Companies such as the CDC realised this already in the case of follow-on suits. It is all the more true when the goal of deterrence should also be reached by increasing the probability of being caught and convicted for potential infringers. In that respect, both US American and European commentators may have a very valid point when they argue that the European group litigation may fail to be effective when the entrepreneurial side of lawyers (or other agents) is simply denied.[770]

---

[770] Issacharoff, *Will Aggregate Litigation Come to Europe?*, http://ssrn.com/abstract=1296843; Schnell, Class action madness in Europe – a call for a more balanced debate, 2007 (11) E.C.L.R., 617–619; Weth, Die Rolle des Anwaltes, German Working Papers in Law and Economics (8) 2008, 10; Eger, Kommentar zu Stephan Weth: Die Rolle des Anwaltes, German Working Papers in Law and Economics (9) 2008; Micklitz, *Collective Private Enforcement of Consumer Law: The Key Questions.* in *Collective Enforcement of Consumer Law.* eds. Van Boom and Loos. Europa Law Publishing (2007), 13, 25.

Developing the right design of a group litigation mechanism is a very complex task and the governments of the Member States need to approach this issue with great care in order to avoid the costly introduction of systems that turn out to be inefficient in the end.

CHAPTER 6

SUMMARY, POLICY IMPLICATIONS AND FUTURE RESEARCH

A. SUMMARY

In this thesis, insights of the Law and Economics literature were collected in order to develop the features of an optimal group litigation concerning the deterrence of European competition law violation and these were then compared to the proposals of the European Commission in the White Paper on damages actions.

Chapter 1 and 2 provide the basis for the analysis conducted in remainder of this thesis. Chapter 1 provides an overview of the enforcement of European competition law including the rationale of European competition law, the debate about private versus public enforcement in general, and the discussed legal changes to enhance private enforcement. Chapter 2 provides the economic and legal framework used to analyse the efficiency of group litigation mechanisms with regard to deterrence of competition law infringements. This structure is mainly based on economic insights and knowledge developed in the Law and Economics literature. Such an economics based approach entails a choice as to the goal to be pursued by private enforcement to be that of deterrence of unlawful conduct, in this specific case, the (inefficient) breach of competition law and the focus on total welfare. Therefore, the insights of the theories on optimal deterrence are applied to the setting of private enforcement of competition law.

Using the economic framework laid out in chapters 1 and 2, chapter 3 turns to two necessarily slightly abstract forms of existing group litigation mechanisms, i.e. collective actions and representative actions. These different actions were analysed with regard to their potential to achieve deterrence. Outcomes resulting from an initial analysis showed that the optimal group litigation mechanisms from the point of view of society at large (total welfare approach), would be a stand-alone action brought in the form of a mandatory group litigation, including all losses caused to society at large. The main arguments for that outcome are that to reach optimal deterrence, the penalty imposed on the infringer, in the form of damages to be paid, should be based on total harm caused to society, and therefore include all losses caused to all different members of society. This leads to the conclusion that the optimal group litigation should incorporate all individual losses in one proceeding, to be (cost-) efficient. Therefore, and because free riding problems can be eliminated, the optimal system would be a mandatory one, rather than opt-in or opt-out mechanism. It is shown that stand-alone actions are to be preferred over follow-on actions from an efficient deterrence perspective, as only the former increase the rate of detection. This is important as it is increased detection that decreases the amount of the optimal sanction, which otherwise may be prohibitively large, and also when the availability bias leads to a greater value of the risk of detection compared to an increase in the damage awards, i.e. the imposed monetary penalties. Follow-on actions merely contribute to the amount of sanction faced by the infringer when public fines are too low to deter. However, it would be more (cost) efficient in such cases, where the public fine is too low, that the public fine be instead raised sufficiently. Therefore, the analysis continued focusing on mandatory stand-alone group actions.

In the analysis of the two abstract forms of existing group litigation systems of collective and representative actions, problems and obstacles to private litigation for damages specific to certain types of breaches of European competition law were taken into account. The analysis suggests that neither collective nor representative actions will be the optimal group litigation mechanism in the sense of the best group litigation to reach the goal of efficient deterrence, unless the existing systems were to be substantially altered. Problems specific to collective actions, such as the necessity of one of the victim (lead plaintiff) to become active on behalf of himself and other victims of the infringement, render that particular system of bundling similar claims into one procedure less efficient. This is especially so in those cases where the information asymmetry on the side of the victims is large. One way to reduce such problems would be to motivate the lawyer representing the group of victims to become the actual driving force and the active party. However, as the analysis shows, problems and large inefficiencies occur when the collective action is not adequately and explicitly designed to have a lead lawyer, rather than a lead plaintiff. Similar outcomes result in the analysis of representative actions brought by associations on behalf of the victims.

One particular necessity crystallised out of this analysis: the incentives given to the acting agent need to be adequately taken into account and designed in any form of group litigation. In cases where typically individual victims (such as end consumers) will not be the acting agent themselves, this insight has large implications for other goals that one may pursue, such as complete compensation of individual losses of these victims. This important insight is the corner stone of the idea of a market-based approach to private enforcement, where agents compete with each other for detection and litigation of competition law infringements. As has been shown, such a market may heal many of the problems and inefficiencies that would remain in the two stylised forms of existing mechanisms described before. Such a market with competing enforcement agents would, however, face similar problems as those unearthed in the discussion of the economic analysis of competition in research and development. Both are characterised by large upfront investments that are necessary in order to gain profits that are highly uncertain. Therefore, under a first-come, first-served mechanism, there will be many resources wasted in the competitive process. Solutions to these market failures presented included the use of auctions for the right to litigate after detection of a certain infringement has taken place. This solution would not only increase the efficiency of the market idea in general, but also those of other systems of collective actions or representative actions when characterised by strong competition and races to the courts.

After the features of the theoretical optimal system of group litigation with regard to deterrence were determined, the insights gained are used in chapter 4 to compare and discuss the efficiency of the Commission's proposal against this benchmark. The analysis shows that the proposed mechanisms do not reach the potential efficiency of the theoretical optimal solution developed in the previous chapter. This result was no surprise, as the starting point or goal to be achieved though private enforcement in the Commission's point of view, is presumably not deterrence – at least not the dominating one. Moreover, while the theoretical analysis in chapter 3 focuses on stand-alone actions, the Commission wants to encourage follow-on actions in addition to stand-alone actions. The examination nevertheless highlights the inefficiencies, necessary trade-offs, and some of the costs imposed on society should those particular mechanisms suggested by the Commission be chosen. These considerations are also relevant for follow-on actions and for achieving other goals. A discussion of the goals other than deterrence also shows that even these goals may not be achieved to the highest degree possible. After all, the choices made by the Commission can be interpreted to stem from compromises made in the issues (e.g. the goals) themselves and in the political arena (e.g. taking harmonisation and implementation costs into account).

Chapter 5 illustrates the basic features of three selected legal systems, i.e., the group litigation mechanisms as developed in the USA, UK and Germany. These are then compared to the features of the theoretical optimal solution developed in chapter 3. As these existing mechanisms deviate substantially from the theoretical benchmark, they are unlikely to achieve the optimal deterrence results the optimal group litigation mechanisms are argued to achieve. However, the stark differences between the developed systems and their experienced effectiveness and difficulties provide some partial support to the insights gained in the theoretical part of chapter 3. In very broad terms, it seems that the less attention was paid to the question of who would actually have incentives to become active under the current systems, and which problems might occur or what possible regulative remedies to these might be enacted, the less effective the systems turned out to be. This outcome would also hold, if the goal to be achieved would be anything other than deterrence, for example corrective justice as compensation of individual victims. If the incentives structures that the economic analysis highlights are neglected neither deterrence not compensation can be achieved in any efficient or even just effective way.

B. POLICY IMPLICATIONS

It is acknowledged that this analysis largely neglects other relevant aspects, such as strictly legal issues and debates, as well as the political choices involved. However, as has been stated several times throughout the text, the insights gained by conducting an economic cost-benefit analysis, albeit only in qualitative terms, helps to clarify and highlight many issues that are currently discussed in the European Union. The conflicts between different goals and necessary trade-offs identified here remain relevant under any other approach. Even when the discussion should be a purely legal one, or a chiefly political one, the costs and benefits of specific choices concerning the design of a particular group litigation mechanism are still relevant when it comes to implementation of the results of the discussion in reality. Moreover, specific choices made between one option and another should be explicitly stated and justified whenever they entail trade-offs. This can only increase the transparency and enhance the quality of the debate and the resulting choices.

The policy implications of the analysis conducted here are manifold. The most important one is that policy makers faced with the task of developing a group litigation mechanism and imbedding it into their existing legal framework should pay attention to the incentive structures their choices will provide to the relevant subjects of the legal rules. Not only economic theoretical, but also some empirical research exists and experiences have been made in several countries with different systems, which provide essential insights into these incentive structures and the legal rules creating or governing them. Moreover, as should have become clear in the analysis conducted here, policy makers should not rush or be rushed regarding the decision on a particular form of group litigation to be implemented in their legal system.

The theoretical analysis of this thesis demonstrates that policy makers should not attempt to design one solution that would be applied to all types of competition law infringements, at least not without explicitly acknowledging the resulting inefficiencies. Instead, it might be more efficient end effective to tailor specific instruments to the particular circumstances they should and could be applied in, provided the costs of doing so will be outweighed by the additional benefits. Moreover, in cases where the traditional concepts of group litigation would prove to be inefficient, other mechanisms may be considered. Though some of the concepts raised here, like the idea of professional enforcement agents may sound strange at first glance, the basic arguments supporting such an avenue are not merely theoretical. Similar deliberations are already taking place, for example in the debate about passing-on defence and indirect purchaser standing, where some argue that indirect purchasers should not be granted standing due to efficiency reasons. Overall, policy makers should be aware that lip service paid to a "one size fits all" group litigation system where the victims are merely supposedly enabled to claim and fight for their rights, does a disservice not only to the victims in question but to society at large.

Experiences of some European Member States suggest, *inter alia*, that the use of opt-in requirements in group litigation may inhibit the efficiency of group actions. That is not a unique experience of the GLO of the UK, but also Sweden, for example, has made such observations with regard to their collective action processes.[771] Consequently, both countries are debating reform steps. On the other hand, Portugal with opt-out solutions in collective/representative actions seems to report much more favourable experiences[772] and there are more countries having similar experiences with opt-in and opt-out systems.[773] With regard to representative actions by associations, experiences in the UK and Germany identified larger potential obstacles to the efficiency of such systems. Portugal however is planning to introduce consumer representative actions including aggregate damages and representation also of unidentified consumers. It seems that they are experiencing far fewer problems with the implementation of features, which may make such a system much more effective.[774] Therefore, instead of rejecting certain ideas from the outset as being against the "*ordre*

771 See Chapter 5 section B for the UK and Lindblom, "Sweden," *The Annals of the American Academy of Political and Social Science* 622 (2009): 231; reporting only 11 cases in over 5 years.

772 Antunes, "Portugal," *The Annals of the American Academy of Political and Social Science* 622 (2009): 161.

773 Apart from the US, also Denmark, Norway, the Netherlands, see Gaudet Jr, "Turning a blind eye: The Commission's rejection of opt-out class actions overlooks Swedish, Norwegian, Danish and Dutch experience – Swedish, Norwegian, Danish, and Dutch experiences contradict" *European Competition Law Review* 30 (2009): 107.

774 See Chapter 5 B and C for the German and UK experience, and Antunes, *Portugal* 161, 166 f for a description of the envisioned consumer representative action.

public" or constitutional rights on a general European level, further investigating the solutions being implemented in other countries to address these dilemmas may bare fruit. Of paramount importance is first an acceptance that exemptions to general principles might be found in many areas of law, and second, that reform will not be possible without changes of the *status quo*.

Another relevant implication of the results of the analysis conducted here is that trade-offs between different goals, explicitly or implicitly pursued at the same time through the same means, are inescapable. Compensatory justice, despite lacking a clear definition, can often be in conflict with deterrence effects. The protection of consumer welfare can be in conflict with dynamic efficiency of markets. In addition, sustaining old traditions and principles, for example focusing on the compensatory function of tort law and neglecting its potential deterrence function, might be in conflict with progress and reform. Whilst unavoidable, in order to promote economic efficiency such trade-offs should be made unambiguous and choices made for one or the other side of these trade-offs should be justified in order to enhance transparency of the political process, both on European and on national levels. Important and difficult choices will have to be made and those governed by the rules should be informed about the reasons for particular choices. This would strengthen transparency and the democratic process.

In a broader framework, one may ask whether the individual members of society supposed to be better protected against the losses caused by competition law infringements, i.e. end consumers, may not be served better by a system designed to achieve *ex ante* deterrence rather than just compensatory justice after the harming incident has taken place.[775] As stated before, measuring deterrence is a difficult task, but the necessary methods and tools are in the process of being developed and sometimes already being employed. A very simplistic comparison of a few numbers may help to clarify this point.[776]

Taking the figures provided by the OFT[777] on the amount of losses avoided by detecting and ending price fixing agreements to increase the price of replica

775 Even Nelie Kroes stated clearly "Most people would agree that prevention through deterrence is better than cure", Kroes, *Damages Actions for Breaches of EU Competition Rules: Realities and Potentials Opening speech at the conference 'La reparation du prejudice cause par une pratique anti-concurentielle en France et à l'étranger: bilan et perspectives ', Cour de Cassation.*

776 Following an example by Nelie Kroes, *Consumers at the heart of EU Competition Policy SPEECH/08/212*, calculating a direct benefit of the Commissions activities to consumer of 30 EUR for each European citizen.

777 Office of Fair Trading, *Private actions in competition law: effective redress for consumers and business, OFT Discussion Paper 916*, 6. Available at www.oft.gov.uk/shared_oft/reports/comp_policy/oft916.pdf.

football kits in the *Replica Football Kit*[778] case, the abortion of the price-fixing agreement saved the consumers over £50 million in losses. Estimated 1,2 to 1,5 million consumers were affected,[779] so that the savings in future losses due to the abortion of the detected offence alone mounted to up to £ 41, 66 for each affected consumer. Moreover, this figure was not even taking the additional saved losses due to deterrence of similar competition law infringements into account. Due to the same competition law infringement, the consumer organisation *Which?* was claiming £ 20 in damages per consumer in its one and only follow-on case against JJB Sports PLC, and was able to achieve a settlement providing consumers compensation of £ 10 for many and £ 20 for few.[780] Competition law infringements occur across industries and products, as well as over time, so that consumers may well be harmed by one or the other at some point. However, it is possible that the value of avoided future losses caused by the detection and ending of certain infringements already outweigh the value of individual harm that can or will be compensated. If that is not the case, one may then want to add the value of the losses avoided, because (similar) infringements were deterred, or abandoned, because of the detection and prosecution of just one offence. Studies conducted in the UK, for example, report cautious estimates of deterrence ratios and estimate that for one detected cartel case, the number of deterred or abandoned cartels ranged between 5 and 16.[781] Taking these values into account, would increase the total amount of avoided future losses significantly.

C. FUTURE RESEARCH

If further research conducted in the area of estimating and measuring deterrence effects shows that the benefits for end consumers gained by increasing deterrence will outweigh the potential value of compensation in individual cases then the argument for protection of consumers should be made to primarily favour *ex ante* deterrence systems rather than *ex post* compensation systems. That is, that focus should shift to designing compensation systems in a way that they would lead to deterrence, as prevention can be argued to be better than cure. Therefore, another policy implication would be to foster important research in the relevant areas of estimating deterrence effects and costs of enforcement activities. The results of this research would be relevant in several areas, not only to the debate about private enforcement in general, and group litigation in particular, but also

778 Office of Fair Trading, *Decision of the Office of Fair Trading No. CA98/06/2003, Price-fixing of Replica Football Kit* (2003).

779 Final Report for the Civil Justice Council, *"Improving Access to Justice through Collective Actions", Developing a More Efficient and Effective Procedure for Collective Actions*, 88.

780 Competition Appeal Tribunal, *The Consumers Association v JJB Sports PLC, case number 1078/7/9/07*. See also Chapter 5 on this case and the problems encountered by Which?

781 Deloitte & Touche LLP, *The deterrence effect of competition enforcement by the OFT*, 8 f.

for the accountability of enforcement measures of competition law. Such research is also necessary to establish the optimal resources spent on enforcement and may provide better answers to the question whether the theoretical enforcement agent described in chapter 3 would need to be awarded all of the sanction to have the right incentives to invest in detection efforts, or whether indeed a fraction of this sum would suffice.

In light of such research, it might also turn out that the changes necessary to make private enforcement of competition law efficient, or even just more effective, especially through the introduction of group litigation mechanisms, are simply not desirable, or too costly from a society point of view. That may be the case, for example, when it is considered simply impossible to introduce a system that goes farther than a very elaborate opt-in mechanism in order to protect individual rights. If this is the case, policy makers should consequently reconsider whether the fostering of private enforcement really is the right way to proceed. After using more accurate estimates to compare the costs and benefits of private, as well as public enforcement, it may turn out that resources otherwise spent on the reform of civil procedure rules to introduce half hearted group litigation tools would be more efficiently spent on improving and/or extending public enforcement of competition law, to the benefit of all. In such a case, the enforcement of competition law may indeed remain very different in the European Union compared to the enforcement of competition in the USA. While the former would concentrate and mostly rely on public enforcement activities, the latter would have a strong part of private enforcement and there would be less convergence, at least with regard to enforcement activities.

REFERENCE LIST

COURT DECISIONS

GERMANY

BGH. 16.06.2009, case no XI ZB 33/08. 2009.

BGH. Decision of July 4, 2009 – KZR 42/08. 2009.

BGH. Caroline of Monaco BGHZ (15th November, 1994 – VI 56/94). 1994.

BGH. Decision of June 4, 1992 (file Ni. IX 149/91).1992.

BGH. Decision of September 30, 2003 (file No.X ZR 114/00). 2003.

BVerfG, (Bundesverfassungsgericht – Federal Constitutional Court). Beschluss vom 12. Dezember 2006 – 1 BvR 2576/04.

LG Dortmund. "1.4.2004, 13 O 55/02 (Kart);".

LG Düsseldorf. 21.2.2007 – 34 O (Kart) 14705. 2007.

LG Mannheim. 11.07.2003 – 7 O 326/02.

UK

England and Wales Court of Appeal (UK). Devenish Nutrition Ltd v Sanofi-Aventis SA (France) and others [2008] EWCA Civ 1086; [2008] WLR (D) 317. 2008.

High Court of England and Wales. Devenish Nutrition Ltd v Sanofi-Aventis SA (France) and others [2007] EWHC 2394. 2008.

High Court of England and Wales. Emerald Supplies Ltd v British Airways plc [2009] EWHC 741 (Ch); [2009] WLR (D) 136. 2009.

United Kingdom Competition Appeals Tribunal. BCL Old Co Ltd & Ors v Aventis SA & Ors, Court of Appeal – United Kingdom Competition Appeals Tribunal, January 28, 2005. 2005.

Competition Appeal Tribunal. The Consumers Association v JJB Sports PLC, case number 1078/7

EUROPEAN UNION

Court of First Instance of the European Communities. Case T-201/04 Microsoft Corp. v Commission of the European Communities. 2007.

European Court of Justice. Case 170/83, Hydrotherm Gerätebau GmbH v Compact del Dott. 1984.

European Court of Justice. Case 26/62 Algemene Transport- en Expeditie Onderneming van Gend & Loos v Nederlandse administratie der belastingen. 1963.
European Court of Justice. Case C-453/99 Courage Ltd v Bernard Crehan [2001] ECR I-6297. 2001.
European Court of Justice. Cases C-295/04 to C-298/04 Vincenzo Manfredi and Others v. Lloyd Adriatico Assicurazioni SpA and Others ECR I-6619. 2006.
European Court of Justice. Sabine von Colson and Elisabeth Kamann v Land Nordrhein-Westfalen, Case – 14/83. 1984.

USA

U.S. District Courts. In re Auction Houses Antitrust Litigation., 164 F. Supp. 2d 345 (S.D.N.Y. 2001). 2001.
U.S. District Courts. Table C-4, U.S. District Courts – Civil Cases Terminated, by Nature of Suit and Action Taken, during the 12-Month Period Ending September 30, 2005. (2005).
United States Court of Appeals. 8th Circuit, No. 96–2925 KAMPA vs WHITE CONSOLIDATED INDUSTRIES, INC.
U.S. Supreme Court. Eisen v. Carlisle & Jacquelin, 417 U.S. 156. 1974.
U.S. Supreme Court. Hanover Shoe, Inc. v. United Shoe Machinery Corp., 392 U.S. 481. 1968.
U.S. Supreme Court. Illinois Brick Co. v. Illinois, 431 U.S. 720. 1977.
U.S. Supreme Court. Sprague v. Ticonic National Bank 307 U.S. 161,167. 1939.
U.S. Supreme Court. Trustees v. Greenough (1882) 105 U.S. 527. 1882.

ITALY

The Italian Supreme Court. Corte di Cassazione, 1183/2007. 2007.

REFERENCES

Abramowicz, M. "On the Alienability of Legal Claims." *The Yale Law Journal* 114 (2004): 697.
Abramowicz, M. "The Uneasy Case For Patent Races over Auctions." *Stanford Law Review* 60 (2007): 803.
Alexander, J.C. "An introduction to class action procedure", available at www.law.duke.edu/grouplit/papers/classactionalexander.pdf." *Online* (2000).
American Bar Association, Chicago, US (ABA). "ABA Comments on the Commission's Green Paper on damages actions for breach of the EC antitrust rules." (2006). Available at: http://ec.europa.eu/competition/antitrust/actionsdamages/green_paper_comments.html

Amtenbrink, F. and Van de Gronden, J. *Economic Law and the Treaty of Lisbon I: Competition and Internal Market.* Tijdschrift voor Europees en Economisch Recht, Vol. 56, pp. 323–329, 2008–9

Andrelang, C. "Damages for the Infringement of Article 81 EC by Cartel Agreements According to sec. 33 (3) GWB The Changes of Law Concerning" Protective Law" Requirement and the"Passing-On" Defence." *World Competition* 30 (2007): 573.

Antunes, H.S. "Portugal." *The Annals of the American Academy of Political and Social Science* 622 (2009): 161.

Apple, J.G. and Deyling, R.P. *A primer on the civil-law system.* Federal Judicial Center (1995).

Associazione fra le società italiane per azioni. "Comments on the Green Paper on damages actions for breach of the EC antitrust rules." (2006). Available at: http://ec.europa.eu/competition/antitrust/actionsdamages/green_paper_comments.html

Audretsch, D.B., Baumol, W.J. and Burke, A.E. "Competition policy in dynamic markets." *International Journal of Industrial Organization* 19 (2001): 613.

Baetge, D. "National report Germany: Class Actions, Group Litigation & Other Forms of Collective Litigation." *Global Class Actions* (2007). Available at: www.law.stanford.edu/display/images/dynamic/events_media/Germany_National_Report.pdf

Baker, J.B. "The case for antitrust enforcement." *Journal of Economic Perspectives* 17 (2003): 27.

Baker, J.B. "Private information and the deterrent effect of antitrust damage remedies." *Journal of Law, Economics, & Organization* 4 (1988): 385.

Bar-Gill, O. and Parchomovsky, G. "A marketplace for Ideas?" *Texas Law Review* 84 (2005): 395.

Baumol, W.J. and Ordover, J.A. "Use of antitrust to subvert competition." *Journal of Law & Economics* 28 (1985): 247.

Bebchuk, L.A. "Negative Expected Value Suits." *NBER Working Paper Series Paper no. W6474* (1998).

Bebchuk, L.A. "Optimal sanctions when individuals are imperfectly informed about the probability of apprehension." *The Journal of Legal Studies* 21 (1992): 365.

Bebchuk, L.A. "Suing solely to extract a settlement offer." *Journal of Legal Studies* 17 (1988): 437.

Bebchuk, L.A. and Chang, H.F. "Analysis of Fee Shifting Based on the Margin of Victory: On Frivolous Suits, Meritorious Suits, and the Role of Rule 11, An." *Journal of Legal Studies* 25 (1996): 371.

Bebchuk, L.A. and Guzman, A.T. "How Would You Like to Pay for That--The Strategic Effects of Fee Arrangements on Settlement Terms." *Harvard Negotiation Law Review* 1 (1996): 53.

Beccaria, C. "On Crime and Punishment." Pages 117 in *Theories of Punishment.* Edited by Stanley E. Grupp. Bloomington: Indiana University Press (1971).

Bechtold, R. *Kartellgesetz: Gesetz gegen Wettbewerbsbeschränkungen: Kommentar.* München: CH Beck (2008).

Becker, G.S. "Crime and Punishment: An Economic Approach." *The Journal of Political Economy* 76 (1968): 169.

Becker, G.S. "The economic way of looking at life." *Nobel Lecture, Journal of Political Economy* 101 (1993): 385.

Becker, G.S. and Landes, W.M. *Essays in the Economics of Crime and Punishment.* New York: Columbia University Press (1974).

Becker, G.S. and Stigler, G.J. "Law enforcement, malfeasance, and compensation of Enforces." *The Journal of Legal Studies* 3 (1974): 1.

Behr, V. "Punitive Damages in America and German Law-Tendencies towards Approximation of Apparently Irreconcilable Concepts." *Chicago-Kent Law Review* 78 (2003): 105.

Behrens, P. "Theoretische und Praktische Probleme einer Ökonomisierung der Kartellrechtsanwendung." Pages 457 in *Internationalisierung des Rechts und seine ökonomische Analyse.* Edited by Thomas Eger, Claus Ott, Jochen Bigus and Georg von Wangenheim. (2008).

Bentham, J. *Principles of penal law.* The Works of Jeremy Benthem (1843).

Beuchler, H. "Länderbericht Frankreich." Page 57 in *Das Verbandsklagerecht in der Informations-und Dienstleistungsgesellschaft.* Edited by Hans-W Micklitz and Astrid Stadler. Münster: Landwirtschaftsverlag (2005).

Beuchler, H. "Länderbericht Vereinigte Staaten." Pages 941 in *Das Verbandsklagerecht in der Informations-und Dienstleistungsgesellschaft.* Edited by Hans-W Micklitz and Astrid Stadler. Münster: Landwirtschaftsverlag (2005).

Block, M.K. "Optimal penalties, criminal law and the control of corporate behavior." *Boston University Law Review* 71 (1991): 395.

Böge, U. and Ost, K. "Up and Running, or is it? Private enforcement-the Situation in Germany and Policy Perspectives." *European Competition Law Review* 27 (2006): 197.

Bohn, J. and Choi, S.J. "Fraud in the new-issues market: Empirical evidence on securities class actions." *University of Pennsylvania Law Review* 144 (1995): 903.

Bolotova, Y.V. "Cartel overcharges: An empirical analysis." *Journal of Economic Behavior and Organization* 70 (2009): 321.

Bone, R. G. "Modeling Frivolous Suits." *University of Pennsylvania Law Review* 145 (1996): 519.

Bonelli Erede Pappalardo, Bredin Prat, Hengeler Mueller, Slaughter and May and Uría Menéndez. "Damages Actions for Breach of the EC Antitrust Rules, Comments on the Commission's White Paper." (30 June 2008). Available at: http://ec.europa.eu/competition/antitrust/actionsdamages/white_paper_comments.html

Bork, R.H. *The antitrust paradox: A policy at war with itself.* Basic Books New York (1978).

Bouckaert, B. "Original assignment of private property." Pages 1 in: *Encyclopedia of Law and Economics.* (2000).

Bowles, R., Faure, M. and Garoupa, N. "Forfeiture of Illegal Gain: An Economic Perspective." *Oxford Journal of Legal Studies* 25 (2005): 275.

Braun, D.D. "Principal-agent theory and research policy: an introduction." *Science & Public Policy* 30 (2003): 302.

Breit, W. and Elzinga, K.G. "Private antitrust enforcement: the new learning." *Journal of Law & Economics* 28 (1985): 405.

Brickman, L. "Effective Hourly Rates of Contingency Fee Lawyers: Competing Data and Non-Competitive Fees." *Washington University Law Quarterly* 81 (2003): 653.

Brodley, J.F. "Antitrust Standing in Private Merger Cases: Reconciling Private Incentives and Public Enforcement." *Michigan Law Review* 94 (1995): 1.

Budzinski, O. "Monoculture versus diversity in competition economics." *Cambridge Journal of Economics* 32 (2007): 295.

Bulst, F.W. " Damages Actions for breach of EC Antitrust Rules." (2006). Available at: http://ec.europa.eu/competition/antitrust/actionsdamages/green_paper_comments.html

Bundeskartellamt. "Private Kartellrechtsdurchsetzung, Stand, Probleme, Perspektiven – Diskussionspapier." (2005). Availabe at: www.bundeskartellamt.de/wDeutsch/download/pdf/Diskussionsbeitraege/05_Proftag.pdf

Bundestag, D. "Beschlussempfehlung und Bericht des Ausschusses für Wirtschaft und Arbeit zu dem Gesetzentwurf der Bundesregierung: Drucksache 15/3640, Entwurf eines Siebten Gesetzes zur Änderung des Gesetzes gegen Wettbewerbs-beschränkungen, BT-Drucks. 15/5049." *Bundestags-Drucksache* 15 (2005): 5049.

Bundesverfassungsgericht – Pressestelle. *Pressemitteilung Nr. 27/2007 Vom 7. März 2007,Zum Beschluss Vom 12. Dezember 2006 – 1 BvR 2576/04 (Press Release 27/2007).* (2007).

Burroughs, A. F. "Mythed It Again: The Myth of Discovery Abuse and Federal Rule of Civil Procedure 26 (b)(1)." *McGeorge Law Review* 33 (2001): 75.

Cafaggi, F. and Micklitz, H. "Administrative and Judicial Collective Enforcement of Consumer Law in the US and the European Community." *EUI LAW Working Paper no. 2007/22* (2007).

Camerer, C. "Behavioral economics: Reunifying psychology and economics." *Proceedings of the National Academy of Sciences of the United States of America* 96 (1999): 10575.

Camilli, E.L. "Optimal Fines in Cartel Cases and the Actual EC Fining Policy." *World Competition* 29 (2006): 575.

Canoy, M., Rey, P. and van Damme, E. "Dominance and Monopolization." *TILEC Discussion Paper DP 2004-022* (2004).

CDC, Cartel Damage Claims. "Comments on the European Commission's White Paper on Damages actions for breach of EC antitrust rules.". Available at: http://ec.europa.eu/competition/antitrust/actionsdamages/white_paper_comments.html

CEFIC, European Chemical Industry Council. "The comments of the chemical industry on the commission GREEN PAPER on damages actions for breach of EC Antitrust rules." *CEFIC* (12 Apr 2006). Available at: http://ec.europa.eu/competition/antitrust/actionsdamages/green_paper_comments.html

Choi, S.J. "Evidence on Securities Class Actions, The." *Vanderbilt Law Review* 57 (2004): 1465.

Clark, E., Hughes, M. and Wirt, D. "Study on the conditions of claims for damages in case of infringement of EC competition rules-Analysis of economic models for the calculation of damages." (2004).

Clermont, K.M. and Currivan, J.D. "Improving on the Contingent Fee." *Cornell Law Review* 63 (1977): 529.

Clermont, K.M. and Eisenberg, T. "Trial by jury or judge: Transcending empiricism." *Cornell Law Review* 77 (1991): 1124.

Coffee Jr, J.C. "Regulation of Entrepreneurial Litigation: Balancing Fairness and Efficiency in the Large Class Action, The." *The University of Chicago Law Review* 54 (1987): 877.

Coffee Jr, J.C. "Rescuing the Private Attorney General: Why the Model of the Lawyer as Bounty Hunter Is Not Working." *Maryland Law Review* 42 (1983): 215.

Coffee Jr, J.C. "Understanding the Plaintiff's Attorney: The Implications of Economic Theory for Private Enforcement of Law through Class and Derivative Actions." *Columbia Law Review* 86 (1986): 669.

Collins, D. "Public Funding of Class Actions and the Experience with English Group Proceedings." *Manitoba Law Journal* 31 (2005): 211.

Competition Law Research Centre (Hungary). "Comments on the White Paper". Available at: http://ec.europa.eu/competition/antitrust/actionsdamages/white_paper_comments.html

Connor, J.M. *Global price fixing.* Berlin: Springer (2008).

Connor, J.M. "Optimal deterrence and private international cartels." *Purdue University, Working Paper Series* (2007).

Connor, J.M. and Helmers, C. G. "Statistics on Modern Private International Cartels, 1990–2005, AAI Working Paper No. 07–01." *The American Antitrust Institute* (2007).

Cooper, J.C., Froeb, L., O'Brien, D.P. and Vita, M. "Vertical Restrictions and Antitrust Policy: What About the Evidence?, Vanderbilt Public Law Research Paper No. 05–32." *Competition Policy International* 1 (2005): 45.

Cooter, R. and Ulen, T.S. *Law and Economics.* Pearson (2003).

Council of the European Union. *Council Regulation (EC) no. 1/2003 of 16 December 2002 on the Implementation of the Rules on Competition Laid Down in Articles 81 and 82 of the Treaty.* (2003).

Cox, J.D. and Thomas, R.S. "Does the plaintiff matter? An empirical analysis of lead plaintiffs in securities class actions." *Columbia Law Review* 106 (2006): 1587.

Crane, D.A. "Antitrust Antifederalism." *California Law Review* 96 (2008): 1.

Crane, D.A. "Antitrust Modesty." *Michigan Law Review* 105 (2006): 1193.

Crane, D.A. "The Paradox of Predatory Pricing." *Cornell Law Review* 91 (2005): 1.

Cumming, G., Spitz, B. and Janal, R. *Civil Procedure Used for Enforcement of EC Competition Law by the English, French and German Civil Courts.* Alphen aan de Rijn: Kluwer Law International (2007).

Dana, J.D. and Speir, K.E. "Expertise and contingent fees: The role of asymmetric information in attorney compensation." *Journal of Law, Economics, and Organization* 9 (1993): 349.

Danzon, P.M. "Contingent Fees for Personal Injury Litigation." *The Bell Journal of Economics* 14 (1983): 213.

Danzon, P.M. and Lillard, L.A. "Settlement out of court: The disposition of medical malpractice claims." *Journal of Legal Studies* 12 (1983): 345.

Dasgupta, P. and Stiglitz, J.E. "Uncertainty, industrial structure, and the speed of R&D." *The Bell Journal of Economics* (1980): 1.

Daughety, A.F. "*Settlement.*" Pages 95 in *Encyclopedia of Law and Economics, Volume I. The History and Methodology of Law and Economics.* Edited by Boudewijn Bouckaert and Gerrit De Geest. Cheltenham: Edward Elgar (2000).

Dawes, A. "The English High Court strikes out a representative claim brought on behalf of "all other direct or indirect purchasers of air freight services", refusing to stretch the scope of the English civil procedure rules in order to encourage the bringing of private damages actions (Emerald Supplies & ANR / British Airways), No 26352." *E-Competitions* (Jun 2009).

Dayagi-Epstein, O. "Representation of Consumer Interest By Consumer Associations-Salvation for the Masses?" *Competition Law Review* 3 (2006): 209.

Deloitte & Touche LLP. *The Deterrence Effect of Competition Enforcement by the OFT* (Nov 2007). Available at: www.oft.gov.uk/shared_oft/reports/Evaluating-OFTs-work/oft962.pdf

DeLong, J.V. "The New 'Criminal' Classes: Legal Sanctions and Business Managers." Pages 9 in: *Go directly to jail: the criminalization of almost everything.* Edited by Gene Healy. Washington DC: Cato Institute (2004).

Deutscher Bundesrat. " Weißbuch der Kommission der Europäischen Gemeinschaften über Schadenersatzklagen wegen Verletzung des EG-Wettbewerbsrechts" BR-Drucksache 248/08." (2008). Available at: http://ec.europa.eu/competition/antitrust/actionsdamages/white_paper_comments.html

Deutscher Bundestag (German Parliament). *Entwurf eines Gesetzes gegen den unlauteren Wettbewerb (UWG), BT-Drucks. 15/1487.*

Deutscher Bundestag (German Parliament). *Entwurf eines Gesetzes zur Einführung von Kapitalanleger-Musterverfahren, BT-Drucks. 15/5091.* (2005).

Duffy, J.F. "Rethinking the prospect theory of patents." *University of Chicago Law Review* 71 (2004): 439.

Easterbrook, F.H. "Detrebling antitrust damages." *Journal of Law & Economics* 28 (1985): 445.

Easterbrook, F.H. "Predatory strategies and counterstrategies." *The University of Chicago Law Review* 48 (1981): 263.

Eger, T. and Weise, P. "Limits to the private enforcement of antitrust law." *German Working Papers in Law and Economics* 2007 (2007).

Eichholtz, S. *Die US-amerikanische Class Action und ihre deutschen Funktionsäquivalente.* Tübingen: Mohr Siebeck (2002).

Eide, E. "*Economics of Criminal Behavior.*" Page 345 in: *Encyclopedia of Law and Economics, Volume I. The History and Methodology of Law and Economics.* Edited by Boudewijn Bouckaert and Gerrit De Geest. Cheltenham: Edward Elgar (2000).

Eilmansberger, T. "The Green Paper on Damages Actions for Breach of the Ec Antitrust Rules and Beyond: Reflections on the Utility and Feasibility of Stimulating Private Enforcement through Legislative Action." *Common Market Law Review* 44 (2007): 431.

Eisenberg, T., Miller, G.P. and Hall, M.T. "Attorneys Fees in Class Action Settlements: An Empirical Study." *Journal of Empirical Legal Studies* 1 (2004): 27.

Eisenberg, T. and Miller, G.P. "Role of Opt-outs and Objectors in Class Action Litigation: Theoretical and Empirical Issues, The." *Vanderbilt Law Review* 57 (2004): 1529.

Eisenhardt, K.M. "Agency theory: An assessment and review." *The Academy of Management Review* 14 (1989): 57.

Emanuelson, D., Normann, P. and Ostoyich, J. "More of the same: growth in private antitrust litigation and cutbacks by the US Supreme Court." *The Antitrust Review of the Americas* (2009).

Emmerich, V. "§33 GWB." in: *Wettbewerbsrecht.* Edited by U. Immenga and E. -J Mestmäcker. (2007).

Emmerich, V. *Kartellrecht.* München: Beck (2001).

Emons, W. and Garoupa, N. "The economics of US-style contingent fees and UK-style conditional fees." *Centre for Economic Policy Research (CEPR) Discussion Paper no. 4473* (2004).

European Commission. "*Block Exemptions for Horizontal Agreements: Commission Regulation no 2658/2000 of 29 November 2000 on the Application of Article 81 (3) of the Treaty to Categories of Specialisation Agreements* " OJ 2000 L304/3 (2000).

European Commission. " Guidelines on the applicability of Article 81 of the EC Treaty to horizontal cooperation agreements (2001/C 3/02)." OJ 2001 C3/2 (2001).

European Commission. *COMMISSION REGULATION (EC) no 2790/1999 of 22 December 1999 on the Application of Article 81(3) of the Treaty to Categories of Vertical Agreements and Concerted Practices* OJ L336/21 (1999).

European Commission. *Commission Regulation no 2659/2000 of 29 November 2000 on the Application of Article 81 (3) of the Treaty to Categories of Research and Development Agreements.* OJ 2000 L304/7, (2000).

European Commission. "Commission Staff Working Document, Accompanying document to the White Paper on Damages actions for breach of the EC antitrust rules, Impact Assessment, {COM (2008) 165 final} {SEC(2008) 404} {SEC(2008) 406}." (2008).

European Commission. "Commission Staff Working Paper, Annex to the Green Paper Damages actions for breach of the EC antitrust rules, (COM(2005) 672 final)." (2005).

European Commission. " Commission Notice- Guidelines on the application of Article 81(3) of the Treaty" Guidelines on the application of article 81 of the EC Treaty to technology transfer agreements, OJ 2004 C 101/2.

European Commission. "*Guidance on the Commission's Enforcement Priorities in Applying Article 82 of the EC Treaty to Abusive Exclusionary Conduct by Dominant Undertakings*". OJ C 45/7(2009).

European Commission. "Discussion Paper on the Application of Article 82 of the Treaty to Exclusionary Abuses" *Brussels, (Online Publication)* (2005).

European Commission. "Green Paper: Damages actions for breach of the EC antitrust rules." COM(2005) 672 final (2005).

European Commission. "Commission Notice – Guidelines on the application of vertical restraints" OJ 291/01. (2000).

European Commission. "*White Paper on Damages actions for breach of the EC antitrust Rules COM(2008) 165 final, SEC(2008) 404.*" COM(2008) 165 final (2008).

European Commission for the Efficiency of Justice (CEPEJ). "*European Judicial Systems 2002, Facts and Figures on the Basis of a Survey Conducted in 40 Council of Europe Member States*". Council of European Publishing (2002).

European Commission for the Efficiency of Justice (CEPEJ). "*European Judicial Systems 2006, Facts and Figures on the Basis of a Survey Conducted in 40 Council of Europe Member States*". Council of European Publishing (2006).

European Group on Tort Law. *Principles of European tort law: text and commentary.* Wein, New York: Springer (2005).

Farmer, S.B. "More Lessons from the Laboratories: Cy Pres Distributions in Parens Patriae Antitrust Actions Brought by State Attorneys General." *Fordham Law Review* 68 (1999): 361.

Farrell, J. and Katz, M.L. "The economics of welfare standards in antitrust." *Competition Policy International* 2 (2006): 3.

Farrell, L. and Ince, S. "UK: Private Enforcement." *The 2009 European Antitrust Review – a Global Competition Review special report.* Global Competition Review (2009).

Faure, M. and Van Boom, W. "Introducing "Shifts in Compensation Between Private and Public Systems"." Pages 1 in *Shifts in Compensation Between Private and Public Systems.* Edited by Michael Faure and Willem Van Boom. Wien: Springer (2007).

Federal Ministry of Economics and Technology, Federal Ministry of Justice, the Federal Ministry of Food, Agriculture and Consumer Protection and Bundeskartellamt. "*Comments of the Federal Ministry of Economics and Technology, the Federal Ministry of Justice, the Federal Ministry of Food, Agriculture and Consumer Protection and the Bundeskartellamt on the EU Commission's White Paper on "Damages actions for breach of the EC antitrust rules.*" (2008). Available at: http://ec.europa.eu/competition/antitrust/actionsdamages/white_paper_comments.html

Feinberg, R.M. "The Enforcement and Effects of European Competition Policy: Results of a Survey of Legal Opinion." *Journal of Common Market Studies* 23 (1985): 373.

Feuerstein, L.W. "Two-Way Fee Shifting on Summary Judgment or Dismissal: An Equitable Deterrent to Unmeritorious Lawsuits." *Pepperdine Law Review* 23 (1995): 125.

Fisch, J.E. "Lawyers on the Auction Block: Evaluating the Selection of Class Counsel by Auction." *Columbia Law Review* 102 (2002): 650.

Fisher, F.M. "Economic Analysis and Antitrust Damages." *World Competition* 29 (2006): 383.

Foer, A. "The Goals of Antitrust: Thoughts on Consumer Welfare in the US." *American Antitrust Institute Working Paper no. 05–09* (2005).

Fox, E.M. "'We Protect Competition, You Protect Competitors'." *World Competition* 26 (2003): 149.

Franke, J., Härdle, W.K. and Hafner, C.M. *Statistics of financial markets: an introduction.* Berlin: Springer (2008).

Franke, N. and Puttfarken, H. "*Die Action Civile der Verbände in Frankreich.*" Pages 149 in *Die Bü ndelung gleichgerichteter Interesssen im Prozess.* Edited by Jürgen Basedow, Hopt J. Klaus, Kötz Hein and Baetge Dietmar. Tübingen: Mohr Siebeck (1999).

Friedman, M.W. "Constrained Individualism in Group Litigation: Requiring Class Members to Make a Good Cause Showing before Opting Out of a Federal Class Action." *The Yale Law Journal* 100 (1990): 745.

Fullerton, R.L., Linster, B.G., McKee, M. and Slate, S. "Using auctions to reward tournament winners: Theory and experimental investigations." *RAND Journal of Economics* 33 (2002): 62.

Garoupa, N. "The Theory of Optimal Law Enforcement." *Journal of Economic Surveys* 11 (1997): 267.

Gaudet Jr, R. "Turning a blind eye: The Commission's rejection of opt-out class actions overlooks Swedish, Norwegian, Danish and Dutch experience - Swedish, Norwegian, Danish, and Dutch experiences contradict " *European Competition Law Review* 30 (2009): 107.

German Monopolies Commission (Monopolkommission). *Das Allgemeine Wettbewerbsrecht in Der Siebten GWB-Novelle, Sondergutachten Der Monopolkommission Gemäß, §44 Abs. 1 Satz 4 GWB* (2004).

Gibbons, S.M.C. "Group Litigation, Class Actions and Lord Woolf's Three Objectives - A Critical Analysis." *Civil Justice Quarterly* 27 (2008): 208.

Ginsburg, D.H. "Comparing antitrust enforcement in the United States and Europe." *Journal of Competition Law & Economics* 1 (2005): 427.

Gordon, F. and Squires, D. "The Deterrent Effect of UK Competition Enforcement." *De Economist* 156 (2008): 411.

Gravelle, H. "The efficiency implications of cost-shifting rules." *International Review of Law and Economics* 13 (1993): 3.

Gravelle, H. and Waterson, M. "No Win, No Fee: Some Economics of Contingent Legal Fees." *The Economic Journal* 103 (1993): 1205.

Gross, S.R. and Syverud, K.D. "Getting to no: A study of settlement negotiations and the selection of cases for trial." *Michigan Law Review* 90 (1991): 319.

Halfmeier, A. *Popularklagen im Privatrecht: zugleich ein Beitrag zur Theorie der Verbandsklage.* Tübingen: Mohr Siebeck (2006).

Halpern, P.J. and Turnbull, S.M. "Legal fees contracts and alternative cost rules: An economic analysis." *International Review of Law and Economics* 3 (1983): 3.

Harris, R.G. and Sullivan, L.A. "Passing on the Monopoly Overcharge: A Comprehensive Policy Analysis." *University of Pennsylvania Law Review* 128 (1979): 269.

Haucap, J. and Stühmeier, T. "Wie hoch sind durch Kartelle verursachte Schäden: Anworten aus Sicht der Wirtschaftstheorie." *Wirtschaft Und Wettbewerb* 58 (2008): 413.

Hay, B.L. "Contingent fees and agency costs." *Journal of Legal Studies* 25 (1996): 503.

Hay, B.L. and Rosenberg, D. "'Sweetheart' and 'Blackmail' Settlements in Class Actions: Reality and Remedy." *Notre Dame Law Review* 75 (2000): 1377.

Hehne, M., Herrmann, M., Fellbaum, B. and Matthes, D. "Die Eignung des deutschen Zivilprozessrechts zur Durchsetzung des europäischen Kartellrechts im Lichte der 7. GWB-Novelle." Pages 86 in: *Das europäische Kartellrecht nach der VO 1/03 im Wechselverhältnis von europäischem Recht und innerstaatlichem Verfahrensrecht.* Edited by Christian Tietje and Werner Blau. Berlin: Berliner Wissenschafts-Verlag (2005).

Helland, E. and Tabarrok, A. "Contingency fees, settlement delay, and low-quality litigation: Empirical evidence from two datasets." *Journal of Law, Economics, and Organization* 19 (2003): 517.

Hellwig, M. "Private Damage Claims and the Passing On Defense in Horizontal Price Fixing Cases: An Economistks Perspective." Pages 121 in *Private Enforcement of EC Competition Law.* Edited by Jürgen Basedow. Alphen aan den Rijn: Kluver Law International (2007).

Helsel, S.D. "Preventing Predatory Abuses in Litigation between Business Competitors: Focusing on a Litigant's Reasons for Initiating the Litigation to Ensure a Balance between the Constitutional Right to Petition and the Sherman Acts Guarantee of Fair Competition in Business." *William.& Mary Law Review* 36 (1994): 1135.

Hensler, D.R., Dombey-Moore, B., Giddens, B., Gross, J. et al. *"Class action dilemmas: pursuing public goals for private gain".* Rand Corporation (2000).

Heyer, K. "Welfare standards and merger analysis: Why not the best?" *U.S. Department of Justice Working Paper* (2006).

Hill, J. "Litigation and Negligence: A Comparative Study." *Oxford Journal of Legal Studies* 6 (1986): 183.

Hodges, C. "Competition enforcement, regulation and civil justice: what is the case?" *Common Market Law Review* 43 (2006): 1381.

Hodges, C. "Country Report: England and Wales." (2007). Available at: www.law.stanford.edu/display/images/dynamic/events_media/England_Legislation.pdf.

Hörmann, G. "Sammelklagen Im Energie- Und Versicherungsrecht." Paper presented at Kollektive Rechtsdurchsetzung - Chancen Und Risiken. Bamberg, 2006.

Hoseinian, F. "Passing-on Damages and Community Antitrust Policy - An Economic Background." *World Competition: Law and Economics Review* 28 (2005): 3.

Hubbard, R. and O'Brien, A. *Microeconomics.* London: Prentice Hall (2008).

Hyde, C.E. "Conditional versus contingent fees: Litigation expenditure incentives." *International Review of Law & Economics* 26 (2006): 180.

Hylton, K.N. "The theory of penalties and the economics of criminal law." *Review of Law and Economics* 1 (2005): 175.

International Chamber of Commerce (ICC). "ICC Comments on the Commission's Green Paper on damages actions for breach of the EC antitrust rules." Available at: http://ec.europa.eu/competition/antitrust/actionsdamages/green_paper_comments.html

Issacharoff, S. and Miller, G.P. "Will Aggregate Litigation Come to Europe?" *NYU Law and Economics Research Paper no. 08-46* (2008).

Jablonski, S.R. "Translation and Comment: Enforcing US Punitive Damages Awards in Foreign Courts-A Recent Case in the Supreme Court of Spain." *The Journal of Law and Commerce* 24 (2004): 225.

Joint Working Party of the Bars and Law Societies of the United Kingdom ("JWP"). "Response to the Commission White Paper on Damages Actions for Breach of the EC Competition Rules." (2008). Available at: http://ec.europa.eu/competition/antitrust/actionsdamages/white_paper_comments.html

Jones, A. and Sufrin, B. *EC Competition Law: text, cases and materials.* Oxford: Oxford University Press, USA (2007).

Jones, C.A. "Private Antitrust Enforcement in Europe: A Policy Analysis and Reality Check." *World Competition* 27 (2004): 13.

Judge Macduff. *Dawson & Others v. First Choice Holidays & Flights Limited.* 2007.

Kalven Jr, H. and Rosenfield, M. "Contemporary Function of the Class Suit." *The University of Chicago Law Review* 8 (1941): 684.
Kaplow, L. "Shifting plaintiffs' fees versus increasing damage awards." *The Rand Journal of Economics* 24 (1993): 625.
Kaplow, L. and Shavell, S. "Fairness versus welfare." *Harvard Law Review* 114 (2000): 961.
Kaplow, L. and Shavell, S. *Fairness versus Welfare.* Harvard University Press (2002).
Katz, A. "The effect of frivolous lawsuits on the settlement of litigation." *International Review of Law and Economics* 10 (1990): 3.
Kauper, T.E. and Snyder, E.A. "Inquiry into the Efficiency of Private Antitrust Enforcement: Follow-on and Independently Initiated Cases Compared, An." *Georgetown Law Journal* 74 (1985): 1163.
Kerber, W. "Should Competition Law Promote Efficiency? Some Reflections of an Economist on the Normative Foundations of Competition Law." Pages 93 in *Economic theory and competition law.* Edited by Josef Drexl. Cheltenham: Edward Elgar (2009).
Kersting, C. "Perspectives for Private Enforcement in European Antitrust Law (Perspektiven der privaten Rechtsdurchsetzung im Kartellrecht)." *Zeitschrift Für Wettbewerbsrecht (ZWeR) - Journal of Competition Law* 3 (2008): 252.
Kilian, M. "Alternatives to Public Provision: The Role of Legal Expenses Insurance in Broadening Access to Justice: The German Experience." *Journal of Law and Society* 30 (2003): 31.
Kilian, M. "Das Gesetz zur Neuregelung des Verbots der Vereinbarung von Erfolgshonoraren." *Neue Juristische Wochenschrift* 61 (2008): 1905.
Kilian, M. and Regan, F. "Legal expenses insurance and legal aid - two sides of the same coin? The experience from Germany and Sweden." *International Journal of the Legal Profession* 11 (2004): 233.
Kionka, E. J. *Torts in a Nutshell.* St. Paul: Thomson West (1999).
Kirstein, R. "Risk Neutrality and Strategic Insurance." *Geneva Papers on Risk and Insurance.Issues and Practice* 25 (2000): 251.
Klemperer, P. "Auction theory: A guide to the literature." *Journal of Economic Surveys* 13 (1999): 227.
Klemperer, P. "What really matters in auction design." *Journal of Economic Perspectives* 16 (2002): 169.
Koch, H. "Non-Class Group Litigation Under EU and German Law." *Duke Journal of Comparative and International Law* 11 (2001): 355.
Korobkin, R.B. and Ulen, T.S. "Law ansd Behavioral Science: Removing the Rationality Assumption from Law and Economics." *California Law Review* 88 (2000): 1051.
Kötz, H. "Ziele des Haftungsrechts." Pages 643 in: *Festschrift für Ernst Steindorff.* Edited by Jürgen F. Baur. Berlin: Walter de Gruyter & Co. (1990).
Kritzer, H.M. "Contingency fee lawyers as gatekeepers in the civil justice system." *Judicature* 81 (1997): 22.
Kroes, N. "Consumers at the Heart of EU Competition Policy" SPEECH/08/212. 2008.
Kroes, N. "Damages Actions for Breaches of EU Competition Rules: Realities and Potentials Opening Speech at the Conference 'La Reparation Du Prejudice Cause Par Une Pratique Anti-Concurentielle En France Et à l'étranger: Bilan Et Perspectives ', Cour De Cassation." 2005.

Kroes, N. "Enforcement of Prohibition of Cartels in Europe." *Proceedings of 2006 EU* (2006).

Kroes, N. "Enhancing Actions for Damages for Breach of Competition Rules in Europe". SPEECH/05/533. 2005.

Kroes, N. "Introductory Speech, ICN Seminar on Competition Agency Effectiveness, Summary Report, Brussels, January 2009." 2009.

Kroes, N. "More private antitrust enforcement through better access to damages: an invitation for an open debate." *Opening Speech at the Conference 'Private Enforcement in EC Competition Law: The Green Paper on Damages Actions'* (9 March 2006).

Krüger, H. *Öffentliche und private Durchsetzung des Kartellverbots von Article 81 EG.* Wiesbaden: Deutscher Universitaets-Verlag (2007).

Kurpas, S. *The Treaty of Lisbon – How Much 'Constitution' is Left? An Overview of the Main Changes.* CEPS Policy Brief, No. 147, December 2007. Available at SSRN: http://ssrn.com/abstract=1334072

Lafontaine, F. and Slade, M. "Exclusive contracts and vertical restraints: Empirical evidence and public policy." *Handbook of Antitrust Economics*, P. Buccirossi (Ed.) Cambridge: MIT Press (2008).

Lampe, M.W. and Rossman, M.E. "Procedural Approaches for Countering the Dual-Filed FLSA Collective Action and State-Law Wage Class Action." *Labor Lawyer* 20 (2004): 311.

Lande, R.H. "Are Antitrust 'Treble' Damages Really Single Damages?" *Ohio State Law Journal* 54 (1993): 115.

Lande, R.H. "Five Myths about Antitrust Damages." *University of San Francisco Law Review* 40 (2005): 651.

Lande, R.H. and Davis, J.P. "Benefits from Private Antitrust Enforcement: An Analysis of Forty Cases." *University of San Francisco Law Review* 42 (2008): 879.

Lande, R.H. and Davis, J.P. "An Evaluation of Private Antitrust Enforcement: 29 Case Studies." *Interim Report Submitted to the Antitrust Modernization Commission* (2006).

Landes, W.M. "Optimal sanctions for antitrust violations." *The University of Chicago Law Review* 50 (1983): 652.

Landes, W.M. and Posner, R.A. "The Private Enforcement of Law." *The Journal of Legal Studies* 4 (1975): 1.

Landes, W.M. and Posner, R.A. "Should Indirect Purchasers Have Standing to Sue under the Antitrust Laws – An Economic Analysis of the Rule of Illinois Brick." *The University of Chicago Law Review* 46 (1978): 602.

Langen, E. and Bunte, H.J., eds. *Kommentar zum deutschen und europäischen Kartellrecht.* 9th ed. Luchterhand (2001).

Leslie, C.R. "Antitrust Damages and Deadweight Loss." *Antitrust Bulletin* 51 (2006): 521.

Lindblom, H. "Sweden." *The ANNALS of the American Academy of Political and Social Science* 622 (2009): 231.

Lipczynski, J., Wilson, J.O.S. and Goddard, J. *Industrial organization: competition, strategy, policy.* Financial Times/Prentice Hall (2005).

Lopatka, J.E. and Page, W.H. "Indirect Purchaser Suits and the Consumer Interest." *Antitrust Bulletin* 48 (2003): 531.

Lord Justice Jackson. " The Funding of Civil Litigation " in: *Review of Civil Litigation Costs*. Preliminary Report by Lord Justice Jackson, Vol. 1 (2009).

Lott, J.R. "*Corporate Criminal liability*." Pages 492 in: *Encyclopedia of Law and Economics, Volume I. The History and Methodology of Law and Economics*. Edited by Boudewijn Bouckaert and Gerrit De Geest. Cheltenham: Edward Elgar (2000).

Luna, E. "Overextending the Criminal Law." Pages 1 in: *Go directly to jail: the criminalization of almost everything*. Edited by Gene Healy. Washington DC: Cato Institute (2004).

Macey, J.R. and Miller, G. P. "Auctioning Class Action and Derivative Suits: A Rejoinder." *Northwestern University Law Review* 87 (1992): 458.

Mackenrodt, M. "Private Incentive, Optimal Deterrence and Damage Claims for Abuses of Dominant Positions– The Interaction between the Economic Review of the Prohibition of Abuses of Dominant Positions and Private Enforcement." Pages 165 in: *Abuse of Dominant Position: New Interpretation, New Enforcement Mechanisms?*. Edited by Mark-Oliver Mackenrodt, Gallego Conde Beatriz and Stefan Enchelmaier. Berlin: Springer (2008).

Magnus, U. *Unification of tort law: Damages, Principles of European Tort Law*. The Hague, London, Boston: Kluwer Law International (2001).

Max Planck Institute for Intellectual Property, Competition and Tax Law. "Comments of the Max Planck Institute for Intellectual Property, Competition and Tax Law (Munich) on the DC Competition Green Paper of December 2005." (2006).

McAfee, P.R., Mialon, H.M. and Mialon, S.H. "Private v. public antitrust enforcement: A strategic analysis." *Journal of Public Economics* 92 (2008): 1863.

McAfee, P.R. and Vakkur, N. "The Strategic Abuse of the Antitrust Laws." *Journal of Strategic Management Education* 1 (2004): 1.

Mcdougall, A. and Verzariu, A. "Vitamins Litigation: Unavailability of Exemplary Damages, Restitutionary Damages and Account of Profits in Private Competition Law Claims." *European Competition Law Review* 29 (2008): 181.

Merges, R.P. and Nelson, R.R. "On the complex economics of patent scope." *Columbia Law Review* 90 (1990): 839.

Miceli, T.J. "Do contingent fees promote excessive litigation." *The Journal of Legal Studies* 23 (1994): 211.

Micklitz, H. "Collective Private Enforcement of Consumer Law: The Key Questions." Pages 13 in *Collective Enforcement of Consumer Law*. Edited by Willem Van Boom and Marco Loos. Europa Law Publishing (2007).

Micklitz, H. and Stadler, A. "The Development of Collective Legal Actions in Europe, Especially in German Civil Procedure." *European Business Law Review* 17 (2006): 1473.

Micklitz, H. and Stadler, A. "Leistungsklagen von Verbänden." Page 1309 in *Das Verbandsklagerecht in der Informations-und Dienstleistungsgesellschaft*. Edited by Hans-W Micklitz and Astrid Stadler. (2005).

Micklitz, H. and Stadler, A. *Das Verbandsklagerecht in der Informations-und Dienstleistungsgesellschaft*. (2005).

Miller, G.P. and Singer, L.S. "Nonpecuniary Class Action Settlements." *Law and Contemporary Problems* 60 (1997): 97.

Miller, G.P. "Some agency problems in settlement." *The Journal of Legal Studies* 16 (1987): 189.

Mom, A. "*Länderbericht Spanien.*" Pages 655 in *Das Verbandsklagerecht in der Informations- und Dienstleistungsgesellschaft.* Edited by Hans-W Micklitz and Astrid Stadler. Münster: Landwirtschaftsverlag (2005).

Monti, M. " A Reformed Competition Policy: Achievements and Challenges for the Future." SPEECH/04/477 (2004).

Monti, M. "Private Litigation as a Key Complement to Public Enforcement of Competition Rules and the First Conclusions on the Implementation of the New Merger Regulation." SPEECH/04/403 (2004).

Möschel, W. "Kommentar: Erweiterter Privatrechtsschutz im Kartellrecht." *Wirtschaft Und Wettbewerb* (2006): 115.

Möschel, W. "Law and Market Organization: The Historical Experience in Germany From 1900 to the Law Against Restraints of Competition (1957)-Comment." *Journal of Institutional and Theoretical Economics* 151 (1995): 21.

Möschel, W. *Recht der Wettbewerbsbeschränkungen.* Köln: Heymann (1983).

Motta, M. *Competition policy: theory and practice.* Cambridge: Cambridge University Press (2004).

Mühlbach, T. and Rinne, A. "Germany: Private Antitrust Litigation " *The 2009 European Antitrust Review - a Global Competition Review special report.* Global Competition Review (2009).

Mulheron, R.P. *The class action in common law legal systems: a comparative perspective.* Portland: Hart publishing (2004).

Mulheron, R.P. *Competition Law Cases Under the Opt-Out Regimes of Australia, Canada and Portugal: A Research Paper for the Department for Business, Enterprise and Regulatory Reform.* Research Paper (2008). Available at: www.berr.gov.uk/files/file49008.pdf

Mulheron, R.P. "From representative rule to class action: steps rather than leaps." *Civil Justice Quarterly* 24 (2005): 424.

Mulheron, R.P. "Reform of collective redress in England and Wales." Research Paper, (2008). Available at: www.civiljusticecouncil.gov.uk/files/collective_redress.pdf

Mulheron, R.P. "Some Difficulties with Group Litigation Orders-and Why a Class Action is Superior." *Civil Justice Quarterly* 24 (2005): 40.

Mulheron, R.P. and Cashman, P. "Third party funding: A changing landscape." *Civil Justice Quarterly* 27 (2008): 312.

Nicholson, M. and Hersh, C. "Canada." Pages 13 in: *Private Antitrust Litigation 2007 - in 19 Jurisdictions Worldwide.* Edited by Samantha Mobley. Global Competition Review (2007).

Nordh, R. "Group Actions - the Swedish Experience." 2005. Avialable at: www.courdecassation.fr/IMG/File/judge_nordh.pdf

Office of Fair Trading. *Decision of the Office of Fair Trading No. CA98/06/2003, Price-fixing of Replica Football Kit.* 2003.

Office of Fair Trading. "*Private actions in competition law: effective redress for consumers and business, OFT Discussion Paper 916.*" (April 2007). Availabe at: www.oft.gov.uk/shared_oft/reports/comp_policy/oft916.pdf

Office of Fair Trading. "*Private actions in competition law: effective redress for consumers and business, Recommendations by the Office of Fair Traiding.*" OFT916resp (November 2007). Available at: www.oft.gov.uk/shared_oft/reports/comp_policy/oft916resp.pdf

Organization for Economic Co-operation and Development. "Competition Policy and Efficiency Claims in Horizontal Agreements." Paris, 1995. Available at: www.oecd.org/dataoecd/1/4/2379526.pdf

Organization for Economic Co-operation and Development. *Report on the Nature and Impact of Hard Core Cartels and Sanctions Against Cartels Under National Competition Laws.* DAFFE/COMP(2002)7 (2002).

Organization for Economic Co-operation and Development. *The Role of Competition Policy in Regulatory Reform, OECD Reviews of Regulatory Reform, Reform of the United Kingdom* (2002). Available at:

Oxera and Komninos, A. "Quantifying antitrust damages – Towards non-binding guidance for courts," (2009) (published online): European Commision (2010)

Pace, N.M. *Class Actions in the United States of America: An Overview of the Process and the Empirical Literature*Santa Monica, California, USA: Rand Institute for Civil Justice (2007).

Paulis, E. "Policy Issues in the Private Enforcement of EC Competition Law." Pages 7 in *Private enforcement of EC competition law.* Edited by Jürgen Basedow. Alphen aan den Rijn: Kluwer Law International (2007).

Pera, A. "Changing Views of Competition, Economic Analysis and EC Antitrust Law." *European Competition Journal* 4 (2008): 127.

Perry, M. and Vincent, D.R. "The Optimal Timing of Procurement Decisions and Patent Allocations." *International Economic Review* 43 (2002): 1035.

Pindyck, R.S. and Rubinfeld, D.L. *Microeconomics.* International Edition, Singapore: Prentice Hall (2005).

Pirker-Hörmann, B. and P. Kolba. "Österreich: Von Der Verbandsklage Zur Sammelklage." Paper presented at Kollektive Rechtsdurchsetzung – Chancen Und Risiken. Bamberg, 2006.

Polinsky, M.A. "Detrebling Versus Decoupling Antitrust Damages: Lessons from the Theory of Enforcement." *Georgetown Law Journal* 74 (1986): 1231.

Polinsky, M.A. and Rubenfield, A.M. "A note on settlements under the contingent fee method of compensating lawyers." *International Review of Law and Economics* 22 (2002): 217.

Polinsky, M.A. and Rubinfeld, D.L. "A damage-revelation rationale for coupon remedies." *Journal of Law, Economics, and Organization* 23 (2007): 653.

Polinsky, M.A. and Rubinfeld, D.L. "Optimal awards and penalties when the probability of prevailing varies among plaintiffs." *The Rand Journal of Economics* 27 (1996): 269.

Polinsky, M.A. and Shavell, S. "Enforcement costs and the optimal magnitude and probability of fines." *The Journal of Law & Economics* 35 (1992): 133.

Polinsky, M.A. and Shavell, S. "A note on optimal fines when wealth varies among individuals." *The American Economic Review* 81 (1991): 618.

Polinsky, M.A. and Shavell, S. "Public Enforcement of Law." Pages 307 in *Encyclopedia of Law and Economics.* Edited by Boudewijn Bouckaert and Gerrit De Geest. Cheltenham: Edward Elgar (2000).

Polinsky, M.A. and Shavell, S. "Punitive Damages." Pages 228 in *Tort Law and Ecomomics, Encyclopedia of Law and Economics.* Edited by Michael Faure. Cheltenham: Edward Elgar Publishing Limited (2009).

Polinsky, M.A. and Shavell, S. "Should Liability Be Based on the Harm to the Victim or the Gain to the Injurer?" *Journal of Law, Economics, and Organization* 10 (1994): 427.

Polverino, F. and Cengiz, F. "A Class Action Model for Antitrust Damages Litigation in the European Union." *World Comeptition* 30 (2007): 479.

Posner, R.A. *Antitrust Law: Economic Perspective.* Chicago, London: The University of Chicago Press (1976).

Posner, R.A. *Economic analysis of law.* Boston: Little, Brown and Company (2003).

Prichard, J.R.S. "Private Enforcement and Class Actions." Pages 217 in *Canadian Competition Policy: Essays in Law and Economics.* Edited by J. Robert S. Prichard, W.T. Stanbury and Thomas A. Wilson. Butterworths (1979).

Priest, G. L. and Klein, B. "The Selection of Disputes for Litigation." *The Journal of Legal Studies* 13 (1984): 1.

Quarta, F. "Recognition and Enforcement of US Punitive Damages Awards in Continental Europe: The Italian Supreme Court's Veto." *Hastings International and Comparative Law Review* 31 (2008): 753.

Randall, J. "Does De-Trebling Sacrifice Recoverability of Antitrust Awards." *Yale J.on Reg.* 23 (2006): 311.

Renda, A., Van Den Bergh, R., Keske, S., Pardolesi, R. et al. *Making Antitrust Damages Actions in the EU More Effective. Study in Support of the Impact Assessment of the EC White Paper on Antitrust Damages Actions* (published online): European Commision (2007).

Richman, B.D. and Murray, C.R. "Rebuilding Illinois Brick: A Functionalist Approach to the Indirect Purchaser Rule." *Southern California Law Review* 81 (2007): 69.

Riley, A. *The EU Reform Treaty and the Competition Protocol: Undermining EC Competition Law*, CEPS Policy Brief No. 142, September 2007.

Riley, A.J. and Peysner, J. "Damages in EC antitrust actions: who pays the piper?" *European Law Review* 31 (2006): 748.

Rodger, B.J. "Private Enforcement of Competition Law: The Hidden Story." *European Competition Law Review* (2008).

Röhling, A. "Die passing-on defence im deutschen Recht." Page 1117 in *Festschrift für Ulrich Huber zum siebzigsten Geburtstag.* Edited by T. Baums, M. Lutter, K. Schmidt and J. Wertenbruch. Tübingen: Mohr Siebeck (2006).

Rosenberg, D. "Casual Connection in Mass Exposure Cases: A Public Law Vision of the Tort System, The." *Harvard Law Review* 97 (1983): 849.

Rosenberg, D. and Kozel, R. J. "Solving the Nuisance-Value Settlement Problem: Mandatory Summary Judgment." *Harvard Law and Economics Discussion Paper no. 469; Harvard Public Law Working Paper no. 90* (2004).

Rosenberg, D. and Shavell, S. "A model in which suits are brought for their nuisance value." *International Review of Law and Economics* 5 (1985): 3.

Rosenberg, D. and Sullivan, J. P. "Coordinating Private Class Action and Public Agency Enforcement of Antitrust Law." *Journal of Competition Law and Economics* 2 (2006): 159.

Roth, W.H. "§33 GWB." *Frankfurter Kommentar zum Kartellrecht.* Edited by von Hahn Helmuth. Köln: O. Schmidt (2001).

Roth, W.H. "*Private enforcement of European competition law – recommendations flowing from the German experience.*" Pages 61 in *Private Enforcement of EC Competition Law.* Edited by Jürgen Basedow. Alphen aan den Rijn: Kluver Law International (2007).

Rowe Jr, T.D. "State and Foreign Class-Action Rules and Statutes: Differences from – and Lessons for? – Federal Rule 23." *Western State University Law Review* 35 (2007): 147.

Rubinfeld, D.L. and Scotchmer, S. "Contingent fees." Pages 415 in *The New Palgrave Dictionary of Economics and the Law.* Edited by P. Newman. London: Macmillan (1998).

Rubinstein, A., von Neumann, J., Morgenstern, O. and Kuhn, H.W. *Theory of Games and Economic Behavior.* Princeton University Press (2007).

Säcker, F.J. *Die Einordnung der Verbandsklage in das System des Privatrechts.* CH Beck (2006).

Schäfer, H.B. "The Bundling of Similar Interests in Litigation. The Incentives for Class Action and Legal Actions taken by Associations." *European Journal of Law and Economics* 9 (2000): 183.

Schäfer, H.B. and Ott, C. *Lehrbuch der ökonomischen Analyse des Zivilrechts.* Berlin, Heidelberg, New York: Springer (2005).

Schilken, E. "Der Zweck des Zivilprozesses und der kollektive Rechtsschutz." Pages 21 in *Kollektiver Rechtsschutz im Zivilprozess.* Edited by Caroline Meller-Hannich. Baden-Baden: Nomos (2008).

Schinkel, M.P. "Effective Cartel Enforcement in Europe." *World Competition* 30 (2007): 539.

Schinkel, M.P. and Rüggeberg, J. "Consolidating Antitrust Damages in Europe: A Proposal for Standing in Line With Efficient Private Enforcement, Amsterdam Center for Law & Economics Working Paper No. 2006–04." *World Competition: Law and Economics Review* 29 (2006): 395.

Schneider, B. "Auf dem Weg zu Securities Class Actions in Deutschland? – Auswirkungen des KapMuG auf die Praxis kapitalmarktrechtlicher Streitigkeiten." *Betriebsberater (BB)* 60 (2005): 2249.

Schnell, G. "Class Action Madness in Europe – a Call for a More Balanced Debate." *European Competition Law Review* 28 (2007): 617.

Schwartz, M.L. and Mitchell, D.J.B. "Economic Analysis of the Contingent Fee in Personal-Injury Litigation, An." *Stan.L.Rev.* 22 (1969): 1125.

Scotchmer, S. "*Incentives to Innovate.*" Pages 273 in *The New Palgrave Dictionary of Economics and the Law.* Edited by P. Newman. London: Macmillan (1998).

Secretary of State, (UK) *Claims of behalf of consumers, guidance for prospective specified bodies.*

Seeliger, D. "Kollektiver Rechtsschutz im Kartell- und Wettbewerbsrecht." Pages 73 in *Kollektiver Rechtsschutz im Zivilprozess.* Edited by Caroline Meller-Hannich. Baden-Baden: Nomos (2008).

Segal, I.R. and Whinston, M.D. "Public vs. private enforcement of antitrust law: A survey." *Stanford Law and Economics Olin Working Paper no. 335* (2006).

Sen, A. "Rational Behaviour." *The New Palgrave Dictionary of Economics.* Edited by Steven N. Durlauf and Lawrence E. Blume. (2008).

Sergius Koku, P. "An analysis and the effects of class-action lawsuits." *Journal of Business Research* 59 (2006): 508.

Shavell, S. "Criminal law and the optimal use of nonmonetary sanctions as a deterrent." *Columbia Law Review* (1985): 1232.

Shavell, S. "Economic analysis of litigation and the legal process." *Harvard Law School: Harvard Law School John M. Olin Center for Law, Economics and Business Discussion Paper Series, Paper 404* (2004).

Shavell, S. "The level of litigation: Private versus social optimality of suit and of settlement." *International Review of Law & Economics* 19 (1999): 99.

Shavell, S. "Liability for harm versus regulation of safety." *The Journal of Legal Studies* 13 (1984): 357.

Shavell, S. "A note on marginal deterrence." *International Review of Law and Economics* 12 (1992): 345.

Shavell, S. "Social versus the Private Incentive to Bring Suit in a Costly Legal System, The." *The Journal of Legal Studies* 11 (1982): 333.

Shepherd, S.R. "Damage Distribution in Class Actions: The Cy Pres Remedy." *University of Chicago Law Review* 39 (1971): 448.

Silver, C. "'We're scared to death': Class certification and blackmail." *NYU Law Review* 78 (2003): 1357.

Silver, C. "*Class Actions – Representative Proceedings.*" Pages 194 in *Encyclopedia of Law and Economics, Volume I. The History and Methodology of Law and Economics.* Edited by Boudewijn Bouckaert and Gerrit De Geest. Cheltenham: Edward Elgar (2000).

Simmons, M.Q. "Damages for economic loss: Questions of procedure." *Competition Appeals Tribunal* (2007).

Snyder, E.A. and Huges, J.W. "The English rule for allocating legal costs: evidence confronts theory." *Journal of Law, Economics, & Organization* 6 (1990): 345.

Snyder, E.A. and Kauper, T.E. "Misuse of the Antitrust Laws: The Competitor Plaintiff." *Michigan Law Review* 90 (1991): 551.

Sorabji, J., Napier, M.C.Q. and Musgrove, R. "*Improving Access to Justice through Collective Actions: Developing a More Efficient and Effective Procedure for Collective Actions*". Edited by Sorabji, J., Napier, M. C. Q. and Musgrove, R. (2008).

Souam, S. "Optimal antitrust policy under different regimes of fines." *International Journal of Industrial Organization* 19 (2001): 1.

Spagnolo, G. "Leniency and whistleblowers in antitrust." *Centre for Economic Policy Research (CEPR) Discussion Paper no. 5794* (2006).

Stadler, A. "Grenzüberschreitender kollektiver Rechtsschutz in Europa." *JuristenZeitung* 64 (February 2009): 121.

Stein, A. and Harel, A. "Law & Economics at the Animal Farm: Offering a New Solution to the Class Action Agency Problem." *Working Paper Series.*

Stigler, G.J. "Free riders and collective action: An appendix to theories of economic regulation." *The Bell Journal of Economics and Management Science* 5 (1974): 359.

Stigler, G.J. "The Optimum Enforcement of Laws." *The Journal of Political Economy* 78 (1970): 526.

Stiglitz, J.E. and Walsh, C.E. *Economics.* New York: W. W. Norton (2006).

Study Group on a European Civil Code in co-authorship with the Research Group on EC Private Law. "Book III: Obligations and corresponding rights." Pages 141 in *Principles, Definitions and Model Rules ofEuropean Private Law, Draft Common Frame of Reference (DCFR) Interim Outline Edition.*

Stürner, M. "Model case proceedings in the Capital Markets." *Civil Justice Quarterly* 26 (2007): 250.

Stuyck, J., Terryn, E., Colaert, V., Van Dyck, T. et al. *"An Analysis and Evaluation of Alternative Means of Consumer Redress Other than Redress through Ordinary Judicial Proceedings" Final Report.* SANCO/2005/B5/010 (2007).

The European Consumers' Association (BEUC). *"Damages Actions for breach of EC anti-trust rules: BEUC position on the Commission's Green Paper."* (2006).

The Law Commission. *Sixth Programme of Law Reform: Damages, LAW COM no. 247, 1997* (1997).

The Law Reform Commission. *Report on Aggravated, Exemplary and Restitutionary Damages*LRC 60–2000 (2000).

Tirole, J. *The theory of industrial organization.* MIT press (1993).

Ulen, T.S. "Rational Choice Theory in Law and Economics." Pages 790 in *Encyclopedia of Law and Economics, Volume I. The History and Methodology of Law and Economics.* Edited by Boudewijn Bouckaert and Gerrit De Geest. Cheltenham: Edward Elgar (2000).

United Kingdom Competition Appeals Tribunal. *BCL Old Co Ltd & Ors v Aventis SA & Ors, Court of Appeal – United Kingdom Competition Appeals Tribunal, January 28, 2005.* 2005.

United States Court of Appeals. *8th Circuit, No. 96-2925 KAMPA vs WHITE CONSOLIDATED INDUSTRIES, INC.*

Van Boom, W. and Loos, M. "Effective Enforcement of consumer law in Europe." Pages 231 in *Collective Enforcement of Consumer Law.* Edited by Willem Van Boom and Marco Loos. Europa Law Publishing (2007).

Van Den Bergh, R. and Camesasca, P. D. *European competition law and economics: a comparative perspective.* London: Sweet & Maxwell (2006).

Van Den Bergh, R. and Keske, S. "Private Enforcement of European Competition Law: Quo Vadis?" *European Review of Contract Law* 3 (2007): 468.

Van den Hauwe, L. "Public Choice, Constitutional Political Economy and Law and Economics." Pages 603 in *Encyclopedia of Law and Economics.* Edited by Boudewijn Bouckaert and Gerrit De Geest. Cheltenham: Edward Elgar (2000).

Van Velthoven, B. "Legal cost insurance and social welfare." *Economics Letters* 72 (2001): 387.

Vanberg, V.J. "Consumer Welfare, Total Welfare and Economic Freedom – On the Normative Foundations of Competition Policy." *Freiburg Discussion Papers on Constitutional Economics* 09/3 (2009).

Vidmar, N. "The American Civil Jury for Auslander (Foreigners)." *Duke Journal of Comparative & International Law* 13 (2003): 95.

Waelbroeck, D., Slater, D. and Even-Shoshan, G. "Study on the Conditions for Claims for Damages in Case of Infringement of EC Competition Rules: Comparative Report, Open Procedure COMP/2003/A1/22, Ashurst Study for Directorate General Competition of the EU Commission, London, England." (2004).

Wagener, W.H. "Modelling the effect of one-way fee shifting on discovery abuse for private antitrust litigation." *New York University Law Review* 78 (2003): 1887.

Wagner, G. "Kollektiver Rechtsschutz – Regelungsbedarf bei Massen- und Streuschäden." Pages 41 in: *Auf dem Weg zu einer europäischen Sammelklage?* Edited by Matthias Casper, André Janssen, Petra Pohlmann and Reiner Schulze. Munchen: European law publishers GmBH (2009).

Wagner, G. "Schadensersatz bei Kartelldelikten." *German Working Papers in Law and Economics* 2007 (2007): 18.

Waye, V. "Conflicts of Interests between Claimholders, Lawyers and Litigation Entrepreneurs." *Bond Law Review* 19 (2007): 9.

Werden, G. J. and Schwartz, M. "Illinois Brick and the Deterrence of Antitrust Violations - An Economic Analysis." *The Hastings Law Journal* 35 (1983): 629.

Willging, T.E., Hooper, L.L. and Niemic, R.J. "Empirical study of class actions in four federal district courts: Final report to the advisory committee on civil rules." *Washington, DC: Federal Judicial Center* (1996).

Wils, W.P.J. "The combination of the investigative and prosecutorial function and the adjudicative function in EC antitrust enforcement: A legal and economic analysis." *World Competition* 27 (2003): 201.

Wils, W.P.J. "Is criminalization of EU competition law the answer?" *World Competition: Law and Economics Review* 28 (2005): 117.

Wils, W.P.J. "Optimal antitrust fines: theory and practice." *World Competition* 29 (2006): 183.

Wils, W.P.J. *The optimal enforcement of EC antitrust law: essays in law & economics.* The Hague: Kluwer Law International (2002).

Wils, W.P.J. "The Relationship between Public Antitrust Enforcement and Private Actions for Damages." *World Competition* 32 (2009): 3.

Wils, W.P.J. "Should private antitrust enforcement be encouraged in Europe?" *World Competition* 26 (2003): 473.

Wissenbach, K. "Schadenersatzklagen gegen Kartellmitglieder." Pages 21 in *Beiträge zum Transnationalen Wirtschaftsrecht.* Edited by Christian Tietje, J. Kraft and R. Sethe. (2006).

Wright, J.L. and Williams, M.M. "Remember the Alamo: The Seventh Amendment of the United States Constitution, the Doctrine of Incorporation, and State Caps on Jury Awards." *South Texas Law Review* 45 (2003): 449.

European Studies in Law and Economics

The series '*European Studies in Law and Economics*' is devoted to further the understanding of Law and Economics in Europe. The volumes published in this series present an interdisciplinary perspective on the effects of laws on people's behaviour and on the economic system. The ample topics address a wide audience, including policy makers, legislators, economists, lawyers and judges. The series is peer-reviewed.

The series is an initiative of the PhD programme '*European Doctorate in Law and Economics*' (EDLE). The EDLE is the academic response to the increasing importance of the economic analysis of law in Europe. The programme is offered by the Universities of Bologna, Hamburg and Rotterdam in association with the Indira Gandhi Institute of Development Research, Mumbai (India). PhD students receive the unique opportunity to study law and economics in three different countries. The programme prepares economists and lawyers of high promise for an academic career in a research field of growing importance or for responsible positions in government, research organisations and international consulting firms.

The European Commission sponsors the EDLE as an excellence programme under the prestigious Erasmus Mundus scheme. For further information please visit: www.edle-phd.eu.

www.ingramcontent.com/pod-product-compliance
Ingram Content Group UK Ltd.
Pitfield, Milton Keynes, MK11 3LW, UK
UKHW051921100926
8556IPUK00021B/1301